T0211034

Patricia Pesado

Editor

Computer Science – CACIC 2022

28th Argentine Congress, CACIC 2022
La Rioja, Argentina, October 3–6, 2022
Revised Selected Papers

 Springer

Editor
Patricia Pesado (iD)
Universidad Nacional de La Plata
La Plata, Argentina

ISSN 1865-0929   ISSN 1865-0937 (electronic)
Communications in Computer and Information Science
ISBN 978-3-031-34146-5   ISBN 978-3-031-34147-2 (eBook)
https://doi.org/10.1007/978-3-031-34147-2

This Springer imprint is published by the registered company Springer Nature Switzerland AG
The registered company address is: Gewerbestrasse 11, 6330 Cham, Switzerland

Communications
in Computer and Information Science 1778

Rationale

The CCIS series is devoted to the publication of proceedings of computer science conferences. Its aim is to efficiently disseminate original research results in informatics in printed and electronic form. While the focus is on publication of peer-reviewed full papers presenting mature work, inclusion of reviewed short papers reporting on work in progress is welcome, too. Besides globally relevant meetings with internationally representative program committees guaranteeing a strict peer-reviewing and paper selection process, conferences run by societies or of high regional or national relevance are also considered for publication.

Topics

The topical scope of CCIS spans the entire spectrum of informatics ranging from foundational topics in the theory of computing to information and communications science and technology and a broad variety of interdisciplinary application fields.

Information for Volume Editors and Authors

Publication in CCIS is free of charge. No royalties are paid, however, we offer registered conference participants temporary free access to the online version of the conference proceedings on SpringerLink (http://link.springer.com) by means of an http referrer from the conference website and/or a number of complimentary printed copies, as specified in the official acceptance email of the event.

CCIS proceedings can be published in time for distribution at conferences or as post-proceedings, and delivered in the form of printed books and/or electronically as USBs and/or e-content licenses for accessing proceedings at SpringerLink. Furthermore, CCIS proceedings are included in the CCIS electronic book series hosted in the SpringerLink digital library at http://link.springer.com/bookseries/7899. Conferences publishing in CCIS are allowed to use Online Conference Service (OCS) for managing the whole proceedings lifecycle (from submission and reviewing to preparing for publication) free of charge.

Publication process

The language of publication is exclusively English. Authors publishing in CCIS have to sign the Springer CCIS copyright transfer form, however, they are free to use their material published in CCIS for substantially changed, more elaborate subsequent publications elsewhere. For the preparation of the camera-ready papers/files, authors have to strictly adhere to the Springer CCIS Authors' Instructions and are strongly encouraged to use the CCIS LaTeX style files or templates.

Abstracting/Indexing

CCIS is abstracted/indexed in DBLP, Google Scholar, EI-Compendex, Mathematical Reviews, SCImago, Scopus. CCIS volumes are also submitted for the inclusion in ISI Proceedings.

How to start

To start the evaluation of your proposal for inclusion in the CCIS series, please send an e-mail to ccis@springer.com.

Preface

Welcome to the selected papers of the XXVIII Argentine Congress of Computer Science (CACIC 2022), held in La Rioja, La Rioja, Argentina, during October 3–6, 2022. CACIC 2022 was organized by the National University of La Rioja (La Rioja) on behalf of the Network of National Universities with Computer Science Degrees (RedUNCI).

CACIC is an annual congress dedicated to the promotion and advancement of all aspects of computer science. Its aim is to provide a forum within which the development of computer science as an academic discipline with industrial applications is promoted, trying to extend the frontier of both the state of the art and the state of the practice. The main audience for and participants of CACIC are seen as researchers in academic departments, laboratories, and industrial software organizations.

CACIC 2022 covered the following topics: intelligent agents and systems; software engineering; hardware architecture; networks and operating systems; graphic computation, visualization, and image processing; computer technology applied to education; databases and data mining; innovation in software systems; innovation in computer science education; signal processing and real-time systems; digital governance and smart cities.

This year, the congress received 184 submissions. Each submission was reviewed by at least 3, and on average 3.2 Program Committee members and/or external reviewers, following a single-blind peer-review scheme. A total of 69 full papers, involving 236 different authors from 43 universities, were accepted. According to the recommendations of the reviewers, 20 of them were selected for this book.

During CACIC 2022, special activities were also carried out, including one plenary lecture, one discussion panel, a special track on Digital Governance and Smart Cities, and an International School with four courses.

Special thanks to the members of the different committees for their support and collaboration. Also, we would like to thank the local Organizing Committee, reviewers, lecturers, speakers, authors, and all conference attendees. Finally, we want to thank Springer for their support of this publication.

April 2023   Patricia Pesado

Organization

Editor

Patricia Pesado[1]   National University of La Plata, Argentina

Editorial Assistant

Pablo Thomas   National University of La Plata, Argentina

Program Committee

Maria Jose Abásolo   National University of La Plata, Argentina
Claudio Aciti   National University of Central Buenos Aires,
                                          Argentina
Hugo Alfonso   National University of La Pampa, Argentina
Jorge Ardenghi   National University of the South, Argentina
Marcelo Arroyo   National University of Río Cuarto, Argentina
Hernan Astudillo   Technical University Federico Santa María, Chile
Sandra Baldasarri   University of Zaragoza, Spain
Javier Balladini   National University of Comahue, Argentina
Luis Soares Barbosa   University of Minho, Portugal
Rodolfo Bertone   National University of La Plata, Argentina
Oscar Bria   National University of La Plata, Argentina
Nieves R. Brisaboa   University of La Coruña, Spain
Carlos Buckle   National University of Patagonia San Juan Bosco,
                                          Argentina
Alberto Cañas   University of West Florida, USA
Ana Casali   National University of Rosario, Argentina
Silvia Castro   National University of the South, Argentina
Alejandra Cechich   National University of Comahue, Argentina
Edgar Chávez   Michoacan University of San Nicolás de Hidalgo,
                                          Mexico
Carlos Coello Coello   CINVESTAV, Mexico
Uriel Cuckierman   National Technological University, Argentina
Armando E. De Giusti   National University of La Plata, Argentina

---

[1] RedUNCI Chair

Sponsors

Network of Universities with Careers in Computer Science (RedUNCI)

National University of Salta

Invap

Sadosky Foundation

Federal Investment Council

Contents

Databases and Data Mining

Hardware Architectures, Networks, and Operating Systems

Innovation in Software Systems

Signal Processing and Real-Time Systems

Innovation in Computer Science Education

Digital Governance and Smart Cities

Agents and Systems

VNS Variant Approach Metaheuristics for Parallel Machines Scheduling Problem

Claudia R. Gatica(✉), Silvia M. Molina, and Guillermo Leguizamón

Lab. de Investigación y Desarrollo en Inteligencia Computacional (LIDIC), University National of San Luis (UNSL), Argentine, Ejército de los Andes 950, (5700) San Luis, Argentina
{crgatica,smolina,legui}@unsl.edu.ar

Abstract. VNS (*Variable Neighborhood Search*) is a trajectory metaheuristic that uses different neighborhood structures following some pre-established criteria to perform the search. In this work, variants of the standard VNS (or simply VNS) are proposed to improve its performance by introducing changes in the order of their application, neighborhood sequences used, and/or exploration mechanisms considering the Parallel Machines Scheduling Problem to minimize the Maximum Tardiness. The proposed variants are VNS+R (VNS *Random*) with random neighborhood selection; VNS+LHS (VNS *Latin Hypercube Sample*) with pre-selection of neighborhoods through Latin Squares; VNS+E (VNS *Exploratory*) which intensifies the exploration of the search space and finally, VNS+ER (VNS *Exploratory&Random*) which combines functional aspects of both VNS+R and VNS+E. The results show that the variants that intensify the exploration in the search space, and the variant with the scheme of Latin squares, improve the performance of VNS.

Keywords: Parallel Machine Scheduling · Maximum Tardiness · Metaheuristics · Variable Neighborhood Search

1 Introduction

Trajectory metaheuristics (S-metaheuristics, hereafter) are search algorithms used to solve NP-hard problems such are scheduling problems. In particular, VNS (Mladenović and Hansen [9]) perform a systematic search through neighborhood structures, where the exploration sequence and size of each neighborhood are crucial in the design of the algorithm [20].

Activity scheduling is a decision-making process that plays an important role in production and multiprocessor systems, in manufacturing and information distribution, and transportation environments. The parallel machine environment has been studied for several years due to its importance both academically and industrially.

This article considers the identical parallel machines scheduling problem without restrictions in order to minimize the *maximum tardiness*, and besides it

P. Pesado (Ed.): CACIC 2022, CCIS 1778, pp. 3–18, 2023.
https://doi.org/10.1007/978-3-031-34147-2_1

is an extension of the work presented in CACIC [8] regarding the bibliographical review in Sect. 2, and the experiments in Sect. 5.

As regards the bibliographical review, we search the recently published articles emphasizing the observation of characteristics such as schemes or strategies in the search of the VNS algorithms applied to scheduling problems, neighborhood structures, and instance size problems. Regarding the extended experiments, three aspects are taken into account based on the latest obtained results, and the revised publications: a) the size of the instances; b) the number of neighbors in the local search; and c) the number of neighborhood structures.

The organization of this work is as follows. Section 2 details a review of the recent literature related to our topic of study. Section 3 presents and formulates the parallel machine scheduling problem. Section 4 describes the proposed variants of VNS. Section 5 details the design of the experiments. Section 6 shows and analyzes the results obtained. Finally, in Sect. 7 the conclusions are given.

2   Literature Review

The bibliographical review presents in this article takes into account publications already included in CACIC [8] between 2012-2019, adding the ones between 2021-2023. Table 1 shows a brief of the found characteristics according to the year published.

The presented review is mainly based on three aspects: neighborhood search scheme [20], characteristics of the neighborhood structures, and the size of the instances of the problem.

We observe that the VNS metaheuristic has been applied to various academic and real-world problems, applied alone or in a hybrid way in combination with other metaheuristics. Regarding the characteristics of the neighborhood search scheme, we quote two recent examples: collaborative, presented in [2], in which the neighborhood search is made through a combined process between two VNS, and global VNS. Another example is found in [14] where the authors compare two variants VNS^0 and VNS^{NL}; in each variant, it is used the same neighborhood structures and, in their experiments, they compare two structural properties for the local search that lead to the two proposed variants.

Regarding the characteristics of the operators of the neighborhood structures and of the local search, we see in various works such as [2, 12, 18], and [22] that are implemented on a specific representation of the solution of scheduling problem. Besides we have seen that they are implemented from 1, 2, 3, 4, 5, 6, 7, 8, and 9 as numbers of VNS neighborhood structures, and the involved local search operators can be the same or different, in which case such could be 1 or 2 different ones.

As regards the size of the instances, different complexity instances are taken into account, thus differentiating them into three categories which can be classified in the following manner: *Small* to the ones that use between 2 and 5 machines, and from 2-100 jobs, *Medium*; the ones that work with 5-10 machines and more than 100 jobs, and lastly the *Large* that use 10, 20, or more machines, and a number higher or equal to 500 jobs. The classification is based on the number of jobs.

Table 1. Recent research in the relevant field.

Publication	Neighborhood search scheme	Structure features	Problem instance sizes
Maecker et al. (2023) [14]	VNS algorithm where two scheme variants are compared	Six neighborhood structures and two structural properties	small: 20,40,80 jobs and medium: 160,320 jobs
Shaojun Lu et al. (2022) [13]	A variable neighborhood search (VNS) algorithm	Three structures for the investigated problem	small: 30,40,100 jobs and medium: 200 jobs
Deming Lei et al. (2022) [12]	Reduced variable neighborhood search (RVNS)	Five neighborhood structures specific operators	small: 20,25,50 jobs and medium: 150, 250 jobs
Cai et al. (2022) [2]	A collaborative variable neighborhood search (CVNS)	Eight neighborhood structures and two global search operators	small: 30,40,50,60,70,80, 90,100 jobs and medium: 120,150
Zhang et al. (2022) [22]	A general variable neighborhood search (GVNS)	Two intra-machine and inter-machine moves by four neighborhoods	small: 40,50,70,80, 100 jobs and medium: 120 jobs
Rudek et al. (2021) [18]	Fast search scheme in a neighborhood	Only structure used as an operator	small: 100 jobs and medium: 200, 400 and large: 800
García-Guarín et al. (2019) [7]	VNS that allow a continuous representation	Implement algebraic equations and differential equations	competition instance problems
Erden et al. (2019) [4]	VNS is used for initial solution construction	The neighborhood structures are based in dispatching rules	small: 25, 50, 75, 100 medium: 125, 150, 175, and 200 jobs
Jun Pei et al. (2019) [16]	Hybrid VNS-GSA VNS and Gravitational search algorithm (GSA)	Use GSA as local search operator and n-swap as neighborhood structure	small: 60,70,80,90, 100, medium: 200,300, 400, large: 500,600 jobs
Vargas Fortes et al. (2018) [21]	The VNS algorithm where the neighborhoods are defined on continuous space as a distance function	The local search step of the VNS apply the cyclic coordinate method	tested on three simulation systems of the real world
Senne et al. (2013) [19]	VNS heuristic with representation based on solution	Considers three machine movements and nine neighborhoods	small: 5 to 100 jobs and medium: 120, 150,170 and 200 jobs
Cheng et al. (2012) [3]	VNS algorithm use representation based on solution	Use five search structures based on insertion, swap, and inversion	small: 20, 40, 60, 80, 100 jobs

In other research studies, we found that in [4] a VNS is presented to provide initial solutions to other metaheuristics implemented to solve the dynamic process scheduling and due date assignment (DIPPSDDA) problem, where the objective function was to minimize punctuality and tardiness (E/T). In [19] it is applied to the problem of scheduling a set of independent jobs, with sequence-dependent setup times and task compatibility constraints, on a set of parallel machines, with the aim of minimizing the maximum completion time (makespan). In [16] a hybrid VNS-GSA algorithm (VNS and the Gravity Search Algorithm) is applied for a single machine and parallel machine scheduling, the objectives of minimizing maximum earliness and the number of late jobs with effect position-based learning (where the actual processing time of the job is a function of its position) and configuration-dependent processing times. In [3] a VNS is presented for the scheduling problem of identical parallel machines, with the objective of minimizing the total completion time. For the configuration of parameters, in [21] a VNS is presented for the design of the parameters of the damping controllers in multi-machine power systems: such as power system stabilizers (PSS) and the power flux controller. interline-power swing damping (IPFC-POD). For the real-world problem called energy dispatch in smart distributed grids, the hybrid algorithm VNS-DEEPSO (Differential Evolutionary Particle Swarm) is proposed in [7], to obtain solutions to minimize operational costs and maximize smart grid revenues. This algorithm was designed with some improvements that allow the evaluation of equations formed from nonlinear algebraic equations and differential equations in which it is impossible to obtain their derivative with an exact mathematical model [21].

In the present work, different variants of the VNS algorithm are presented and analyzed. These variants (VNS+R, VNS+LHS, VNS+E, and VNS+ER) arise from changes in the basic neighborhood search and selection scheme, in order to improve their performance on the minimization problem of the maximum tardiness.

3   The Parallel Machines Scheduling Problem

The unrestricted parallel machine scheduling problem is a common problem in real manufacturing and production systems, and it is also a problem of interest from theoretical and practical points of view. In the literature, the problem studied is denoted as $P_m||T_{max}$. The first field describes the environment of the P_m machines, and the second contains the constraints, here it can be noted that the problem has no constraints, therefore the field is empty, and the third provides the objective function to be minimized T_{max} [15, 17].

This scheduling problem can be expressed as follows: there are n tasks to be processed without interruption on some of the m identical machines belonging to the system P_m; each machine cannot process more than one task at a time. The task t_j, $(j = 1, 2, 3, ..., n)$ is available at time zero. It requires a positive and uninterrupted processing time p_j on a machine and also has a due date d_j by which its processing should be finished. For a given task processing order (schedule), the earliest completion time C_j and the maximum tardiness time $T_j = \{C_j - d_j, 0\}$, are easily calculated. The problem is to find an optimal order (schedule) that minimizes the value of the objective function:

$$Maximum\,Tardiness : T_{max} = max(T_j) \tag{1}$$

This problem is considered NP-hard when $2 \leq m \leq n$ [15,17]. An instance of the problem with $n = 5$ tasks and $m = 2$ machines is shown in Example 1.

	t_1	t_2	t_3	t_4	t_5		t_j
	(4, 15)	(7, 20)	(8,19)	(2, 6)	(3, 8)		(p_j, d_j)

Fig. 1. Instance with $n = 5$ tasks t_j, $m = 2$, with processing times p_j and due dates d_j; for $j = 1, ..., 5$.

Example 1: Instance with $n = 5$ tasks t_j, $m = 2$, with processing times p_j and due dates d_j; for $j = 1, ..., 5$ (see Fig. 1).

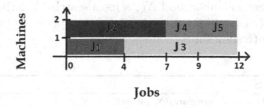

Fig. 2. Gantt chart of a possible solution for Example 1.

The Gantt chart in Fig. 2 describes a possible solution or schedule S (by schedule) of tasks on two machines m_1 and m_2, where

$$S = [\{m_1, (t_1, p_1, d_1), (t_3, p_3, d_3)\}, \{m_2, (t_2, p_2, d_2), (t_4, p_4, d_4), (t_5, p_5, d_5)\}]$$

and the distribution of $tasks = t_1, t_2, t_3, t_4, t_5$ is: t_1 and t_3 runs on m_1 and t_2, t_4 and t_5 run on m_2. Therefore, the respective completion times are $C_j = ((t_1, 4), (t_2, 7), (t_3, 12), (t_4, 9), (t_5, 12))$ and the tardiness times computed in each task $T_j = (0, 0, 0, 3, 4)$, where the maximum tardiness is $T_{max} = 4$.

4   VNS S-metaheuristics and Proposed Variants

The S-metaheuristics have shown their effectiveness in addressing several problems of optimization in different domains [4,7,16,19], among others. They make an exploration through neighborhood structures [20] using a procedure iterative starting from an initial solution, generally random, and applying operators that define the search trajectory.

VNS sequentially considers a set of different neighborhood structures N_i where $i = 1, 2, 3, ..., k_{max}$, are defined in the solution space of the issue. The previous sequence is carried out systematically or randomly in order to obtain high-quality solutions for the purpose of escaping from local optima. A neighborhood structure N in the space of solutions X of a given solution x is denoted as $N(x) \subset X$, where $N : X \rightarrow P(X)$, being $P(X)$ is the power set x [10].

In our work, the sequence of neighborhood structures is understood as the inspection order of each of the N_i neighborhood structures defined as the input of the VNS algorithm. An interesting aspect of VNS is that it presents a basic scheme that serves as a flexible framework for implementing heuristic variants [10] and they also demonstrate good performance in solving complex problems.

4.1   Standard VNS Algorithm

VNS (Algorithm 1) receives as input a set of neighborhood structures defined in advance N_i, $i = 1, ..., k_{max}$. Each iteration of the algorithm is composed of three steps: (1) shaking, (2) local search, and (3) move. The initial solution S_0 is shaken in the current neighborhood N_k, a local search (Algorithm 2) is applied to the solution S_1 (S_1 is obtained by means of the operator of disturbance N_k) to obtain a candidate solution S_2.

Algorithm 1 VNS

1: Input: a set of neighborhood structures N_i for i=1,...,k_{max}
2: $S=S_0$ {Generate the initial solution}
3: **repeat**
4:     $k=1$
5:     **while** $k \leq k_{max}$ **do**
6:         $S_1=N_k(S)$ {Shaking: take a random solution S_1 from k_{th} neighborhood N_k}
7:         $S_2=LS(S_1)$ {LS: Local Search on N_k}
8:         **if** $f(S_2) \leq f(S)$ **then**
9:             $S = S_2$
10:            $k = 1$
11:        **else**
12:            $k = k + 1$ {Move to next neighborhood}
13:        **end if**
14:    **end while**
15: **until** Stopping criteria
16: Output: Best solution S

The current solution S is replaced by the new local optimum S_2, if and only if S_2 is better than S and the same procedure is restarted in N_1, if S_2 is not better, the search is moved to the next neighborhood N_{k+1}, and a new solution is generated in N_{k+1} and that VNS tries to improve until exhausting the available neighborhood structures. The study of the variants of the VNS algorithm was based on the hypothesis that a change in the choice of the sequence of neighborhoods could help escape efficiently from local minima and thus improve its performance. In the following subsections describe the variants implemented and studied in the present work.

Algorithm 2 LS

1: Input: $s=s_0$
2: $i = 0$
3: **repeat**
4: $\quad s_1 = N(s)$ {Generate a candidate neighbor from s}
5: $\quad$ **if** $f(s_1) \leq f(s)$ **then**
6: $\quad\quad s=s_1$
7: $\quad$ **else**
8: $\quad\quad$ Stop
9: $\quad$ **end if**
10: **until** Stopping
11: Output: Final solution found s (local optima)

4.2 Variant Algorithm VNS+R

The VNS+R algorithm (Algorithm 3) uses a sequence of structures random input neighborhoods, the selection of the next neighborhood structure N_i is obtained from some of the N_r (Algorithm 3, lines 12-13).

Algorithm 3 VNS+R

1: Input: a set of neighborhood structures N_i for i=1,...,k_{max}
2: $S=S_0$ {Generate the initial solution}
3: **repeat**
4: $\quad k=1$
5: $\quad$ **while** $k \leq k_{max}$ **do**
6: $\quad\quad S_1=N_k(S)$ {Shaking: take a random solution S_1 from k_{th} neighborhood N_k}
7: $\quad\quad S_2=LS(S_1)$ {LS: Local Search on N_k}
8: $\quad\quad$ **if** $f(S_2) \leq f(S)$ **then**
9: $\quad\quad\quad S = S_2$
10: $\quad\quad\quad k = 1$
11: $\quad\quad$ **else**
12: $\quad\quad\quad r = \text{random}(0, k_{max}\text{-}1)$
13: $\quad\quad\quad k = r$ {Move to another neighborhood $r! = k$}
14: $\quad\quad$ **end if**
15: $\quad$ **end while**
16: **until** Stopping criteria
17: Output: Best solution S

4.3 VNS+LHS Variant

VNS+LHS has a previous stage where a set of data structures of neighborhoods $\{N_1, ..., N_{k_{max}}\}$ is processed to generate the sequence to apply during the search. This is selected from a set of possible sequences of structure structures and neighborhoods built with Latin squares. Therefore, in order to build such set of possible sequences of neighborhood structures and then choose the most expediently, it was proposed: 1) generate a combination of uniform sequences in a design space with the Latin squares approach, 2) evaluate the sequences with the objective function of the problem on a bounded set of instances and applying appropriate statistical tests, and finally 3) choose the one that has been the most convenient. From there, VNS+LHS behaves like VNS.

4.4   Variant VNS+E

The VNS+E variant (Algorithm 4) was implemented by extending the local search (Algorithm 4, line 7) to a number greater than 1, with respect to possible immediate neighbors of the current solution. A ranking is then performed by evaluating the function objective and the best quality solution is selected as the best solution with respect to the current solution (LSE, Algorithm 5).

Algorithm 4 VNS+E

```
1: Input: a set of neighborhood structures N_i for i=1,...,k_max
2: S=S_0 {Generate the initial solution}
3: repeat
4:     k=1
5:     while k ≤ k_max do
6:         S_1=N_k(S) {Shaking: take a random solution S_1 from k_th neighborhood N_k}
7:         S_2=LSE(S_1) {LS: Local Search exploratory on N_k}
8:         if f(S_2) ≤ f(S) then
9:             S = S_2
10:            k = 1
11:        else
12:            k = k + 1 {Move to next neighborhood}
13:        end if
14:    end while
15: until Stopping criteria
16: Output: Best solution S
```

4.5   Variant VNS+ER

The VNS+ER algorithm is the last variant that is proposed, which is obtained through the combination of VNS+E and VNS+R. It also uses the LSE search (Algorithm 5). To perform the move, use the strategy of the algorithm (Algorithm 3) in lines 12 and 13.

Algorithm 5 LSE

```
1: Input: s=s_0
2: i = 0
3: repeat
4:     Generate(s) {Generate n candidate neighbors from s applying N_k}
5:     s_1= rank-best-neighbor() {Order and select the best neighbor of s}
6:     if f(s_1) ≤ f(s) then
7:         s=s_1
8:     else
9:         Stopping
10:    end if
11: until Stopping
12: Output: Final solution found s (local optima)
```

5   Design of Experiments

All the algorithms were implemented in C++ language, in the MALLBA library [1]. 90 instances of the problem are established, for each of these instances the algorithms are executed 30 times and the maximum number of evaluations is set to 360,000 as stopping criteria. The experiments were executed in a sub-cluster formed by eleven nodes whose characteristics are the following: 64-bit CPUs each with Intel Q9550 Quad Core 2.83 GHz, 4 GB DDR3 1333 Mz memory, 160 Gb SATA hard drive and Asus P5Q3 motherboard.

5.1   Instances of the Problem

In order to find test instances of the problem, a review of the literature where the parallel machine scheduling problem is addressed [3,16,19] among others. While it was noted that there are instances of the problem of scheduling of parallel machines, the same ones, in general, involve more information depending on the objective function studied and the restrictions of the problem such as setup times, or release times to the system, times of deterioration of tasks (or jobs). However, for our unrestricted problem (on assignments) we do not none were found, for this reason, the set of instances was built from data obtained by random generator for parallel scheduling problem. These data consisted of pairs (p_j, d_j), where p_j is the time of processing and d_j is the due date of the task t_j for different sizes of problem instances. For the experiments, 90 instances were generated using a random generator by different problem sizes which were: *Small* of 100 tasks with 2 and 5 machines; *Medium* of 120, 150, 200 tasks and 5, 10, and 20 machines; *Large* of 500 tasks and 10 number of machines. Such are available upon request (email: crgatica@email.unsl.edu.ar). The solution evaluation function takes an instance as input and calculates the value of *maximum tardiness* according to Eq. (1) in Sect. 3.

5.2   Parameter Settings

One of the advantages of the VNS algorithms consists of a scarce number of parameters to set up, regardless of the establishing the stop criteria, and define the set of neighborhood structures of entry which are: the number of structures of neighborhood $k_{max} = 6$ (for the instances of 500 tasks is $k_{max} = 8$), the maximum number of iterations in the local search is 1,000, number of additional neighbors in the local exploration search is 10. Whereas, for the 500 tasks is 50. The maximum number of evaluations of the objective function is 360,000, which is defined as the stopping criterion. The neighborhood structures N_k are given by the disturbing operators N-swap (N_1), 2-opt (N_2), 3-opt (N_3), 4-opt (N_4), Shift (N_5), Scramble (N_6), Insertion (N_7) and Inversion (N_8). A description of such operators is found in [20]. The representation of the solution used in algorithms is an integer permutation.

5.3   Algorithm Performance Evaluation Metrics

The metrics defined for the experimental study were: *Bench*, which is the reference value, or, so far, reference value, or optimum known for now, which is obtained by applying the heuristics and dispatch rules [15]; *Best*, the best value of the objective found function.

$$Ebest = \frac{Best - Bench}{Bench} * 100 \qquad (2)$$

This is the percentage error. *Mbest*, the mid value of Best; *Mebest*, the mid value of *Ebest*; *Median*, is the central value of the set of *Best* values sorted from smallest to largest; *Mevals*, the mid value of objective function evaluations where *Best* value was found; *M. Times Runs*, the average execution time in nanoseconds.

6   Analysis of Results

In this section is presented an analysis of the results of the computational results considering the 90 instances, ten units of each of the following sizes: (a) $n = 100$ and $m = 5$; (b) $n = 100$ and $m = 10$; (c) $n = 120$ and $m = 5$; (d) $n = 120$ and $m = 10$; (e) $n = 150$ and $m = 5$; (f) $n = 150$ and $m = 10$; (g) $n = 200$ and $m = 10$; (h) $n = 200$ and $m = 20$ and (i) $n = 500$ and $m = 10$.

Table 2 synthesizes the obtained results obtained by VNS and the variants VNS+R, VNS+LHS, VNS+E and VNS+ER. The average values of *Mbest*, *Best* are shown, and the percentage error value *Ebest*, are separated into groups according to the size of the instances of the problem *Small, Medium* and *Large*.

The table entries for the metrics *Mbest* and *Best* correspond to the average values found by the algorithm VNS and its variants. The minimum values are seen in bold font. Regarding the metric *Ebest* are the values of the percentage error obtained by the Eq. (2) of the Sect. 5.3, and correspond to average, same, or minor values of *Best* regarding the reference values *Bench*. Said values of *Ebest* can be zero or negative, and are also marked in bold font.

We have included the results obtained in our previous CACIC work [8] that correspond to the group of size *small* size: $n = 100$ and $m = 5$. For the rest of the group, starting from *small*: $n = 100$ and $m = 10$ new results are reported.

If we see the results previously mentioned of instances *Small* $n = 100$ and $m = 5$, the best average values correspond to the VNS+ER variant related to *Best* and *Ebest*, and to the variant VNS+LHS related to *Mbest*. Then, continuing with the size group of small instances: $n = 100$ but with $m = 10$ machines, which are new results, we see in the column corresponding to VNS+E, the values *Mbest*, *Best* and *Ebest* are minimum in the three metrics with respect to the rest of the algorithms.

For the group of instances *Medium*: $n = 120$, $n = 150$ and $n = 200$ some minimum values of the metric *Mbest* relate to VNS+LHS, and others to the variant VNS+E. The minimum values of the metric *Best* and *Ebest* are found in the column of the variant VNS+E.

For the group of instances *Large*: $n = 500$ tasks, the variant VNS+LHS obtains the minimum values of the three evaluation metrics *Mbest*, *Best* and *Ebest* regarding the rest of the algorithms.

Briefly, for the different sizes of the problem *Small*, *Medium*, and *Large* we can see that the variants VNS+ER, VNS+E and VNS+LHS find minimum values in the *Mbest*, *Best* and *Ebest* metrics. Therefore, the suggested hypothesis in this study establishes that some of the variants better the performance of VNS.

Table 2. Comparison of VNS methaheuristic variants with respect to *Mbest*, *Best* and *Ebest*.

Size	n	m	Avg. values	VNS	VNS+R	VNS+LHS	VNS+E	VNS+ER
Small	100	5	Mbest	2,469.05	2,570.58	**2,402.37**	2,459.41	2,466.10
			Best	2,376.95	2,415.15	2,341.35	2,342.45	**2,329.15**
			Ebest	3.94	6.83	1.69	0.95	**-0.26**
		10	Mbest	9,317.35	9,319.21	9,318.57	**9,299.55**	9,307.00
			Best	9,279.60	9,265.50	9,275.20	**9,221.30**	9,232.10
			Ebest	-0.47	-0.62	-0.51	**-1.09**	-0.97
Medium	120	5	Mbest	10,036.35	10,025.59	**9,764.68**	9,780.10	9,828.20
			Best	9823.8	9,798.70	9,710.40	**9,704.00**	9,706.70
			Ebest	1.03	0.77	-0.14	**-0.20**	-0.17
		10	Mbest	11,316.00	11,203.31	11,128.80	**11,111.76**	11,127.93
			Best	11,093.20	11,123.20	11,081.50	**11,030.60**	11,053.10
			Ebest	-0.42	-0.17	-0.40	**-0.84**	-0.67
	150	5	Mbest	17,028.92	17,025.83	**16,414.83**	16,436.83	16,584.56
			Best	16,693.80	16,655.70	16,312.40	**16,302.60**	16,371.20
			Ebest	2.27	2.06	-0.03	**-0.07**	0.34
		10	Mbest	13,965.51	13,957.42	13,842.22	**13,839.43**	13,853.77
			Best	13,819.90	13,829.90	13,790.90	**13,782.70**	13,787.90
			Ebest	-0.17	-0.09	-0.38	**-0.44**	-0.40
	200	10	Mbest	18,631.72	18,630.30	**18,354.99**	18,367.97	18,439.44
			Best	18,440.50	18,414.30	18,285.30	**18,266.00**	18,284.90
			Ebest	0.76	0.61	-0.09	**-0.20**	-0.09
		20	Mbest	19,739.73	19,728.15	19,609.03	**19,604.22**	19,622.15
			Best	19,598.50	19,598.80	19,578.40	**19,538.90**	19,539.60
			Ebest	-0.05	-0.05	-0.16	**-0.36**	-0.35
Large	500	10	Mbest	46,323.71	46,299.29	**45,948.44**	46,023.70	46,018.91
			Best	45,835.10	45,731.20	**45,480.90**	45,551.60	45,552.60
			Ebest	1.12	0.89	**0.34**	0.49	0.50

Figure 3 illustrates the box diagrams according to the evaluation metric *Ebest* of the algorithm VNS, and the variants VNS+R, VNS+LHS, VNS+E and VNS+ER, separated in groups of different instance sizes of the problem.

In the box diagrams, we can see the metric of evaluation *Median* represented by a horizontal line in bold. If such lines are centered in zero, it means that the obtained values *Best* are close to the *Bench*, that is, to the optimum known.

Besides, if the graphic of the box diagrams are below zero it means that the values *Best* are better than the values *Bench*, meaning that there were found new optimums or better reference values close to the optimums.

For the group of instances *Small* (a) and (b), all the algorithms reach the optimum known value. It can observed that the mid of the *Ebest* below zero, even reaching negative values, which indicate that the algorithms get up to better values than the known optimum.

For the group of instances *Medium*, for the instances (c), (d), and (e) it can be seen that the difference in the performance of the algorithms, the standard VNS, and the VNS+R do not reach the optimum value; Its values of *Ebest* are always higher or even zero. In the best-case scenario, algorithms VNS+E and VNS+LHS stand out. In (e), an increase of the *Ebest* is noticeable for the algorithm VNS+ER. For all the instances you can see that the algorithm VNS+E and the VNS+LHS have a tendency to find closer and better values to the *Ebest*.

For the group of instances *Large* no algorithm with the chosen parametric configurations reaches the optimum value, being algorithm VNS+LHS the one that stands out. It is worth mentioning that studies were undertaken with different numbers of neighborhoods, augmenting said number k_{max} from 6 to 8 as the entrance. It was also augmented the exploratory potential of the variants VNS+E and VNS+ER sets the number of neighbors from 10 to 50 in the local search.

Figure 4 shows a convergence graph of the computational effort of the algorithms according to the evaluation metric *Mevals* separated by the groups of the different sizes of the instances from (a) to (i). Here, the number of evaluations that the algorithms need in the search process to find the optimum until reaching the stop criteria, which was set at 360,000.

In summary, the exploratory variants (VNS+E and VNS+ER) need a higher number of evaluations in the search processing. This, at the same time, needs longer execution times of the algorithms according to the measuring variable in nanoseconds *M. Time Runs* managing to avoid a premature convergence. This happens when there is a stagnation toward optimum locals to explore in more promising space search areas.

6.1 Statistical Test

We use the non-parametric statistic test (Friedman Ranking) [6], and [5] to make a comparison of the experimental media, obtained by taking as an evaluation metric, the average value of the Media (*Mbest*). Thus, we obtained a ranking of the algorithms, which represents the algorithm with the best performance in each group, separated by the size of the instances.

To compare each algorithm with each other, and verify if there are any differences between them, we use a process *post-hoc*, that as the same test aforementioned, this one is also provided for by the tool *Controlltest*, [11].

In applying the procedure *Controlltest*, [11] of comparisons in pairs between the control algorithm, the algorithm with best performance, in comparison with the others, comparing in pairs, if the Holm adjusted values p-*values* are inferior than 0.05, the pears are significantly different. On the other hand, if the p-*values* is more than, or equal to 0.05, it implies that such algorithms in the pair, are not statistically different with respect to the control algorithm.

For the group of instances *Small*, in groups (a) and (b) it was found that the VNS+ER and VNS+E variants were the best and there were no significant differences between the two, but with the rest of the algorithms.

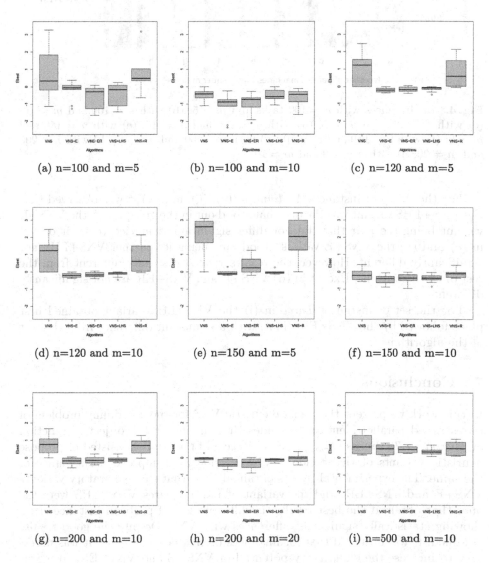

(a) n=100 and m=5   (b) n=100 and m=10   (c) n=120 and m=5

(d) n=120 and m=10   (e) n=150 and m=5   (f) n=150 and m=10

(g) n=200 and m=10   (h) n=200 and m=20   (i) n=500 and m=10

Fig. 3. Boxplots of problem instances comparing VNS variants about *Ebest*

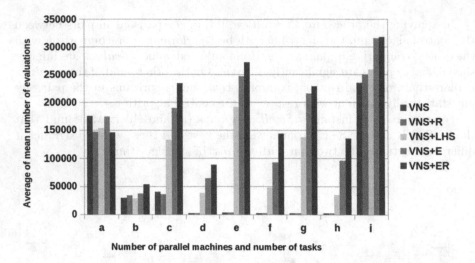

Fig. 4. (a) Instances with $n = 100$ tasks and $m = 5$, (b) with $n = 100$ and $m = 10$; (c) with $n = 120$ and $m = 5$; (d) with $n = 120$ and $m = 10$; (e) with $n = 150$ and $m = 5$; (f) with $n = 150$ and $m = 10$; (g) with $n = 200$ and $m = 10$; (h) with $n = 200$ and $m = 20$; (i) with $n = 500$ and $m = 10$.

For the group of instances *Medium*, in (c), (g), and (f) it was observed that the VNS+LHS variant was the one that stood out in the group, with the VNS+E variant being the pair that did not differ significantly; in vice versa, it occurs in (e) and (h) the VNS+E variant stood out, being its partner VNS+LHS not significantly different. However, the results were statistically different from the rest of the algorithms. Except in (d) VNS+E and VNS+ER are not significantly different.

For the set of instances *Large* in (i) the VNS+LHS variant obtained first place followed by the VNS+E variant, with a significant difference from the rest of the algorithms.

7   Conclusions

In this work we present the S-metaheuristic VNS for the scheduling problem of unrestricted parallel identical machines that minimizes the objective function of *Maximum Tardiness* (T_{max}). The objective of the study consisted of propose heuristic variants of the standard VNS version that improve performance of the same. The experimental results obtained show that the exploratory variants VNS+E and VNS+ER, and the variant of Latin squares VNS+LHS were the ones that obtained the best results, in different sets of problem instance sizes, showing statistically significant differences with VNS. Despite the good results obtained, it was observed that for instances of greater complexity, it was necessary to increase the exploratory potential of VNS+E and VNS+ER, so it was increased the number of neighbors of the current solution in the exploratory local search, and it was also required to increase the number of neighborhood structures available to explore. This implied an increase in the execution time of such variants, but less convergence toward local optima is achieved. The VNS+LHS variant obtains a good performance in each set of problem sizes, is expensive in its execution times, and requires extra time for the construction of the possible sequences of neighborhood structures using a Latin square. This allows us to conclude that in future work it will be necessary to carry out experiments to implement new strategies and search operators, especially to solve a set of instances of the problem of large size, as well as an analysis of the behavior of the algorithms and strategies that are proposed.

Acknowledgments. The authors are grateful for the continuous support of the Universidad Nacional de San Luis (UNSL) through the Research Project PROICO 03-1018 and the Departamento de Informática in the Facultad de Ciencias Físico Matemáticas y Naturales in the UNSL.

References

1. Alba, et al.: MALLBA: a library of skeletons for combinatorial optimisation. In: Monien, B., Feldmann, R. (eds.) Euro-Par 2002. LNCS, vol. 2400, pp. 927–932. Springer, Heidelberg (2002). https://doi.org/10.1007/3-540-45706-2_132
2. Cai, J., Lu, S., Cheng, J., Wang, L., Gao, Y., Tan, T.: Collaborative variable neighborhood search for multi-objective distributed scheduling in two-stage hybrid flow shop with sequence-dependent setup times. Sci. Rep. **12**(1), 1–19 (2022)
3. Cheng, W., Guo, P., Zhang, Z., Zeng, M., Liang, J.: Variable neighborhood search for parallel machines scheduling problem with step deteriorating jobs. Math. Prob. Eng. **2012**, 928312 (2012)
4. Erden, C., Demir, H.I., Kökçam, A.H.: Solving integrated process planning, dynamic scheduling, and due date assignment using metaheuristic algorithms. Math. Prob. Eng. **2019**, 1572614 (2019)
5. Friedman, M.: A comparison of alternative test of significance for the problem of the m rankings. Ann. Math. Stat. **11**, 86–92 (1940)
6. Friedman, M.: The use of ranks to avoid the assumption of normality implicit in the analysis of variance. J. Am. Stat. Assoc. **3**, 674–701 (1937)
7. García-Guarín, P.J., Cantor, J., Cortés-Guerrero, C., Guzmán Pardo, M.A., Rivera Rascón, S.A.: Implementación del algoritmo vns-deepso para el despacho de energía en redes distribuidas inteligentes. Inge Cuc (2019)
8. Gatica, C., Molina, S., Leguizamón, G.: Evaluation of variants of the VNS metaheuristics for the parallel machines scheduling problem. XXVIII Congreso Argentino de Ciencias de la Computación, La Rioja Argentina (2022)
9. Hansen, P., Mladenović, N.: Variable neighborhood search: principles and applications. Eur. J. Oper. Res. **130**(3), 449–467 (2001)
10. Hansen, P., Mladenović, N., Todosijević, R., Hanafi, S.: Variable neighborhood search: basics and variants. EURO J. Comput. Optimiz. **5**(3), 423–454 (2017)
11. J. Derrac, S. García, D.M., Herrera, F.: A practical tutorial on the use of nonparametric statistical tests as a methodology for comparing evolutionary and swarm intelligence algorithms. Swarm Evolut. Comput. **1**, 3–18 (2011)

12. Lei, Deming y He, S.: An adaptive artificial bee colony for unrelated parallel machine scheduling with additional resource and maintenance. Exp. Syst. Appl. **205**, 117577 (2022)
13. Lu, S., Ma, C., Kong, M., Zhou, Z., Liu, X.: Solving a stochastic hierarchical scheduling problem by VNS-based metaheuristic with locally assisted algorithms. Appl. Soft Comput. **130**, 109719 (2022)
14. Maecker, S., Shen, L., Mönch, L.: Unrelated parallel machine scheduling with eligibility constraints and delivery times to minimize total weighted tardiness. Comput. Oper. Res. **149**, 105999 (2023)
15. Morton, T.E., Pentico, D.W.: Heuristic scheduling systems. John Wiley and Sons, Inc, With Applications to Production Systems and Project Management (1993)
16. Pei, J., Cheng, B., Liu, X., Pardalos, P.M., Kong, M.: Single-machine and parallel-machine serial-batching scheduling problems with position-based learning effect and linear setup time. Ann. Oper. Res. **272**(1), 217–241 (2019)
17. Pinedo, M.: Scheduling Theory, Algorithms, and Systems. PRENTICE HALL (1995)
18. Rudek, R.: A fast neighborhood search scheme for identical parallel machine scheduling problems under general learning curves. Informática blanda aplicada, **113**, 108023 (2021)
19. Senne, E.L.F., Chaves, A.A.: A VNS heuristic for an industrial parallel machine scheduling problem. ICIEOM CIO Valladolid (Spain, 2013)
20. Talbi, E.G.: Metaheuristics from design to implementation. John Wiley & Sons (Canada, 2009)
21. de Vargas Fortes, E., Macedo, L.H., de Araujo, P.B., Romero, R.: A VNS algorithm for the design of supplementary damping controllers for small-signal stability analysis. Int. J. Electr. Power Energy Syst. **94**, 41–56 (2018)
22. Zhang, Xiangyi y Chen, L.: A general variable neighborhood search algorithm for a parallel-machine scheduling problem considering machine health conditions and preventive maintenance. Informática & Investigación de operaciones **143**, 105738 (2022)

Technology Applied to Education

Augmented Reality to Reinforce Working Memory in Children with ASD. A Case Studies

Mónica R. Romero[1]([⊠]) [iD], Ivana Harari[1] [iD], Javier Diaz[1] [iD], Estela M. Macas[2] [iD], and Nancy Armijos[3] [iD]

[1] Faculty of Computer Science, National University of La Plata, LINTI, Calle 50 y 120, Buenos Aires La Plata, Argentina
monica.romerop@info.unlp.edu.ar
[2] International Ibero-American University, UNINI MX, Calle 15 y 36, Campeche, México
[3] International University of Ecuador UIDE, Loja, Ecuador

Abstract. Are interventions conducted using augmented reality beneficial for the working memory of children with autism spectrum disorder? This article describes a case study, which reviewed working memory in children who used Hope Software, the objective of the study was to assess whether children can remember after one year of the intervention the processes of imitation, perception, visual coordination, motor skills from sequences of auditory, visual stimuli, in direct, reverse and increasing order. The research was worked under the mixed approach, the type of research was experimental, descriptive and purposeful, it had the participation and guidance of a multidisciplinary team, it was carried out at the Ludic Place Therapeutic Center in Quito Ecuador, during the period from June to December 2022, A proposal was built that allows obtaining metrics through an assessment carried out through participatory design methods.

The results obtained indicate that after one year of the intervention the participants remembered the processes, they even repeated some sequences, so we conclude that the use of augmented reality can favors working memory in children with autism.

Keywords: Augmented Reality (AR) · Autism Spectrum Disorder ASD · New information and communication technologies (NTIC) · Teaching learning · Software Hope · Working memory

1 Introduction

Memory is a complex cognitive system that is not understood as "a single entity, it consists of a series of different systems that have in common the capacity to store information" [1], as well as to retrieve it. Said information is obtained through the senses, memory being in a way a record of perceptions [2–5]. Regarding the population with Autism Spectrum Disorder (ASD), working memory problems could arise due to the type of information that must be remembered[6] and the demands of the tasks or the environment, also due to difficulties in the storage and simultaneous processing of information[7, 8].

P. Pesado (Ed.): CACIC 2022, CCIS 1778, pp. 21–32, 2023.
https://doi.org/10.1007/978-3-031-34147-2_2

Previously, an Educational Treatment of Children with ASD mediated through augmented reality (AR) called TEARA was determined, which can be defined as a disruptive method that complements the new information and communication technologies (NTIC) designed to improve the quality of life of children with autism, a training system called Hope is defined, which reinforces and promotes teaching learning processes such as imitation, motor skills and perception[9]. On the other hand, through the work: "Hope Project: Development of mobile applications with augmented reality to teach dance to children with ASD" [10] we executed an intervention plan to improve certain skills in children with autism and we have determined that AR allows improve skills and teaching-learning processes [11–17].

While it is true that there has been much experimentation with the use of Information and Communication Technologies in the treatment, reinforcement, education, routines of children with ASD [18], it is also true; that the biggest problem resides in the fact that the studies carried out are of a brief and specific nature where AR is used in a few sessions and a result is obtained, there is little literature where researchers have focused their attention on verifying what happens with the research participants experimental after the interventions. The idea is to know if indeed the skills that improved with the use of AR have been stored in the working memory, if the children remember what they learned [19–26].

The previous studies served as the basis for the development of the present investigation where new aspects have extended and explored, such as the working memory of ASD children after a year of intervention using TEARA, the perspective of information processing through several experiments that served to evaluate working memory. In this investigation, the investigative background is described, the methodology and work plan to be used, the characteristics and procedure for the selection of the sample and the evaluation instruments are exposed in Sect. 2, the discussion session shows the processing of the data obtained and finally the conclusions, limitations and future work based on the results obtained are detailed.

2 Material and Methods

The study is of a descriptive type and design, of a selective non-probabilistic cross-sectional type. Sampling is non-probabilistic, purposeful, intentional with inclusion and exclusion criteria; since premeditated intentions are being used to choose a group that is typical of the sample. The participants were 05 children with ASD from the Ludic Place Center, between 5 and 8 years old, people who met the inclusion criteria. The instruments used were the tests, corresponding to PMPA (free recall, cued recall, and recognition) and MSCA (visual item recall and prose recall). The information was processed with the IBM SPSS Statistics and Microsoft Excel programs Characteristic of the sample (Inclusion criteria): Neurodevelopmental diagnosis: Autism spectrum disorder, Severity level: 1, Age: between 05 years, 02 months, and 08 years. 04 months, Schooling. From 2 to 4 grades, during the year 2022, Educational situation: included in regular basic education institutions. Gender: Male and educative: female: Spanish. Before the beginning of the sessions, the parents gave their informed consent for the children to participate in the experiment.

Conditions for the administration of the tests to the study sample. The evaluations were carried out individually at the Ludic Place Therapeutic Center in the City of Quito, Ecuador. The evaluation environments were found to be sufficiently illuminated and free of noise. The duration of each evaluation session fluctuated between 25–35 min. The reagents administered strictly following the instructions published in the respective manuals. The characteristics of the participants in the case study shown below in Table 1.

Table 1. Descriptive sheet of participant characteristics.

Participant	Age	IC	Severed ASD	Reciprocal ty social emotion	Communication No-Verbal	Inflexibly to change	Stereotypies and reactivity and sensory
I1	5	Half	Half	Half	Half	Half	Half
I2	6	Half	Half	Half	Half	Half	Half
I3	4	Half	Half	Half	Half	Half	Half
I4	5	Half	Half	Half	Half	Half	Half
I5	7	Low	Low	Low	Low	Low	Low

2.1 Work Plan

ASD are interventions mediated through AR, for this purpose we carry out a work plan where different phase are evidenced.

Phase I: Selection of memory tests.

We then examined recall in a variety of situations: individual difference tests, standard laboratory tests (controlled situations), and recall of an event (natural situation).

Phase II: Testing.

In phase 2 the memory tasks defined. The memory tasks to be used in the experiments were the following:

- Natural Situation: Recall of the introductory event (recall of the event and recall of details)
- Controlled Situations

- PMPA (free recall, cued recall, and recognition)
- MSCA (visual item recall and prose recall)

Phase III: Evaluation of results.

We will therefore have three levels of evaluation, referring to: Natural situation. (Memory and recognition), Controlled Situations (PMPA), (MSCA)

Experiments proposed to measure Working Memory in ASD children.

To conduct the task, posters associated with Software Hope were used, starting by teaching each of the alternatives shown by the software managed by the therapist, introducing the child and interacting with him.

Experiment 1: Recall of the Introductory Event.

Hope Software avatar images. Hence, the therapist asks about the image: "Do you? remember what this image is about" (identity) and after looking at the menu card that.

segregated into 5 options, "Do any of these options bring back any memories?" (action). Additionally, the children were asked if they could identify knowledge, namely: "Do you know how to dance?" (Sensory detail) and "Where did you dance?" (Contextual detail) the order of the questions was established following the logical sequence of the situation. First: the dance memory (Software Hope); then: the context indistinctly (options, music, place); and, finally, the action associated with dancing.

The questions about this episode were developed considering the characteristics of a natural situation. Therefore, it was avoided to pose the task as a succession of questions and answers in the manner of an interrogation or an exam. We have considered that this modality was suitable for a familiar memory format for the child, of a colloquial type, which was also useful when calibrating the type of memory.

The score in this test is 1 point for each correct answer in the 2 questions about memory of the event (identity memory and character action) on the one hand, and 1 point for each correct answer in the 2 questions about memory of details on the other hand. (Sensory detail and software contextual detail). Next, Table 2 shows the resources (image, audio, video) used for the experiment.

Experiment 2: Controlled situations

PMPA (Memory Test). This test made up of pictorial material corresponding to 4 categories (child uses hands, child uses feet, child makes a pose, child makes a line). 16 cards are used (4 per category). The 16 images are presented one by one in random order. The therapist asks the child to name each image once seen. Once the drawing is named, she removes the letter. After presenting the 16 cards in random order, free recall, cued recall, and recognition are requested in that order. Free Recollection After 30 min, the child is asked to name all the pictures that she remembers, in the order she wants. Only hits considered.

I remember with clues. The therapist tells the child: "Very good, now we are going to do it in another way". She is given the name of each category as a clue (e.g., "There were hands") and is asked to name all the pictures on the list that she can remember that correspond to that category. Hits and intrusions, if any, are considered. Recognition: The child with eight pictures for this recognition task. Each sheet presents four illustrations: one of them corresponds to one of the images seen previously and the other three images are distractors from the same conceptual category. The eight plates are presented successively, one by one. In total, eight drawings. The therapist asks the child to point out

Table 2. Recourses utilizes experiment.

Software Hope -	Instrument	Action to perform	Figure
Image	Avatar	Show Hope Software avatar of the	
	Menu	Show each of the menu. options	
	Scenarios	Show game scenarios the various	
Audio	songs	play songs that the game has.	
Video	Video de sessions	of Show child fragments of his stake	

which of the images she has seen before. Hits, false alarms and omissions, if any, are taken into account.

Memory tests of the Mc Carthy Scales of Aptitudes and Psychomotor Skills for Children (MSCA).

These are two tests belonging to the MSCA (general intelligence test for children between 2 1/2 years and 8 1/2 years). The tasks are: free recall of visual items (pictorial) memory) and free recall of prose (verbal memory) [3].

Visual Item Recall

It is an immediate free recall task of images. It is a sheet with illustrations of five dance movements that visually promoting double coding: visual and oral verbal. The therapist names aloud while pointing to them and the child repeats. The sheet is exposed for 10 s, so the children have all 5 objects present during that time. The therapist then puts the slide away and immediately asks the child to remember what she has shown him, in the order she wants. Next, Table 3 shows the visual items used for experiment 2.

Table 3. MSCA memory tests. Item visuals experiment 2.

It is a simple story created in relation to the Software Hope that the therapist reads to the child the story has few words no more than 100. Then she asks him to tell it to her. For the score, the story has divided into 6 elements that contemplate the essential points of the story: 2 characters (teacher and child) and 4 actions (hands, feet, trace a route, pose). Table 4 below shows the items of the prose recall test.

Table 4. Story belonging to the MSCA prose memory test.

One day, a child, attended Ludic Place, when his teacher arrived, she was waiting for him and indicated a new game called Hope, the idea was to follow the avatar(robot)displayed on the screen, and perform. certain actions. this game allowed the child to have fun in addition to moving and dancing. The boy could choose the music and the scenery and some options through the game menu. The boy learned to move his hands, then his feet, he also made some strokes with his hands, and he was able to perform. some poses After a while the boy was dancing in the classroom.

3   Results

The evaluation of the working memory in ASD children after the use of the Hope software, was carried out after 1 semester of intervention and sought to measure the working memory for the effect, 10 sessions were carried out. Of which 05 were predestined to the evaluation of the tests planned in experiment 1 where some natural situations were evaluated, through introductory events about Software Hope and the remaining 5 to the evaluation of experiment 2, which used controlled situations regarding dance, dance, movements. In each of them different activities were proposed including different techniques and materials. Table 5 below shows the summary of the results obtained.

Table 5. Results of Assessment of Working Memory in ASD Children.

Actions experiment 1	Actions experiment 1		Actions experiment 1			
	Event introductory	Hope Software	PMPA		MSCA	
Child with ASD	Memory of event	Memory of details	Test memory free memory	Remember or with indications	Re-sane of Items visuals	Re-sane of prose
Scale ofPunctuation	Score of (0–4)	Score of (0–2)	Score of (0–8)	Score of (0–16)	Score of (0–5)	Score of (0–5)
I1	4	2	7	6	5	3
I2	4	2	8	5	4	4
I3	3	2	7	7	5	3
I4	4	2	6	4	4	4
I5	4	1	4	6	5	2

Adaptation to experience. The participants in the intervention showed their acceptance and comfort. Diverse types of data collected during the intervention. On the one hand, those corresponding to experiment 1 and experiment 2, and on the other, those related to the performance of the participants during the sessions. Two categorical data sets were obtained, which were used to assess participants' progress in working memory.

As shown in Fig. 1, a positive evolution is obtained in all the items for all the participants. The best values are obtained in terms of Experiment 1, especially for recall of details and event memory; however, the result of Experiment 2 in the PMDA test, especially in memories with clues, was not satisfactory and all participants reached scores of below average. All the participants in the intervention presented significant improvements in working memory. From an estimated range of [80%-100%] correct working memory children without ASD, the participants in this case study presented a range estimated [70%-55%] participant I1 had 28 correct answers out of 40 possible with 70%, followed by participant I3 with 67.5%, participant I4 with 62.5% except for I5 who shows a slight decrease with 55%.

Prior to the evaluation, the results of the measurement of working memory for the 2019–2020 period of the members of the case study were available, where natural situations and controlled situations were reviewed, they used PMPA, MSCA scales, we contrasted the results of the evaluation obtained in 2022 making significant progress. We now analyze the progress of the study group using the probabilistic approach. We compared the distributions of responses before and after the intervention, measuring the distances to the mean (normalized to 1) of the evaluations of both distributions. There is progress if the assessment after the intervention is higher than the average, and progress is significant if the distance between both values exceeds 5%. The following results are shown below in Fig. 2:

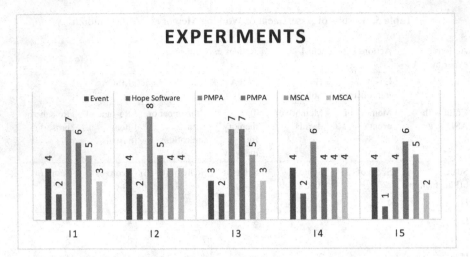

Fig. 1. Individual progress of the participants in terms of working memory before the use of AR and after the use of Software Hope.

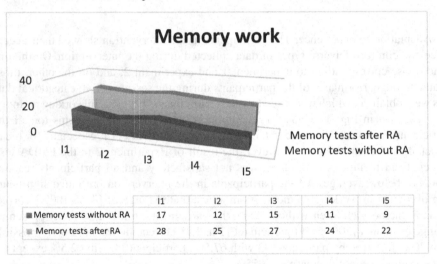

	I1	I2	I3	I4	I5
Memory tests without RA	17	12	15	11	9
Memory tests after RA	28	25	27	24	22

Fig. 2. Individual progress of the participants in terms of working memory before the use of AR and after the use of the Hope Software.

4 Discussion

We have presented an intervention based on two experiments that allowed us to measure the working memory of children with ASD using an experimental design, the results of the intervention allow us to answer our research question positively. Indeed, the intervention carried out has been shown to be effective when it comes to improving working memory, associated with cognitive abilities, it is important to highlight that the abilities have changed significantly in the period considered.

The results confirm that the use of RA as a means of working memory reinforcement helps children with ASD to reinforce cognitive aspects regarding the storage of memories in working memory, which includes the short and long term, additionally contrasting the results. of the participants prior to the RA intervention, it can be indicated that the success of the stimulation through the senses will largely depend on the teaching-learning strategies used [27–30].

The results showed a higher performance in the tests where an evolutionary pattern was determined, especially in experiment 1, whose strategy was to verify aspects generally related to Software Hope, through memory of the event and recall of details. The evaluation of working memory was used, from sequences of stimuli of different order: auditory, in direct, reverse and increasing order. Regarding the nonverbal communication of the participants through the memory of visual items, there is the greatest progress than those associated with the memory of prose [31, 32].

In this study, there was a planning of experiments with concrete material and following a methodology, where the children interacted with their therapist using various resources to carry out the different proposed activities, which provided knowledge mechanisms to the children in a systemic way, generating environments conducive to fostering interest in remembering.

5 Conclusions

Regarding the theoretical justification, the present study will allow us to understand, in greater detail, the working memory in a group of students with regular basic ASD, which will initially provide significant and updated information in the area; therefore, it will become a relevant source of knowledge given the scarce bibliography on the subject, allowing other professionals to carry out studies and expand the content on the subject of the effectiveness of AR in the working memory of ASD children, regarding the As a practical aspect, the execution of this study will initially enable psychologists, teachers and professionals related to the area to develop new evaluation and treatment resources aimed at improving the working memory of children with ASD. In the same way, incipiently it will facilitate the elaboration. of new projects and stimulation programs on working memory in children with ASD mediated through NTIC.

On the other hand, it will make it possible as an initial study, that the different institutions that provide care and education to children with ASD will additionally serve to train teachers, based on the implementation of resources and scientifically proven information for the stimulation using RA of the memory of work of children with ASD.

Finally, regarding the methodological importance, this study will disseminate data that contribute to the validity and reliability of the instrument used for this group of children.

There are, of course, various limitations in the study conducted that indicate that the results must be viewed with caution, the duration of the intervention, and the heterogeneity of the participants prevent generalization of the results. This study is a particular example of the use of AR as an educational tool that can be an instrument with great potential to reinforce working memory in children with ASD.

The analysis of works focused on attention, memory in ASD reflects opposite results, even in works in which the same evaluation tests used, however, there were no works that allow us to compare results after RA interventions. Having controlled for the variables cognitive level and level of language development in all the studies analyzed.

As future work, correlations of working memory and source memory can be made in children with ASD who participated in training using AR. Future studies should include larger groups, a greater number of sessions with alternative creative dynamics in a longer period of intervention, promoting cooperation between researchers and institutions to unify criteria, lengthen interventions, and design follow-up periods, all of which is crucial to improve the reliability of the results. It is expected to expand this study and conduct new research related to the need for greater knowledge about the functioning of working memory and its link with interventions related to the use of NICT in children with autism.

Acknowledgment. We are grateful to the LINTI New Computer Technologies Research Laboratory of the National University of La Plata -Argentina, the National Secretary of Higher Education, Science and Technology SENESCYT- Ecuador, as well as the Ludic Place therapeutic Centre where this project conducted.

References

1. Han, Y.M.Y., Chan, M.C., Chan, M.M.Y., Yeung, M.K., Chan, A.S.: Effects of working memory load on frontal connectivity in children with autism spectrum disorder: a fNIRS study. Sci. Rep. **12**(1), 1–14 (2022). https://doi.org/10.1038/s41598-022-05432-3
2. Acosta, M.T.: Sleep, memory and learning. Medicina (B. Aires), vol. 79, pp. 29–32 (2019)
3. Agudelo Gómez, L., Pulgarín Posada, L.A., Tabares Gil, C.: La estimulación sensorial en el desarrollo cognitivo de la primera infancia. Cypriot J. Educ. Sci. **20**(2), 37–50 (2018)
4. Seijas Gómez, R.: Atención, memoria y funciones ejecutivas en los trastornos del espectro autista: ¿cuánto hemos avanzado desde Leo Kanner? Rev. la Asoc. Española Neuropsiquiatría, **35**(127), 573–586 (2015). https://doi.org/10.4321/s0211-57352015000300009
5. Solcoff, K.: El origen de la Memoria Episódica y de Control de Fuente: Su relación con las capacidades de Teoría de la Mente (2011)
6. Nekar, D.M., et al.: Effects of augmented reality game-based cognitive–motor training on restricted and repetitive behaviors and executive function in patients with autism spectrum disorder. Healthc. **10**(10), 1981 (2022). https://doi.org/10.3390/healthcare10101981
7. Aguiar-Aguiar, G., Mainegra-Fernández, D., García-Reyes, O.: Teaching reading comprehension to school children with autism spectrum disorders: secrets from experience. Rev. Electron. Educ. **24**(2), 1–16 (2020). https://doi.org/10.15359/ree.24-2.22
8. Roma, M.C.: La construcción de la memoria autobiográfica en niños con TEA mediada por los Sistemas Alternativos y Aumentativos de Comunicación: una revisión sistemática. Perspect. Metod. **20**(99), 1–28 (2020). https://doi.org/10.18294/pm.2020.3166
9. Romero, M.R., Harari, I., Diaz, J., Macas, E.: Hope Project : development of mobile applications with augmented reality to teach dance to children with ASD. In: Libro de actas - XXVIII Congreso Argentino de Ciencias de la Computación - CACIC, pp. 734–745 (2022)
10. Romero, M.R., Harari, I., Diaz, J., Macas, E.: TEARA : Educational treatment of children with ASD , mediated through augmented reality. In: Libro de actas - XXVIII Congreso Argentino de Ciencias de la Computación - CACIC, pp. 118–130 (2022)
11. Romero, M.R., Harari, I., Diaz, J., Macas, E.: Hope project : development of mobile applications with augmented reality to teach dance to children with ASD. In: Libro de actas - XXVIII Congreso Argentino de Ciencias de la Computación - CACIC, pp. 734–745 (2022)

12. Romero, M., Harari, I., Diaz, J., Macas, E.: Proyecto esperanza: desarrollo de software con realidad aumentada para enseñanza danza a niños con transtorno del espectro autista. Rev. Investig. Talent. **9**(1), 99–115 (2022)
13. Romero, M.R., Macas, E., Harari, I., Diaz, J.: Is it possible to improve the learning of children with ASD through augmented reality mobile applications? In: Botto-Tobar, M., Zambrano Vizuete, M., Torres-Carrión, P., Montes León, S., Pizarro Vásquez, G., Durakovic, B. (eds.) ICAT 2019. CCIS, vol. 1194, pp. 560–571. Springer, Cham (2020). https://doi.org/10.1007/978-3-030-42520-3_44
14. Romero, M., Harari, I., Diaz, J., Ramon, J.: Augmented reality for children with autism spectrum disorder. A systematic review. Int. Conf. Intell. Syst. Comput. Vision, ISCV 2020 **5**, 9204125 (2020). https://doi.org/10.1109/ISCV49265.2020.9204125
15. Romero, M., Macas, E., Harari, I., Díaz, J.: Eje integrador educativo de las TICS: caso de EstudioNiños con trastorno del espectro autista. SAEI - Simp. Argentino Educ. en Informática, pp. 171–188 (2019)
16. Romero, M., Díaz, J., Harari, I.: Impact of information and communication technologies on teaching-learning processes in children with special needs autism spectrum disorder. XXIII Congr. Argentino Ciencias la Comput, pp. 342–353 (2017). https://www.researchgate.net/publication/341282542
17. Romero, M., Harari, I.: Uso de nuevas tecnologías TICS -realidad aumentada para tratamiento de niños TEA un diagnóstico inicial. CienciAmérica Rev. Divulg. científica la Univ. Tecnológica Indoamérica **6**(1), 131–137 (2017). https://dialnet.unirioja.es/descarga/articulo/6163694.pdf
18. Láinez, B., Chocarro de Luis, E., Héctor Busto Sancirián, J., López Benito, J.R.: Aportaciones de la Realidad Aumentada en la inclusión en el aula de estudiantes con Trastorno del Espectro Autista Contributions of Augmented Reality in inclusive education with students with autism spectrum disorders. Rev. Educ. Mediática y TIC **7**(2), 120–134 (2018). https://doi.org/10.21071/edmetic.v7i2.10134
19. Krause, M., Neto, M.A.C.: Systematic mapping of the literature on mobile apps for people with Autistic Spectrum Disorder. ACM Int. Conf. Proceeding Ser. **5**, 45–52 (2021). https://doi.org/10.1145/3470482.3479616
20. Gali-Perez, O., Sayis, B., Pares, N.: Effectiveness of a mixed reality system in terms of social interaction behaviors in children with and without Autism Spectrum Condition. ACM International Conference Proceedings Series (2021). https://doi.org/10.1145/3471391.3471419
21. Thevin, D.I.L., Rodier, N., Oriola, B., Hachet, M., Jouffrais, C., Brock, A.M.: Inclusive adaptation of existing board games for gamers with and without visual impairments using a spatial augmented reality framework for touch detection and audio feedback. Proc. ACM Human-Computer Interact. **5**(ISS), 3488550 (2021). https://doi.org/10.1145/3488550
22. Zheng, Z.K., Sarkar, N., Swanson, A., Weitlauf, A., Warren, Z., Sarkar, N.: CheerBrush: a novel interactive augmented reality coaching system for toothbrushing skills in children with autism spectrum disorder. ACM Trans. Access. Comput. **14**(4), 1–20 (2021). https://doi.org/10.1145/3481642
23. Putnam, C., Mobasher, B.: Children with autism and technology use: a case study of the diary method. Conference on Human Factors in Computing Systems - Proceedings, pp. 1–8 (2020). https://doi.org/10.1145/3334480.3375218
24. Koumpouros, Y., Toulias, T.: User centered design and assessment of a wearable application for children with autistic spectrum disorder supporting daily activities. ACM International Conference Proceeding Series, pp. 505–513 (2020). https://doi.org/10.1145/3389189.3398002

25. Pamparău, C., Vatavu, R.D.: A research agenda Is needed for designing for the user experience of augmented and mixed reality: a position paper. ACM International Conference Proceeding Series, pp. 323–325 (2020). https://doi.org/10.1145/3428361.3432088

26. Li, J., et al.: Non-participatory user-centered design of accessible teacher-teleoperated robot and tablets for minimally verbal autistic children. ACM International Conference Proceeding Series, pp. 51–59 (2020). https://doi.org/10.1145/3389189.3393738

27. Barquero, D.D.: El Trastorno del Espectro Autista (TEA) y el uso de las Tecnologías de la información y comunicación (TIC). Int. J. New Educ. **4**, 7447 (2019). https://doi.org/10.24310/ijne2.2.2019.7447

28. Singh, K., Srivastava, A., Achary, K., Dey, A., Sharma, O.: Augmented reality-based procedural task training application for less privileged children and autistic individuals. In: Proceedings - VRCAI 2019 17th ACM SIGGRAPH International Conference on Virtual-Reality Continuum and its Applications in Industry (2019) https://doi.org/10.1145/3359997.3365703

29. Rouhi, A., Spitale, M., Catania, F., Cosentino, G., Gelsomini, M., Garzotto, F.: Emotify: emotional game for children with autism spectrum disorder based-on machine learning. International Conference on Intelligent User Interfaces, Proceedings IUI, pp. 31–32 (2019). https://doi.org/10.1145/3308557.3308688

30. Jamiat, N., Othman, N.F.N.: Effects of augmented reality mobile apps on early childhood education students' achievement. ACM International Conference Proceedings Series, pp. 30–33 (2019). https://doi.org/10.1145/3369199.3369203

31. Te Tsai, W., Chen, C.H.: The use of augmented reality to represent gamification theory in user story training. ACM International Conference Proceedings Series, pp. 265–268 (2019). https://doi.org/10.1145/3345120.3345131

32. Tarantino, L., De Gasperis, G., Di Mascio, T., Pino, M.C.: Immersive applications: what if users are in the autism spectrum? An experience of headsets engagement evaluation with ASD users. Proceedings - VRCAI 2019 17th ACM SIGGRAPH International Conference on Virtual-Reality Continuum and its Applications in Industry (2019) https://doi.org/10.1145/3359997.3365696

A Review of Intelligent Tutoring in Secondary Education

María Cecilia Pezzini[1](✉) and Pablo Thomas[2]

[1] School of Computer Science, National University of La Plata, La Plata, Argentina
c_pezzini@hotmail.com
[2] School of Computer Science, Council of Scientific Research Associate Center of the Province of Buenos Aires (CIC), Computer - Science Research Institute LIDI (III-LIDI, National Universityof La Plata, La Plata, Argentina
pthomas@lidi.info.unlp.edu.ar

Abstract. The use of intelligent tutoring systems may be useful to support the teaching and learning process, especially in the area of Math, in order to contribute to improve the students' academic level.

The selection strategies and evaluation criteria were defined in a previous work about Intelligent Tutoring in Teaching [11]. The present paper delves into the analysis of the selected intelligent tutoring systems taking their functional characteristics into consideration.

Keywords: Intelligent tutoring systems · Secondary education · Math teaching

1 Introduction

In 2018, Argentina participated in PISA (Programme for International Student Assessment). This is a triennial series of tests intended for students aged 15 years who are enrolled in 7th grade or more. The details from this testing survey show that a great proportion of students could not satisfactorily solve problems requiring routine procedures, following simple instructions with information available. [28].

In the testing called 'Aprender 2019' conducted by the National Ministry of Education through the Secretary of Educational Information and Evaluation (SEIE), Mathematics is the subject in which students show the greatest number of difficulties and in which only a 29% showed a satisfactory or advanced performance (the two upper categories of the four used to classify students according to their performance in the test) and a 43% of students performed below the basic level [28].

The evolution of technology has led to develop software systems using artificial intelligence techniques with the aim of supporting customized education by serving as a personal tutor for each student, with the capacity of discerning his/her needs and the meta-cognitive processes required in learning.

The selection strategies and evaluation criteria were defined in a previous work about Intelligent Tutoring in Teaching [11].

P. Pesado (Ed.): CACIC 2022, CCIS 1778, pp. 33–46, 2023.
https://doi.org/10.1007/978-3-031-34147-2_3

The present paper delves into the analysis of the selected intelligent tutoring systems taking their functional characteristics into consideration.

Special emphasis shall be put on Intelligent Tutoring Systems (hereinafter, ITS) in relation to the teaching of Math.

The preference in the selection is based on the fact that the mathematical thinking is that which presents the greatest difficulty for students, and improving it will provide certain tools to develop analytical thinking and help learn content from other disciplines, enabling its consideration as a game-changing learning tool.

In addition, it promotes an advancement in reasoning and abstraction skills, contributing to the analysis of strategies both in relation to problem-solving and dealing with specific situations.

Section 2 describes the selection of intelligent tutoring systems. Section 3 shows the analysis of intelligent tutoring systems. Section 4 details the selected intelligent tutoring systems. Section 5 describes the functional characteristics of the selected intelligent tutoring systems, and Sect. 6 presents conclusions and future works.

2 Selection of Intelligent Tutoring Systems

Intelligent tutoring systems make up three basic areas: educational research by means of tools which enable a customized teaching process ensuring the student's learning success; artificial intelligence by applying user modeling techniques, representation of knowledge and reasoning, and cognitive or educational psychology, upon the application of the cognitive simulation of the behavior of a tutor: reasoning, learning, and knowledge.

Intelligent tutoring systems enable the emulation of a human tutor in the sense of knowing what to teach, how to teach and who to teach.

On the other hand, tutors may also be implemented to help gradually solve misconceptions, contributing to a conceptual change [34] [35] in the way of constructing knowledge in a meaningful way.

The bibliographic search was conducted in academic research databases, based on specific strings, as shown in Table 1.

A total of 183 papers were found that address the subject of interest, from which 10 intelligent tutoring systems were selected, in relation to the subject of ITS in secondary education, preferably in the area of Mathematics, which may in some cases model affectivity; their publication dates correspond to the last five years.

The following items were taken into account as selection strategies:

- The title of the publication; publications whose title is not related to the object of the work were not considered.
- Exclusion based on the abstract: publications were excluded if the abstract or keywords were not related to the focus of the review.
- Exclusion based on a quick review: a quick reading of sections and subsections, figures, tables and references was performed to exclude publications that were not related to the aim of the review.

– Exclusion based on the complete article: the complete reading of the publication was carried out and those that did not match the inclusion and exclusion criteria were left out of consideration.

Table 2 shows the selected intelligent tutoring systems and the reference source.

Table 1. Search engines and search string

Digital Library	Search filters
ACM Digital Library [14] SEDICI [9] IEEE *Xplore* [7] Springer [5]	Intelligent tutoring systems; year range; mathematics o stem; affective intelligent tutoring systems

Table 2. Selected intelligent tutoring systems

Name of ITS	Description	Source
Al-Tutor	Generating Tailored Remedial Questions and Answers Based on Cognitive Diagnostic Assessment	[19]
Aleks	Assessment and Learning in Knowledge Spaces	[30, 1]
Auto-Tutor	SKOPE-IT (Shareable Knowledge Objects as Portable Intelligent Tutors): overlaying natural language tutoring on an adaptive learning system for mathematics (2018)	[22, 31]
SKOPE IT	SKOPE-IT (Shareable Knowledge Objects as Portable Intelligent Tutors): overlaying natural language tutoring on an adaptive learning system for mathematics (2018)	[32]
Lexue 100	Evaluating an Intelligent Tutoring System for Personalized Math Teaching	[36]
An Intelligent Math Electronic Tutoring System for Students with Specific Learning Disabilities (SLDs)	An Intelligent Math Electronic Tutoring System for Students with Specific Learning Disabilities (SLDs)	[20]
SIMPLIFY ITS	An intelligent tutoring system based on cognitive diagnosis models and spaced learning	[42]
MathSpring	Advances from the Office of Naval Research STEM Grand Challenge: expanding the boundaries of intelligent tutoring systems	[16]
ASSISTments	Advances from the Office of Naval Research STEM Grand Challenge: expanding the boundaries of intelligent tutoring systems	[25]
WAYANG OUTPOST	Advances from the Office of Naval Research STEM Grand Challenge: expanding the boundaries of intelligent tutoring systems	[4]

3 Analysis of Intelligent Tutoring Systems

According to the advancements observed in intelligent tutoring systems [10] in recent years, this work proposes a new study approach based on the evaluation of four aspects: general aspects, aspects related to ITS feedback, methodological-educational aspects, and intelligent tutoring system evaluation items.

Each of the proposed criteria is described below.

- General aspects: The criteria included in this category are associated with the contextualization of intelligent tutoring systems and a general characterization of said systems. Based on these indicators, the type of article, the source country and university and the target educational level can be determined.

  - Type of article: This criterion aims to determine the reference format in which it was published. This may be in a conference, in a journal, in a workshop or if it is a chapter in a book, as applicable.
  - Research country: This criterion aims to investigate in which countries experiences are carried out with the selected ITS. This may then allow for a summary of countries showing the highest concentration of research projects focused on the development of intelligent tutoring systems. The potential values for this criterion are country names.
  - Research University: This criterion aims to investigate the universities in which the experiences with the selected ITSs are explored, tested and/or developed. This may then allow for a summary of universities showing the highest concentration of research projects focused on the development of ITSs. The potential values for this criterion are university names.
  - Educational level, the potential values are:

    - Special Education. It identifies the experiences carried out with people in special education. It details, if applicable, the particular characteristics of the target population.
    - Pre-school. This label determines whether ITSs are applicable to recipients between the ages of 3 and up to 5 or 6 years.
    - Primary. This label determines whether ITSs are applicable to recipients between the ages of 6 and up to 12 or 13 years.
    - Secondary. This label identifies ITSs in which recipients are teenagers and young people with an average age between 13 and 18 years.
    - Tertiary/University. It identifies ITSs in which recipients are studying at university or at a tertiary/higher education institution, or are researchers for an educational institution.

  - Domain: This criterion indicates the domain of application of the intelligent tutoring system (Mathematics, Language, etc.).

- Aspects related to ITS feedback. The criteria included in this category seek to show the strategies and techniques with which the ITS is planned to be developed, its possible association with other ITS and its feedback with the student.

- Methodological-educational aspects. Since these ITS are oriented towards the teaching and learning process, we seek to know the type of educational process that is being carried out and the goals that are proposed to be achieved with their use. They can be grouped into intelligent tutoring system functions and tools.

  – ITS functions.

    - To determine the student's level of initial diagnosis. The method used to determine the initial diagnosis shall be indicated.
    - To establish a customized learning path. The methodology implemented to guide the student's learning process in the ITS shall be indicated.
    - To integrate a natural language teaching agent to the ITS. It shall indicate whether the ITS has a natural language teaching agent interacting with the student or not. In other words, whether there is a natural language user interface.
    - To model the students' behavior to determine their emotional state.

  – ITS tools: An intelligent tutoring system should be adapted to the student's needs and preferences in order to achieve better results. It is necessary to have computational models that diagnose student performance and provide the ITS with predictive data in order to change the teaching strategy when necessary, or simply to recommend new exercises and problems. These computational models can be: neural networks, genetic algorithms, theory of knowledge spaces, among others.

- Evaluation of intelligent tutoring systems: It allows to determine if the selected intelligent tutoring systems were subjected to an evaluation process. This may consist of tests in laboratories, verification in controlled environments, and/or demonstration in real scenarios; with the possibility of determining the main techniques used and the results achieved. The potential values are: qualitative, quantitative, quasi-experimental.

4 Introduction of the Selected Intelligent Tutoring Systems

4.1 AI-Tutor: Generating Tailored Remedial Questions

AI-Tutor [19] is an intelligent tutoring system jointly developed by the National Institute of Computer Science, Sokendai, Tokyo, Japan and the Chinese Academy of Sciences University, Beijing, which not only incorporates the basic functions of general tutoring systems, but also adds three functions to it: cognitive diagnostic assessment, generation of customized corrective questions and automatic problem solving.

Cognitive diagnostic assessment acts as an effective way to assess students in a detailed manner.

To refine the student's level of knowledge, Al Tutor proposes a cognitive diagnosis based on the model of Chen [12], who proposed a personalized e-learning system based on Item Response Theory to provide individual learning paths for students.

Wongwatkit [8] conducted experiments and showed that those students who used the diagnostic assessment system had significantly better learning achievements than those who learned with the conventional system. These results show the advantage of the cognitive diagnostic assessment as an effective way to help students discover their failings and provide active learning.

Al-Tutor automatically generates quality corrective questions to cover the students' knowledge weaknesses, rather than selecting learning materials from a bank of items, which makes it more efficient to learn the knowledge domain in a short time.

4.2 Aleks (Assessment and Learning in Knowledge Spaces)

The ITS consists of a Placement Test (PT) and five preparation modules (PM), aligned with the Mathematics contents of secondary school between 7th and 11th grade, as shown in Table 3.

The PT probes the student's previous knowledge of Mathematics and identifies the topics he/she has mastered and those he/she needs to learn. Based on the results of this diagnostic PT, the ITS generates a learning path according to the needs of each student within the PM.

The platform automatically records the data of the student-ITS interaction. The reports it generates contain the following information: date, duration, result of each PT (on a scale of 0 - 100 points); percentage of PM topics initially mastered by the student (prorated directly from the result of the initial PT) and percentage of topics mastered at the time of requesting the report (determined from the last PT completed); total study time in the PM.

Table 3. Placement levels and recommended ranges [30]

PT result	Placement level	Coding level
< 10	Pre-Algebra (7th grade)	1
10–24	Basic Algebra (8th grade)	2
25–39	Intermediate Algebra (9th grade)	3
40–54	Advanced Algebra (10th grade)	4
> 55	Pre-Calculation (11th grade)	5

4.3 Auto-tutor

AutoTutor is a teaching agent that has a natural language conversation with students, and simulates the dialogues of human tutors, as well as their teaching strategies [23, 24, 31].

An affection-sensitive AutoTutor was also developed, which responds intelligently to student's emotions such as confusion, frustration, and boredom [17].

Experiments have been conducted through comparisons with trained human tutors, and the use of AutoTutor and other ITSs using the conversational technique, and no major differences have been found [33,38, 41].

The characteristics of AutoTutor that explain the improvements in learning [21, 26, 40] are: the content of what the agent says and the robustness of the conversational mechanisms.

One conversational mechanism used in both AutoTutor and human tutoring is the so-called expectation & misconception-tailored dialogue (EMT dialogue).

As students give their responses distributed over multiple conversational turns, their contributions are compared to expectations and misconceptions by matching semantic patterns.

4.4 Skope-It

SKOPE-IT (Shareable Knowledge Objects as Portable Intelligent Tutors): overlay of natural language tutoring on an adaptive learning system for Mathematics [32], it stores and delivers web-based services. It is designed to integrate multiple applications, using semantic messaging.

SKOPE-IT was used to integrate AutoTutor [32] and ALEKS (Assessment and Learning in Knowledge Spaces), a commercial Mathematics learning system [18].

When building SKOPE-IT the goal is to combine: solved examples, self-explanation [2] and dead-end driven learning [39].

SKOPE-IT integrates dialogues using HTML and coordinates real-time communication between a variety of web services [31]. In SKOPE-IT, each service communicates with another service using semantic messages, which pass through link nodes (e.g., a request using text).

The link nodes determine the structure of the network, communicating with each other through standardized protocols (HTML5 postMessage).

4.5 Lexue 100

Lexue is defined as an intelligent system for teaching and learning Mathematics.

Lexue 100 consists of a teaching method based on 3I, Individualized Adaptation, Incremental Mastery, and Interactive discovery.

It employs Big Data techniques to guide students through customized pathways, it adapts lessons to the students' knowledge, and it identifies their learning needs.

4.6 Design Prototype of an Intelligent Math E-Tutoring System for Students with Specific Learning Disabilities

Students with specific learning disabilities (SLDs) often experience negative emotions when solving Math problems, and have difficulty in managing them. This is one of the reasons why Mathematics e-learning tools are not effective (e.g., Khan Academy (2019), STMath (2019) [20].

The e-tutoring prototype for students with specific learning disabilities combines eye-tracking data, touchscreen inputs, and response time to model student behavior.

Many students with SLDs exhibit specific negative emotional behaviors. The system detects three types of negative emotional behaviors:

– Distraction: if the eyes do not look at the screen for more than 1 min.

- Situation of tension, confusion or irritability, if the screen is pressed more than three times in 1 s.
- Hesitation, if the screen has not been touched for more than 2 min and more than 70% of the time has been spent looking at user interface buttons.

After detecting that the student is exhibiting one of the three behaviors mentioned above, it rectifies it through dialogue.

Following the guidelines for tutoring students with SLDs [37], two methods were added to the design to help maintain or restore good emotion: praising correct problem-solving behavior or providing brain breaks. Besides, in order to collaborate with those students who do not know how to solve the problem, two methods are presented: giving hints or switching to a simpler problem.

4.7 Simplify ITS

Simplify ITS [42] is part of a larger system called SIMPLIFY (Smart Tutor System based on Cognitive Diagnostic and Spatial Learning Models), which consists of several modules where the most important ones are student tracking, student reports and activity recommendations.

Simplify ITS is the module based on activity recommendations, which helps teachers to select the most appropriate activity for each student based on the his/her previous interactions with the learning platform.

The student's skill profile is determined automatically by using Cognitive Diagnosis Models (CDMs).

If there is no information about the student in the system, the system will offer activities randomly, until a minimum sample size is achieved. Once there is enough data about the student's learning experience in the course, the system recommends activities if the student does not yet have all the skills in the domain.

If it has been a long time since the student has mastered an activity, the system sends reinforcement activities about already-learned concepts, thus avoiding the loss of mastered skills. Simplify ITS prioritizes reinforcement over learning new skills.

One of the objectives of Simplify ITS is to support teachers by providing information that helps them adapt the learning experience to their students. It is the teacher who accepts or rejects the activity suggested by the ITS for a particular student.

4.8 MathSpring

MathSpring is a Math practice environment within an adaptive tutor, which provides math instruction, and merges hints, help, and links to external educational videos.

MathSpring integrates Wayang Outpost and ASSISTments.

4.9 Wayang Outpost

It is an instructional system, which contains the empirical model of the student, his/her behaviors and interventions; it focuses on the affective, cognitive and meta-cognitive nature of the student. That is to say, it works on three areas: cognition, engagement and affection [4].

The tutor supports strategic and problem-solving skills based on the cognitive learning theory [13], this occurring when the teacher teaches skills to a learner.

The expert is Wayang Outpost, which collaborates with the student in solving mathematical problems.

Hints are an important component of the tutor, to help students learn strategies for approaching mathematical problems; using the learning theory proposed by Mayer [27].

An important element of cognitive learning is to challenge students by providing them with problems that are slightly more difficult than those they could solve on their own.

Vygotsky [43] referred to this as the zone of proximal development, and suggested that encouraging development within this zone leads to faster learning [29]. The software provides an adaptive selection of problems with greater or lesser difficulty depending on the student's recent success and effort [3,15].

Students go through three cyclical phases: anticipation, performance, and self-reflection.

The anticipation phase refers to the motivational/affective processes that precede efforts to learn, and that influence the students' predisposition to initiate or continue the learning process.

Performance involves processes that occur during study and/or problem solving, and that impact concentration and outcomes (including monitoring during the execution of problem solving).

The self-reflection phase involves processes that follow problem solving or study efforts, with a focus on the student's reactions to the experience (including self-assessment and self-judgment). These self-reflections, in turn, influence the anticipation with respect to subsequent learning efforts, completing the self-regulation cycle.

The system also incorporates the use of Math Facts Retrieval (MFR) training software. Returning to already-mastered topics is an efficient strategy that facilitates learning mastery.

4.10 ASSISTments

ASSISTments is a formative assessment system rather than a means to assess students.

ASSISTment consists of a main question (also known as the original question) and a tutoring session to accomplish the desired learning. It can be included in the category of cognitive tutors; it does not monitor student learning; it monitors student progress in problem-solving.

5 General Characteristics of the Selected Intelligent Tutoring Systems

Table 4 shows a summary of the general characteristics of the intelligent tutoring systems under study.

Table 4. General characteristics of ITS.

ITS Characteristics					Aleks	AI-Tutor	Assistments	Auto-Tutor	Lexue 100	MathSpring	Simplify ITS	SLDs	Skope IT	Wayang Outpost
General Description		Type of article	Document		X									X
			Conference			X						X	X	
			Symposium							X				
			Journal				X	X	X		X			
		Country/University	Japan	Computer Science Institute		X								
			China	Educational Technology Department					X					
			US	University of California	X									
				University of Memphis				X						
				University of Wisconsin								X		
				University of Massachusetts						X				X
				Worcester Polytechnic Institute and Carnegie Mellon University			X							
			Spain	Research and Development Center in Advanced Telecommunications (Galicia)							X			
			Canada	University of Ottawa									X	
		Domain	Math		X	X	X	X		X		X	X	X
			Multiple						X					
			Not specified								X			
		Educational Level	Special									X		
			Pre-school											
			Primary							X		X		
			Secondary		X		X	X	X	X	X	X	X	X
			Tertiary/University											
Feedback with the ITS		Feedback with other ITS			X		X	X		X	X		X	X
		Feedback with the activity	On the task		X	X	X	X	X		X	X		X
			Task processing		X	X	X	X	X		X	X		X
			Self-adjustment					X	X		X	X		X
			Affective							X		X	X	X
Methodological-educational	ITS functions	Initial diagnosis methodology			X	X								
		Learning customization methodology			X	X		X						X
		Natural language teaching agent						X					X	X
		Student behavior modeling											X	X
	ITS tools	Rules clustering, classification, decision tree						X						
		Knowledge Space Theory			X									
		Genetic algorithms						X						
		Other							X	X		X		X
Evaluation Technique			Quantitative		X		X						X	X
			Qualitative		X	X	X	X			X	X	X	X
			Quasi-experimental							X				

6 Conclusions and Future Works

The analysis of the selected works reveals the trends towards which ITS developments are moving forward. These trends involve:

- Incorporation of conversational computer agents, aiding electronic tutoring, through dialogue.
- Cognitive diagnostics to determine the student's level in the subject under study, generating a customized learning path according to the student's needs.
- Integration of intelligent tutoring systems with complementary strengths to enhance learning and enable the complementarity of learning resources. This is the case of SKOPE-IT and MathSpring. SKOPE-IT integrated AutoTutor and ALEKS.

In terms of Bloom's taxonomy, ALEKS (outer loop) focuses primarily on applying Math skills, while AutoTutor (inner loop) questions help students understand, analyze, and evaluate mathematical concepts.

Solved examples, self-explanation and dead-end driven learning were combined when building SKOPE-IT.

MathSpring integrates Wayang Outpost and ASSISTments. Wayang Outpost [6] is an online tutoring system that focuses on Math skills for secondary school students, and ASSISTments is a platform used by teachers to assign digital homework and classroom activities [26].

That is to say, Wayang Outpost is located in the outer loop, selecting appropriate problems to be solved by a student; while ASSISTments founds itself in the inner loop; the tutor provides support to the student when solving a problem, including step-by-step guidance, reflection and solution review at the end.

The use of hybrid systems reduces the effort in ITS development.

From the research conducted, it is clear that ITSs place the student at the core of the educational process by allowing him/her to regulate his/her own learning.

Self-regulated study habits are then transformed into a determining factor for a successful educational process. It has also been observed that the use of an ITS as a complementary tool reduces the differences among students from the same Math course and enlightens teachers about the degree of learning of every student, making it possible to keep track of the difficulties and knowledge attained by each student.

The evaluation of intelligent tutoring systems shows that tutoring systems outperform non-expert tutors and may even match up to human expert tutors in some topics.

The results of this work serve as a starting point to continue with the challenge of improving students' learning in the area of Mathematics, in which deficiencies have been further aggravated as a result of the COVID-19 pandemic.

As part of our future work, the aim is to implement the use of at least one of the ITSs under study in students enrolled in 1st grade of secondary education and analyze its impact on learning.

References

1. Aleks.https://www.aleks.com/. Último acceso: 5/02/2023
2. Aleven, V., McLaren, B., Roll, I., Koedinger, K.: Toward Tutoring Help Seeking. In: Lester, J.C., Vicari, R.M., Paraguaçu, F. (eds.) ITS 2004. LNCS, vol. 3220, pp. 227–239. Springer, Heidelberg (2004). https://doi.org/10.1007/978-3-540-30139-4_22
3. Arroyo, I., Cooper, D., Burleson, W., Woolf, B.P.: Bayesian networks and linear regression models of students' goals, moods, and emotions. In: Romero, C., Ventura, S., Pechenizkiy, M., Baker, R. (eds.) Handbook of Educational Data Mining, pp. 323–338. CRC Press, Boca Raton (2010)
4. Arroyo, I., Woolf, B.P., Burelson, W., et al.: A multimedia adaptive tutoring system for mathematics that addresses cognition, metacognition and affect. Int. J. Artif. Intell. Educ. **24**(387–426) (2014). https://doi.org/10.1007/s40593-014-0023-y. Últimoacceso 7 Feb 2023
5. Springer link. https://link.springer.com/.Último acceso: febrero 2023
6. Beal, C.R., Walles, R., Arroyo, I., Woolf, B.P.: On-line tutoring for math achievement testing: a controlled evaluation. J. Interact. Online Learn. **6**(1), 43–55 (2007)
7. IEEE *Xplore*. https://www.ieee.org/.Último acceso: febrero 2023
8. Wongwatkit, C., Srisawasdi, N., Hwang, G.-J., Panjaburee, P.: Influence of an integrated learning diagnosis and formative assessment-based personalized web learning approach on students learning performances and perceptions. Interact. Learn. Environ. **25**(7), 889–903 (2017)
9. PREBI - SEDICI (UNLP).http://sedici.unlp.edu.ar/.Último aceso: febrero 2023
10. Casanovas, I.: La didáctica en el diseño de simuladores digitales para la formación universitaria en la toma de decisiones. Tesis de Magíster en Docencia Universitaria, UTN-FRBA (2005)
11. Pezzini C, Thomas P, Tutores inteligentes en la enseñanza: Una revision y análisis en la educación secundaria. XXVIII Congreso Argentino de Ciencias de la Computación - CACIC 2022. Editorial de la Universidad Nacional de La Rioja (EUDELAR). ISBN: 978–987–1364–31–2
12. Chen, C.-M., Lee, H.-M., Chen, Y.-H.: Personalized e-learning system using item response theory. Comput. Educ. **44**(3), 237–255 (2005)
13. Collins, A., Brown, J.S., Newman, S.E.: Cognitive apprenticeship: Teaching the crafts of reading, writing, and mathematics. In: Resnick, L.B. (ed.) Knowing, Learning, and Instruction: essays in honor of robert glaser, pp. 453–494. Lawrence Erlbaum Associates, Hillsdale (1989)
14. ACM, Association for computing Machinery. https://www.acm.org/. Último acceso: febrero 2023
15. Corbett, A.T., Anderson, J.R.: Knowledge tracing: Modeling the acquisition of procedural knowledge. User Model. User Adapted Interact. **4**, 253–278 (1995)
16. Craig, S.D., Graesser, A.C., Perez, R.S.: Advances from the Office of Naval Research STEM Grand Challenge: expanding the boundaries of intelligent tutoring systems. IJ STEM Ed **5**, 11 (2018). https://doi.org/10.1186/s40594-018-0111-x. Últimoacceso 5 Feb 2023
17. D'Mello, S.K., Graesser, A.C.: AutoTutor and affective AutoTutor: learning by talking with cognitively and emotionally intelligent computers that talk back. ACM Trans. Interact. Intel. Syst. **2**, 1–39 (2012)
18. Falmagne, J. C., Albert, D., Doble, C., Eppstein, D., & Hu, X. (Eds.). (2013). Knowledge spaces: Applications in education. Springer Science & Business Media
19. Gan, W., Sun, Y., Ye, S., Fan, Y., Sun, Y.: AI-Tutor: Generating Tailored Remedial Questions and Answers Based on Cognitive Diagnostic Assessment. In: 2019 6th International Conference on Behavioral, Economic and Socio-Cultural Computing (BESC), Beijing, China, 2019, pp. 1–6 https://doi.org/10.1109/BESC48373.2019.8963236. Último Acceso: 5/02/2023

20. Wen, Z.A., Silverstein, E., Zhao, Y., Amog, A.L., Garnett, K., Azenkot, S.: Teacher Views of Math E-learning Tools for Students with Specific Learning Disabilities. In The 22nd International ACM SIGACCESS Conference on Computers and Accessibility, Association for computing Machinery (ACM), New York, NY, USA, 1–13 (2020)
21. Graesser, A.C., Wiemer-Hastings, K., Wiemer-Hastings, P., Kreuz, R.: TRG AutoTutor: a simulation of a human tutor.J. Cognit. Syst. Res. **1**, 35–51 (1999)
22. Graesser, A.C., Chipman, P., Haynes, B.C., Olney, A.: AutoTutor: an intelligent tutoring system with mixed-initiative dialogue. IEEE Trans. Educ. **48**(4), 612–618 (2005)
23. Graesser, A.C., Lu, S., Jackson, G.T., Mitchell, H., Ventura, M., Olney, A., et al.: AutoTutor: a tutor with dialogue in natural language. Behav. Res. Meth. Instruments Comput. **36**, 180–193 (2004)
24. Graesser, A.C., Jeon, M., Dufty, D.: Agent technologies designed to facilitate interactive knowledge construction. Discourse Process. **45**, 298–322 (2008)
25. Heffernan, N.T., Heffernan, C.L.: The ASSISTments ecosystem: building a platform that brings scientists and teachers together for minimally invasive research on human learning and teaching. Int. J. Artif. Intell. Educ. **24**(4), 470–497 (2014). https://doi.org/10.1007/s40 593-014-0024-x
26. Samantha, J., Reyes, J.-R., Víctor, C., Alan, R.N.: An affective learning ontology for educational systems (2016)
27. Mayer, R.E.: Multimedia Learning. Cambridge University Press, New York (2001)
28. Ministerio de Educación de la República Argentina. https://www.argentina.gob.ar/educacion/ evaluacion-e-informacion-educativa. Último acceso: 8/02/2023
29. Murray, T., Arroyo, I.: Towards measuring and maintaining the zone of proximal development in adaptive instructional systems. In: Proceedings of the 6th International Conference on Intelligent Tutoring Systems. 749–758 (2002)
30. N. L. Miller, J. E. Sanchez-Galan and B. E. FernándezUse of an Intelligent Tutoring System for Mathematics by Students Who Aspire to Enter the Technological University of Panama. In: 7th International Engineering. Sciences and Technology Conference (IESTEC) **2019**, 255–260 (2019). https://doi.org/10.1109/IESTEC46403.2019.00-66
31. Nye, B.D., Graesser, A.C., Hu, X.: AutoTutor and family: a review of 17 years of science and math tutoring. Int. J. Artif. Intell. Educ. **24**(4), 427–469 (2014)
32. Nye, B., Pavlik, P., Windsor, A., et al.: SKOPE-IT (Shareable Knowledge Objects as Portable Intelligent Tutors): overlaying natural language tutoring on an adaptive learning system for mathematics. IJ STEM Ed **5**, 12 (2018). https://doi.org/10.1186/s40594-018-0109-4. Últimoacceso 07 Feb 2023
33. Olney, A.M., et al.: Guru: A Computer Tutor That Models Expert Human Tutors. In: Cerri, S.A., Clancey, W.J., Papadourakis, G., Panourgia, K. (eds.) ITS 2012. LNCS, vol. 7315, pp. 256–261. Springer, Heidelberg (2012). https://doi.org/10.1007/978-3-642-30950-2_32
34. Perkins, D. (1995) La escuela inteligente. Gedisa
35. Pozo, J. I. (1998). Aprendices y maestros. Alianza
36. Zhang, B., Jia, J.: Evaluating an intelligent tutoring system for personalized math teaching. Int. Symp. Edu. Technol. (ISET) **2017**, 126–130 (2017)
37. Rosen. P.: Tutoring Kids With Dyscalculia | Tutors for Math Issues. https://www.unders tood.org/en/articles/tutoring-kids-with-dyscalculia-what-you-need-to-know. Último Acceso: 8/02/2023
38. Understood -For learning and thinking differences. Brain Breaks for Kids
39. VanLehn, K., Siler, S., Murray, C., Yamauchi, T., Baggett, W.B.: Why do only some events cause learning during human tutoring? Cogn. Instr. **21**(3), 209–249 (2003)
40. VanLehn, K., Graesser, A.C., Jackson, G.T., Jordan, P., Olney, A., Rose, C.P.: When are tutorial dialogues more effective than reading? Cogn. Sci. **31**, 3–62 (2007)

41. VanLehn, K.: The relative effectiveness of human tutoring, intelligent tutoring systems and other tutoring systems. Educ. Psychol. **46**, 197–221 (2011)
42. Villanueva, N.M., Costas, A.E., Hermida, D.F., Rodríguez, A.C.: SIMPLIFY ITS: An intelligent tutoring system based on cognitive diagnosis models and spaced learning. IEEE Global Eng. Educ. Conf. (EDUCON) **2018**, 1703–1712 (2018). https://doi.org/10.1109/EDUCON. 2018.8363440
43. Vygotsky, L.: Mind in society: The development of higher psychological processes: Harvard University Press (1978)

Analyzing Attendance Indicators in Digital Technologies-Mediated Courses in Tertiary Technician Education

Omar Spandre[1]([✉]), Paula Dieser[1], and Cecilia Sanz[2,3]

[1] Master'S Degree in Application of Computer Technology in Education.
School of Computer Sciences, Argentine UNLP, Buenos Aires, Argentina
spandreomar@gmail.com

[2] Institute of Research in Computer Sciences LIDI – CIC. School of Computer Sciences,
Argentine UNLP, Buenos Aires, Argentina
csanz@lidi.info.unlp.edu.ar

[3] Scientific Research Commission From the Province of Buenos Aires, Buenos Aires, Argentina

Summary. The Community of Inquiry (CoI) model has been used as a theoretical framework to analyze online learning, recognizing the importance of having three types of presence: Cognitive, Teaching and Social. In particular, this model gained visibility after the interruption of face-to-face classes due to the COVID-19 pandemic. In this context, higher education institutions adapted their courses to a virtual format to serve students during this period of time. This work addresses a case study in which indicators of the three presences in tertiary technician education courses are analyzed during the years 2020 and 2021 at the Higher Institute of Teacher and Technical Training No. 93 (ISFDyT 93) of the city of San Vicente. To this end, a survey was implemented, which was answered by 119 students. The results obtain indicate that both the Educational and Cognitive presences are highly valued, the Social presence a bit less, as well as the indicators that refer to the dialog between the students.

Keywords: Community of Inquiry · higher education · education mediated by digital technology · emergency remote education · types of presences

1 Introduction

In this article, the interactions between the members of an educational community are analyzed. It focuses on a population of tertiary-level students that carried out their pedagogical activities between 2020 and 2021, during the period locally referred to as ASPO (preventive and mandatory social isolation). Additionally, it is an extended article, with an in-depth presentation of the results and with an enriched discussion of the previous article published by the authors at the CACIC 2022 congress held in the city of La Rioja in October of that year. The work focuses on analyzing dialog components, mediated by virtual teaching and learning environments. In a period of compulsory online education due to the pandemic, these components, and their relationships, are affected by the use

P. Pesado (Ed.): CACIC 2022, CCIS 1778, pp. 47–58, 2023.
https://doi.org/10.1007/978-3-031-34147-2_4

of current digital technologies, and, therefore, by the gap between those who have the resources to access them and those who have had to learn how to use them quickly and in an improvised manner. Due to the ASPO, a large number of teachers and students carried out their activities in virtual classrooms, interacting with each other in different environments, producing knowledge through various teaching strategies, and adapting their plans to the new context. At the same time, synchronous and asynchronous dialog alternatives have been developed, which can be studied from various dimensions. According to [1], these dimensions or presences and the interrelation between them are necessary for online learning.

This article analyzes the relationships between the presences and how students perceive them, based on the dimensions and indicators of the CoI Model [1]. It should be noted that, regardless of the pandemic, this is a relevant and current topic, since it relates to educational processes mediated by digital technologies. Thus, the results found here will be a contribution to the design of future courses with hybrid modalities.

From now on, this article is organized as follows: Sect. 2 includes the theoretical framework and the survey following the CoI Model. Section 3 summarizes some background information, Sect. 4 details the methodological aspects used to review the different types of presences under the CoI Model that are applied to the case study addressed here, and Sect. 5 presents an analysis and discussion of the results obtained. Finally, in Sect. 6, conclusions and future works are presented.

2 Theoretical Framework

2.1 The Community of Inquiry Model

The CoI (Community of Inquiry) model is a theoretical framework developed by Garrison and Anderson [1]. According to this model, for online learning to be possible, the interrelation of three dimensions or presences is necessary: Social Presence, Cognitive Presence and Teaching Presence [2]. These three types of presences are described in greater detail below:

Cognitive Presence. It indicates to what extent students are able to construct meaning through continuous reflection in a community of critical investigation/inquiry [1, 3], through sustained communication [4]. The proposed model identifies four non-sequential phases in Cognitive Presence: activation, exploration, integration and resolution [1, 3].

Social Presence. It is the capacity of participants to project themselves socially and emotionally as individuals, to promote direct communication between individuals, and to make explicit personal representation. Social Presence marks a qualitative difference between a collaborative research/action community and the process of merely downloading information [3].

Teaching Presence. It is defined in the CoI model as the act of designing, facilitating and guiding the teaching and learning processes to obtain the expected results according to students needs and abilities [5].

2.2 The Community of Inquiry Survey

The CoI framework has been adopted as a guide for research and practice in online learning. However, in 2006, two issues were challenging CoI research in particular. The first was the lack of common measures in studies about individual presences, which made making generalizations difficult. The second issue was that few studies before that date explored all three presences and, more importantly, the interactions between them, and these are fundamental to the model itself [6].

In 2006, several leading researchers in relation to the CoI Model began working on the creation of a survey instrument to measure the three presences and agreed that a self-report survey would be appropriate to measure presences, since they are based on student perceptions, using a 5-point Likert scale (1: strongly disagree; 5: strongly agree). The points in common between the existing elements were reconciled to capture each one of the presences [6] and the result was a 34-item instrument [7], which is presented here later through a link, since this is the survey that was used for the case study in this paper. Items 1–13 refer to the Teaching Presence, items 14–22 correspond to the Social Presence, and items 23–34 are related to the Cognitive Presence.

In order to process the results, a scale is used in this work to assess each answer, where 1 = Strongly disagree; 2 = Disagree; 3 = Neutral; 4 = Agree; 5 = Strongly agree; then the average is calculated for each of the statements.

3 Background Analysis

In a previous work carried out by the authors [8], the strategies used during the lockdown period in several countries of the region are analyzed in light of the theoretical framework of the CoI Model, to which end a systematic review of 24 published articles between 2020 and 2021 was carried out. These works address the problem in Higher Education, in communities that sorted to virtual education during that period due to the suspension of face-to-face activities.

In the preceding article, the implications of reorganizing the teaching and learning processes are analyzed; the results show that a high percentage of research focuses on the teaching Presence, particularly for the educational and organizational design, with much less emphasis on the Cognitive Presence. Additionally, there is little production on the Social Presence dimension and the analysis of indicators that reinforce learning [8].

The results reveal a scarce production on the Social Presence dimension, as well as on the analysis that focuses on affection, group cohesion and open communication, which are indicators that reinforce learning and maintain a positive social relationship dynamic. This aspect is only dealt with in some articles from the perspective of cohesion among students, in particular in one work it is addressed with first-year students in Higher Education institutions, and as a dropout variable, taking into account the high alphabetization level of students who have completed the secondary level [8].

The aforementioned aspects motivated this new work, in which a survey is carried out based on the proposal of the CoI model. The survey is applied to a case study with students from a Higher Education educational community who took only online courses in 2020 and 2021. Thus, the objective of this work is to analyze the relationships between the presences of the CoI model, using the survey instrument indicated in Subsect. 2.2, in light of this theoretical framework.

In this sense, for this background analysis, the research articles selected are those whose titles indicate the specific study of Social Presence within the framework of the Community of Inquiry model.

As a first observation, it can be said that most of the referenced authors agree in defining the close relationship that exists between Social Presence, Cognitive Presence and Teaching Presence in the Community of Inquiry model [9–13].

In this regard, the authors in [10] postulate a series of statements that are worth highlighting: the articulation between the three presences is evidenced in the mediating role that the Social Presence acquires in relation to the other two presences, since the Social Presence is a condition to achieve critical thinking (Cognitive Presence) and it is, in turn, the responsibility of the teacher based on the activities proposed and carried out.

In the online educational practice, the Social Presence is revealed through the interaction and collaboration that are originates, developed and boosted by the affective communication, open communication and cohesion of the members that make up the community [9].

The findings of some of these studies [11, 12] seem to indicate that Social Presence is relevant as a predictor of successful learning processes, given its close relationship with the Cognitive Presence in certain practices in virtual environments, such as forums, where friendly and relaxed environments that contribute to group cohesion and collaborative work are more easily formed [9].

4   Methodological Aspects for the Case Study about Presence Analysis in the Community of Inquiry Model

The results of the previous article [8] and the aforementioned background motivated this work and the need to delve into the case study presented here – the assessment of students in relation to the presence of the CoI Model in educational processes in which they have participated and that were mediated by digital technologies. In particular, new research questions are raised:

Q1. What are the perceptions of the students participating in the survey in relation to the CoI model presences?

Q2. Are there any differences between the presences based on these perceptions?

Q3. Are there any differences in these presences based on major and student age range?

To find answers to these research questions, the aforementioned CoI model survey is used, which is presented in the following link: https://drive.google.com/file/d/1MZlcT BJpEnVEOUEail6gBYSbKtDSFxEB/view.

In this case study, the community is made up of 1st, 2nd and 3rd year students of the Instituto Superior de Formación Técnica No. 93 (ISFT 93) of the city of San Vicente who took higher technical courses during the years 2020 and 2021, while the ASPO mandate required all education activities to be carried out virtually. The higher technical courses involved are: Accounting Administration; Accounting Administration with a focus on Marketing; Public Administration; Application Analysis, Development and Programming; Nursing; and Tour Guide.

The survey presented in Subsect. 2.2 on the aforementioned group was distributed. In addition, variables were included for further analysis, such as participant gender and age.

To fill out the survey, a Google form was used, which was initially sent to key students and professors in each course who, in turn, distributed the forms through their corresponding relevant WhatsApp groups. As a result of this process, 50 responses were received. Then, additional dissemination was achieved through an institutional email to all the students of the mentioned courses, and 70 more responses were received. A filter was applied to remove duplicates, leaving a total of 119 unique responses, which are analyzed in this paper.

Analyzing the sample (see Fig. 1), the responses received were distributed as follows: 5 students from Accounting Administration, 11 from Accounting Administration with a focus on Marketing, 7 from Public Administration, 26 from Application Analysis, Development and Programming, 60 from Nursing, and 10 from Tour Guide.

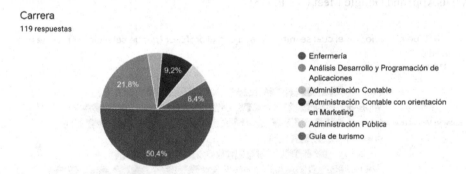

Fig. 1. Number of students by major; sample total = 119 surveys

In relation to the profile of the students who answered the survey, the majority were female between 26–41 years old (see Fig. 2).

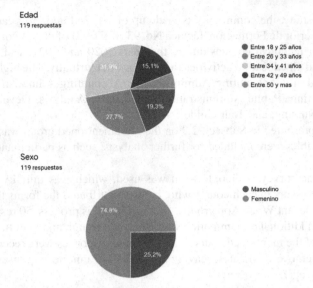

Fig. 2. Upper: Number of students by age range; Bottom: Participating students by gender.

As regards teacher-student communications, students had several options available, and mostly chose the institution's Virtual Teaching and Learning Environment (VTLE), WhatsApp, and Google Meet (see Fig. 3).

Fig. 3. Digital tools used for communication according to participant survey responses

5   Results Obtained

In this section, the results obtained in relation to each research question are presented.

As regards research question Q1, What are the perceptions of the students participating in the survey in relation to the CoI model presences?, the Teaching Presence (items 1–13) is the one with the highest level of satisfaction, since its mean assessment is 4.10.

There are responses that confirm a disagreement in relation to the statements that refer to Social Presence (items 14–22), since the mean assessment is 3.70, where items 16, 17 and 18 are below that value.

Student perception in the case survey items involving the Cognitive Presence (23–34), shows a higher level of agreement, since the mean assessment is 4 (Agree).

Mean student assessments for each of the 34 survey items are presented in Fig. 4.

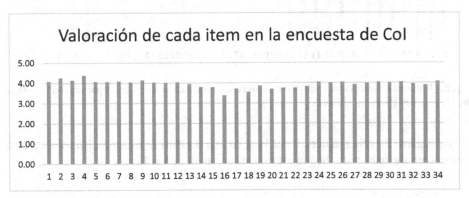

Fig. 4. Mean assessments for each of the items based on the answers given by participants through the CoI survey.

As regards question Q2, Are there any differences between the presences based on these perceptions?, it can be seen that the highest assessment corresponds to the Teaching Presence, and mainly to those items that focus on course design and organization (items 1–4); the mean in this case is 4.24. Items 16–18, pertaining to Social Presence, are the least valued, with a mean of 3.55. These include the following statements: "Web-based or online communication is an excellent medium for social interaction.", "I felt comfortable chatting online," and "I felt comfortable participating in course discussions." Finally, item 23 of Cognitive Presence ("The issues discussed increased my interest in course topics.") is the least valued within this presence, with a mean of 3.82.

To address question Q3, Are there any differences in these presences based on major and student age range?, a filter was applied to separate Nursing students, since they made up 50% of the sample being analyzed.

Within this major, there is a higher level of agreement regarding all three presences, and these students recorded the highest mean values in all survey item, as shown in Fig. 5.

Fig. 5. Mean assessments for each of the items based on the answers given by participants through the CoI survey (Nursing students).

As regards the other majors, it can be seen that students from Administration-related courses are the ones with the lowest evaluation, as shown in Fig. 6.

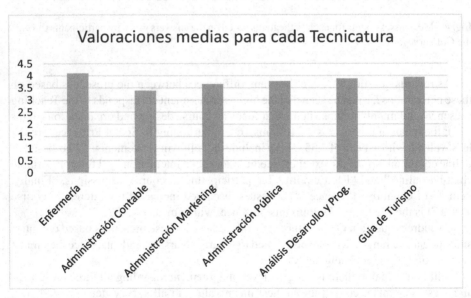

Fig. 6. Mean assessments for each of the items based on the answers given by participants through the CoI survey for each of the technical majors.

As regards student ages, they were split into two groups: 18–33 and +33 years old. The results show a lower average evaluation for the three presences in the youngest group compared to the rest of the sample.

The values that reflect disagreement among the younger population, which intensify in Social Presence and items 16–18, refer directly to web-mediated communication and to the participation of students in group conversations, as shown in Fig. 7.

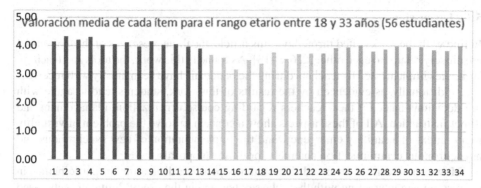

Fig. 7. Mean assessments for each of the items based on the answers given by participants through the CoI survey; 18–33 years old.

In summary, as shown in Fig. 8, the mean assessment among Nursing students is higher for all three presences, compared to the mean assessment of the entire group.

Another aspect to highlight is that the mean assessment of the 18–33 year-olds is lower for all three presences compared to the entire group.

The mean assessment for Social Presence is lower in all cases, compared to the other two presences.

	Teaching Presence	Social Presence	Cognitive Presence	Total
Mean assessment for the entire sample (119)	Mean assessment 4.10	Mean assessment 3.70	Mean assessment 3.98	Mean assessment 3.95
Mean assessment, Nursing major (60)	Mean assessment 4.30	Mean assessment 3.71	Mean assessment 4.17	Mean assessment 4.10
Mean assessment, 18-33 years old (56)	Mean assessment 4.09	Mean assessment 3.55	Mean assessment 3.90	Mean assessment 3.88

Fig. 8. Mean assessments for each presence considering the entire group, only Nursing students, and only students within the 18–33 year-old range.

5.1 Discussion

In line with the works cited throughout this article, the three presences of the CoI model are closely related to each other [2, 6, 8–13]. As found in this work, the tools and teaching strategies implemented by teachers during the pandemic have been mostly well received.

Additionally, as evidenced by the results of this work, students tend to agree with the decisions made by their teachers regarding course organization, management and direct instruction. All of these aspects show a concern to solve the problem of virtuality in a context of a sanitary emergency, and the implementation of new synchronous and asynchronous communication channels for online proposals.

However, it can be observed that students perceive difficulties in participating in discussions, in interacting with their classmates, and in the use of digital or web-based tools. This is in agreement with the results obtained in a previous work [8], in which the scarce production on the Social Presence dimension is identified, especially with focus on affection, group cohesion and open communication [8]. Then, the Social Presence was found to be the least valued of the presences by the students in their perception of the experiences lived during the ASPO period.

As a consequence, it could be thought that students have not been able to have a fully positive interaction with their peers and teachers, or that this has been not enough, with insufficient opportunities for dialog. As a hypothesis, it is possible that teachers have used face-to-face class formats in virtual reality, with greater emphasis on study materials and having tools, but perhaps less attention on promoting interaction. The lack of connectivity, the time allocated to virtual classes, and insufficient preparation in the management of digital tools may be the variables that affected the teaching and learning processes so that the dimension of Social Presence is less valued in the survey used in this work. For this reason, the need to implement strategies that strengthen the indicators that maintain a dynamic of positive social relations is reinforced, as stated in the previously mentioned works [11, 12].

The average assessment of the indicators that refer to the Teaching Presence accounts for the work that was carried out in the first months of the pandemic, and relates to the appropriation of communication tools and the organization of the courses, but, even so, students have not been able to actively participate in classes.

The youngest students, according to their survey assessments, are the most dissatisfied with respect to the items that refer directly to web-mediated communication and the participation of students in group conversations. Even though it could be thought that this age group (18–33 years old) is the one with the best technological mastery, perhaps they have not been able to communicate correctly among peers or with their teacher. One hypothesis could be linked to the use of other types of communication tools in their daily lives within this age group, tools that have not been part of the ecosystem proposed by teachers and the institution. This could also be due to the lack of teacher training in the proposal of more activities related to promoting dialog among peers and with teachers.

In a post-pandemic world, it forces us to rethink the strategies used in courses mediated by technology, and to look for those that focus on components where students can interact with each other, based on the least valued items from the entire sample: 16-Web-based or online communication is an excellent medium for social interaction; 17-I felt comfortable chatting online; 18-I felt comfortable participating in course discussions; 19-I felt comfortable interacting with other course participants.

6 Conclusions and Future Work

In this paper, a case study was presented in which the three types of presences are analyzed: Social, Cognitive and Teaching, which are proposed as part of the Community of Inquiry model. These presences are considered essential for the development of effective educational proposals mediated by digital technologies. Based on the results obtained, it can be observed that the dialog component linked to the Social Presence should be strengthened when designing the courses. At the same time, there is a positive perception about teacher efforts to design and address educational proposals during the ASPO period. Some results will also shed light on the work in some of the courses of studies included in the sample, since some differences have been found in this sense, as well as in relation to age, which opens the door to drill deeper into these variables.

The conclusions of this article will be considered in the process of advancing a thesis developed within the framework of the Master in Information Technologies Applied to Education: of the School of Computer Science of the UNLP. Additionally, progress will be made in the design of educational proposals that take into account the three dimensions, given the incidence that these have on the educational process.

This work is an extended version of the article presented at CACIC 2022 [14], with an improvement and greater level of detail of the results obtained, in addition to a richer discussion in relation to future work.

References

1. Garrison, D.R., Anderson, T.: E–Learning in the 21st Century: A Framework for Research and Practice. Routledge Falmer, London (2003)
2. Garrison, R., Cleveland-Innes, M., Fung, T.S.: Exploring causal relationships among teaching, cognitive and social presence: student perceptions of the community of inquiry framework. Internet High. Educ. **13**(1–2), 31–36 (2010). https://doi.org/10.1016/j.iheduc.2009.10.002
3. Garrison, R., Anderson, T., Archer, W.: Critical inquiry in a text based environment: computer conferencing in higher education. Internet High. Educ. **11**(2), 1–14 (2000). https://doi.org/10.1016/S1096-7516(00)00016-6
4. Gunawardena, C.N., Lowe, C.E., Anderson, T.: Analysis of a global online debate and the development of an interaction analysis model for examining social construction of knowledge in computer conferencing. J. Ed. Comp. Res. **17**(4), 397–431 (1997)
5. Gutiérrez-Santiuste, E., Rodríguez-Sabiote, C., Gallego-Arrufat, M-J.: Cognitive presence through social and teaching presence in communities of inquiry: a correlational–predictive study. Australas. J. Educ. Technol. **31**(3), 349–362 (2015)
6. Arbaugh, B., et al.: Community of inquiry framework: validation and instrument development. Int. Rev. Res. Open Distrib. Learn. **9**(2), 1492–3831 (2008). https://doi.org/10.19173/irrodl.v9i2.573
7. Richardson, J.C., et al.: Uso del marco de la comunidad de investigación para informar un diseño instruccional eficaz. En: Moller L., Huett J. (eds) La próxima generación de educación a distancia. Springer, Boston, MA (2012). https://doi.org/10.1007/978-1-4614-1785-9_7

8. Spandre, O., Dieser, P., Sanz, C.: Revisión Sistemática de Metodologías Educativas Implementadas Durante la Pandemia del COVID-19 en la Educación Superior en Iberoamérica. En Congreso Argentino de Informática, pp. 49–63. Springer, Cham (2022)

9. Ferreyra, E.G., Strieder, S., Valenti, N.B.: La presencia social en la educación en línea según el Modelo Comunidad de Indagación. Abordajes. Revista de Ciencias Sociales y Humanas. vol. 6, núm. 12 (2022)

10. Gutiérrez-Santiuste, E., Gallego-Arrufat, M.J.: Presencia social en un ambiente colaborativo virtual de aprendizaje: análisis de una comunidad orientada a la indagación. Revista mexicana de investigación educativa. vol. 22, núm 75, 1169–1186 (2017) Recuperado http://www.scielo. org.mx/scielo.php?script=sci_arttext&pid=S1405-66662017000401169&lng=es&tlng=es

11. Gutiérrez-Santiuste, E., Rodríguez-Sabiote, C. Gallego-Arrufat, M. J.: Cognitive presence through social and teaching presence in communities of inquiry: a correlational-predictive study. Australas. J. Educ. Technol. **31**(3), 349–362 (2015). Disponible en: http://ajet.org.au/ index.php/AJET/issue/view/112

12. Costley, J., Lange, C.: The Relationship between Social Presence and Critical Thinking: Results from Learner Discourse in an Asynchronous Learning Environment. J. Inf. Technol. Educ. Res. **15**, 89–108 (2016). https://doi.org/10.28945/3418

13. Yang, J.C., Quadir, B., Chen, N., Miao, Q.: Effects of online presence on learning performance in a blog-based online course. Int. High. Educ. **30**, 11–20 (2016). https://doi.org/10.1016/j. iheduc.2016.04.002

14. Spandre, O., Dieser, M.P., Sanz, C.V.: Análisis de indicadores de presencias en cursos mediados por tecnología digital en tecnicaturas de Educación Superior. In: XXVIII Congreso Argentino de Ciencias de la Computación (CACIC) (La Rioja, 3 al 6 de octubre de 2022) (2023)

Graphic Computation, Images and Visualization

COVID-19 Signs Detection in Chest Radiographs Using Convolutional Neural Networks

Guido Sebastián Armoa(✉), Nuria Isabel Vega Lencina, and Karina Beatriz Eckert

Universidad Gastón Dachary, Posadas, Misiones, Argentina
guidoarmoa777@gmail.com

Abstract. COVID-19 pandemic that affected the entire world since late 2019 and the need to collaborate with the healthcare system gave rise to this article. Early diagnosis of the disease caused by the coronavirus is crucial for the treatment and control of this type of illness. In this context, chest radiography plays an important role as an alternative test to confirm or rule out an infected person; precisely, this work aims to analyze and develop a software prototype for COVID-19 signs recognition in chest radiographs, based on image processing using convolutional neural network model. Proposal is based on CRISP-ML methodology, following its phases of understanding the business and data, adapting the latter, generating the model and then evaluating it; experimentation and analysis of the behavior of the network were carried out by training it using different publicly available datasets. Experimental results demonstrate the proposed prototype effectiveness and limitations, with classification accuracy close to 80%.

Keywords: Digital image processing · Artificial neural networks · Convolutional neural networks · Chest radiography

1 Introduction

Coronavirus 2019 (COVID-19) is an infectious disease that has affected over 650 million individuals worldwide and caused over 6 million deaths as of February 2023 [1].

Traditionally, to determine whether a patient is infected or not, Reverse Transcription Polymerase Chain Reaction (RT-PCR) and rapid antibody tests are used. Former is considered more reliable, but it takes 4 to 6 h to obtain results. In addition, high demand for authorized laboratories can result in delays of several days, and there is also a shortage of PCR test kit centers. On other hand, rapid tests allow results to be obtained in 10 to 15 min, but they have a sensitivity of less than 30%, making them not recommended for routine diagnosis [2].

Early COVID-19 diagnosis is crucial for its treatment and control. This motivates alternative testing methods study, such as Chest X-rays (CXR). Imaging tests play an important role in patient management; they have been used to support diagnosis, determine the disease severity, guide treatment and assess its response. In contrast to

© The Author(s), under exclusive license to Springer Nature Switzerland AG 2023
P. Pesado (Ed.): CACIC 2022, CCIS 1778, pp. 61–75, 2023.
https://doi.org/10.1007/978-3-031-34147-2_5

PCR, CXR can be a more cost-effective and faster method to diagnose signs caused by COVID-19 [3].

CXR is generally the first-line imaging study in the evaluation of patients with suspected COVID-19 due to its usefulness, availability and low cost. Along with clinical evaluation and laboratory tests, it contributes to the initial assessment and disease monitoring. CXR also has sufficient sensitivity for detecting COVID-19, suggesting its utility as a complementary diagnostic tool [4, 5].

There are significant differences in sensitivity between PCR and CXR, but it is accepted that the latter can be used as a method for organizing the care of individuals according to existing resources and their needs in certain scenarios. These scenarios include environments with high disease prevalence (community transmission), centers with limited access to tests (PCR or rapid tests) and available portable CXR equipment, or in patients with severe symptoms, allowing for faster triage, hospitalization, and treatment [6].

Currently, there is unprecedented progress in Artificial Intelligence (AI) technology, which has led to the creation of new tools and applications. AI represents an attempt to mimic human intelligence, and systems based on it incorporate algorithms such as machine learning and deep learning in complex environments, facilitating the automation of multiple processes [7].

Thanks to deep learning, a computer can acquire the ability to perform classification tasks from images. Automatic feature extraction allows models to perform very well when used for computer vision activities, such as object identification. By using this tool, a computational system can develop the ability to classify tasks from images. Feature extraction automation makes these models very accurate in computer vision tasks, such as object identification. Among the most popular types of ANN (Artificial Neural Network) are CNNs (Convolutional Neural Networks). These networks do not require manual feature extraction, so it is not necessary to determine in advance which features are used to classify images, as in classic image processing. Instead, they rely on automatic extraction, obtaining this information directly from training images. Important features are acquired as the network evolves and learns through its experience from the input image set [8].

Proposal is to develop and train a CNN to analyze patients chest X-rays with suspected COVID-19 in an automated way, taking into account the situation of the pandemic in Argentina and the province of Misiones. This will allow doctors to quickly determine if a patient shows typical signs of the disease, and assist in making decisions about hospitalization and immediate treatment while waiting for laboratory results.

Present article is structured in the following manner: Sect. 2 presents a proposal. Section 3 describes the methodology. Evaluation for prototype can be found in Sect. 4. Finally, in Sect. 5, conclusions and future research are thoroughly explained.

2 Proposal

This paper presents an extension of the project presented at CACIC 2022 [9] entitled 'Detección de signos de COVID-19 en radiografías de tórax a través del procesamiento digital de imágenes con redes neuronales convolucionales'.

Several steps were followed for CNN implementation, starting with the loading and configuration of the dataset, followed by the creation of the network model with each of its layers. Finally, network was trained and tested. Prototype development is based on the CRISP-ML(Q) methodology [10], methodology phases include: business understanding, data understanding, data preparation, modeling and evaluation, excluding the last deployment phase as it is not relevant to the project objective (a prototype).

3   Methodology

CRISP-ML(Q) methodology was chosen because it provides a clear structure under a systematic approach for developing machine learning models, which helps ensure that all necessary phases for building an effective model are covered. It allows the project to be transparent and reproducible, aiding in effectively communicating the model's results. [10, 11].

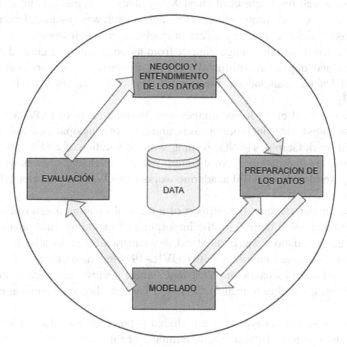

Fig. 1. Adapted CRISP-ML(Q) Methodology.

CRISP-ML(Q) is based on CRISP-DM CRoss-Industry Standard Process (CRISP) for Data Mining (DM) [12], basically consists of CRISP for development of Machine Learning (ML) applications with assurance of the Quality (Quality).

In Fig. 1, see a general methodology adaptation from project. As can be noted, the process begins with defining business and data understanding. Last phases such as deployment, monitoring and maintenance were excluded as they were not considered relevant to the project's goal, which is a prototype. Additionally, there is a back-and-forth between the data preparation and modeling phase as different training iterations are conducted, and based on results, dataset is modified to achieve better performance, and if necessary, model is also modified to evolve until obtaining a model that meets the requirements. Lastly, results are evaluated and if necessary, all activities are repeated until the objectives are met.

3.1 Business and Data Understanding

Business and data understanding are part of methodology first phase. Business involves defining the problem that proposed model aims to solve, which in this case is described in Sect. 1. Main project objective is to develop a software prototype to signs COVID-19 detection in chest radiographs of patients using convolutional neural networks.

Data Understanding

As a first step, search for a dataset of chest X-ray images was carried out, as it was the primary factor to start with prototype development. Search was conducted using various means such as publicly accessible sources or published research works.

It was decided to use the image dataset from an open database created by a team of researchers and physicians affiliated with the University of Qatar, Doha, and the University of Dhaka, Bangladesh, along with their collaborators from Pakistan and Malaysia [13].

Dataset consists of chest X-ray images with positive cases of COVID-19, normal cases (healthy lungs), viral pneumonia cases, and cases of lung opacities. All images are in Portable Network Graphics (PNG) format, with a resolution of 299×299 pixels.

Researchers created dataset from different publicly available sources with the aim of producing useful and impactful academic works on COVID-19 that can help address the pandemic.

To aid data understanding, the support of a medical imaging diagnostician professional was enlisted. With their help, the importance of including viral pneumonia and lung opacity cases in dataset was understood, as a patient affected by advanced COVID-19 can present with these conditions, with COVID-19 being the root cause. Additionally, it was confirmed that in a pandemic alert state, where positive cases are abundant, any sign of pneumonia, whether typical of COVID-19 or not, should be considered and not dismissed.

Therefore, these images types were included to positive cases dataset increase and allow the network to learn from a greater number of examples.

3.2 Data Preparation

This phase involves preparation and pre-processing of the images that will be used to train the network, as well as the division into training, validation, and testing sets. Once the original dataset was obtained, different configurations of it were generated, meaning different distributions of images in different datasets were created for testing purposes to see which gave better or worse results.

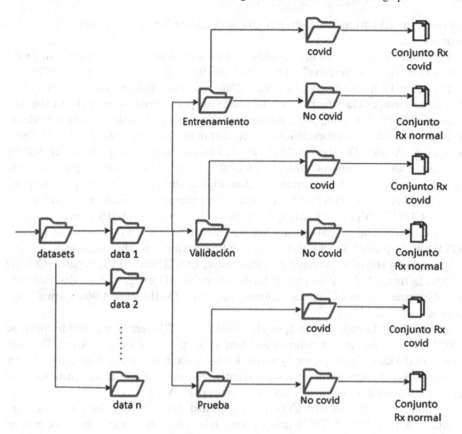

Fig. 2. Distribution of folders

Factors taken into account for datasets generation were as follows: whether the dataset was curated, meaning if images with errors or poor quality that could skew the results were removed and whether lungs with pneumonia images (as COVID positive) or opacity lungs images and pneumonia images (as COVID positive) were considered.

As a first step, each dataset characteristics were decided and then for each one, following structuring was carried out: each dataset was divided into three folders, with 80% of the selected images forming part to training set, 10% for validation set and remaining 10% for test set. It was sought to make all sets as diverse as possible.

Furthermore, within each subset of each dataset (training, validation and test), two folders were created representing each possible classification, the images classified as COVID positive and the images classified as COVID negative.

Figure 2 shows folders distribution and files mentioned above and all created configurations are stored within datasets folder.

For the first dataset (data 1), it was decided to test with all available images, taking as COVID positive all images of COVID, viral pneumonia, and lung opacities. Inclusion of viral pneumonia images and lung opacities images within COVID positive classification was done in order to increase dataset size and achieve better neural network training accuracy.

For negative COVID, all images classified as normal were taken, resulting in a total of 10,972 images for "positive" COVID and 10,192 images for "negative" COVID.

For second dataset, images classified as "normal" were used as examples of negative COVID and images classified as COVID and "viral pneumonia" were used as examples of positive COVID, leaving aside images of lung opacity. This decision was made on Dr. Luqui Osvaldo recommendation, a specialist in diagnostic imaging at the "Hospital Escuela de Agudos Dr. Ramón Madariaga", because lung opacity can be caused by many diseases and is not a common sign of disease in question, which could obscure the study. Moreover, given current epidemiological situation, in practice, there is no distinction between COVID pneumonia and viral pneumonia. Both are considered as positive COVID, although there may be signs that differ from each other, given that each case is different, and a viral pneumonia may have been caused by a previous positive COVID in the patient. In another context, without a pandemic, this could vary.

A total of 4,960 images were taken for positive COVID and 10,192 negative COVID images. In turn, a balance was made for negative COVID images set, so that both sets have the same number of images, reducing negative COVID set to 4,960 normal lungs images.

For the third dataset, only images classified as COVID were considered for positive COVID set, that is, viral pneumonia and lung opacity images were not used. This was done with the idea of giving exactly network what it needs to learn, although the number of images used to network train is significantly reduced, it is still an adequate size and better quality since it only has X-rays with positive COVID.

A total of 3,615 positive COVID images and 3,615 normal lung images were obtained. All available COVID images were taken, and the same number of normal lung images was selected, trying to select the "best quality" images.

Finally, for fourth dataset, only COVID and normal lung images were considered, like dataset number 3, with difference that for the latter, in order to improve the results and reduce bias, it was necessary to "purge" the images, for this, the images had to be viewed individually and those that were very blurry or defective were eliminated as they could bias the results obtained, resulting in poor quality classifications.

This activity was carried out without professional help, as it is a task that takes a lot of time and we did not have the availability of doctors. That is why the purge was exclusively of radiographs that were noticeably poorly executed.

For last dataset, after the purge, a total of 2,462 positive COVID images were obtained, and the same number of normal lung images were selected for positive COVID.

3.3 Modeling

Modeling phase of the network includes its development, optimization and training. These activities are described in detail below.

Prototype Development

Developed prototype was implemented in Python, since it is a multi-paradigm and multi-level open-source and free language. It was chosen because it is ideal for AI techniques implementation. In turn, Anaconda platform was used since it can create and implement deep learning models that use neural networks. Additionally, it integrates easily with tools such as TensorFlow and Keras to create and train neural network models, including convolutional neural networks [14–17].

For CNN implementation, a series steps were followed, starting with loading and dataset configuring, followed by creating the network and each of its layers, including convolutional layers, max pooling layers, flattening layer, and dense layer.

Decision on the number of applied filters, parameters used and layers number was made after performing different network configurations and selecting the architecture that demonstrated the best performance in training, thus determining the final configuration of chosen model, by iterating back and forth between previous phase, modifying data used and model repeatedly testing.

Network performance was evaluated based on accuracy and validation error set, training time and computational cost, in addition to results of testing with test images.

To objectively test each network, the same dataset was used. Different training sessions were performed for each network configuration, selecting neural network model that achieved the best results. These tests are not presented in this work since only the tests performed on final model and its validation are considered relevant.

Subsequently, a graph was implemented to track each training session and evaluate the behavior of the network during the training, as well as to evaluate the performance of the validation set.

CNN Creation

Sequential() function was used to create the neural network, which groups a linear stack of layers into a tf.keras.Model file [18].

Then, each layer was added to the network using the add() function. Parameters received by this function are as follows: filters number used, filter size, padding variable referring to corners filter, height and length of input images and activation function used. Additionally, a MaxPooling layer was added using a 2x2 filter size.

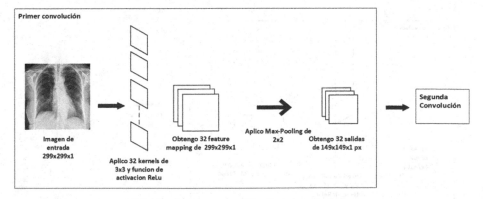

Fig. 3. Architecture of the first convolution.

With this last layer, first convolution ends and in Fig. 3, its architecture can be observed graphically. Next, as shown in Fig. 4, second and third convolutional layers are added, in this case, hidden layers, so the size of image (inputShape) is not specified.

In both cases, the parameters they receive are as follows: filters number, filter size, padding variable and activation function used.

At the end, a MaxPooling layer is added, for which a filter of size 2x2 was used, thereby concluding the convolutions.

Finally, a flattening layer is added to transform the multidimensional network into a one-dimensional network, which is then passed to a traditional neural network. In Fig. 5, complete final convolutional neural network architecture can be seen, formed by the 3 convolutional layers, flattening layer and multilayer perceptron (MLP). MLP outputs MLP represent the entire network outputs, resulting in each class accuracy percentage.

3.4 Network Optimization

After finishing building the network, optimization process was carried out. To do this, optimization parameters of the algorithm were used through the compile() function,

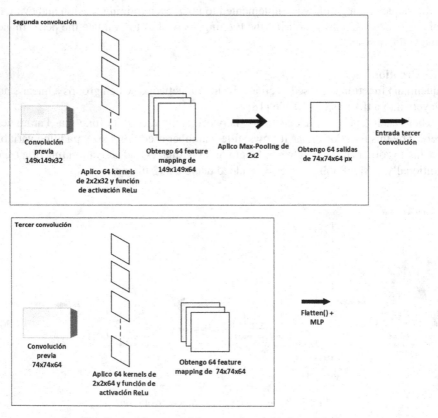

Fig. 4. Architecture of the second and third convolution.

which takes as parameters a loss function, an optimizer along with learning rate and a metric. These parameters help to evaluate network during training performance.

Optimizer used for the learning function was Adam, which uses gradient descent. It takes the learning rate (lr) as a parameter, in this case, a lr = 0.0005 was used.

Loss function chosen was categorical crossentropy, which is used in multi-class classification tasks. These are tasks where an example can only belong to one of several possible categories, and the model must decide which one. Formally, it is designed to quantify the difference between two probability distributions. [19]. Metric used was accuracy, which represents the percentage of correct predictions made by the network. It calculates how often the predictions are correct.

3.5 Network Training

Next step is to specify training and dataset. To do this, we use the fit_generator() function, which receives the following parameters: training set, steps per epoch number, epochs number (in this case, 20), validation set and validation steps number [20].

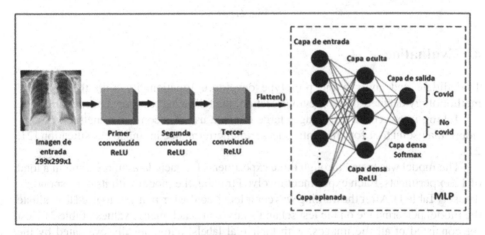

Fig. 5. Complete prototype architecture with CNN

Once network is trained, model is saved in corresponding directory, in this case, in the specific folder named "modelo", the structure is saved under the name "modelo.h5" and the weights under the name "pesos.h5".

After saving the model, training a line plot and validation learning is generated as epochs function, as shown in Fig. 6, the plot displays 4 metrics.

Four metrics mentioned above are train_acc (training accuracy) and val_acc (validation accuracy), which represent accuracy of learning for both the training and validation sets, respectively. On other hand, we have train_loss (training loss) and val_loss (validation loss), which represent the training and validation sets learning error of.

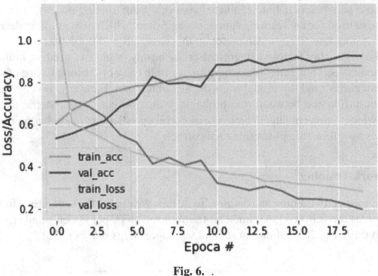

Fig. 6. .

4 Evaluation

To validate and analyze the prototype developed functionality with the proposed methodology detailed in the previous section, the following tests have been planned:

Taking into account test images large number, use of a confusion matrix was considered, a useful tool for efficiently measuring performance in image classification [21, 22].

The model was tested through three experiments for each dataset, resulting in a total of 12 experiments. Each experiment involved training the model with its corresponding dataset (Table 1). After the training was completed, confusion matrix was used to evaluate the model performance on the test set and analyze the each metric values (Table 2). Test set consisted of all the images, with their real labels, automatically evaluated by the model and compared to their predicted labels.

Table 1 presents a comparative summary of error and accuracy results obtained during each model training. Additionally, Table 2 shows metric values obtained from confusion matrices generated in each experiment.

Table 1. Training results summary.

Dataset	Test	Training Error	Validation Error	Training Accuracy	Validation Accuracy
1	1	0,3840	0,3319	0,8292	0,8552
	2	0,3575	0,3030	0,8478	0,8725

(*continued*)

Table 1. (*continued*)

Dataset	Test	Training Error	Validation Error	Training Accuracy	Validation Accuracy
	3	0,3478	0,2951	0,8511	0,8730
2	4	0,2956	0,6591	0,8715	0,6099
	5	0,2928	0,6354	0,8806	0,6069
	6	0,2939	0,5788	0,8752	0,6633
3	7	0,3993	0,2759	0,8009	0,8920
	8	0,3993	0,2759	0,8009	0,8920
	9	0,3602	0,2588	0,8387	0,9034
4	10	0,3510	0,3900	0,8410	0,8208
	11	0,3971	0,3815	0,8122	0,8562
	12	0,4212	0,3944	0,7909	0,8375

In Table 1, it can be observed that the vast majority of the trainings had results that at first glance seem promising. Test 9 training stands out for achieving an 90% accuracy and only 0.25 validation set error. On the other hand, test 5 was the test with least favorable results, with 0.63 error and validation set 60% accuracy.

Table 2. Summary of tests.

Dataset	Test	Precision		Sensitivity		F1-score		Accuracy
		Covid	No Covid	Covid	No Covid	Covid	No Covid	
1	1	0,66	0,77	0,83	0,58	0,73	0,66	70,78%
	2	0,58	0,85	0,94	0,31	0,71	0,46	63,11%
	3	0,51	0,91	0,99	0,06	0,67	0,11	52,75%
2	4	0,49	0,50	0,94	0,05	0,65	0,09	49,95%
	5	0,49	0,44	0,91	0,06	0,64	0,11	49,04%
	6	0,49	0,00	1,00	0,00	0,66	0,00	49,95%
3	7	0,51	0,95	0,99	0,05	0,67	0,10	52,76%
	8	0,53	0,83	0,96	0,17	0,69	0,28	56,91%
	9	0,47	0,47	0,54	0,40	0,51	0,43	47,65%
4	10	0,79	0,79	0,80	0,78	0,79	0,79	79,47%
	11	0,65	0,68	0,71	0,63	0,68	0,65	67,07%
	12	0,66	0,65	0,64	0,67	0,65	0,66	66,06%

In Table 2, it can be observed that all tests performed with the same dataset gave similar results.

Dataset 1 is set that shows the greatest variation in its results, achieving an 71% accuracy in test 1 (Table 2).

Tests performed with dataset number 2 stand out for obtaining least favorable results, in no case did it manage to exceed 50% accuracy. The fact of having same amount of images for each class, a 50% accuracy indicates that the network classifies practically all images as the same class.

For dataset number 3 case, a similar behavior to tests performed with dataset number 2 is observed, with little notable results. It is convenient to note that test 9 performed with this dataset presents the best accuracy value, reaching 90% on the validation set during training (Table 1). It is important to note that, although the accuracy value in training is high, it does not ensure good performance in classifying images, as can be seen in the classification results in Table 2.

Finally, dataset number 4 stands out for obtaining best results, exceeding 66% accuracy on the test set in all cases. Test 10, where an accuracy of 79% was achieved in classifying test set images, stands out and confusion matrix generated is shown in Fig. 7.

4.1 Network Validation

Based on the results of the previous tests, the best-performing network in image classification was selected, which was obtained in test 10 with dataset 4 (achieving 79% accuracy), and validation was performed with the help of a professional in the of diagnostic imaging field from the Hospital Escuela de Agudos Dr. Ramón Madariaga.

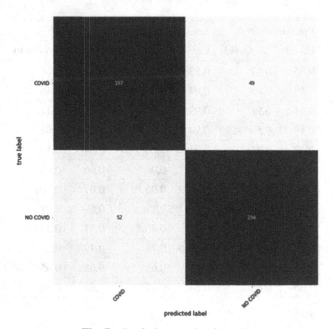

Fig. 7. Confusion matrix of test 10.

A dataset containing 52 unlabeled images from test set of the dataset used to train the network was provided to the professional, who was asked to classify them according to their criteria. Of the 52 chest X-ray images, 37 were classified by the professional in the same way as the network, 3 could not be defined under any classification, so they were not taken into account, and the remaining 12 images were classified in contradiction to the outputs obtained by the network.

A 75% agreement was obtained with classification performed by the doctor. It is worth noting that classification criteria may vary depending on each person, as factors such as experience or human error may affect decision made. Therefore, the validation results are considered favorable.

5 Conclusions

In order to meet this work objectives, an exhaustive research process and COVID-19 signs analysis in lung radiographs was necessary, as well as a deeper understanding of convolutional neural networks application in image classification, network architecture designing and different datasets, prototype implementing, network training and testing with each dataset, and validating the prototype's performance with a professional. Finally, the results were analyzed to determine proposal feasibility.

After analysis, it can be observed that result tables and confusion matrices demonstrate that dataset number 4 showed best performance in image classification, achieving 79% accuracy. Based on this, it can be deduced that refinement performed on dataset was the key factor in achieving this improvement. In this sense, tests indicate that removing low-quality images produces an exponential improvement in classification results, demonstrating the sensitivity that CNNs have to these images types and having a representative dataset importance.

Within exposed analysis, it is possible to observe that trained network has two major limitations: used to radiograph perform technique, which can affect image quality and chronic conditions that patient may present. On other hand, it is important to highlight high computational cost demanded to CNNs development.

As it has been shown, prototype obtained was promising for specialist physician in diagnostic imaging, as it was able to effectively classify lung radiographs with COVID-19 signs in a matter of seconds once the radiograph was obtained. In this way, an alternative could be generated to cooperate with health organizations in COVID-19 diagnosis.

According to what has been expressed above, it has been demonstrated that with convolutional neural networks application, a prototype capable of effectively recognizing COVID-19 signs in lung radiographs was built. Thus, it is evident this study successfully fulfilled the objectives proposed at the beginning of the research.

In this work, CRISP-ML(Q) methodology application allowed classifying problem lung radiograph images with COVID-19 signs to be addressed in a rigorous and structured manner, which led to effective prototype development for this disease diagnosis. Use this methodology allowed for adequate and structured project management. It is highly recommended for machine learning projects, as it provides a structured and rigorous approach to problem-solving.

Finally, it should be noted that since pandemic beginning, numerous research projects of same nature as this one have emerged, resulting in many cases with excellent results, confirming the usefulness of these tools in the field. All of this leads to future improvements for this work, one of which could be implementing a network that, instead of performing binary classification, performs multi-class classification. Additionally, transfer learning could be utilized given that it presents numerous advantages and currently there are many works that support its efficiency (ResNet, VGG, etc.).

References

1. COVID-19 Visualizer. https://www.covidvisualizer.com/. Accessed 07 Dec 2022
2. Martínez Chamorro, E., Díez Tascón, A., Ibáñez Sanz, L., Ossaba Vélez, S., Borruel Nacenta, S.: Radiologic diagnosis of patients with COVID-19. Radiologia **63**(1), 56–73 (2021). https://doi.org/10.1016/j.rx.2020.11.001
3. ¿Qué es una red neuronal? - MATLAB & Simulink. https://la.mathworks.com/discovery/neural-network.html. Accessed 24 Sep 2020
4. The Handbook of Artificial Intelligence. Elsevier (1981)
5. Introducción al Aprendizaje Automático - Fernando Sancho Caparrini. http://www.cs.us.es/~fsancho/?e=75. Accessed 07 Sep 2020
6. ¿Qué es el Deep Learning? | SmartPanel. https://www.smartpanel.com/que-es-deep-learning/. Accessed 07 Sep 2020
7. Deep Learning - Libro online de IAAR. https://iaarbook.github.io/deeplearning/. Accessed 17 Nov 2021
8. Bagnato, J.I.: Aprende Machine Learning en Español, p. 164 (2020). https://www.aprendemachinelearning.com/
9. Armoa, G.S., Vega Lencina, N.I., Eckert, K.B.: Detección de signos de COVID-19 en radiografías de tórax a través del procesamiento digital de imágenes con redes neuronales convolucionales. XXVIII Congr. Argentino Ciencias la Comput. (CACIC), Ciudad La Rioja, La Rioja, Argentina (2022)
10. Studer, S., et al.: Towards CRISP-ML(Q): a machine learning process model with quality assurance methodology. Mach. Learn. Knowl. Extr. **3**(2), 392–413 (2021). https://doi.org/10.3390/make3020020
11. CRISP-ML(Q). https://ml-ops.org/content/crisp-ml. Accessed 07 Dec 2022
12. Chapman, P., et al.: Step-by-step Data Mining Guide. SPSS inc. vol. 78, pp. 1–78 (2000). https://www.semanticscholar.org/paper/CRISP-DM-1.0%3A-Step-by-step-data-mining-guide-Chapman-Clinton/54bad20bbc7938991bf34f86dde0babfbd2d5a72%0A http://www.crisp-dm.org/CRISPWP-0800.pdf
13. COVID-19 Radiography Database | Kaggle. https://www.kaggle.com/tawsifurrahman/covid19-radiography-database. Accessed 21 May 2021
14. Anaconda | Use Cases. https://www.anaconda.com/use-cases. Accessed 17 Feb 2022
15. Librerías, M.L.: TensorFlow, Scikit-learn, Pytorch y Keras - Platzi. https://platzi.com/blog/librerias-de-machine-learning-tensorflow-scikit-learn-pythorch-y-keras/?gclid=CjwKCAiA4KaRBhBdEiwAZi1zzrm5QrcLNP_R6BqpM9DZj0H6v9yvzsHEXltymGQzgu3FfBQaImjc_hoCmHMQAvD_BwE&gclsrc=aw.ds. Accessed 10 Mar 2022
16. Keras: the Python deep learning API. https://keras.io/. Accessed 04 Jul 2022
17. TensorFlow. https://www.tensorflow.org/?hl=es-419. Accessed 04 Jul 2022
18. The Sequential class. https://keras.io/api/models/sequential/. Accessed 02 Mar 2022
19. Función de pérdida de entropía cruzada categórica | Plataforma Peltarion. https://peltarion.com/knowledge-center/documentation/modeling-view/build-an-ai-model/loss-functions/categorical-crossentropy. Accessed 17 Mar 2022

20. fit_generator function - RDocumentation. https://www.rdocumentation.org/packages/keras/versions/2.4.0/topics/fit_generator. Accessed 04 Jul 2022
21. La matriz de confusión y sus métricas – Inteligencia Artificial –. https://www.juanbarrios.com/la-matriz-de-confusion-y-sus-metricas/. Accessed 15 Mar 2022
22. Evaluando los modelos de Clasificación en Aprendizaje Automático: La matriz de confusión.| profesorDATA.com. https://profesordata.com/2020/08/07/evaluando-los-modelos-de-clasificacion-en-aprendizaje-automatico-la-matriz-de-confusion-claramente-explicada/. Accessed 04 Apr 2022

A Digital Zen Garden for Mental Health Conditions Treatment

Nicolás Jofré$^{(\boxtimes)}$, Graciela Rodríguez, Yoselie Alvarado, Jacqueline Fernandez, and Roberto Guerrero

Laboratorio de Computación Gráfica (LCG), Universidad Nacional de San Luis, San Luis, Argentina
{npasinetti,gbrodriguez,ymalvarado,jmfer,rag}@unsl.edu.ar

Abstract. From the beginning of the COVID-19 pandemic, the severity and prevalence of symptoms of psychological distress, fatigue, brain fog, and other conditions have increased considerably, including among people who have not been infected with SARS-CoV-2. Many studies summarize the effect of the pandemic on the availability of mental health services and how this has changed during the pandemic. Concerned that potential increases in mental health conditions, had already prompted 90% of countries surveyed to include mental health and psychosocial support in their post COVID-19 response plans, but major gaps and concerns remain. In this paper we developed a de-stress proposal through a digital zen garden by using an augmented reality sandbox. The system provides patients with flexible interaction and easy control of the scenario, while making real time data recording. Three evaluation methods were developed to review the effectiveness of the therapy. According to the evaluation results of patients' training, the system is a low cost entertainment tool that augments patients' motivation, and helps to increase the effectiveness of therapy.

Keywords: Mental Health · Cognitive Disorders · Virtual Reality · Augmented Reality · COVID-19

1 Introduction

In terms of pathophysiology, a closely related coronavirus (SARS-CoV) is reported to be neurotoxic and affect mental health. Furthermore, among the survivors of SARS infection, patients were reported to have persistent elevated stress, and over 64% of the survivors are reported to have a combination of stress, anxiety, and depression [1].

Only in the first year of the COVID-19 pandemic, global prevalence of anxiety and depression increased by a massive 25%, according to a scientific brief released by the World Health Organization (WHO). WHO Director-General, said that the information gathered about the impact of COVID-19 on the world's mental health is just the tip of an iceberg. As a consequence, this is a wake-up call

P. Pesado (Ed.): CACIC 2022, CCIS 1778, pp. 76–87, 2023.
https://doi.org/10.1007/978-3-031-34147-2_6

to all countries to pay more attention to mental health and do a better job of supporting their populations' mental health. One major explanation for the increase is the unprecedented stress caused by the social isolation resulting from the pandemic. Linked to this were constraints on people's ability to work, seek support from loved ones and engage in their communities. Loneliness, fear of infection, suffering and death for oneself and for loved ones, grief after bereavement and financial worries have also all been cited as stressors leading to anxiety and depression [2]. Among health workers, exhaustion has been a major trigger for suicidal thinking [3].

Some studies show that the pandemic has affected the mental health of young people and that they are disproportionally at risk of suicidal and self-harming behaviours. It also indicates that women have been more severely impacted than men and that people with pre-existing physical health conditions, such as asthma, cancer and heart disease, were more likely to develop symptoms of mental disorders [4].

Data suggests that people with pre-existing mental disorders do not appear to be disproportionately vulnerable to COVID-19 infection. Yet, when these people do become infected, they are more likely to suffer hospitalization, severe illness and death compared with people without mental disorders. People with more severe mental disorders, such as psychoses, and young people with mental disorders, are particularly at risk [5].

While the pandemic has generated interest in and concern for mental health, it has also revealed historical under-investment in mental health services. Countries must act urgently to ensure that mental health support is available to all. In this sense, there is an urgent need for tools to address diseases such as stress, anxiety, among others.

The aim of this paper is to propose a de-stress therapeutic tool by approximating the ancient method of Japanese Zen Garden through Augmented Reality (AR).

Section 2 gives a brief overview of Japanese Zen Garden. Section 3 describes the proposed Augmented Reality Sandbox Architecture System. Section 4 details the evaluation method to review the effectiveness of the therapy with a preliminary evaluation published in [6], that evaluation was extended to more participants. Additionally, two user experience evaluations were conducted based on participant emotion and perception. Section 5 provides a small discussion and future guidelines.

Section 4 details evaluation methods reviewing the effectiveness of the therapy. Evaluations methods extend participants number and method suggested in a preliminary publication [6]. Evaluations involve one objective and two subjective analysis. Subjective user experience evaluations were conducted based on participant emotion and perception. Section 5 provides a small discussion and future guidelines.

2   Japanese Zen Garden

Japanese gardens create their own styles and one of the most famous are the so-called Zen gardens that seek to go beyond and create a place conducive to meditation and contemplation (See Fig. 1).

The japanese zen garden creates a miniature stylized landscape through carefully composed arrangements of rocks, water features, moss, pruned trees and bushes, and uses gravel or sand that is raked to represent ripples in water. Zen gardens are commonly found at temples or monasteries. A zen garden is usually relatively small, surrounded by a wall or buildings, and is usually meant to be seen while seated from a single viewpoint outside the garden, such as the porch of the hojo, the residence of the chief monk of the temple or monastery. Many, with gravel rather than grass, are only stepped into for maintenance. Classical zen gardens were created at temples of Zen Buddhism in Kyoto during the Muromachi period. They were intended to imitate the essence of nature, not its actual appearance, and to serve as an aid for meditation [7].

It is important to understand that the word zen means meditation. Monks used zen garden as an ideal place for meditation. They are areas that transmit tranquility, inner serenity and reduce stress through their beauty [8].

Sand represents the vastness of the ocean and rocks represent the mountains. One of the many benefits of zen gardens is to de-stress their owners by playing with the rake, creating shapes in the sand. We can give movement to our garden, for example by creating designs with "stacked stones" which signify stability.

Zen gardens bring us serenity and relaxation; they stimulate creativity and the best thing is that we do not need a large space to create one, we can assemble them in any corner of our home or office.

Fig. 1. Photo courtesy of John S. Lander [9].

3   Augmented Reality Sandbox

When referring to an augmented reality environment it talks about any real-world environment with elements augmented or supplemented by computer-generated input [10].

Since their conception in 2012 [11,12], the AR sandbox system is used to teach geographical, geological, and hydrological concepts such as how to read topographic maps, the meaning of contour lines, watersheds, catchment areas, levees, etc. It is a tool that combines 3-dimensional visualization applications with a hands-on sandbox. Users can create topography models by shaping real sand, which is then augmented in real time by an elevation color map, topographic contour lines, and simulated water flow.

However, in many cases AR sandbox can be seen as a form of non-verbal therapeutic intervention [13–15]. Patients (often, children) can use sand to portray their experiences that they cannot express verbally. Moreover, many psychologists leverage this tool to treat psychic disorders due to its proven efficiency.

Given this background it would be interesting to evaluate how an AR sandbox can contribute to reducing stress resulting from everyday life problems and the well-known Covid-19 pandemic.

3.1   System Description

As mentioned in Sect. 2, sand represents the vastness of the ocean and rocks represent the mountains. One of the many benefits of zen gardens is to de-stress their owners by playing with the rake, creating shapes in the sand. In relation to this, the sand in our sandbox is initially flattened and unrelieved, and the user has a set of tools such as trowel, rake and ruler. Using these tools, the user can perform different actions such as:

- to create indentations or mountains by the trowel,
- to create ripples that can represent water by the rake, and clean up and redraw them by a ruler,
- to clean and redraw the relief until the desired relief is achieved by a ruler.

It is expected that the user can visualize an analyze the projected textures in each sandbox section so they can determine and materialize the landscape appearance by means of the tools based on their observation.

3.2   Architecture System

Our AR sandbox prototype system comprises the following hardware components:

- A computer with a high-end graphics card, running Linux.
- A Microsoft Kinect 3D camera.
- A digital video short-throw projector with a digital video interface, such as HDMI or DVI.

- A mirror.
- A sandbox with a way to mount the Kinect camera, the mirror and the projector above the sandbox.
- Sand.

The architecture was designed for a medium sandbox of 120 × 100cm. These measurements determined that the depth sensor is suspended 2.2m above the sandbox. Having a regular projector, the ideal projection aperture is projecting to a screen located at a distance of more than 3 m, that is, the projector position has to be higher than the position of the depth sensor. This feature gives a resulting sensor shadow on the sandbox. The sensor-projector height problem can be solved by using a conveniently placed mirror to simplify the structure that supports all the devices. The mirror size results in 60 × 60cm.

The developed prototype used for this work is shown below (Fig. 2). Figure 3 shows in detail the resulting visualized sand landscape.

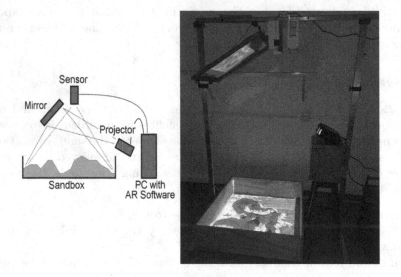

Fig. 2. Sandbox architecture system.

4   Experiences and Results

The present research carried out three experimental methodologies using a group of fifty participants between 12 and 60 years old, all of them from San Luis, Argentina.

Firstly, we implemented a physiological evaluation method based on user's heart rate. Secondly, we apply a technique that directly measures emotions through a questionnaire. Finally, we performed a quantitative study for measuring the perception of the interface.

Fig. 3. Sandbox projected.

se presentan 3 evaluaciones, una objetiva y 2 subejtivas basadas en la experiencia del usuario

4.1 Physiological Evaluation

We performed an objective evaluation method to review the effectiveness of the therapy training. The training consisted of measuring the level of participants' stress before and after the experience with our sandbox prototype through 5–20 minutes user free actions. Actions were detailed in Sect. 3.1.

Stress level monitoring enables to check how much stress the user has. For experimental data acquisition, a smart band was used [16]. The smart band measures the user's heart rate and determines the current stress level based on its variability according to Jachymek et al. work [17]. Range values are suggested by the smart band's application as shown in Table 1 [16].

Table 1. Stress level description

Levels of stress			
Relaxed	Mild	Moderate	High
0-39	40-59	60-79	80-100

Table 2 shows the stress level measured at two different time slices: before and after the sandbox experience (second, third, fifth and sixth columns from left to right).

Table 2. Stress level of the fifty participants before and after to the experience

# User	A Priori Level	A Posteriori Level	# User	A Priori Level	A Posteriori Level
1	35	24	26	48	40
2	29	21	27	47	39
3	34	25	28	44	35
4	29	23	29	42	31
5	40	31	30	30	24
6	64	34	31	41	28
7	38	28	32	34	27
8	27	22	33	48	35
9	38	28	34	49	40
10	59	33	35	41	28
11	43	26	36	45	36
12	47	29	37	41	29
13	44	35	38	44	30
14	42	31	39	46	36
15	30	24	40	46	35
16	41	28	41	43	28
17	35	27	42	40	27
18	44	35	43	44	38
19	49	38	44	50	38
20	42	28	45	41	28
21	60	39	46	41	30
22	45	38	47	38	37
23	47	42	48	44	38
24	45	38	49	41	32
25	45	33	50	42	37

4.2 Emotional Evaluation

Spending time doing an enjoyable activity can help relieve stress and anxiety, improve your mood and enhance feelings of happiness and well-being. Accordingly, measuring user emotions is an interesting strategy to analyze. The Self-Assessment Manikin (SAM) is a non-verbal pictorial assessment technique that directly measures the pleasure, arousal, and dominance associated with a person's affective reaction to a wide variety of stimuli [18].

Pictograms provide the SAM scale with a great advantage since the verbal component and language are eliminated, making the evaluation of the dimensions based on drawings. Each pictogram of the scale represents an increasing score between 1 and 9, including the points between the drawings (Fig. 4).

For this experiment only the pleasure dimension was studied since we are interested in how it affects the decrease of stress. Each participant was instructed to use the right extreme SAM rating if the reaction was one of feeling happy/pleased/satisfied/contented/hopeful/relaxed, and to use the other extreme if he felt unhappy/annoyed/unsatisfied/melancholic/despairing/bored.

Fig. 4. SAM Scale: Pleasure dimension.

Table 3 shows the level of pleasure measured after the sandbox experience, considering the average of the users and the standard deviation of the values obtained.

Table 3. Result SAM Scale: Pleasure

	SAM 1-9
Average	7
Standard deviation	1.25

4.3   Interface Evaluation

Since we have increased the number of users, we thought it would be useful to carry out a quantitative study of user experience to understand and evaluate the user's perception of the interface. Therefore, we have chosen to use the standardized AttrakDiff questionnaire [19] that allows us to rate an experience with an overall score, using several different metrics. AttrakDiff is composed of 4 dimensions, each one of them with 7 items. All these 28 items are scored from -3 to 3. The advantage of this measure is that it gives a broad view of taking into account the ergonomics, usability and the pragmatic and hedonic dimensions.

The 4 dimensions are detailed as PQ, HQ-I, HQ-S and ATT, where:

- PQ (Pragmatic Quality): describes the functional quality of an application and indicates the degree of success through the user's objectives achieved using it;
- HQ-I (Hedonic Quality - Identity): indicates the level of immediate identification of the user with the application;
- HQ-S (Hedonic Quality - Stimulus): indicates if the application supports the user's needs concerning originality, interest and, especially, stimulus;
- ATT (Attractiveness): it is the most comprehensive measure that quantifies the overall attractiveness of the application, based on the perception of quality by the user.

For the evaluation, fifty users freely experimented with the application, executing the tasks mentioned in Sect. 3.1. For our study, only 12 attributes from the all 28 original method attributes were selected (Table 4). These were considered the most appropriate to analyze modifications and/or improvements to our technological prototype. The results obtained can be seen in Fig. 5.

Table 4. 12 selected attributes from the original AttrakDiff questionnaire

Dimension	Attribute
PQ	Human - Technical
	Unpredictable - Predictable
	Unruly - Manageable
HQ-I	Unimaginative - Creative
	Dull - Captivating
	Undemanding - Challenging
HQ-S	Isolating - Connective
	Unprofessional - Professional
	Cheap - Premium
ATT	Rejecting - Inviting
	Repelling - Appealing
	Discouraging - Motivating

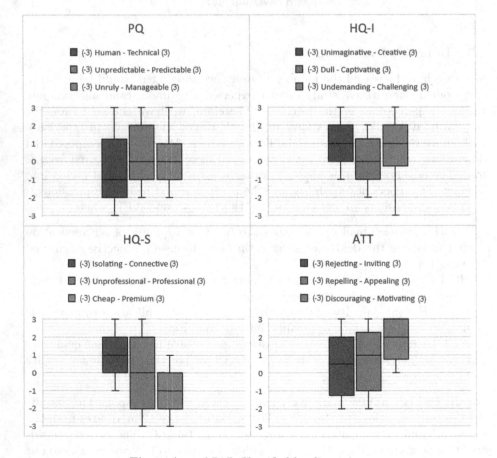

Fig. 5. AttrackDiff: Classified by dimension.

In Fig. 5, the analysed attribute in each dimension is represented by a boxplot. Every boxplot clearly determines the trends of the samples by showing their distribution.

5 Discussion and Conclusions

In this paper we developed a therapy system by using the augmented reality technique, a Kinect 3D camera and a sandbox. The system mimics a Japanese Zen Garden de-stress process by using a digital strategy through an augmented reality sandbox. The system provides users with flexible interaction and easy sand control, and also presents real time data recording.

From the objective evaluation method, results show that the level of stress after the experience decreases by 20 to 30 percent according to the measurements of the smartwatch used. Gathered data show that the system enables to provide an experience that reduces the participants' stress.

While considering SAM technique, average and standard deviation parameters are evaluated. According to SAM scale establish values (between 1 and 9), evaluated groups highlight that pleasure dimension is near to 80% with a considerably low dispersion degree. These results show that, for most of the users, the obtained values in the evaluation of pleasure dimension are positive.

On the other hand, the standardized evaluation AttrakDiff express the following behaviors according to each dimension:

- PQ (Pragmatic Quality):
  - The Human - Technical attribute, shows that the system adapts to more human/natural use.
  - The Unpredictable - Predictable attribute, exhibit that the system is mostly predictable according to user requirements.
  - The Unruly - Manageable attribute, highlights that the system is moderately controllable.
  Finally, the dimension reflects that the system is optimal, but should be improved in aspects such as system control.
- HQ-I (Hedonic Quality - Identity):
  - The Unimaginative - Creative attribute reflects that the system encourages the user to be creative, with the particularity that no user considered the system to have uninspiring characteristics.
  - The Dull - Captivating attribute shows that users consider the system to be moderately charming without being totally enchanted or totally bored.
  - The Undemanding - Challenging attribute shows that the system naturally motivated users to generate different garden design proposals by trying to make them original.
  Finally, this dimension shows that users quickly felt identified with the final objective of the prototype leading them to compete with their own creations.

- HQ-S (Hedonic Quality - Stimulus):
    - The Isolating - Connective attribute shows that the system is highly convective, where in particular no user considered it as a stand-alone system.
    - The Unprofessional - Professional attribute shows that no major skills are required to be able to use and understand the system as a whole.
    - The Cheap - Premium attribute attribute reflects that the designed prototype is clearly considered by the users as a low-cost system. Moreover, no user evaluated the system as being of considerable cost.

  Finally, this dimension reflects that the system is highly stimulating thanks to its connectivity, its ease of use and understanding, and its low cost.
- ATT (Attractiveness):
    - The Rejecting - Inviting attribute shows that users consider the system to be considerably inviting. In particular, no user considered that the system possessed features that would generate rejection.
    - The Repelling - Appealing attribute shows that the prototype is remarkably appealing, as no user expressed dislike.
    - The Discouraging - Motivating attribute shows that the system is highly motivating with the particularity that no user considered the system to have dissuasive aspects.

  Finally, this dimension shows that the system as a whole has engaging qualities that inspire the user.

As a result, the experiment provides a new insight into the relationship between these types of technologies and traditional mindfullness methods.

The experiences here considered gave users free will at the moment of actions' choice. Robust experiments should consider an actions' protocol to be followed by users. Additionally, real time digital sandbox elements interaction is beyond the scope of this work.

Future studies will take into account the development of a virtual reality Japanese Zen Garden including both headsets and gestural sensing devices. The system should immerse the user inside the virtual garden and give him the possibility to affect the scene through his avatar in the same way as it is done in a real zen garden.

References

1. Mahalakshmi, A.M., et al.: Does COVID-19 contribute to development of neurological disease? Immun. Inflam. Dis. **9**(1), 48–58 (2021)
2. Elena Dragioti, E., et al.: A large-scale meta-analytic atlas of mental health problems prevalence during the COVID-19 early pandemic. J. Med. Virology **94**(5), 1935–1949 (2022)
3. Johns, G., Samuel, V., Freemantle, L., Lewis, J., Waddington, L.: The global prevalence of depression and anxiety among doctors during the COVID-19 pandemic: systematic review and meta-analysis. J. Affect. Disord. **298**, 431–441 (2022)
4. Pınar IRMAK VURAL, Nazife BAKIR, Cuma Demir, and Pınar IRMAK VURAL. The effect of religious coping on geriatric anxiety in a group of older turkish women during the covid-19 pandemic period. Turkish Journal of Geriatrics, 25(2), 282–290, 2022

5. Hassan, L., et al.: Disparities in COVID-19 infection, hospitalisation and death in people with schizophrenia, bipolar disorder, and major depressive disorder: a cohort study of the UK biobank. Mol. psychiatry **27**(2), 1248–1255 (2022)

6. Jofré, N., et al.: Prototyping a digital zen garden. In: Editorial de la Universidad Nacional de La Rioja (EUDELAR), editor, Libro de actas - XXVIII Congreso Argentino de Ciencias de la Computación - CACIC 2022 (2022)

7. Locher, M., Fujimori, T.: Zen Garden Design: Mindful Spaces by Shunmyo Masuno Japan's Leading Garden Designer. Tuttle Publishing (2020)

8. Locher, M., Shigeru, U.: Zen Gardens: The Complete Works of Shunmyo Masuno. Tuttle Publishing, Japan's Leading Garden Designer (2012)

9. Lander, J., Garden. Z.: https://www.gettyimages.in/photos/john-lander-?ass ettype=image&phrase=john%20lander%20&sort=mostpopular&license=rf%2Crm (2022). Accessed: 2023–02–20

10. Azuma, R.T.: A survey of augmented reality. Presence Teleoperators Virtual Environ. **6**(4), 355–385 (1997)

11. https://eos.org/science-updates/augmented-reality-turns-a-sandbox-into-a-geoscience-lesson

12. Kreylos, O., et al.: The AR sandbox: augmented reality in geoscience education. In: AGU Fall Meeting Abstracts. vol. 2016, p. ED51H-0843 (2016)

13. Gabele, M., Schröer, S., Husslein, S., Hansen, C.: An AR sandbox as a collaborative multiplayer rehabilitation tool for children with adhd. In: Mensch und Computer 2019 - Workshopband, Bonn, 2019. Gesellschaft für Informatik e.V

14. Lindner, P., Hamilton, W., Miloff, A., Carlbring, P.: How to treat depression with low-intensity virtual reality interventions: Perspectives on translating cognitive behavioral techniques into the virtual reality modality and how to make anti-depressive use of virtual reality-unique experiences. Front. Psychiatry **10**, 792 (2019)

15. https://ar-sandbox.com/augmented-reality-sandbox-for-therapy/

16. Xiaomi Inc., Zepp life. Google Play Store, 2022

17. Jachymek, M., et al.: Wristbands in home-based rehabilitation - validation of heart rate measurement. Sensors **22**(1), 60 (2022)

18. Bradley, M.M., Peter, J, L.: measuring emotion: the self-assessment manikin and the semantic differential. J. Behav. Ther. Exp. Psychiatry **25**(1), 49–59 (1994)

19. Ribeiro, Iara Margolis, Providência, Bernardo: Quality Perception with Attrakdiff Method: A Study in Higher Education During the Covid-19 Period. In: Martins, Nuno, Brandão, Daniel, Moreira da Silva, Fernando (eds.) Perspectives on Design and Digital Communication II. SSDI, vol. 14, pp. 217–231. Springer, Cham (2021). https://doi.org/10.1007/978-3-030-75867-7_14

Software Engineering

Toward an Execution Trace Standard: An MDE Approach

Claudia Pereira[1]([⊠]) [iD], Liliana Martinez[1] [iD], and Liliana Favre[1,2] [iD]

[1] Universidad Nacional del Centro de la Provincia de Buenos Aires, Tandil, Argentina
{cpereira,lmartine,lfavre}@exa.unicen.edu.ar
[2] Comisión de Investigaciones Científicas de la Provincia de Buenos Aires, La Plata, Argentina

Abstract. Dynamic analysis extracts information that describes the structure of the runtime behavior of a software system. This information, typically represented in the form of execution traces, is useful in many software modernization activities, such as reverse engineering and program analysis. The Architecture-Driven Modernization initiative has defined standards to support the modernization process in the context of Model-Driven Engineering (MDE). However, to date, there is no standard for representing runtime information that allows the specification of dynamic information independent of any programming language. In light of this, we present TRACEM, a metamodel for representing trace information under a standard representation that would allow traces to become a new domain in software engineering. The purpose of defining TRACEM is to complement an MDE framework for software modernization that aims to integrate static and dynamic analysis techniques during the reverse engineering process. This article contains a description of TRACEM and a case study that illustrates how dynamic information combined with static information allows for improving the whole reverse engineering process.

Keywords: Architecture-Driven Modernization · Reverse Engineering · Metamodeling · Transformation · Static Analysis · Dynamic Analysis · Legacy System

1 Introduction

In the software modernization context, reverse engineering techniques play an important role, specifically, they cover the process of analyzing available software artifacts such as requirements, design, architectures, or code, with the goal of extracting information and providing high-level views of the underlying system. Thus, software modernization starts from an existing implementation and requires an evaluation of every part of the system that could be transformed or implemented anew from scratch. The great advance of mobile technologies and the emergence of new paradigms such as cloud computing and the Internet of Things have led to a growing demand for software modernization. Many companies are faced with the need to modernize or replace their legacy software systems, which have involved the investment of money, time, and other resources over the years. Many of them are still business critical and their replacement represents a high risk.

© The Author(s), under exclusive license to Springer Nature Switzerland AG 2023
P. Pesado (Ed.): CACIC 2022, CCIS 1778, pp. 91–106, 2023.
https://doi.org/10.1007/978-3-031-34147-2_7

As regards the systematic modernization process, novel technical frameworks for information integration, tool interoperability, and reuse have emerged. Specifically, Model-Driven Engineering (MDE) is a software engineering discipline in which software development can be broken down into standardized, highly automated activities that can mass-produce software applications reducing costs, development time, and risks. MDE emphasizes the use of models and model transformations to raise the abstraction level and the automation degree in software development. Productivity and aspects of software quality such as interoperability and maintainability are goals of MDE [1].

Regarding MDE, recent OMG contributions to modernization are aligned with the Architecture-Driven Modernization (ADM) proposal. It is defined as "the process of understanding and evolving existing software assets for the purpose of software improvement, modifications, interoperability, refactoring, restructuring, reuse, porting, migration, translation, integration, service-oriented architecture deployment" [2]. The OMG ADM Task Force is developing a set of standards (metamodels) to facilitate interoperability between modernization tools, such as the Knowledge Discovery Metamodel (KDM) [3] and the Abstract Syntax Tree Metamodel (ASTM) [4]. ADM has emerged complementing the Model-Driven Architecture (MDA) [5], an OMG initiative that manages the software evolution from abstract models to implementations. The essence of MDA is the Meta Object Facility metamodel (MOF) [6] which allows the interoperability of different types of artifacts from different technologies. Metamodeling is an essential technique of MDA whose advantages are widely known. A standard machine-processable language can be used to check whether models are valid instances. On the other hand, a metamodel that has been defined with the core of UML [7] class diagrams is an accessible language, easy to understand and maintain, and therefore contributes to easy adaptation, allowing language evolution. Based on the meta-metamodel level, tools that allow exchanging formats may be developed to manipulate models, regardless of the modeling language used [1].

ADM standards enable the extraction of models from code representing static information. Despite the increasing interest in dynamic analysis techniques in reverse engineering, there is no standard for representing runtime information. Such a standard could be used by tools for visualization and analysis of execution traces, facilitating interoperability and data exchange. In previous work, we showed how to reverse engineer models from code through static analysis, including class diagrams, use case diagrams, behavioral diagrams, and state diagrams [8–10]. In [11] we have presented TRACEM, a trace metamodel that is the foundation for dynamic analysis in the ADM context. This metamodel allows trace information to be represented in a standard way supporting extensibility, interoperability, abstraction, and expressiveness. An execution trace model is obtained each time the program runs. Then, by running the program with a significant set of test cases, we obtain a set of trace models that will be analyzed to obtain relevant dynamic information. The ultimate goal is to integrate dynamic and static analysis techniques combining the strengths of both approaches in the reverse engineering process within an MDE framework. In this article, we extend the previous work [11] by providing a more detailed description of our proposal, particularly, how the dynamic information specified in TRACEM allows complementing the information obtained statically and is exemplified on the models obtained in previous works [8–10].

This article is organized as follows. Section 2 presents the background. Section 3 describes a framework for reverse engineering in the MDE context. Section 4 details the TRACEM metamodel. In Sect. 5, we analyze the impact of dynamic analysis through a case study that illustrates how dynamic information combined with static information allows improving the whole reverse engineering process. Section 6 discusses related work. Finally, Sect. 7 presents conclusions and future work.

2 Background

2.1 Standards for Modernization

The purpose of standardization is to achieve well-defined interfaces and formats for the interchange of information about software models to facilitate interoperability between the software modernization tools and services of the adherents of the standards. This will enable a new generation of solutions to benefit the whole industry and encourage collaboration among complementary vendors.

In the MDA context, the most relevant OMG standards for our research are:

- The MOF (Meta Object Facility) metamodel enables metadata management and modeling language definition and is based on a simplification of UML structural modeling capabilities [6].
- Object Constraint Language is a typed, declarative and side effect-free specification language. OCL is used to complement models and metamodels with a set of constraints and queries [12].
- XML Metadata Interchange is a common model interchange format that allows serializing and sharing the MOF-based metamodels and models in a uniform way [13].
- The Query-View-Transformation is a metamodel for expressing transformation in MDA-based processes [14].

In the ADM context, the OMG ADM Task Force is developing a set of standards (metamodels) such as KDM and ASTM, both metamodels are defined via MOF.

- KDM is a metamodel for knowledge discovery in software that allows representing information related to existing software assets, their associations, and operational environments regardless of the implementation programming language and runtime platform. KDM is the foundation for software modernization representing entire enterprise software systems, not just code.
- ASTM is a specification for modeling elements to express abstract syntax trees (AST). In particular, the ASTM specification mainly includes the following metamodels:

- Generic Abstract Syntax Tree Metamodel (GASTM), a generic set of language modeling elements common across numerous languages establishes a common core for language modeling.

- Language Specific Abstract Syntax Tree Metamodels (SASTM) for particular languages such as Ada, C, Fortran and Java, that are modeled in MOF or MOF compatible forms.

We defined TRACEM with the aim of complementing the existing set of standards, which would allow considering traces as a new domain in software engineering and representing them independently of any programming language. Dynamic information can be used for different purposes such as reverse engineering or program analysis.

2.2 Static and Dynamic Analysis

Static analysis extracts information that describes the software structure reflected in the source code, whereas dynamic analysis extracts information that describes the structure of the runtime behavior. Ernst [15] compares both analyses from the point of view of their synergy and duality. He states that static analysis is conservative and sound. Conservatism means reporting weak properties that are guaranteed to be true, preserving soundness, but not strong enough to be useful. Soundness guarantees that static analysis provides an accurate description of the behavior, no matter on what input or in what execution environment the program is run. Dynamic analysis is precise, it examines the actual runtime behavior of the program, however, the results of executions may not generalize to other executions. The main challenge to carry out the right dynamic analysis is selecting a representative set of test cases. A test set can help to detect properties of the program; however, it can be difficult to detect whether results of a test set are true program properties or properties of a particular execution context.

The combination of static and dynamic analysis can enrich the reverse engineering process. There are different ways of combination, for instance performing first static analysis and then dynamic one or perhaps, iterating static and dynamic analysis.

3   Reverse Engineering into the MDE Framework

We propose a framework to reverse engineering models that combines the advantages of static and dynamic analysis (Fig. 1). This framework is based on the MDE principles: all artifacts involved can be viewed as models and the process can be viewed as a sequence of model-to-model transformations where the extracted information is represented in a standard way. Each model can be reused, refactored, modified or extended for reverse engineering purposes or for other purposes. Metamodels are defined via MOF and the transformations are specified between source and target metamodels. Then, MOF metamodels "control" the consistency of these transformations.

In previous work, we presented a process to reverse engineering models from code through static analysis, that includes class diagrams, use case diagrams, behavioral diagrams, and state diagrams [8–10]. In the framework, as shown in Fig. 1, the first step of the static analysis is to extract the code model, that is an abstract syntax tree model instance of the SASTM (Specific ASTM), using a model injector. Next, a model-to-model transformation is performed to generate an instance of GASTM from the previous model. Finally, using a KDM model as an intermediate representation of the software system, high-level

UML models are obtained through a chain of model-to-model transformations. The first step of the process requires implementing an injector and transformations to obtain the GASTM model for each programming language, while the sequence of transformations in subsequent steps is independent of the legacy language.

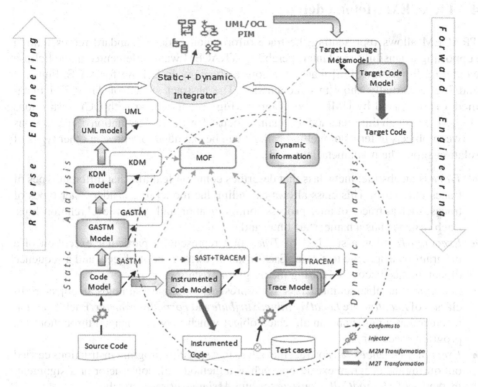

Fig. 1. MDE Modernization Process

In this article, we present TRACEM, a trace metamodel that is the foundation for dynamic analysis (see the dotted circle in Fig. 1). This metamodel allows us to obtain and record trace information. Dynamic analysis is a valuable technique for reverse engineering by providing information about the runtime behavior of software systems. However, dynamic analysis requires both a complete and executable system and the instrumentation of the code to detect and record relevant events at runtime for subsequent offline analysis.

To reverse engineering models from code execution, the first step is to record trace data. This includes a set of objects, a set of attributes for each object, a location and type for each object, a set of messages, and timestamp for each event. This dynamic information is obtained through source code instrumentation, a process in which additional code fragments are inserted into the code being analyzed.

An execution trace model, instance of TRACEM, is obtained each time the program runs. A set of trace models is then obtained by running the program with a significant set of test cases. These models will be analyzed to obtain relevant dynamic information that, in combination with static information, can be used to improve the reverse engineering process. Then, the resulting models would be the starting point for the forward engineering process.

4   TRACEM Metamodel

TRACEM allows representing the trace information under a standard representation supporting extensibility and interoperability. TRACEM was implemented in the Eclipse Modeling Framework [16] that is the core technology in Eclipse for MDE. Figure 2 and Fig. 3 partially show this metamodel. The abstract syntax of TRACEM metamodel is described by UML class diagram (Fig. 2) augmented with OCL restrictions (Fig. 3). Although this metamodel is mainly focused on the representation of interactions between objects in terms of method calls, it can be extended to represent other types of relationships. The main metaclasses are:

- *Trace* is an abstract metaclass that describes common features that different types of traces may have. This class allows extending the model to consider other types of traces, such as traces of inter-process communication and system-level relationships. Each instance has a name, start time, and end time.
- *ExecutionTrace* is a subclass of *Trace* that represents a particular execution of a program on a specific test case. Each instance owns a set of objects and a sequence of statements discovered during the program execution.
- *Location* is an abstract metaclass that represents a storage that holds an object. Subclasses of *Location* are *LocalVariable*, *Attribute* and *FormalParameter*. Each *Location* instance has a name and an allocated object which may be changed throughout the program execution.
- *ExecutionSentence* is an abstract metaclass that specifies program instructions carried out during the program execution, such as a method call, constructor or assignment, instances of *MethodCall*, *Constructor* and *Assignment* respectively.
- *Object* is a metaclass that represents objects created during the program execution. Each instance has an identifier, creation time, destruction time, and owns attributes and objects. It can be stored in different locations during the program execution.
- *Call* is an abstract metaclass that represents both method calls and constructors. Each instance has a name and owns a subtrace.
- *MethodCall* is a metaclass that represents actual method invocations that are executed during program execution. Each instance has a caller, a target and can have actual parameters and a returned object, all of them are *Object* instances.
- *Constructor* is a metaclass that represents invocations to the class constructor that is automatically called when an object is created.

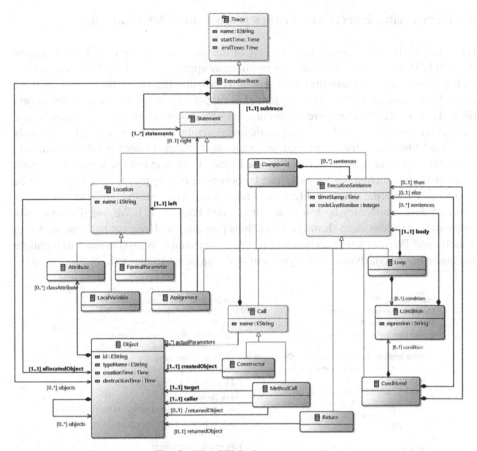

Fig. 2. TRACEM: abstract syntax

-- *the returned object of a method call corresponds to the object returned by its return sentence*
context MethodCall::returnedObject:Object
derived: returnedObject = subtrace.statements->collect (s| s.ocllsTypeOf(return).returnedObject)

context Assignment -- *restrictions on the right and left parts of an assignment*
inv: right.OcllsKindOf(location) **or** right.OcllsKindOf(MethodCall) **or**
    right.OcllsKindOf(Constructor) **and** left.allocatedObject =
      if right.ocllsTypeOf(Location) **then** right.allocatedObject
      else   **if** right.ocllsTypeOf(MethodCall) **then** right.returnedObject
      else   **if** right.ocllsTypeOf(Constructor) **then** right.createdObject **endif endif   endif**

context Compound -- *compound only has local variables as locations*
inv: statements->select(s | s.ocllsKindOf(Location))-> forAll (l| l.ocllsTypeOf (localVariable))

context MethodCall -- *relationship between formal and actual parameter*
inv: actualParameters->forAll (ap| self.subtrace.statements->
    collect(ocllsTypeOf(FormalParameter)) ->exists(fp| fp.allocatedObjet = ap)

Fig. 3. TRACEM: OCL restrictions

5   Recovering Execution Traces from Code: An Example

Dynamic analysis is exemplified in terms of the same case study used in Tonella and Potrich [17], which describe a reverse engineering approach based on classical compiler techniques and abstract interpretation to obtain UML diagrams from Java object-oriented code. In the case study, the Java program *eLib* supports the main functions of the library (Fig. 4). It contains an archive of documents of different kinds, books, journals, and technical reports. Each of them has specific functionality. Each document can be uniquely identified, and library users can request documents for loan. To borrow a document, both user and document must be verified by the library. Users can borrow up to a maximum number of documents; while books can be borrowed by any user, journals can only be borrowed by internal users, and technical reports can be consulted but not borrowed. A detailed description may be found at Tonella and Potrich [17]. We use the same case study in previous work to show the extensions proposed with respect to the approach of Tonella and Potrich [8–10]. In this article, the same example is used in order to highlight the contributions of dynamic analysis within the proposal framework.

```
class Library {                                   private void addLoan(Loan loan) {
   Map documents = new HashMap();                    if (loan == null) return;
   Map users = new HashMap();                         User user = loan.getUser();
   Collection loans = new LinkedList();              Document doc = loan.getDocument();
   ...                                               loans.add(loan);
   private boolean verifyData (User u, Document d)   user.addLoan(loan);
   {  if (u == null || d == null) return false;      doc.addLoan(loan);  }
      if (u.numberOfLoans() <                     ...} // end class Library
         MAX_NUMBER_OF_LOANS &&                    class Document {...
         d.isAvailable() && d.authorizedLoan(u))      public boolean isAvailable() {return loan==null;}
                 return true;                         public boolean authorizedLoan(User user) {
      return false;                                       return true;      }
   }                                               } // end class Document
   public boolean borrowDocument
           (User user, Document doc) {             class Book extends Document {...}
   if (verifyData (user, doc) {                    class InternalReport extends Document {...}
        Loan loan = new Loan(user, doc);           class User {... }
        addLoan(loan);                             class InternalUser extends User {}
        return true;        }                      class Loan {
   return false;                                      User user;  Document document;
   }                                                  public Loan(User usr, Document doc) {
   public int numberOfLoans() {                           user = usr;    document = doc;
      return loans.size();      }                   } // end class Loan
```

Fig. 4.   Source code of the *eLib* program

   Dynamic analysis produces a set of execution trace instances, one for each test case. Although each instance represents a different interaction between objects, there is no guarantee that all interactions are considered. Conversely, in static analysis, all possible behaviors are represented. As an example, Fig. 5 partially shows an instance of the trace metamodel obtained from the execution of the method *borrowDocument* resulting in a successful loan of the *book1* (instance of Book) to the *internalUser1* (instance of InternalUser). Each time an object is created, it is identified by the class name concatenated with a numeric value.

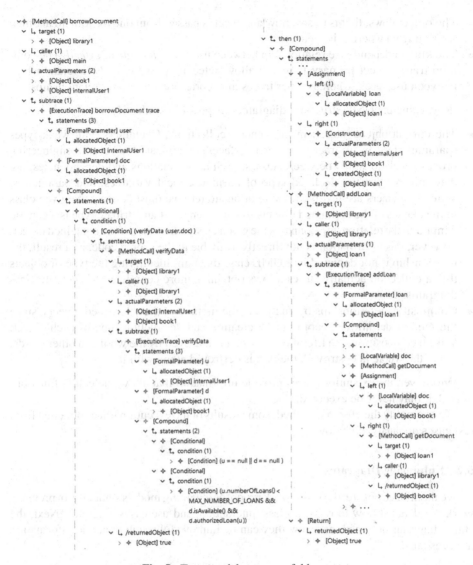

Fig. 5. Trace model: a successful loan

5.1 Dynamic Information Impact

The execution traces provide information that allows complementing the models obtained through static analysis.

Regarding the UML behavioral diagram, it is possible to identify:

- The current object that invokes the method (*caller*) and the one that receives the message (*target*).
- The current parameter linked to each formal parameter, that is, which object is actually stored in each formal parameter for a particular trace.

- The object flows, that is to say, how an object is passed from one location to another, starting from where it is created.
- The kind of dependence relationship between use cases, *include* or *extend*. The common traces reflect primary flow and allow detecting possible *include* relationships between use cases, whereas other traces may correspond to *extend* relationships.

Regarding the UML structural diagram, it is possible to identify:

- The current objects stored in the generic collections. Containers with weak types (parameterized in abstract types or interfaces) complicate the reverse engineering process. Relationships between classes, such as associations and dependencies, are determined from the declared type of attributes, local variables, and parameters. When containers are involved, the relations to retrieve must connect the given class to the classes of the contained objects. As an example, if an attribute type is a generic container, the relationship connects the given class to the class of the contained object, however, this information is not directly available in the source code, as a result, the relationship is not depicted in a UML class diagram. Identifying the type of objects that a collection actually stores allows obtaining more complete and accurate class diagrams.
- Composition relationships by analyzing the lifetime of the referenced objects, since the metamodel allows recording the creation and destruction time of each object. Within composition, the lifetime of the part is managed by the whole, in other words, when the whole is destroyed, the part is destroyed along with it.

Moreover, the execution traces provide information that allows detecting functionality that may never be executed.

To exemplify the aforementioned, some results of the execution traces obtained from test cases are analyzed below.

5.2   Enhancing Diagrams

As we mentioned before, the framework proposes obtaining models statically. In previous work we detailed how to recover class, interaction, and use cases diagrams. Next, the static diagrams obtained, and how they can be improved through dynamic information are presented.

Enhancing Behavioral Diagrams.   A detailed description of how to obtain sequence diagrams from source code of methods is presented in [9]. Figure 6 partially shows the diagrams obtained by static analysis corresponding to *borrowdocument*, *verifydata*, and *addloan* methods, in particular. In these diagrams appear instances of types, such as *doc* and *d* of *document* type (allocations are enclosed in boxes in Fig. 6). However, there is no information about the allocated object in each instance.

From dynamic analysis, trace model allows identifying the object flow through the *allocatedObject* reference, then it is possible to realize that the object *book1* allocated in the formal parameter *"doc"* of the *borrowDocument* method, is the same object as the one allocated in:

- the formal parameter *"d"* of the *verifyData* method;
- the actual parameter *"doc"* of the constructor that create a new *Loan* object called *loan1*;
- the class attribute *"doc"* of the *loan1* object;
- the local variable *"doc"* in the *addLoan* method.

From this information, UML behavioral diagrams, such as interaction or collaboration, will show only one object of *Document* type even if there is more than one variable of this type. The same situation occurs with objects *internalUser1* and *loan1*. The contribution of dynamic analysis results in more accurate diagrams in terms of identifying current objects that send and receive messages.

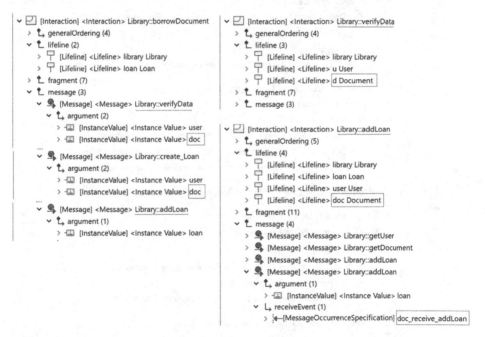

Fig. 6. Sequence diagrams

Enhancing Use Case Diagrams. A detailed description of how to obtain use case diagrams from source code of methods is presented in [8, 10]. Figure 7 partially shows some use cases and their relationships obtained by static analysis, which allows obtaining generalization and dependency relationships, however the particular kind of dependency cannot be distinguished. Execution traces allow improving these diagrams. The trace models resulting from the execution of a set of test cases allow distinguishing primary from alternative paths. As we mentioned before, the common sub-trace reflects primary flow and allows detecting *include* relationships between use cases. The other sub-traces (alternative paths) may correspond to *extend* relationships. Thus, in the case of *borrow-document* method execution, it can be observed that the *verifydata* method is executed on each execution trace. In this particular case, both methods are considered use cases through static analysis, then, the dynamic analysis infers that dependency relationship between them may be an *include*.

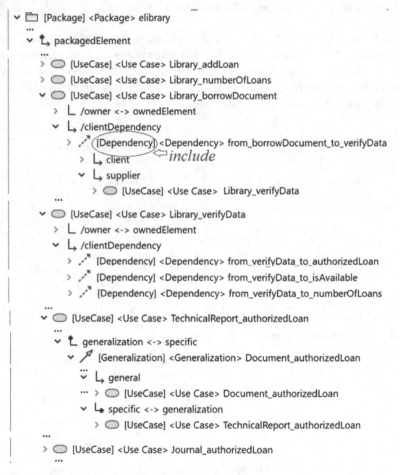

Fig. 7. Use cases diagram

Enhancing Class Diagrams. Modisco was used to recover uml class diagrams from *elib* code. Figure 8 partially shows the *elibrary* package obtained by static analysis, some classes and their properties and operations are depicted in particular. The class *library* owns documents, users and loans, all of them stored in generic collections. As an example, the Fig. 8 highlights the property *documents* of *map* type from which the association between the classes *library* and *map* (*a_documents_library*) is deduced. In trace models, the *documents* collection will only contain objects of *document* subtypes, thus, an association between *library* and *document* will be inferred.

On the other hand, by analyzing the creation and destruction times of the *library1* object and the objects of type *Loan* added to the *loans* collection of *Library*, it is possible to infer that the association between *Library* and *Loan* is indeed a composition.

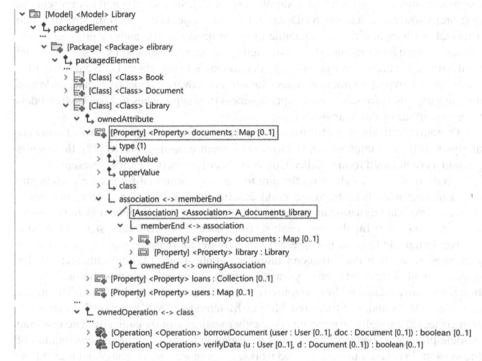

Fig. 8. Class diagram

6   Related Work

The search for related work on the definition of metamodels for representing execution traces did not yield many results, which was one of the reasons for advancing our approach to contribute to the construction of a standard.

Reverse engineering models from legacy code is not new in software engineering. Many works have contributed to the reverse engineering of object-oriented code, in particular dynamic analysis techniques. [17] and [18] perform dynamic analysis to complement static analysis of Java code. Trace information obtained from program execution is represented by UML models.

With the growing adoption of MDE principles and techniques, which consider models as first-class entities in all processes, new approaches for reverse engineering have been developed. Among the proposals that propose metamodels to represent the traces of execution it is worth mentioning [19] and [20]. The former proposes an open framework for reverse engineering of executable behavior from existing software code. The standard OMG fUML language is used as an executable pivot format for dynamic analysis. The authors use transformations to generate fUML models from code, which can then be executed directly by the fUML VM. They extended this virtual machine to record execution traces as instances of a simple metamodel. In [20], the authors present the first steps towards extending MoDisco [21], which injects the program structure into a model, with capabilities for dynamic program analysis. The authors propose to add execution trace information to the model during program execution. The resulting model conforms to the impact analysis metamodel that authors introduce. Unlike these works, we propose to represent traces as a new domain in software engineering, independent of any language and providing more expressiveness than approaches that use UML models to represent the dynamic analysis results.

Dynamic analysis is useful not only in reverse engineering, but also in software analysis, software maintenance, software performance, testing, etc. In [22], the authors present a graph-based format, called Compact Trace Format (CTF), for representing trace information of routine calls with the aim to develop a standard format for exchanging traces among analysis tools. Some works describe model-driven approaches in specific domains involving dynamic analysis. [23] focuses on reverse engineering AUTOSAR-compliant models using dynamic analysis from traces of a real-time system in the automotive domain. In [24], authors present a metamodel for representing trace information generated from High Performance Computing applications. [25] presents methods for dynamic analysis applied to energy-aware software engineering. In this approach execution traces are modeled within the source code model generated by MoDisco. The author uses the OMG standard Structured Metrics Metamodel (SMM) to model all information collected through software analysis, either statically or dynamically. The resulting models provide relevant energy-related information to improve the implementation of the system. In contrast to these related works, we propose a MOF-compliant trace metamodel for representing execution traces. This metamodel is the basis for dynamic analysis within a framework in the MDE context, specifically based on ADM standards.

7 Conclusions

In the MDE context, particularly in the area of software modernization, OMG has defined several standards to represent information of existing software systems. However, there is no standard to represent runtime information, for this reason, we promote the creation of a standard that allows the specification of dynamic information independently of any programming language. Thus, trace analysis can be considered as a new domain of the software engineering.

This article presents the basis for dynamic analysis in the reverse engineering process by integrating static analysis, dynamic analysis, and metamodeling in the ADM context. The main contribution is TRACEM, a metamodel that captures the concepts and relationships present in the information obtained from program execution. It allows the specification of execution trace information under a standard representation. Thus, the traces are considered as first-class entities that provide relevant dynamic information. This information can be used for different purposes such as reverse engineering or program analysis. Our objective is to combine the strengths of static and dynamic analysis within an MDE framework to improve the whole reverse engineering process.

TRACEM together with the metamodels of the different programming languages will allow the automatic instrumentation of code and, from this, the injection of trace models that allow decoupling from source technologies. However, injectors and metamodels for different programming languages are not available and must be implemented.

We foresee experimenting with different programming languages to implement injector prototypes. We will also investigate execution trace analysis techniques to understand and manipulate the models obtained from program executions.

References

1. Brambilla, M., Cabot, J., Wimmer, M.: Model-Driven Software Engineering in Practice. 2nd edn. Morgan & Claypool Publishers (2017)
2. Architecture-Driven Modernization (ADM), http://www.omg.org/adm, Accessed 2023 Feb 14
3. Knowledge Discovery Metamodel (KDM), Version 1.4, OMG Document Number: formal/2016–09–01, http://www.omg.org/spec/KDM/1.4 (2016)
4. Abstract Syntax Tree Metamodel (ASTM), Version 1.0, OMG Document Number: formal/2011–01–05. Standard document URL: http://www.omg.org/spec/ASTM (2011)
5. Model-Driven Architecture (MDA), http://www.omg.org/mda/, Accessed 2023 Feb 14
6. OMG Meta Object Facility (MOF) Core Specification, Version 2.5.1, OMG Document Number: formal/2019–10–01. https://www.omg.org/spec/MOF/2.5.1 (2019)
7. OMG Unified Modeling Language (OMG UML), Version 2.5.1, OMG Document Number: formal/2017–12–05. http://www.omg.org/spec/UML/2.5.1 (2017)
8. Favre, L., Martinez, L., Pereira, C.: Reverse engineering of object-oriented code: an ADM approach. In: Handbook of Research on Innovations in Systems and Software Engineering, pp. 386–410. IGI Global (2015)
9. Martinez, L., Pereira, C., Favre, L.: Recovering sequence diagrams from object-oriented Code - an ADM approach. In: Proceedings of the 9th International Conference on Evaluation of Novel Approaches to Software Engineering (ENASE 2014), pp. 188–195 (2014)
10. Pereira, C., Martinez, L., Favre, L.: Recovering Use Case Diagrams from Object-Oriented Code: an MDA-based Approach. Int. J. Softw. Eng. (IJSE), **5** (2), 3–23 (2012)
11. Pereira, C., Martinez, L., Favre, L.: TRACEM - Towards a standard metamodel for execution traces in model-driven reverse engineering. In: Libro de Actas del XXVIII Congreso Argentino de Ciencia de la Computación (CACIC 2022), pp. 272–281 (2023)
12. Object Constraint Language (OCL), Version 2.4, OMG Document Number: formal/2014–02–03, Standard document (2014) http://www.omg.org/spec/OCL/2.4
13. XML Metadata Interchange (XMI) Specification, Version 2.5.1, OMG Document Number: formal/2015–06–07, Standard document (2015) http://www.omg.org/spec/XMI/2.5.1
14. Query/View/Transformation Specification (QVT), Version 1.3, OMG Document Number: formal/2016–06–03, Standard document (2016) http://www.omg.org/spec/QVT/1.3
15. Ernst, M.: Static and dynamic analysis: synergy and duality. In: Proceedings of ICSE Workshop on Dynamic Analysis (WODA 2003), pp. 24–27 (2003)

16. Eclipse Modeling Framework (EMF), http://www.eclipse.org/modeling/emf, Accessed 2023 Feb 14
17. Tonella, P., Potrich, A.: Reverse Engineering of Object-Oriented Code. Monographs in Computer Science. Heidelberg: Springer-Verlag (2005) https://doi.org/10.1007/b102522
18. Systa, T.: Static and Dynamic Reverse Engineering Techniques for Java Software Systems. Ph.D Thesis, University of Tampere, Report A-2000–4 (2000)
19. Bergmayr, A., Bruneliere, H., Cabot, J., Garcia, J., Mayerhofer, T., Wimmer, M. fREX: fUML-based reverse engineering of executable behavior for software dynamic analysis. In:IEEE/ACM 8th International Workshop on Modeling in Software Engineering (MiSE), Austin, TX, pp. 20–26 (2016)
20. Béziers la Fosse, T., Tisi, M., Mottu, J.-M.: Injecting Execution Traces into a Model-Driven Framework for Program Analysis. In: Seidl, M., Zschaler, S. (eds.) STAF 2017. LNCS, vol. 10748, pp. 3–13. Springer, Cham (2018). https://doi.org/10.1007/978-3-319-74730-9_1
21. MoDisco, https://www.eclipse.org/MoDisco, Accessed 2023 Feb 14
22. Hamou-Lhadj, A., Lethbridge, T.C.: A metamodel for the compact but lossless exchange of execution traces. Softw. Syst. Model. **11**, 77–98 (2012)
23. Sailer, A.: Reverse Engineering of Real-Time System Models from Event Trace Recordings. University of Bamberg Press (2019)
24. Alawneh L., Hamou-Lhadj A., Hassine J.: Towards a common metamodel for traces of high performance computing systems to enable software analysis tasks. In: IEEE 22nd International Conference on Software Analysis, Evolution, and Reengineering (SANER 2015), pp. 111–120 (2015)
25. Beziers La Fosse, T.: Model-driven methods for dynamic analysis applied to energy-aware software engineering. Software Engineering [cs.SE]. Ecole nationale supérieure Mines-Télécom Atlantique (2021)

New Horizons for Metamorphic Relationships in Formal Verification

Fernando Asteasuain[1,2]([⊠])([iD])

[1] Universidad Nacional de Avellaneda, Buenos Aires, Argentina
fasteasuain@undav.edu.ar
[2] Universidad Abierta Interamericana - Centro de Altos Estudios CAETI, Buenos
Aires, Argentina

Abstract. In this work we broadened the impact of the so called
Metamorphic relationships (MR's) in the formal verification phase. We
showed the potential of our behavioral framework called FVS (Feather
Weight Visual Scenarios) to successfully denote metamorphic properties
in diverse, complex and meaningful domains such as UAV's flying missions and operating systems for On Board Computers (OBC) for nano
satellites. We employed MR's to validate behavior in a BIG-DATA context, where possible a large amount of data and information seen as
traces must be verified but also a novel way to relate different goals and
UAV's configurations in the context of the dynamic adaption of AUV's
missions due to changes in the requirements. In addition, we explored
complementary behavior as a possible source for obtaining MR's.

Keywords: Metamorphic behavior · Adaptive Systems · Temporal
Planning

1 Introduction

Software engineering can be described as a set of techniques, tools and processes
aiming to produce quality software while minimizing its possible flaws and errors.
Typical software engineering phases include, among others, exploring and specifying system requirements, to analyze and design its features, to describe high
level or architectural interactions between the system's main components, to
implement it in some framework or language, and to validate and verify the
expected behavior of the system.

Since it was born, Software Engineering has been evolving to cope with the
challenges that new software visions and new computer software paradigms bring
along. Just to mention two examples architectural aspects were incorporated as
a separate and a stand-alone software engineering phase to specify high level
components' interactions as the complexity of software system grow and grow
[34]. As a second example, agile methodologies [10] were born to leverage the
bureaucracy involved in software development processes.

P. Pesado (Ed.): CACIC 2022, CCIS 1778, pp. 107–122, 2023.
https://doi.org/10.1007/978-3-031-34147-2_8

Unarguable the data science big bang can be pointed out as one of the most revolutionary domains in the compute science field in the last few years. Nowadays almost any modern device can send and receive information and as a consequence a huge amount of information is out there available to be explored and analyzed. Important software areas like Machine Learning [28], Data Science [1] or BIG DATA [31] are gaining each day more relevance in order to extract, scrutinize and learn from gathered data. These areas deal with distinctive characteristics and requirements. Some of them include handling volatile, unstructured, diverse and heterogeneous tons of data, managing new ways of dealing with information flow and communication between components and a much more rigorous approach to cope with performance and availability concerns. In this context, some Software Engineering techniques need to evolve somehow to face these new elements [11,14,22–24,30,36]. Formal verification and validation has been pinpointed as one of the areas that more urgently need to be tackled. Data Science systems need to be formally verified. According to [17,23], only two of nearly one hundred analyzed approaches addressing new software engineering methods for big data were related to formal validation. These kinds of systems have been defined as "non testeable' software [17,30] because the lack of a proper testing oracle to check their behavior. The problem can be stated as: How the new version of the system, which now includes the analyzed information, can be tested? How can the new system be checked against its expected behavior? How can the expected behavior be specified? How can the software engineer verify if the system is producing the expected outputs?

Metamorphic Relationships (or more simply MRs) [16,33] have been recently applied as a way to handle this problematic issue. The objective of MR's is to construct connections between behavior and data that help to verify the system, linking the old version of the system with its newer version. Probably the most iconic example is a machine learning system focusing on sentiment analysis classifying a given sentence as positive, neutral or negative. So as to verify the system MR's are defined in the following manner: for positive sentences, a new sentence is build using synonyms of the sentence's words. This new word should be classified as positive in the newer version of the system. Similarly, if the new sentence is build using antonyms instead, then the expected outcome should be negative. However, how to specify and define the MR's for every system is an extremely arduous and error-prone task. Also, defining how many MR's are enough is also a tricky point [17].

In [3] we explore FVS (Feather Weight Visual Scenarios) [5–7] as an specification language to model and specify MR's. FVS is a very simple, graphical and declarative language which holds a very flexible and expressive power notation. We now build on the top of that work expanding the horizon for MR's in the formal verification phase. In this work we applied MR's in meaningful domains: Adaptive Systems and Temporal Planning for UAV's (Unmanned Aerial Vehicle) [25,38–40], and Operating Systems for OnBoard Computers (OBC) for nano satellites such as CubeSats [32]. This shows the potential of MR's as a powerful technique to formally verify a system and the applicability of FVS as an specification language for MR's. We employed MR's in two orthogonal styles: in the usual manner as a way to build a verification oracle but also a a way to relate two different goals and configuration for UAV's, which is a very useful feature when dealing with Adaptive Systems. Finally, we inspected complementary behavior as a valuable source to define MR's. This is a very reachable feature in FVS since it can be automatically generated [8,13].

1.1 Summary

The main contributions of this work can be outlined as:

– Showing the potential of FVS to describe MR's for UAV's Adaptive Systems.
– Showing the potential of FVS to describe MR's for UAV's Temporal Planning.
– Showing the potential of FVS to describe MR's for nano satellites' OBC.
– Exploring the possibility to analyze different goals and UAV's configurations employing MR's
– Automatic generation of MR's reasoning about complementary behavior.

The rest of this work is organized as follows. Section 2 presents FVS, and some basic notions of the techniques employed such as Adaptive Systems, Temporal Plannings and OBC's. The next three Sections describe all the case of studies: Sect. 3 is focused on FVS and MR's for Adaptive Systems, Sect. 4 deals with Temporal Planning and Sect. 5 handles MR's for a particular OBC operating systems. Section 6 presents some observations and final remarks regarding the analyzed examples. Finally, Sect. 7 outlines related work and future lines of research that may continue this work whereas Sect. 8 concludes.

2   Background

In this section we give some preliminaries notions about FVS, Adaptive Systems, Temporal Planning and OBC.

2.1   FVS

We now briefly introduce FVS main features. The reader is referred to [5] for a formal characterization of the language. FVS is a graphical language based on scenarios. Scenarios are partial order of events, consisting of points, which are labeled with a logic formula expressing the possible events occurring at that point, and arrows connecting them. An arrow connecting two points simply indicates a precedence relationship. The events occurring at the origin of arrow occur before the events occurring at the destiny point of the arrow. For instance, in Fig. 1-(a) A-event precedes B-event. Sometimes is necessary to refer to the very next or previous occurrence of an event. This is shown graphically with a double ended arrow (see Figs. 1-(b) and 1-(c)). Precedence relationship can be labeled to restrict behavior between events. For example, consider the FVS scenario in Fig. 1-d. This scenario is stating that an A-event precedes B-event such that C-event does not occur between them. FVS features aliasing between points. Scenario in Fig. 1-e indicates that a point labeled with A is also labeled with $A \wedge B$. It is worth noticing that A-event is repeated on the labeling of the second point just because of FVS formal syntaxis. Finally, two special points are introduced as delimiters of the language: a big black circle representing the beginning of the execution of the system and rounded version standing for the end of an execution (see Fig. 1-f).

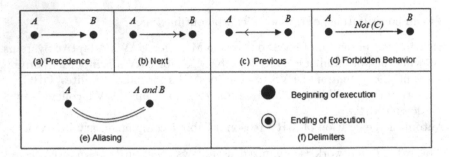

Fig. 1. Basic Elements in FVS

We now introduce the concept of FVS Rules, a fundamental constructor of the language. FVS Rules take the form of an implication: an antecedent scenario and one or more consequent scenarios. They work following this concept: whenever a trace "matches" a given antecedent scenario, then it must also match at least one of the consequent ones. The antecedent is a common substructure of all consequents, enabling complex relationship between points in antecedent and consequents: our rules are not limited, like most triggered scenario notions, to feature antecedent as a pre-chart where events should precede consequent events. Thus, rules can state expected behavior happening in the past or in the middle of a bunch of events. Graphically, the antecedent is shown in black, and consequent ones in grey. Since a rule can feature more than one consequent, elements which do not belong to the antecedent scenario are numbered to identify the consequent they belong to. An example is shown in Fig. 2. The rule describes a requirement for the FreeRTOS[1] operating system used in OBC: the system must start in the *Boot* phase of the operating system, and not in the *Scheduling* or the *ProcessingTasks* phase.

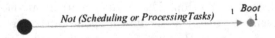

Fig. 2. An FVS rule example

---

[1] https://www.freertos.org/.

We now introduce the concept of anti-scenarios. Anti-scenarios can be automatically generated from rule scenarios. Roughly speaking, they provide valuable information for the developer since they represent a sketch of how things could go wrong and violate the rule. The complete procedure is detailed in [8,13], but informally the algorithm obtains all the situations where the antecedent is found but none of the consequents is feasible. For example, a possible anti scenario for the previous rule in Fig. 2 is shown in Fig. 3. In this anti scenario a *Scheduling* event or an *ProcessingTasks* event occur prior the occurrence of a *Boot* event, thus violating the rule in Fig. 2.

Fig. 3. An anti-scenario example

2.2 Adaptive Systems

Adaptive Systems can be defined as systems that can change their behaviour to account for conditions that were not foreseen at design time [40]. There is a tremendous challenge involved in these kind of systems: goals and configuration of the system must be able to change dynamically. In order to fulfill this objective a meticulous and rigorous architectural approach must be carefully designed. Different layers of abstraction are usually introduced to produced satisfactory results. Lower layers deal with ordinary events while upper layers handle the non-trivial transition going from the old specification to the new specification. A clear example of such approaches is described in [40], presenting a hybrid control architecture that supports runtime swapping of plans, and runtime binding and unbinding of hybrid components.

In that work a motivating example is given. Suppose a UAV is initially on a photographic mission over a certain region. Goals and configuration in the form of temporal logics are provided so that the controller of the UAV can carry on with its mission successfully. While the mission is on course, a missing person alert is issued. If the UAV was designed as an adaptive system, its mission objectives can be dynamically modified without the need for the UAV to return to the central base to be re started.

2.3 Temporal Planning

Temporal planning [39] guarantees that a certain automated device such as robot or an UAV will succeed in its task as long as certain explicit and implicit assumptions about the robot's operating environment, sensors, and capabilities hold. A given plan can fail if any of the assumptions are violated at runtime. An illustrative example is facilitated in [39]. The system is in charge of an UAV taking photographes in a certain region. An possible planning assumption is that requesting a photograph upon flying into a discrete region will be actually taken before exiting that region. Another possible assumption is that a photograph will completely cover a discrete region if the plane's roll and pitch are within certain bounds. These conditions are dynamically verified in [39] employing a so called monitor that checks that the specified conditions are met during execution.

2.4   OBC and Nano Satellites

In the past ten years the nanosatellite industry grow by a factor of 10x, from as few as 20 satellites in 2011 to nearly 200 in 2019, and it is estimated that 1800 to 2400 nano/microsatellites will need to be launched over the next 5 years [18, 38]. In particular, CubeSats, have turned out lately as one of the most popular microsatellites [32]. The CubeSat program was initiated at Stanford University in 1999 for the purpose of building a low-cost and low-weight satellite.

There are a plethora of different domains where CubeSats satellites are directly involved: communications, earth remote sensing, space tethering, biology, astronomy, space weather exploration and planetary science [32], just to mention a few.

On BOARD Computers (OBC) must be carefully designed, planned, developed and verified. For example, battery consumption and other resources are extremely important since the services the satellites provide heavily rely on them. An OBC is in charge of the all the satellites services, it monitors them to ensure their health, and also monitors the status of all the subsystems. An OBC also interacts with the ground station to send the required telemetry data and satellite status [19].

One of the most important aspects to decide when developing a OBC is the operating system to be installed on it. One of the most widely operating systems used is FreeRTOS. As described on its website, FreeRTOS, originally created as a real time operating system for micro controllers, is distributed freely under the MIT open source license, and includes a kernel and a growing set of IoT libraries suitable for use across all industry sectors.

In [4] the formal verification of the FreeRTOS operating system using FVS as the specification language is fully provided.

3   FVS and Metamorphic Relationships(MRs) for UAV's Missions Adaptation

In this section we define MRs for different planning goals and behavior for UAV's missions. The analyzed system is based on the example fully described in [40]. In that work, several goals and UAV's configurations are properly defined so that the artifact can adapt to new missions in a dynamic way. In this example, the UAV serves as a delivery vehicle transporting packages among some locations. In particular, the mission for the UAV is the following. There are three locations, namely A, B and C; and three packages to be delivered: $P1$, $P2$ and $P3$. Package $P1$ must be delivered to C from A, $P2$ to A from C and finally, $P3$ to C from B. Additionally, it is required that the UAV must not move between locations without a package to preserve a minimum weight requirement. An initial plan obtained to achieve UAV's goals is the following: Starting from location A, the it grabs $P1$ and goes to location B, it grabs $P3$ and then carrying $P1$ and $P3$ goes to location C and releases $P1$ and $P3$ there. Finally, the UAV grabs $P2$, goes to location A and releases $P2$ there.

We first model this initial behavior in FVS and then we define MR's relating old and new plans later in the next subsection. Following the vocabulary introduced in [40] we employ some of the followings events in the specification: $atLocation$ (the UAV is the mentioned location), $grabP_i$ (the UAV grabs package P_i) or $releaseP_i$ (the UAV releases package P_i).

The first two rules (depicted in Fig. 4) defines the expected behavior for transporting package $P1$. These FVS rules say that packaged $P1$ must be grabbed by the UAV when arriving at location A, and must be released when arriving to location C.

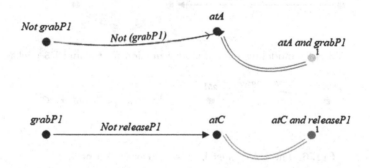

Fig. 4. FVS rules modeling UAV delivery mission for P1 packages

Similarly, rules for packages P2 and P3 are show in Fig. 5.

Now we specify the requirement that establish that the UAV must be always transporting at least one package. The rule in Fig. 6 shapes the behavior starting from location A and ending in location B or C. We use the meta event P_i standing for any type of packages $P1$, $P2$ or $P3$. In few words, the rule says that in every flight starting from location A carrying an package, the UAV must arrive in a different location without releasing it. Two analogues rules using location B and location C as the origin point should be added to complete the requirement specification.

3.1   MRs for UAV's Adaptation to New Plans

When new requirements are introduced in the UAV's missions' new properties, new planning strategies and new UAV configurations may be needed. We now

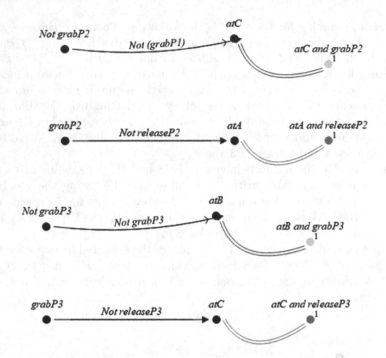

Fig. 5. FVS rules modeling UAV delivery mission for P2 and P3 packages

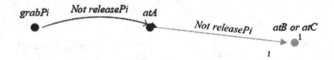

Fig. 6. The UAV must be always carrying a package

define MR's establishing well founded relationships between different plans and behavior. Following the terminology introduced in [40] we use events as *OldSpec* and *NewSpec*, representing the old specification (prior the introduction of the new requirements) and new specification (the new configuration for the UAV).

For example, a new location *D* can be introduced in the system described earlier, with new delivering instructions: package *P1* must be carried from location *A* to location D and package *P3* from *B* to *D*. Instructions for packages P2 remain unchanged. The new planning for the UAV is the following: Starting from location *A*, grabs *P1* and goes to location *B*, grabs *P3*, then with *P1* and *P3* goes to location *C*, it grabs *P3* and flying with the three packages arrives at D where *P1* and *P3* are released. Finally, the UAV grabs *P2*, goes to location *A* and releases *P2* there.

These changes imply that some rules shaping the behavior for translating packages must be modified while others should not be altered. In particular, the new specification implies that new rules for packages *P1* and *P3* must be introduced while rules for $P2$ suffer no changes. We introduce MR's relating old and new specification. Roughly speaking, if a behavioral property P is changed introducing a new property P', then only P' is valid in the new specification. If P is not modified, then P is valid in the new specification. This general scheme is described in Fig. 7.

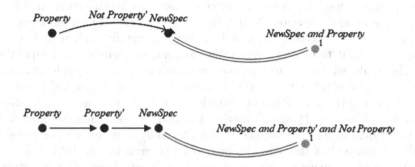

Fig. 7. MRs relating old and new specifications

As explained in [40] in some cases the new specification can not be started immediately due to consistency issues between old and new goals. For example, a statement saying that the UAV artifact can not carry more than two packages due to weight requirements can affect the new planning since three packages are carried out together at some point in the new specification. This is solved introducing a delay between the moment the old specification is dropped and the new specification takes charge. In this delay status the conditions shaping the behavior of the UAV's flight are relaxed so that, for example, a package is released in the next location, therefore waiting until the new specification can be loaded. This can be modeled in FVS as a MRs between specifications as shown in Fig. 8.

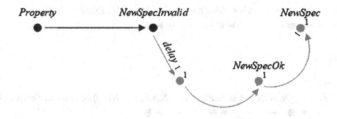

Fig. 8. MRs relating delays betweens specifications

4   FVS and Metamorphic Relationships(MRs) for UAV's Temporal Planning

In this section we define MRs in a more traditional way, employing FVS as a BIG DATA oracle for traces verification. The considered system is based also in defining specifications for UAV's flights, but in this case we focus on temporal planning rather than dynamically switching between specifications like it was shown in the previous Section. As detailed in [39], temporal task planning guarantees a robot will succeed in its task as long as certain explicit and implicit assumptions about the robot's operating environment, sensors, and capabilities hold. The analyzed system in this Section is based on the example introduced in [39]. An UAV artifact must provide surveillance and search and rescue services within a certain region, but considering a non fly zone. Two conditions are monitored in [39]: 1) avoid entering the non fly zone, and, if entered, the degree of violation as the distance inside the no-fly zone mustb me measured and 2): to assure that the area claimed to be covered by the UAV is actually covered, giving no space to measuring errors to occur. Given the specification given in [39] for the UAV's expected behavior we introduce two simple MR's. The objective is very simple: if a target is classified as being in a non fly zone, we change its coordinates so that its included in the fly zone. Similarly, if a person is detected we change the conditions so that the person is not included in the next version of the system. This follows a classic technique to obtain MR's: cases with similar conditions should belong in the same category and cases with opposite conditions should belong in opposite categories. In this Section we focus only in opposite behavior but analogous rules can be introduced considering also similar behavior. Two FVS rules are shown in Fig. 9 modeling two MR's for the UAV's temporal specification. The rule in the top of Fig. 9 says when the position of the UAV is altered (changing not being in the non fly zone to being in the fly zone) then the new result should be ruled out as a fly zone violation. Similarly, rule in the bottom of the Fig. 9 alters an image to that a person is no longer detected.

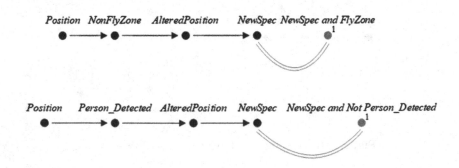

Fig. 9. MRs for temporal planning

5   FVS and Metamorphic Relationships(MRs) for OBC Operating Systems

In this section we build some MR's in a totally different domain: operating systems for OBC designed for nano satellites missions. The behavior of the FreeR-TOS Operating System employing FVS as the specification language is fully detailed in [4]. In this case we build MR's considering the exact opposite behavior of the rules. Since FVS can automatically generate anti-scenarios for every rule, MR's can be automatically generated. This clearly constitute an attractive feature. We took some of the rules specified in [4] and automatically obtain MR's by generating anti-scenarios for every rule. For example, the FVS scenario in the top of Fig. 10 exhibits a behavior that should be classified as an error: the operating system does not start in the boot phase. This MR is an anti scenario for the rule demanding that the system should indeed starts in the boot phase. The scenario in the middle of Fig. 10 is another anti-scenario and should be considered as an error: the operating systems starts to process tasks without entering the scheduling phase. Finally, the scenario in the bottom of Fig. 10 illustrates an scenario which violates the priority-based scheduling policy of the operating system.

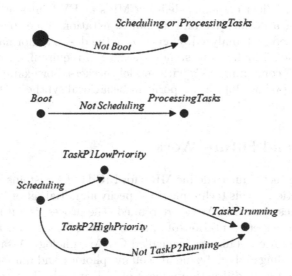

Fig. 10. MRs as FVS anti-scenarios

6   Discussion

In Sects. 3, 4 and 5 we illustrate how FVS can be used as the specification language to successfully denote metamorphic behavior in diverse, complex and meaningful domains such as UAV's flying missions and operating systems for On Board Computers in nano satellites design. We also employed MR's in two flavours: in Sect. 3 we specify MR's to relate different goals and UAV's configurations in the context of a challenging area such as the dynamic adaption of AUV's missions due to changes in the requirements.

In Sect. 4 we continue exploring UAV based system, but we built MR's in a more traditional way: to validate behavior in a BIG-DATA context, where possible a large amount of data and information seen as traces must be checked.

Finally, in Sect. 5 we moved to validate OBC software. In particular we focused on one popular operating called FreeRTOS. We took advantage of FVS's possibility to automatically generate anti-scenarios to build MR's that behave in the exact opposite way to the rules defining the expected behavior of the operating systems. Exploring the opposite behavior of a requirement is an useful way to obtain MR's.

Based on these experiments we can conclude that FVS is an appealing framework to specify metamorphic behavior. FVS expressive power and flexibility is shown in significative domains, from UAV's flying mission to OBC operating systems. In addition, we showed how to denote MR's in two ways: to relate different UAV's configurations and to validate outputs where the vast amount of information make it hard to define. MR's can be automatically generated as anti-scenarios. When manually defining MR's as FVS rules all the desirable characteristics of a declarative and graphical notation shine: behavior can be intuitively explored and analyzed by gathering the desired information from the graphical scenarios. Finally, consistency checking of requirements and MR's can be easily checked combining FVS with model checkers. For example, employing tools like GOAL [37] or [26] we can perform behavioral synthesis [12] and classic behavioral verification [5].

7   Related and Future Work

A very appealing technique to define MR's for BIG DATA systems is presented in [17]. The foundation of this technique is to specify an initial set of MR's and start an iterative process on which MR's are refined. The process is automated, sound and correct. The experimentation of the research is focused on a BIG DATA service implementation. This service, called Cell Morphology Assay (CMA) was designed for modeling and analyzing 3D cell morphology and mining morphology patterns extracted from diffraction images of biology cells. The implementation is able to categorize a huge amount of biology cells images. We believe we can replicate this procedure using FVS, since our language support the refinement operation [3], which constitutes one possible future research line to continue our work. Contrary to FVS, the possibility to check consistency between MRs is not available in this approach.

Other approaches focused on metamorphic properties are [2,16,27]. These options are mostly focused on implementation details such as the actual framework tool to deploy the tests. Our approach is addressing a previous phase which is the exploration and specification of MRs. However, one possible combination is to graphically denote tests as FVS scenarios and trying to explore automatic generation of test cases.

Adaptive System in UAV's control missions is tackled on [40]. This work exhibits how controller synthesis can be used both to guarantee correct transitioning from the old to the new mission goals including architectural reconfiguration to handle new software actuators and sensors if necessary. Adaptation can occur at various levels of abstraction to respond to many different kinds of changes. In particular, [40] deals with mobile robot adaptation that include dynamic responses to changes in the high-level goals that the robot must achieve. Goals and configurations are specified using temporal logics. A very interesting framework based on hybrid components is in charge of performing all the necessary architectural changes in the system to adapt to the new requirements. We were able to reproduce and specify the behavioral specification for some examples of adaptive systems described in [40]. We denote a set of MR's that could be used to relate, explore, and verify goals and requirements from the old and the new specification. We believe this can be a plus in this research line.

Temporal planning for UAV's is addressed on [39]. A monitoring process is implemented to verify that implicit and explicit assumptions of the environment are not violated. If some violation of the requirements occur, it is shown that under certain conditions some corrective actions can be taken to re enter in safe state. The approach can be classified under the Runtime Verification label, a formal methods technique that studies how to synthesize monitors from high-level formal specifications of complex properties [21,39]. In our experimentation we showed how FVS can be used to model MR's for temporal planning and describe how them can be used as a trace oracle and validation in BIG DATA systems.

The specification in [39] is based on the HLOLA specification language [15, 20]. HLOLA is a very rich, expressive and powerful language with the possibility to realize automatic validation tasks. It would be interesting trying to combine this language with FVS's graphical flavour.

Among other future lines of research to continue this work we would like to take one step further FVS's specifications and put them in action in some simulated or real scenarios as described in [39,40]. For example, a possible tool to consider is ArduPilot Software-In-The-Loop (SITL) UAV simulator as in [9,35].

We would also like to explore the interaction between FVS and other tools. For example, [2] extracts MR in runtime checking the different paths in the execution tree. In this context, FVS scenarios could be used as a monitor in the sense given by the model checking techniques. Finally, we are exploring the possibility to interact with automatic code and test generators like [29].

8   Conclusions

In this work we deepened the impact of MR's for formal verification. Besides employing them as a trace oracle for formal validation in BIG DATA we showed how them can be used to explore and reason about different specifications. This is a powerful feature in order to produce the most accurate possible specification of the expected behavior of the system under analysis.

We showed the potential of FVS as a specification language to denote MR's analyzing non trivial examples in cutting-edge and heterogeneous domains such as operating systems for OBC for nano satellites and behavioral specifications for UAV's. In addition, the possibility to automatically generate complementary behavior is a distinctive feature of our approach.

The satisfactory results delineated in this work aim to further blend the interaction between MR's, formal verification and FVS as the underlying specification language and framework.

References

1. Agarwal, R., Dhar, V.: Big data, data science, and analytics: the opportunity and challenge for is research (2014)
2. Asrafi, M., Liu, H., Kuo, F.C.: On testing effectiveness of metamorphic relations: a case study. In: 2011 Fifth International Conference on Secure Software Integration and Reliability Improvement, pp. 147–156. IEEE (2011)
3. Asteasuain, F.: A flexible and expressive formalism to specify metamorphic properties for big data systems validation. In: CACIC, pp 282–291 (2022). ISBN 978-987-1364-31-2
4. Asteasuain, F.: Formalizing operating systems for nano satellites on board computers. In: CONAIISI (2022)
5. Asteasuain, F., Braberman, V.: Declaratively building behavior by means of scenario clauses. Requirements Eng. **22**(2), 239–274 (2016). https://doi.org/10.1007/s00766-015-0242-2
6. Asteasuain, F., Caldeira, L.R.:A sound and correct formalism to specify, verify and synthesize behavior in BIG DATA systems. In: Pesado, P., Gil, G. (eds) Computer Science. CACIC 2021. CCIS, vol. 1584, pp. 109–123. Springer, Cham (2022). https://doi.org/10.1007/978-3-031-05903-2_8
7. Asteasuain, F., Calonge, F., Dubinsky, M., Gamboa, P.: Open and branching behavioral synthesis with scenario clauses. CLEI E-J. **24**(3), 1–20 (2021)
8. Asteasuain, F., Calonge, F., Gamboa, P.: Exploiting anti-scenarios for the non realizability problem. In: Pesado, P., Arroyo, M. (eds.) CACIC 2019. CCIS, vol. 1184, pp. 157–171. Springer, Cham (2020). https://doi.org/10.1007/978-3-030-48325-8_11
9. Baidya, S., Shaikh, Z., Levorato, M.: Flynetsim: an open source synchronized UAV network simulator based on ns-3 and ardupilot. In: Proceedings of the 21st ACM International Conference on Modeling, Analysis and Simulation of Wireless and Mobile Systems, pp. 37–45 (2018)
10. Beck, K., et al.: Manifesto for agile software development (2001)
11. Bellettini, C., Camilli, M., Capra, L., Monga, M.: Distributed CTL model checking using Mapreduce: theory and practice. CCPE **28**(11), 3025–3041 (2016)
12. Bloem, R., Jobstmann, B., Piterman, N., Pnueli, A., Sa'Ar, Y.: Synthesis of reactive (1) designs (2011)
13. Braberman, V., Garbervestky, D., Kicillof, N., Monteverde, D., Olivero, A.: Speeding up model checking of timed-models by combining scenario specialization and

live component analysis. In: Ouaknine, J., Vaandrager, F.W. (eds.) FORMATS 2009. LNCS, vol. 5813, pp. 58–72. Springer, Heidelberg (2009). https://doi.org/10.1007/978-3-642-04368-0_7

14. Camilli, M.: Formal verification problems in a big data world: towards a mighty synergy. In: ICSE, pp. 638–641 (2014)

15. Ceresa, M., Gorostiaga, F., Sánchez, C.: Declarative stream runtime verification (hLola). In: Oliveira, B.C.S. (ed.) APLAS 2020. LNCS, vol. 12470, pp. 25–43. Springer, Cham (2020). https://doi.org/10.1007/978-3-030-64437-6_2

16. Chen, T.Y., Cheung, S.C., Yiu, S.M.: Metamorphic testing: a new approach for generating next test cases. arXiv preprint arXiv:2002.12543 (2020)

17. Ding, J., Zhang, D., Hu, X.H.: A framework for ensuring the quality of a big data service. In: 2016 SCC, pp. 82–89. IEEE (2016)

18. Doncaster, B., Williams, C., Shulman, J.: 2017 nano/microsatellite market forecast. SpaceWorks Enterprises Inc., Atlanta, GA, Technical report (2017)

19. Fernandez, L., Ruiz-De-Azua, J.A., Calveras, A., Camps, A.: Assessing Lora for satellite-to-earth communications considering the impact of ionospheric scintillation. IEEE access 8, 165570–165582 (2020)

20. Gorostiaga, F., Sánchez, C.: HLola: a very functional tool for extensible stream runtime verification. In: TACAS 2021. LNCS, vol. 12652, pp. 349–356. Springer, Cham (2021). https://doi.org/10.1007/978-3-030-72013-1_18

21. Havelund, K., Roşu, G.: Synthesizing monitors for safety properties. In: Katoen, J.-P., Stevens, P. (eds.) TACAS 2002. LNCS, vol. 2280, pp. 342–356. Springer, Heidelberg (2002). https://doi.org/10.1007/3-540-46002-0_24

22. Hummel, O., Eichelberger, H., Giloj, A., Werle, D., Schmid, K.: A collection of software engineering challenges for big data system development. In: SEAA, pp. 362–369. IEEE (2018)

23. Kumar, V.D., Alencar, P.: Software engineering for big data projects: domains, methodologies and gaps. In: IEEEBIGDATA, pp. 2886–2895. IEEE (2016)

24. Laigner, R., Kalinowski, M., Lifschitz, S., Monteiro, R.S., de Oliveira, D.: A systematic mapping of software engineering approaches to develop big data systems. In: SEAA, pp. 446–453. IEEE (2018)

25. Luckcuck, M., Farrell, M., Dennis, L.A., Dixon, C., Fisher, M.: Formal specification and verification of autonomous robotic systems: a survey. ACM Comput. Surv. (CSUR) 52(5), 1–41 (2019)

26. Magee, J., Kramer, J.: State models and Java Programs. Wiley, Chichester (1999)

27. Mayer, J., Guderlei, R.: An empirical study on the selection of good metamorphic relations. In: 30th Annual International Computer Software and Applications Conference (COMPSAC 2006), vol. 1, pp. 475–484. IEEE (2006)

28. Mitchell, T.M., Mitchell, T.M.: Machine LLearning, vol. 1. McGraw-hill New York (1997)

29. Niaz, I.A., Tanaka, J.: Code generation from UML statecharts. In: Proceedings of the 7th IASTED International Conference on Software Engineering and Application (SEA 2003), Marina Del Rey, pp. 315–321 (2003)

30. Otero, C.E., Peter, A.: Research directions for engineering big data analytics software. IEEE Intell. Syst. 30(1), 13–19 (2014)

31. Pramanik, S., Bandyopadhyay, S.K.: Analysis of big data. In: Encyclopedia of Data Science and Machine Learning, pp. 97–115. IGI Global (2023)

32. Saeed, N., Elzanaty, A., Almorad, H., Dahrouj, H., Al-Naffouri, T.Y., Alouini, M.S.: Cubesat communications: recent advances and future challenges. IEEE Commun. Surv. Tutor. 22(3), 1839–1862 (2020)

33. Segura, S., Fraser, G., Sanchez, A.B., Ruiz-Cortés, A.: A survey on metamorphic testing. IEEE Trans. Software Eng. **42**(9), 805–824 (2016)
34. Shaw, M., Garlan, D.: Software Architecture: Perspectives on an Emerging Discipline. Prentice-Hall, Inc., Upper Saddle River (1996)
35. de Sousa Barros, J., Oliveira, T., Nigam, V., Brito, A.V.: A framework for the analysis of UAV strategies using co-simulation. In: 2016 VI Brazilian Symposium on Computing Systems Engineering (SBESC), pp. 9–15. IEEE (2016)
36. Sri, P.A., Anusha, M.: Big data-survey. Indonesian J. Electr. Eng. Inform. (IJEEI) **4**(1), 74–80 (2016)
37. Tsay, Y.-K., Chen, Y.-F., Tsai, M.-H., Wu, K.-N., Chan, W.-C.: GOAL: a graphical tool for manipulating büchi automata and temporal formulae. In: Grumberg, O., Huth, M. (eds.) TACAS 2007. LNCS, vol. 4424, pp. 466–471. Springer, Heidelberg (2007). https://doi.org/10.1007/978-3-540-71209-1_35
38. Ziegert, S., Wehrheim, H.: Temporal plans for software architecture reconfiguration. Comput. Sci.-Res. Dev. **30**, 303–320 (2015)
39. Zudaire, S., Gorostiaga, F., Sánchez, C., Schneider, G., Uchitel, S.: Assumption monitoring using runtime verification for UAV temporal task plan executions. In: 2021 IEEE International Conference on Robotics and Automation (ICRA), pp. 6824–6830. IEEE (2021)
40. Zudaire, S.A., Nahabedian, L., Uchitel, S.: Assured mission adaptation of UAVs. ACM Trans. Auton. Adapt. Syst. (TAAS) **16**(3–4), 1–27 (2022)

Approach to Improving Java Source Code Considering Non-compliance with a Java Style Guide

Pablo Becker⬭, Luis Olsina(✉)⬭, and María Fernanda Papa⬭

GIDIS_Web, Facultad de Ingeniería, UNLPam, General Pico, LP, Argentina
{beckerp,olsinal,pmfer}@ing.unlpam.edu.ar

Abstract. This work shows the betterment of a typical Java source code application by taking into account its non-compliance with a subset of items of the Google Java Style Guide. To get this, an improving strategy is used. The improving strategy has a set of activities that allow defining non-functional requirements in the form of characteristics, attributes, items, and their relationships, as well as designing and implementing measurements, evaluations, analysis, and code changes. The practical case was carried out in the context of an advanced undergraduate subject in System Engineering as a compulsory integrated exam. The results of evaluating attributes/items for compliance with the above coding style guide and improving non-compliances are illustrated in detail. We argue that this study may be of interest to professors and students of other similar degrees.

Keywords: Non-compliance · Source Code · Google Java Style Guide · Improving Strategy

1 Introduction

Elish and Offutt [7] pointed out that *"adherence to standard coding practices is considered to be essential to ensure readable and understandable software, and thus more likely to be easy to maintain and reuse"*. Today, there are well-known coding style guidelines and conventions that arise from different companies and authors for various programming languages intending to make software source code more readable, understandable, and maintainable. For example, regarding readability, dos Santos and Gerosa [5] surveyed a set of 11 coding practices to find out their impact on readability. The authors' findings were that 8 coding practices had evidence of affecting it, while 3 practices had no statistically significant effect.

Furthermore, there is current evidence that programmers and teams work with coding practices in the context of industrial software projects. For example, Broekhuis [4] says that *"teams adopt or adapt coding styles, and in some cases, they are mandatory. This means coding practices are an integral part of software development"*. This author obtained 102 responses from professionals surveyed in the Netherlands in 2021, including 5 project managers, 95 developers, and 2 testers. As a result, more than 90% of

P. Pesado (Ed.): CACIC 2022, CCIS 1778, pp. 123–139, 2023.
https://doi.org/10.1007/978-3-031-34147-2_9

the participants used coding styles in their software projects. As a consideration of his empirical work, Broekhuis highlights *"It is, therefore, reasonable to conclude that they* [coding practices] *have a critical role in industries. This could imply the necessity of teaching these coding styles to students"*.

This paper analyzes the quality evaluation and improvement of a typical Java code application by considering the non-compliance with a selected set of items of the Google Java Style Guide [8]. In a nutshell, this guide serves as the complete definition of Google's coding standards for source code in the Java programming language, which is available online. As in any other coding style guide, the Google Java Style Guide has a set of items grouped in dimensions or sections named 'Source file structure', 'Formatting', and 'Naming', among others, that the assessed code must comply with.

The practical case that we illustrate in the present paper was partially applied in an advanced undergraduate subject in System Engineering as a mandatory exam. The subject called Software Engineering II is taught in the 1st semester of the 5th year of the System Engineering degree. The theoretical content of the subject refers to nonfunctional requirements, measurement, evaluation, and analysis of the quality of a software product or system. Concepts of change and quality improvement are also conveyed. In order to implement these contents from a practical standpoint and promote the technical and transversal competencies of the students, each year, considering the problem to be solved, a strategy is selected from a family of evaluation strategies [14].

In the year 2022, we selected the evaluation strategy with the purpose of understanding and improving the quality of a given Java source code, considering the compliance of the code with a subset of items from [8]. Note that the code we provided to students was deliberately and slightly modified to partially comply with this coding style guide.

The learning goals were mainly two. First of all, as in every academic year, apply the concepts of characteristics, attributes, metrics, and indicators, as well as the concept of analysis of the situation for better recommendations. These concepts and practices are embedded into the processes and methods of any given evaluation strategy [14]. Second, we consider it relevant that students as future professionals learn software coding styles through practice, as Broekhuis suggested above. In short, the contribution of this work is to illustrate both aspects from a practical point of view. Given that this practical case may be of interest to professors and students of other similar degrees, its complete documentation is linked to an additional open resource.

It is important to remark that the current paper is an extended version of the Becker *et al.* work [1]. Unlike this cited conference paper, in this chapter, we present concepts and relationships of the ontological conceptual model for non-functional requirements, which allow a better understanding of the correspondence between requirements in the form of characteristics and attributes with dimensions and items of the coding style guides. Besides, due to the greater availability of space than in that conference paper, we carry out a more extensive analysis of the results of the improving strategy activities.

The remaining sections of this paper are organized as follows. Section 2 provides an overview of the Google Java Style Guide and the evaluation strategy, as well as some descriptions of an ontological conceptual model for non-functional requirements, including the concepts of characteristic, attribute, item, and their relationships. Section 3 describes the motivation and context of the practical case. Section 4 illustrates and implements the strategy activities for the case in detail using a Java source code. Section 5 reviews the related work and finally, Sect. 6 presents the main conclusions.

2 Non-functional Requirements and Improving Strategy: An Overview

For a better understanding of the practical case, in the following three subsections, we would like to go over some fundamentals and elements of dimensions and items of a coding style guide, non-functional requirements, and evaluation strategy activities aimed at improvement.

2.1 Summary of Google's Java Style Guide

As stated above, the practical case is illustrated using the Google Java Style Guide. The online document [8] includes the definition of Google's coding rules and conventions for source code in the Java programming language. It is organized into sections (dimensions) and guidelines (items).

Google's Java Style Guide defines non-functional requirements, that is, the conventions and rules that must be adhered to, by including dimensions and items related to:

- *Source file basics* combine guidelines for filenames, file encoding, whitespace characters, and special characters.
- *Source file structure* that combines guidelines that deal with license information, package and import statements, and class member ordering.
- *Formatting* that aggregates items for braces, indents, line wrapping, whitespace, parentheses, enums, arrays, switch statements, annotations, comments, and modifiers.
- *Naming* deals with items for identifiers such as package, class, method, constant, field, local variable, and type variable.
- *Programming Practices* that deal with @Override, exceptions, static members, and finalizers.
- *Javadoc* states how to format some aspects and where it is required.

For example, the *Naming* section or dimension has guidelines or items labeled as *Class names*, *Method names*, and *Parameter names*, among others.

2.2 Some Concepts and Relationships for Non-Functional Requirements

Non-functional requirements often refer to the concept of a quality aspect of a thing or entity, where an entity can be a resource, process, artifact, or system, among others. In a nutshell, the non-functional requirements are the criteria established to evaluate how an entity should perform, and therefore the concrete entity must have certain quality attributes or items to achieve the non-functional requirements. There is a collection of concepts for this domain, which can be represented in a conceptual model. This model can be structured as an ontology. Figure 1 mainly shows concepts and relationships of the Non-Functional Requirements Top-Domain Ontology (NFRsTDO), in which some terms are semantically enriched with terms of higher-level ontologies such as ThingFO [13]. In the following paragraphs, we would like to define a subset of NFRsTDO concepts and relationships to better understand the present work.

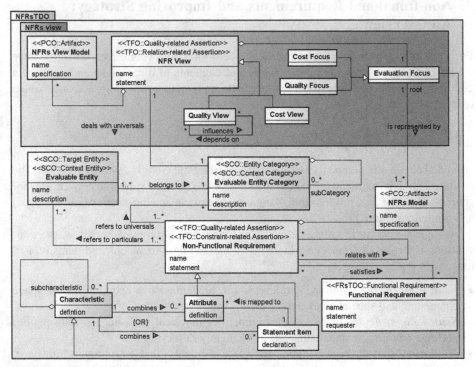

Fig. 1. Concepts and relationships of the Non-Functional Requirements Top-Domain Ontology (NFRsTDO). Note that all the definitions of terms, properties, and relationships can be accessed at https://bit.ly/NFRsTDOv1_2

In particular, we look at the terms *Evaluable Entity, Non-Functional Requirement, Characteristic, Statement Item,* and *Attribute* depicted in Fig. 1.

Evaluable Entity is a Target or Context Entity that represents a particular (concrete) entity to be evaluated. Note that depending on a given situation, an Evaluable Entity has the semantics of a Target Entity, or Context Entity, which in turn are things [13]. An example of an Evaluable Entity is a particular software source code program.

Non-Functional Requirement (NFR) is a Quality-, Constraint-related Assertion [13] that specifies an aspect in the form of a Characteristic, Attribute, or Statement Item to be evaluated on how or how well an Evaluable Entity performs or shall perform.

Characteristic (synonym: Dimension, Factor) is a NFR that represents an evaluable, non-elementary aspect attributed to a particular entity or its category by a human agent. Note that a Characteristic can be evaluated but cannot be measured as an Attribute. Examples of it are *Naming, Compliance,* and *Maintainability,* among many others.

Statement Item –or item for short- is a NFR that represents a declared textual expression of an evaluable physical or abstract aspect asserted for a particular entity or its category by a human agent. Note that a Statement Item can represent for instance an assertive element in a questionnaire instrument, an assertive element in a heuristic check-list, or an assertive element in a guide. The *Class names* Statement Item is an example of this in [8].

Attribute is a NFR that represents a measurable and evaluable physical or abstract aspect attributed to a particular entity or its category by a human agent. Note that an Attribute is a measurable and evaluable elementary NFR, i.e., an elementary quality to be quantified. The *Class naming compliance* is an example of an Attribute name.

Considering the relationships, Fig. 1 shows that a NFR relates with none or many NFRs, where a NFR always refers to an Evaluable Entity. In addition, a Characteristic is a non-elementary NFR, which combines Attributes or Statement Items. For example, in [8], *Class names* and *Method names* are two items combined into the *Naming* dimension. Besides, the *Naming Compliance* sub-characteristic combines Attributes such as *Class naming compliance* and *Method naming compliance*, as we see later.

Finally, a useful relationship that we will put into practice is called is mapped to between the terms Statement Item and Attribute, which we also discuss later on.

2.3 Activities of the Improving Strategy

In Olsina and Becker [14], a family of evaluation strategies guided by measurement and evaluation activities is analyzed. These strategies make it possible to achieve purposes such as understanding, improving, monitoring, and controlling, among others. In this work, the GOCAMEC (*Goal-Oriented Context-Aware Measurement, Evaluation, and Change*) strategy [2] is used, which allows us to understand and improve the current state of an entity. Figure 2 exhibits the GOCAMEC process specification using the UML activity diagram and SPEM notation.

The strategy process starts by enacting the Define Non-Functional Requirements (NFRs) activity (A1), which aims at defining the items/attributes and characteristics to be evaluated. A1 takes as input a quality model and/or guidelines (e.g. as those in [8] and [9]) and produces a "NFRs Specification", which includes a "NFRs Tree".

In the *Design Measurement and Evaluation* activity (A2), metrics and indicators are designed or reused from a repository. Then, the *Implement Measurement and Evaluation* activity (A3) implies producing the measures and indicator values.

A4.1 is called *Design Analysis*, which mainly includes establishing the criteria and instruments for the analysis of the outcomes. As seen in Fig. 2, A4.1 can be performed in parallel with A3. Next, in the *Analyze Results* activity (A4.2), the measures, the indicator values, and the "Analysis Specification" are used as input, to produce the "Conclusion/Recommendation Report". This activity aims at detecting weaknesses in the evaluated entity and recommending changes.

If there are no recommendations for changes, since the level of satisfaction achieved by the indicators is satisfactory, the process ends. But, if there are recommendations for changes due to detected weaknesses, *Design Changes* (A5) is carried out, producing an "Improvement Plan" in which the specific changes to be made are indicated. Then, the plan serves as input to *Implement Changes* (A6). The result is a new version of the entity under study (i.e., a "New Situation").

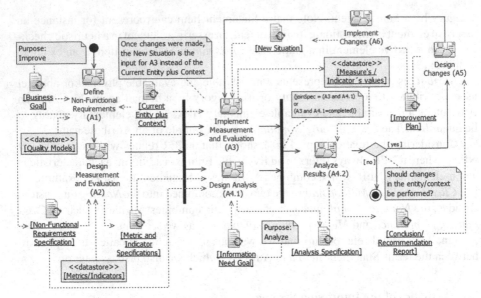

Fig. 2. Generic process specification for the improving strategy called GOCAMEC

Figure 2 shows that after completing activity A6, A3 must be enacted again to perform measurement and evaluation of the new version of the entity. Based on the new results, A4.2 analyzes whether the changes have increased the level of satisfaction achieved by the same NFRs. If the improvement is not enough to meet the main business/information-need goal, new cycles of change, re-evaluation, and analysis can be carried out until the goal set by the organization is achieved.

3 Motivation and Context

As introduced in Sect. 1, the practical case was implemented in the context of the Software Engineering II subject in the first semester of the 5th year of the Systems Engineering degree at the Engineering School of UNLPam. The case is thoroughly developed in Sect. 4, so here we describe a little more about the context.

On the one hand, we chose a Java code because the students spend about 90 h in the previous subject named Object Oriented Programming, in the 1st semester of the 3rd year, using the Java language to program a video game application. The given source code (Evaluable Entity) is called "GUICalculator.java". It has 116 lines of code and the reader can consult it in Appendix IV at https://bit.ly/CCIS_Appendix. We deliberately modified this program a bit to introduce some violations of the [8] coding style items. Code lines with at least one evaluated incident are shaded orange in this Appendix.

On the other hand, the Software Engineering II subject always evaluates the technical skills of students on non-functional requirements using characteristics and attributes to specify them. It also includes measurement and evaluation processes using metrics and indicators as methods to evaluate entities. Note that "*establishing software metrics and quality standards*" is a specific competency in the new curricular standard in Argentina for Information Systems degrees. Therefore, the specification of quality requirements, the design and implementation of metrics and indicators, and the application of an evaluation strategy are key concepts and practices to grade this subject.

Considering the case given to students, we have set the limit that one attribute must map to a single Google Java Style Guide item. In addition, the maximum number of attributes to be evaluated was 8, therefore, mapped to 8 items of this guide. In the present work, we expand the scope of the assignment given to students, by including 11 attributes and by specifying in one instance 3 attributes for 1 item of the guide. Specifically, to the "*3.3.3 Ordering and spacing*" Statement Item in [8], we evaluate the adherence of the GUICalculator.java code to it by using the following Attributes: *1.1.1. Compliance with the ordering of types of imports*; *1.1.2. Spacing compliance between static and non-static import blocks*; and, *1.1.3. Spacing compliance between import sentences*. Thus, we exemplify the relationship is mapped to between the terms Statement Item and Attribute of Fig. 1 using the cardinality 1 to 1 and 1 to many. In summary, this work evaluates 11 attributes mapped to 9 items of the guide, as will be illustrated in detail in the next section.

By assigning this activity to students, which represents an integrated exam that regularly lasts around 35 days, we encourage group work. In the year 2022, there were 10 students, including one international, by an institutional interchange.

The size of the groups varied from 1 group with three members to 3 groups with two members, while 1 student decided to work alone. There were slightly different restrictions on the size of the group, such as the number of attributes/characteristics and the pages of the monograph as the final report to be examined. For example, the group of 3 students must have requirements specified by two sub-characteristics of Compliance [9] and 8 attributes to measure and evaluate. Also, they had to inspect the code beforehand to make sure that the requirements tree included at least 3 attributes that would imply that the code would have to be changed to fully comply with the guide. The resulting monographs were between 33 and 68 pages, including appendices.

In short, we give an account of some transversal skills and competencies gained by the students, by promoting group work, providing all the material in English, and fostering oral and written communication in the Spanish mother tongue.

4   Application of the Improving Strategy to the Practical Case

As commented above, to improve the compliance of the "GUICalculator.java" source code to the Google Java Style Guide, we applied the GOCAMEC strategy. This strategy allows i) to understand the degree of compliance of the source code to the style guide; ii) based on non-compliances, to apply changes to the current version of the source code (v. 1.0) for improving compliance with the style guide; and iii) understand the degree of source code compliance after the changes (that is, to the version 1.1 of the code). Next, we illustrate the activities represented in Fig. 2.

(A1) Define Non-Functional Requirements: Firstly, in this activity, we select a quality model. Since adherence to a coding style guide favors the source code maintainability, we consider the model for external and internal quality proposed in ISO 9126 standard [9], which includes the "*Maintainability*" characteristic. In turn, this characteristic explicitly includes the "*Compliance*" sub-characteristic, which is defined as "*The degree to which the software product (e.g., the source code) adheres to standards or conventions relating to maintainability*". Note that although ISO 25010 [10] replaces ISO 9126, the former does not explicitly include the "*Compliance*" sub-characteristic in its quality models. So, with the intention that students would see the "*Compliance*" sub-characteristic explicitly in the model, the ISO 9126 standard was chosen.

As a second sub-activity in A1, from the Google Java Style Guide, we select a set of items to be evaluated. The selected items are shown in the 1st column of Table 1.

Table 1. Google Java Style Guide items mapped to characteristics and attributes related to "*Maintainability*" and "*Compliance*" of a Java source code and its evaluation results (in [%]). Note: The symbol ● means "Satisfactory"; ◆ "Marginal", and ■ "Unsatisfactory". Additionally, op stands for "operator", EI for "Elementary Indicator" and DI for "Derived Indicator"

Google Java Style Guide Items	Characteristics and Attributes (*in italics*)	op	v1.0 EI/DI	v1.1 EI/DI
	1 Maintainability		73.74 ◆	100 ●
	1.1 Compliance	C-+	73.74 ◆	100 ●
3. Source file structure	1.1.1 Source file structure compliance	A	53.33 ■	100 ●
	1.1.1.1 Compliance with the ordering of types of imports		100 ●	100 ●
3.3.3 Ordering and spacing	*1.1.1.2 Spacing compliance between static and non-static import blocks*		100 ●	100 ●
	1.1.1.3 Spacing compliance between import sentences		0 ■	100 ●
3.4.1 Exactly one top-level class declaration	*1.1.1.4 Compliance with the number of top-level class declarations per source file*		33.33 ■	100 ●
4. Formatting	1.1.2 Formatting compliance	A	72.10 ◆	100 ●
4.1.1 Use of optional braces	*1.1.2.1 Compliance with the use of optional braces*		9.09 ■	100 ●
4.8.2.1 One variable per declaration	*1.1.2.2 Compliance with the number of variables per declaration*		82.61 ◆	100 ●
4.3 One statement per line	*1.1.2.3 Compliance with the number of statements per line*		88.24 ◆	100 ●
4.4 Column limit: 100	*1.1.2.4 Compliance with the maximum line size*		95.15 ◆	100 ●
5. Naming	1.1.3 Naming compliance	C--	82.96 ◆	100 ●
5.2.2 Class names	*1.1.3.1 Class naming compliance*		60.00 ■	100 ●
5.2.3 Method names	*1.1.3.2 Method naming compliance*		100 ●	100 ●
5.2.6 Parameter names	*1.1.3.3 Parameter naming compliance*		100 ●	100 ●

Then, for each item, we define one or more attributes. As exhibited in Fig. 3, for item *3.3.3 Ordering and spacing* we define 3 attributes while for item *3.4.1 Exactly one top-level class declaration* we define just one attribute. It is important to note that mapping a guide item to more than one attribute allows us a more refined evaluation of the item. Figure 3 also shows how different parts of the items' declaration were used to identify attributes. The 2nd column of Table 1 shows in italics all the identified attributes for this study and their mapping to the guide items. The reader can see all the characteristic and attribute definitions in Annex I at https://bit.ly/CCIS_Appendix.

(A2) Design Measurement and Evaluation: As attributes are quantified by metrics, indirect and direct metrics were defined in this activity. For example, to quantify the

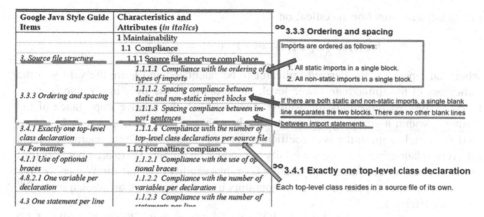

Fig. 3. Example of mapping between Google Java Style Guide items and attributes

attribute *"Compliance with the number of top-level class declarations per source file"* (coded 1.1.1.4 in the 2nd column of Table 1) the indirect metric *"Percentage of valid top-level class declarations"* (%TLC) was defined. The specification of this indirect metric is shown in Table 2. In addition, for each indirect metric, one or more direct metrics were specified. For the foregoing metric, three direct metrics were defined, namely: *"Availability of valid top-level class"* (AVTLC), *"Number of top-level classes"* (#TLC), and *"Number of Java files"* (#JF). Table 3 shows the specification for the direct metric AVTLC. It is important to mention that the measurement procedures must be as clear as possible to favor repeatability and reproducibility. So, some notes were included. For example, Table 3 shows three notes, where one of them (note 1) clarifies what is considered a top-level class.

All the metrics defined for this work can be found in Annex II of the document available at https://bit.ly/CCIS_Appendix.

Since the measured values do not represent the level of satisfaction of an elementary non-functional requirement (e.g. attribute), a transformation must be performed that converts the measured value into a new value that can be interpreted. Therefore, for each attribute, an elementary indicator was specified.

As an example, the elementary indicator specification for attribute 1.1.1.4 is shown in Table 4. This indicator, like the rest of the elementary indicators, has three acceptability levels: *Unsatisfactory* (values less than or equal to 60%), *Marginal* (values greater than 60% and less than 100%), and *Satisfactory* (values that are equal to 100%). We decided to use the traffic light metaphor to facilitate the visualization of the levels of satisfaction achieved: ■red/Unsatisfactory, ◆yellow/Marginal, and ●green/Satisfactory. The reader can find the rest of the elementary indicators in Annex III at https://bit.ly/CCIS_Appendix.

Once all elementary indicators were specified, the next sub-activity was the definition of derived indicators. A derived indicator allows us to interpret a non-functional requirement with a higher level of abstraction, such as the characteristics and sub-characteristics documented in the 2nd column of Table 1. For this study, an aggregation function named Logic Scoring of Preference (LSP) [6] was used for all derived indicators. Particularly, the aggregation function specification is:

$$DI\ (r) = \left(w_1 * I_1^r + w_2 * I_2^r + \ldots + w_m * I_m^r\right)^{1/r}$$

where DI represents the derived indicator to be calculated and I_i are the values of the indicators of the immediate lower level, or grouping in the tree, in a range $0 < = I_i < = 100$; w_i represents the weights that establish the relative importance of the elements within a grouping and must comply with $w_1 + w_2 + \ldots + w_m = 1$, and $w_i > 0$ for $i = 1\ldots$ m; and r is a coefficient for LSP operators. These operators model different relationships among the inputs to produce an output. There are operators (op) of simultaneity or conjunction (operators C), replaceability or disjunction (operators D), and independence (operator A). LSP operators used for this work are shown in the 3rd column of Table 1.

Regarding weights (not shown in Table 1), for this work the dimension called *1.1.3 Naming Compliance* was considered the most relevant, so we set a weight of 0.50. The weight for each element can be seen in Annex VII at https://bit.ly/CCIS_Appendix.

Lastly, acceptability levels were defined for the derived indicators using the same three levels previously defined for the elementary indicators.

Table 2. Indirect metric specification to quantify the *"Compliance with the number of top-level class declarations per source file"* attribute coded 1.1.1.4 in Table 1

Metric Name: Percentage of valid top-level class declarations (%TLC)
Objective: Determine the percentage of valid top-level classes concerning the total of top-level classes in the source code to be measured. **Author:** Pablo Becker and Luis Olsina   **Version:** 1.0
Calculation Procedure **Formula:** $\%TLC = \left(\dfrac{\sum_{i=1}^{\#JF}\sum_{j=1}^{\#TLC} AVTLC_{ij}}{\sum_{i=1}^{\#JF}\#TLC_i}\right) * 100$
Scale: Numeric **Scale Type name:** Ratio   **Value Type:** Real   **Representation:** Continuous
Unit **Name:** Percentage   **Acronym:** %
Related Direct Metrics: AVTLC: Availability of a valid top-level class #TLC: Number of top-level classes #JF: Number of Java files

(A3) Implement Measurement and Evaluation: This activity involves using the metrics and indicators previously defined in A2 to produce metric and indicator values. Thus, the level of satisfaction achieved by the non-functional requirements can be subsequently analyzed.

For example, using the metric *"Percentage of valid top-level class declarations"*, the quantified value for the attribute *"Compliance with the number of top-level class declarations per source file"* is 33.33%. This derived measure is produced by applying the calculation procedure specified in Table 2.

Table 3. Direct metric specification related to the indirect metric *"Percentage of valid top-level class declarations"* (%TLC)

Metric Name: Availability of valid top-level class (**AVTLC**) **Quantified Attribute name:** Valid top-level class
Objective: Determine if a Java file defines a top-level class and the file name is equal to the name of this class **Author:** Pablo Becker and Luis Olsina   **Version:** 1.0

Measurement Procedure   **Type:** Objective
Specification:
`AVTLC = 0`
`if (class declaration defines a top-level class) and`
`    (class name is equal to the source file name)`
`        AVTLC = 1`
Notes:
1. A top-level class is any class that is not a nested class. A nested class is any class whose declaration occurs within the body of another class or interface.
2. The keyword "class" is the tag for any class declaration in Java.
3. Class name and source file name are case-sensitive

Scale: Numeric **Scale Type name:** Absolute   **Value Type:** Integer   **Representation:** Discrete
Unit **Name:** top-level class   **Acronym:** TLC

Table 4. Elementary indicator specification for the attribute *"Compliance with the number of top-level class declarations per source file"* (coded 1.1.1.4 in Table 1). Note: %TLC stands for the *"Percentage of valid top-level class declarations"* metric

Name: Performance Level of the Compliance with the number of top-level class declarations (PL_TLC)
Author: Pablo Becker and Luis Olsina   **Version:** 1.1

Elementary model
Specification: the mapping is PL_TLC = %TLC
  Decision criterion (3 acceptability levels):
    Name 1: ▪ Unsatisfactory;
      Range: [0; 60]
      Description: Indicates that corrective actions must be performed with high priority.
    Name 2: ◆ Marginal;
      Range: (60; 100]
      Description: Indicates that corrective actions should be performed.
    Name 3: ● Satisfactory;
      Range: [100; 100]
      Description: Indicates that corrective actions are not necessary since the attribute meets the required quality satisfaction level.

Scale: Numeric **Scale Type name:** Ratio   **Value Type:** Real   **Representation:** Continuous
Unit **Name:** Percentage   **Acronym:** %

For illustration purposes, Fig. 4 shows a screenshot where we can see that the "GUICalculator.java" file has three top-level classes (highlighted with yellow arrows): "GUICalculator", "calculatorFrame" and "calculatorpanel", but just the class "GUICalculator" is a valid top-level class since its name is equal to the file name. All the base

measures (used to calculate this and other derived measures) can be seen in Annex V of the document at https://bit.ly/CCIS_Appendix.

Once all the indirect metrics' values were obtained, the derived measures were used to calculate all the elementary indicators' values. In turn, these were used to calculate the derived indicators using the LSP aggregation function. Indicators' values both for elementary and derived indicators are shown in the 4th column of Table 1.

(A4.1) Design Analysis: In this activity, it was decided to include in the "Analysis Specification" document that the attributes would be classified using the decision criteria defined for the indicators according to Table 4.

Therefore, attributes that would fall into the Unsatisfactory range (■) should receive attention with the highest priority, followed by those that would fall into the Marginal range (◆). It is important to remark that a guide item reaches the Satisfactory level only if all the mapped attributes fall at the Satisfactory (●) level simultaneously.

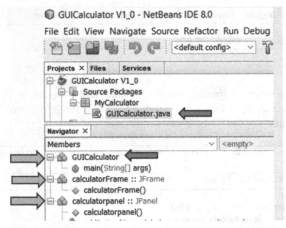

Fig. 4. Screenshot showing the "GUICalculator.java" file and its three top-level classes: "GUICalculator", "calculatorFrame" and "calculatorpanel"

(A4.2) Analyze Results: Following the criteria established in the "Analysis Specification" document, values marked with ■ and ◆ in the 4th column of Table 1 were analyzed, and improvements were recommended.

For example, the *"1.1.1 Source file structure compliance"* characteristic combines 2 attributes with a low level of performance. So, for the *"Spacing compliance between import sentences attribute"* (coded 1.1.1.3) which reached 0% ■ the recommendation was *"Blank lines between import sentences must be eliminated"*, and for the attribute coded 1.1.1.4 which reached 33.33% ■, the recommendation was *"Each top-level class must be defined in a file named as the class considering that names are case-sensitive"*.

Considering the *"1.1.3 Naming compliance"* characteristic, the recommendation for the *"Class naming compliance"* (1.1.3.1) –which got 60% ■- was: *"All class names must be in upper camel case"*.

Finally, the "*1.1.2 Formatting compliance*" characteristic has one attribute that falls at the Unsatisfactory level and three at the Marginal level. Regarding the attribute "*Compliance with the use of optional braces*" (coded 1.1.2.1) –which reached 9.09% ■- the recommendation was: "*Use braces with if, else, for, do, and while statements, even when the body is empty or contains only a single statement*". Similarly, recommendations for attributes that fall at the Marginal level (◆) were addressed.

This activity is where we can observe the importance of having several attributes that map to an item in the guide. For example, as shown in Fig. 3 and Table 1, the item "*3.3.3 Ordering and spacing*" has 3 associated attributes, of which 2 reached 100% ●("*Compliance with the ordering of types of imports*" and "*Spacing compliance between static and non-static import blocks*"). But one had 0% ■, namely "*Spacing compliance between import sentences*". As a consequence, these attributes allow us to judge exactly which parts of the guide item declaration are met, which are not, and at what level.

(A5) Design Changes: Using the "Recommendation Report" generated in A4.2, the changes to be made were designed. For example, to improve the level of satisfaction achieved by the attribute "*Class naming compliance*" (1.1.3.1), it was proposed that the classes named "calculatorFrame" and "calculatorpanel" were renamed as "CalculatorFrame" and "CalculatorPanel", respectively.

Additionally, to improve the attribute "*Compliance with the number of top-level class declarations per source file*" (1.1.1.4), it was proposed that the classes named "CalculatorFrame" and "CalculatorPanel" (which are top-level classes) be defined in separate source files, which should be called "CalculatorFrame.java" and "CalculatorPanel.java", respectively. All proposed changes were recorded in the "Improvement Plan" document.

(A6) Implement Changes: In this activity, the changes proposed in the "Improvement Plan" were carried out. For example, Fig. 5 shows that the new version (v1.1) of the code has renamed the old "calculatorFrame" and "calculatorpanel" classes as "CalculatorFrame" and "CalculatorPanel", respectively. Additionally, Fig. 5 shows that each top-level class was placed in a separate file, which has the same name as the class.

Figure 6 shows some changes made in the source code. For example, in the new code version, every variable declaration declares only one variable (see green box in Fig. 6.b versus Fig. 6.a), and lines do not exceed the limit of 100 characters (see red vertical line). These changes are related to improving the "*Compliance with the number of variables per declaration*" (coded 1.1.2.2) and "*Compliance with the maximum line size*" (coded 1.1.2.4) attributes, respectively.

The new version (v1.1) of the source code is available in Annex VIII at https://bit.ly/CCIS_Appendix.

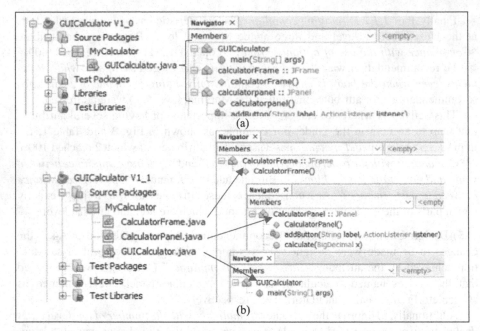

Fig. 5. Source code v1.0 (a) has three top-level classes placed in the "GUICalculator.java" file, while v1.1 (b) has three java files, each of them with a top-level class named as the file name

As shown in the GOCAMEC process of Fig. 2, once A5 and A6 activities were carried out, a re-evaluation must be performed to determine the level of satisfaction achieved by the new version of the source code after the changes. Thus, A3 and A4.2 activities were enacted again.

(A3) Implement Measurement and Evaluation: For this second cycle of measurement and evaluation, we use the same metrics and indicators on version 1.1 of the Java source code. The evaluation results are shown in the 5th column of Table 1.

(A4.2) Analyze Results: As can be seen in column 5th of Table 1, all the attributes reached 100% (●). As a consequence, the new version of the source code satisfies all the Google Java Style Guide items considered for this work. Since new cycles of change, re-evaluation, and analysis are not required because the goal was successfully achieved, the process is finished.

```
class calculatorFrame extends JFrame {
    public calculatorFrame() {
        calculatorpanel panel = new calculatorpanel();
        add(panel);
        pack();
        int w, h, sw, sh;
        w = 350;
        h = 350;
        GraphicsDevice gd = GraphicsEnvironment.getLocalGraphicsEnvironment().getDefaultScreenDevice();
        sw = gd.getDisplayMode().getWidth();
        sh = gd.getDisplayMode().getHeight();
        setBounds(sw / 2 - w / 2, sh / 2 - h / 2, w, h);
    }
}
```

(a)

```
class CalculatorFrame extends JFrame {
    public CalculatorFrame() {
        CalculatorPanel panel = new CalculatorPanel();
        add(panel);
        pack();
        int w;
        int h;
        int sw;
        int sh;
        w = 350;
        h = 350;
        GraphicsDevice gd = GraphicsEnvironment.getLocalGraphicsEnvironment()
                .getDefaultScreenDevice();
        sw = gd.getDisplayMode().getWidth();
        sh = gd.getDisplayMode().getHeight();
        setBounds(sw / 2 - w / 2, sh / 2 - h / 2, w, h);
    }
}
```

(b)

Fig. 6. Snippet of the source code v1.0 (a) versus v1.1 (b)

5 Related Work

Source coding conventions and guidelines that programmers must follow have been introduced since the mid-1970s. Kernighan and Plauger [11] were one of the early promoters of programming style conventions [15], who gave many hints on how to write readable code in the C language using real software examples.

For the Java programming language, one of the first promoters of coding style guidelines was Sun Microsystems in 1997 [17], and the work of Reddy in 2000 [16], who was also a member of this firm. After these contributions, the Google Java Style Guide [8] arose. We have chosen this document for the current practical case, as it has the main dimensions and items to make the code readable, as well as easy formatting and online access for students. Another recent initiative for Java coding conventions and practices is Bogdanovych and Trescak [3].

Many empirical studies have been done on different coding styles that influence code readability, such as those by Elish and Offutt [7], Lee *et al.* [12], dos Santos and Gerosa [5], to cite just a couple. Also, as mentioned in the Introduction Section, according to the survey conducted by Broekhuis, out of 102 responses from software professionals, only 3% did not use a coding style in their enterprise projects. These results may emphasize the role that the learning process in the academy should continue to play in these useful concepts and practices. For the practical case illustrated here, this was one of the learning goals established in the Software Engineering II subject.

As far as we know, what is not present in related works is the mapping of non-functional requirements in the form of dimensions and items of coding style guides with characteristics and attributes to build a quality model –as illustrated in Sect. 4- and supported by ontological concepts and relationships –as seen in Subsect. 2.2. This mapping allows more than one attribute to be assigned to a given item so that finer-grained elementary non-functional requirements can be quantified. Furthermore, it enables systematic understanding and improvement of source code compliance by using metrics, indicators, and refactoring as methods to implement measurement, evaluation, and change activities, all of which are integrated into the GOCAMEC strategy.

The use of the aforementioned concepts and practices was another of the learning goals and objectives set in Software Engineering II. For one of the learning objectives, the employment of tools and analyzers was not promoted as is done in other works. Students were expressly expected, for better understanding, to design metrics and indicators, and manually make code changes from recorded data of non-compliances in the GOCAMEC implementation activities.

6 Conclusions

In this work, we have illustrated the evaluation and improvement of a representative Java source code taking into account the compliance with internal quality attributes duly mapped to a subset of Google Java Style Guide items. To conduct this study, the GOCAMEC strategy was employed, which permits evaluators not only to know the current state of the entity in particular but also to design and implement changes that positively affect the quality of the new version of the target entity.

For the problem posed to the students in the framework of an undergraduate subject, the resulting Java source code was improved justifying the results of the GOCAMEC activities. Furthermore, the learning goals and objectives of the subject and the skills and capabilities expected after passing the course were also addressed.

As a final comment, we would like to emphasize that what is not present in the literature on related work is the mapping of quality requirements (compliance) in the form of characteristics and attributes with dimensions and items of coding style guides, such as illustrated throughout the manuscript.

As a work in progress, we are automating aspects of the presented approach, which is an assignment for an undergraduate thesis in Systems Engineering.

Acknowledgment. This line of research is supported partially by the Engineering School at UNLPam, Argentina, in the project coded 09/F079.

References

1. Becker, P., Olsina, L., Papa, M.F.: Strategy for improving source code compliance to a style guide. In: XXVIII Congreso Argentino de Ciencias de la Computación (CACIC'22), La Rioja, Argentina, pp. 312–321 (2022). http://sedici.unlp.edu.ar/handle/10915/149102

2. Becker, P., Tebes, G., Peppino, D., Olsina, L.: Applying an improving strategy that embeds functional and non-functional requirements concepts. J. Comput. Sci. Technol. **19**(2), 153–175 (2019). https://doi.org/10.24215/16666038.19.e15
3. Bogdanovych, A., Trescak, T.: Coding style and decomposition. In: Bogdanovych, A., Trescak, T. (eds.) Learning Java Programming in Clara's World, pp. 83–100. Springer International Publishing, Cham (2021). https://doi.org/10.1007/978-3-030-75542-3_4
4. Broekhuis, S.: The importance of coding styles within industries. In: 35th Twente Student Conference on IT (TScIT 35), pp. 1–8 (2021)
5. dos Santos, R.M., Gerosa, M.A.: Impacts of coding practices on readability. In: International Conference on Software Engineering, pp. 277–285 (2018)
6. Dujmovic, J.: Continuous preference logic for system evaluation. IEEE Trans. Fuzzy Syst. **15**(6), 1082–1099 (2007)
7. Elish, M., Offutt, J.: The adherence of open source java programmers to standard coding practices. In: 6th IASTED International Conference on Software Engineering and Applications, pp. 1–6 (2002)
8. Google Java Style Guide: https://google.github.io/styleguide/javaguide.html (2022). Last Accessed June 2022
9. ISO/IEC 9126-1: Software Engineering – Software Product Quality – Part 1: Quality Model, International Organization for Standardization, Geneva (2001)
10. ISO/IEC 25010: Systems and Software Engineering – Systems and software product Quality Requirements and Evaluation (SQuaRE) – System and software quality models (2011)
11. Kernighan, B.W., Plauger, P.J.: The Elements of Programming Style, 1st edn. McGraw-Hill, New York (1974)
12. Lee, T., Lee, J.B., In, H.P.: A study of different coding styles affecting code readability. Int. J. Softw. Eng. Appl. **7**(5), 413–422 (2013)
13. Olsina, L.: Applicability of a foundational ontology to semantically enrich the core and domain ontologies. In: 13th International Joint Conference on Knowledge Discovery, Knowledge Engineering and Knowledge Management, vol. 2, pp. 111–119. KEOD (Knowledge Engineering and Ontology Development), Portugal (2021)
14. Olsina, L., Becker, P.: Family of strategies for different evaluation purposes. In: XX CIbSE' 17, Published by Curran Associates, pp. 221–234 (2017)
15. Oman, P.W., Cook, C.R.: A paradigm for programming style research. ACM SIGPLAN Not. **23**(12), 69–78 (1988). https://doi.org/10.1145/57669.57675
16. Reddy, A.: Java™ coding style guide. Sun MicroSystems (2000)
17. Sun Microsystems: Java code conventions. https://www.oracle.com/technetwork/java/codeconventions-150003.pdf (1997)

Quality Management Systems and Blockchain in the 4.0 Era: A Literature Review

Kristian Petkoff Bankoff[✉][iD], Rocío Muñoz[iD], Ariel Pasini[iD], and Patricia Pesado[iD]

Computer Science Research Institute LIDI (III -LIDI), Facultad de Informática, Partner Center of the Scientific Research Agency of the Province of Buenos Aires (CIC), Universidad Nacional de La Plata, La Plata, Argentina
{kpb,rmunoz,apasini,ppesado}@lidi.info.unlp.edu.ar

Abstract. Quality Management Systems emerged in the 20th century, catalyzed by an awareness of quality in organizations, promoting cultural changes to improve not only the quality of the product or service provided, but also all processes and even people. The evolution of computing, along with quality models, helped the use of computer tools to assist in the implementation of Quality Management Systems. However, the rate of change in computing is higher than that of the improvement models used in Quality Management, which prompts reflection on the need to adopt new technologies in these systems as an integral part of them, not just in the context of the business. In this sense, the aim is to analyze publications that relate disruptive technologies, such as Blockchain, to well-established systems or models such as those defined in ISO 9001 in the face of the Fourth Industrial Revolution, and to contextualize those traditional Quality Management Systems in the path to Quality 4.0.

Keywords: Quality Management · Industry 4.0 · Quality 4.0 · Blockchain · Smart Contracts

1 Introduction

Quality Management Systems emerged in the 20th century, catalyzed by a growing awareness of the importance of quality in organizations. This led to cultural changes in order to promote improvement not only in the quality of the products or services provided, but also in all processes and even people.

The Total Quality Management (TQM) approach was based on the philosophy that quality should be a concern of the entire organization and that continuous improvement is essential to maintain long-term competitiveness. Japanese business leaders adopted this philosophy and applied it to all aspects of their operations, from design and production to supplier relationship management

P. Pesado (Ed.): CACIC 2022, CCIS 1778, pp. 140–155, 2023.
https://doi.org/10.1007/978-3-031-34147-2_10

and customer satisfaction. However, the idea of involving the entire organization, its resources, processes, products and services in the quality improvement is not always affordable, which is why other approaches, such as ISO 9001, ISO 14001, ISO/IEC 17025, ISO 45001 and other compatible standards, were defined. These approaches seek to ensure that certain processes, services and products met specific requirements set by customers, by authorities or by the organization itself.

The evolution of computing along with quality models led to the use of computer tools to assist the implementation of Quality Management Systems. However, the rate of change in computing is faster than that of the improvement models used in the late type of Quality Management [3], which prompts reflection on the need to adopt new technologies as an integral part of these systems, not just as a response to the business context. In this sense, we propose to analyze publications that link disruptive technologies such as Blockchain with well-established systems or models, such as those defined in ISO 9001, in the context of the Fourth Industrial Revolution, where the quality of products, services and process optimization is central.

The keyword combinations used in order to search for literature as further described in this article are an increasing number of publications from 2014. Table 1 shows the number of publications found in a preliminary search, while Fig. 1 illustrates this data in a graph[1]. As the main topic of the review is related to Quality, the Blockchain data series is excluded in Fig. 2 to get a detailed view of the stronger Quality-related publications found.

Table 1. Publications per year for each keyword combination

Year	QMS + Blockchain	QMS + Industry 4.0	Quality 4.0	Blockchain + Industry 4.0
2014	0	1	0	0
2015	0	2	1	1
2016	0	7	2	0
2017	3	12	3	6
2018	4	17	3	29
2019	19	30	6	100
2020	18	61	16	164
2021	17	69	29	232
2022	26	94	68	327
2023[1]	2	15	9	48

[1]Until February 16th.

This paper is an extension of "Sistemas de Gestión de Calidad y Blockchain en la era de la Industria 4.0: una revisión de literatura" [27] published in Argentine Congress of Computer Science 2022 (CACIC 2022). The new version incorporates a literature review on Quality 4.0 and places the conclusions of the original paper in the context of TQM and Quality 4.0.

---

[1] 2023 year year data is excluded to avoid biased representation.

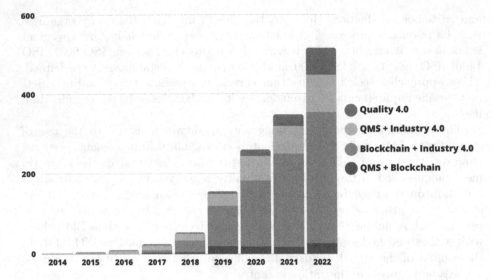

Fig. 1. Number of publications between 2014 and 2022 on this article topics

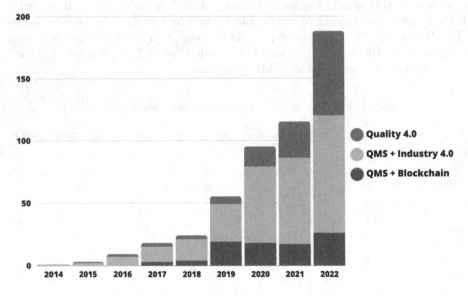

Fig. 2. Number of publications between 2014 and 2022 on Quality topics

2   Context

There are different definitions of *quality* that are focused on concepts such as compliance with requirements, meeting expectations, and suitability for use. In the search of ensuring the quality of its products and services, various Quality Management currents have emerged throughout the 20th century, driven by the so-called quality gurus [28].

The Total Quality Management (TQM) approach emerged in the 1950 s s in Japan, in the context of the country's economic reconstruction following World War II. TQM was developed by Japanese business leaders, such as W. Edwards Deming and Joseph Juran, who introduced new quality management techniques and tools in the Japanese industry. The success of Japanese companies in the 1970 s s and 1980 s,s, such as Toyota, Sony, and Honda, brought increasing global attention to the TQM approach. In the United States, TQM became a popular strategy for improving quality and business competitiveness in the 1980s s and 1990s s [15].

Many key aspects of Quality Management that are reflected in the ISO 9001 standard model involve defining a quality policy, planning, control, assurance, and improvement. A Quality Management System based on ISO 9001 consists of a set of strategic definitions, products, services, customers, and processes necessary for the production of goods and services that are expected to satisfy the customer. These processes (in addition to products) are measured, controlled, and improved by the use of tools such as the PDCA cycle (plan, do, check, act). This model is based on the premise that by applying quality processes, quality products are generated, and that organizations must constantly seek improvement to optimize their productive processes in pursuit of quality. One of the greatest difficulties in implementing a Quality Management System is the effort to generate and maintain a comprehensive set of documents, procedures, and records about its processes and their execution history. However, an organization can only improve and ensure quality if it is first known by itself, and this is only achieved through the availability of data and information.

2.1   Industry 4.0

The concept of Industry 4.0, or the Fourth Industrial Revolution, was first mentioned in Germany in 2011 [35] and represents how the integration of hardware, software, and network resources changes the way industries carry out their operations, producing smart factories rather than just computer-assisted processes. The main features of production modes and organizations within this revolution are global cooperation, permanent exchange of large amounts of data, automatic generation of summaries and information, use of sensors and other digital resources to record all activities more and better. As a result of the integration of digital tools into the entire production, control, and decision-making process, cost-saving benefits are obtained that drive industries 4.0: reduction of operational costs, optimization of waste, optimization of communication among all stakeholders, involvement of customers and obtaining products with higher functionality and quality.

2.2   Quality 4.0

Quality 4.0 is a term that refers to the application of Industry 4.0 technologies and principles to enhance and transform quality management. It involves the integration of digital technologies such as Internet of Things (IoT), Big Data

Analytics, Artificial Intelligence (AI), and Cloud Computing into Quality Management Systems [34].

The term Quality 4.0 emerged from a 2015 report by consulting firm Deloitte entitled "Industry 4.0 and the Future of Quality Management". The report highlighted the potential benefits of integrating Industry 4.0 technologies into quality management, including improved quality and productivity, reduced costs, and enhanced customer satisfaction [12].

Applications of Quality 4.0 include improving efficiency in Quality Management through automation, real-time monitoring, and predictive analysis. It can also enable greater customization of products and services to meet specific customer needs and desires. Additionally, Quality 4.0 can help businesses reduce quality risks, improve decision-making, and increase operational efficiency [7].

2.3   Blockchain

Blockchain is a decentralized database technology that provides a mechanism for immutability guarantee and the absence of a central entity for decision-making in data operations. This is achieved through consensus algorithms, which establish protocols for participating nodes to autonomously decide when a data block is valid and when it is not. Decentralization and immutability (guaranteed by asymmetric cryptography) have led to some successful implementations, especially in the banking and finance business. Over time, it has given way to more businesses in which tools based on this technology make a decisive contribution, even to the extent of suggesting that in a certain degree it is a catalyst for a revolution in computing. One of the most relevant tools based on Blockchain is Smart Contracts. These contracts are software applications programmed to execute predefined actions when agreed conditions are met by two entities or nodes, without the need to trust between them, recording everything in a database that guarantees immutability. It is interesting to note that the record is both the evidence that allows establishing that the conditions are met and the contract itself. The contract, therefore, cannot be altered by neither of the parties or by third parties as it would violate one of the principles of the network. In this sense, this technology, which can be fed by data from other hardware, software, or network pieces, is aligned with principles of process optimization, business and integration of digital tools in the core of the most diverse businesses.

3   Literature Review

In this section, we present the objectives and criteria that were used to carry out the search. It is aimed at establishing connections between pairs of topics to ultimately link the concepts of ISO 9001-based Quality Management Systems, Blockchain, and Industry 4.0 to each other, considering the lack of publications that address this linkage.

Also, an extension of the previous research is proposed so as to compare the Quality Management Systems and the Quality 4.0 concept.

3.1   Goals

The main objective of this work is to verify if there exist, within the literature of each of the main topics, publications from which a network can be established and in the same way it links Quality Management Systems (or other similar systems, such as environmental management systems) with Industry 4.0 and Blockchain technology, with a view to adapting the former to these new industrial and IT trends. To organize the research, this objective was divided into the following sub-objectives:

- To find relationships between publications to determine if ISO 9001-based Management Systems are compatible or adaptable to Industry 4.0 processes.
- To analyze the situation of Quality Management Systems in the context of the Fourth Industrial Revolution.
- To determine if there are other lines of research related to the implementation of Quality Management Systems with Blockchain technology.
- To contextualize the ISO 9001-based management systems with respect to Quality 4.0 and Industry 4.0.

3.2   Search Criteria

The search criteria used for the initial literature review, attached to the first three specified goals were as follows: to collect publications related to quality management, Industry 4.0 and Blockchain, a search was conducted on the Scopus and ResearchGate engines using the expressions "quality management" AND blockchain, "quality management" AND 4.0 AND (industries OR industry), blockchain AND 4.0 AND (industries OR industry). The results were subject to a preliminary analysis based on their abstract to filter those better aligned with the first three goals of the research.

To extend the review to the fourth goal a new search using the "quality management" AND 4.0 (industries OR industry) was carried out, after which a selection of articles aligned to the Quality 4.0 concept were chosen.

3.3   Scope

The scope of the first review was limited to publications related to Quality Management Systems with compatible models or based on the ISO 9001, ISO 14001, ISO/IEC 17025, ISO 45001 standards; also to experiences of management system application in industries, the impact of digitization and the topic of Industry 4.0 on the processes of organizations, whether they have implemented management systems or not. On the other hand, a selection was made to get publications related to Blockchain or Smart Contracts that have a relationship with key aspects of a management system, such as evidence management, versioning and process control.

The first search was carried out between December 2021 and February 2022, and articles were filtered mixing criteria that have the best interrelation among the three proposed topics and that are significantly recent articles. The lack of publications linking the entire theme addressed is seen as a result of the searches even before the decision was made to limit the scope of the first review.

The second search was performed in February 2023 resulting in a list of publications containing some of the filtered ones in the first review but also many published after February 2022. From these results, publications concerning to Quality 4.0 were selected.

3.4 Identified Publications

Table 2 presents the 26 publications collected with their categorization according to the topics that are addressed within the interest of the initial review. Table 3 presents the 6 publications selected for the Quality Management Systems in Quality 4.0 context review.

Table 2. Identified publications for first review

#	Title	B	I4.0	Q
1	"Data quality certification using ISO/IEC 25012: Industrial experiences" [9]			X
2	"The Computerized Maintenance Management System an Essential Tool for World Class Maintenance" [37]			X
3	"A process approach to ISO/IEC 17025 in the implementation of a quality management system in testing laboratories" [14]			X
4	"A proposal of model for a quality management system in research testing laboratories" [23]			X
5	"ISO 9001:2015 Adoption: A Multi-Country Empirical Research" [8]			X
6	"Proposal for a maintenance management system in industrial environments based on ISO 9001 and ISO 14001 standards" [6]			X
7	"Quality of the ISO 9000 series of standards-perceptions of quality management experts" [32]			X
8	"Recertification of a Quality Management System based on ISO 9001 - Is it a must for a modern manufacturing company?" [24]			X
9	"System proposal for implementation of risk management in the context of ISO/IEC 17025" [36]			X
10	"System quality and security certification in seven weeks: A multi-case study in Spanish SMEs" [13]			X
11	"Blockchain Enabled Quality Management in Short Food Supply Chains" [5]	X		X
12	"Evidence Management System Using Blockchain and Distributed File System (IPFS)" [17]	X		X
13	"Are QM models aligned with Industry 4.0? A perspective on current practices" [3]		X	X
14	"Procedure for Defining the System of Objectives in the Initial Phase of an Industry 4.0 Project Focusing on Intelligent Quality Control Systems" [30]		X	X
15	"Quality Culture of Manufacturing Enterprises: A Possible Way to Adaptation to Industry 4.0" [11]		X	X
16	"Quality management in the 21st century enterprises: Research pathway towards Industry 4.0" [16]		X	X
17	"Re-Engineering of Logistics Business Processes Influenced by the Digitalization" [10]		X	
18	"Blockchain Enterprise: Use Cases on Multiple Industries" [25]	X	X	
19	"Blockchain Technology: A Fundamental Overview" [18]	X	X	
20	"Blockchain Technology Applications for Next Generation" [31]	X	X	
21	"EPS-ledger: Blockchain hyperledger sawtooth-enabled distributed power systems chain of operation and control node privacy and security" [19]	X	X	
22	"Significance of Blockchain Technologies in Industry" [26]	X	X	
23	"Blockchain. La revolución industrial de internet" [29]	X	X	
24	Construction of Blockchain Technology Audit System [20]	X		
25	"Decentralized collaborative business process execution using blockchain" [22]	X		
26	"A blockchain-based integrated document management framework for construction applications" [1]	X		

4   Analysis

In this section results from analyzing the publications are shown in two stages, corresponding respectively to the initial review and the extended one.

4.1   First Search

In Fig. 3 the list of items selected to review, related to ISO 9001-based Quality Management Systems, Blockchain and Industry 4.0, is shown, allowing visualization of the location of each publication in the context of the proposed dimensions and the level of cohesion between the terms. To ease the visualization, numbers referring to rows in Table 2 are used.

Analysis. Upon analyzing the relevant articles, it was found that 15% of the selected publications directly responded to the main topics of Quality and Industry 4.0, 24% coincided in the key elements of Blockchain and Industry 4.0, and 8% directly related Blockchain with Quality Management. From the selected literature that addresses individual topics, there are relationships in the text that allow establishing links between Blockchain and Quality Management (8%) and between Quality and Industry 4.0 (8%).

It is also observed that the searches performed did not produce results that directly link to the three topics. However, by analyzing the articles based on a reading of the body of the posts and particularly the conclusions and discussions posed in them, a network of concepts that connect to the searched topics can be established. To start, in [3] concludes that Quality Management as conceived in the 20th century naturally does not contain the fundamentals of Industry 4.0 and that a substantial adaptation incorporating new technologies is necessary in order to be carried out facing the digital industries of the 21st century, as these produce changes and intelligent processes that are faster than today's traditional quality management methods. Some aspects to consider when integrating Quality Management with a business model aligned with Industry 4.0 is quality control in outsourcing and supply chain processes that integrate different organizations, so as to ensure optimization of costs, resource use, and quality itself. In [16], future research questions are proposed, such as: what changes are necessary in Quality Management to engage human development with emerging technologies such as Blockchain, IoT, Big Data, smart supply chains; how to manage outsourcing and integration of multi-organizational processes in the era of Industry 4.0; how to develop quality exchanges with the support of sophisticated methods for smart supply chains. It is of great interest to this analysis to emphasize that resource acquisition is one of the key aspects that must be attended to when implementing a Quality Management System.

Table 3. Identified publications for the extended review

#	Title
Q4-1	"Integrating quality management systems (TQM) in the digital age of intelligent transportation systems industry 4.0" [2]
Q4-2	"Industry 4.0 as a key enabler toward successful implementation of total quality management practices" [33]
Q4-3	"A quality 4.0 assurance framework for the higher education institutes" [21]
Q4-4	"Developing a Quality 4.0 Implementation Framework and Evaluating the Maturity Levels of Industries in Developing Countries" [38]
Q4-5	"Classification of Industry 4.0 for Total Quality Management: A Review" [4]
Q4-6	"Unleashing the Potential of the TQM and Industry 4.0 to Achieve Sustainability Performance in the Context of a Developing Country" [34]

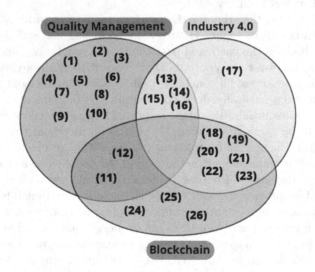

Fig. 3. Relationship between analyzed articles in the first review

The ISO 9001 standard for the implementation of Quality Management Systems can be applied to any type of organization, regardless of the type of industry it operates in. Currently, there are over one million companies and institutions certified under the ISO 9001 standard. Many organizations have started to view Quality Management Systems not only as a mechanism to achieve organizational performance but also as a starting point for the construction of more complex integrated production systems. The implementation of Quality Management Systems improves the predictability of process behavior and, therefore, improves the efficiency of organizations and optimizes resource use [24], which coincides with fundamental principles of Industry 4.0. Among the most highlighted aspects during a search presented in [24] it can be found the reduction of costs and elimination of records that affect work efficiency without providing relevant information to the processes in order to optimize them.

Other management systems are compatible with ISO 9001 without being specifically for quality, as in recent years many of the models have been adapted to have a standardized document body. One of these cases are environmental management systems defined in the ISO 14000 family. The control of the materials used is a key aspect for environmental management system certification; Castillo-Martinez et al. in [6] propose a system architecture that optimizes the exchange of information between different areas through the adoption of tools and technology that automate these processes, emphasizing the recording of each use of the different materials and the tracking of their life cycle. Although the main objectivo of environmental management systems is to improve environmental practices, cost optimization, especially in waste management, is within their responsibilities and is consistent with Industry 4.0.

The topic of Blockchain arises when analyzing the requirements of Quality Management Systems, which rely on evidence registration to support decision-making and monitoring of improvement or correction actions during maintenance. Audits also control the proper execution of pre-defined procedures and the integrity of the corresponding record, which are generally well covered by tools implemented on Blockchain [1,17]. On the other hand, Blockchain technology is gaining more and more ground in various use cases, and therefore, ensuring the quality of an organization whose processes are supported by this technology would catalyze a migration of Quality Management Systems towards Blockchain technologies such as Smart Contracts [19,31].

4.2 Quality Management in Quality 4.0 Context

A relationship between Quality Management Systems, such as those based on ISO 9001, and Industry 4.0 emerges when the concept of Quality 4.0 is considered. Quality 4.0 is a set of practices that aim to integrate the Industry 4.0 tools as well as to adapt Quality Management principles to a fully digitalized context, taking the whole Total Quality Management components [34]; Saha et al. explore the potential benefits of combining TQM and Industry 4.0 for enhancing organizational sustainability performance. The authors suggest that the integration of TQM and Industry 4.0 can lead to more effective resource utilization, improved quality control processes, and increased customer satisfaction. However, the successful implementation of Industry 4.0 requires top management involvement, collaboration with external stakeholders, and a flexible organizational structure.

While there are challenges to adopt Industry 4.0, the authors suggest that its characteristics offer a solid foundation for supporting business success. Overall, the authors conclude that the adoption of Industry 4.0 positively impacts TQM implementation and contributes to enhance organizational sustainability performance.

A classification of Industry 4.0 for TQM is proposed by Baran and Korkusuz Polat in in [4] using the Smart Contracts, Big Data, Cloud Computing, Blockchain and Cyber-phisical Systems as keys among several other. In particular, Smart Contracts enable the creation of production ecosystems driven by intelligent systems with autonomous features such as automatic evidence decision-making. Also, Blockchain can assist ensuring the traceability of quality improvement process, so businesses can identify any coordination problems and take corrective action. One of the reasons of the relation being stronger between Industry 4.0 and TQM appears to be the fact that the later is a superset of practices for the organization to achieve continuous improvement compromising the whole human resources, customers, processes, services, products and tools to it in order to gain cost and resource efficiency and reduce waste, both of which are key principles to the Fourth Industry Revolution. On the other hand, TQM suggests paths to achieve its goals but does not explicitly define concrete procedures while ISO 9000 family (and compatible ISO standards) set the requirements to get a working Quality Management System not focusing in the digitalization but leaving freedom to the organization to implement it [2].

On the other hand, Quality 4.0 can be decomposed in eleven axis [21,38] as shown in Fig. 4, each of one is taken into analysis so as to propose an implementation of TQM using Industry 4.0 tools. Lodi et al. propose the use of autonomous software to monitor changes to regulatory bodies published in government (or any other authority) repositories or websites so as to improve the compliance of the TQM automatically [21]. Also Zulqarnain, Wasif, and Iqbal analyze the challenges in developing countries when it comes to integrate Industry 4.0 technology due to the lack of infrastructure, skilled human resources, as well as cultural, economic, politic, and social treats. Overall, in [38] the authors conclude that Quality 4.0 is not well developed neither in small organizations nor in big enterprises in Pakistan. Furthermore, compliance in one axis of Quality 4.0 can lead to improvements on other dimensions, at the same time that it is observed that most difficult implementations arise at compliance, app development, scalability and culture axis. In Fig. 4 the relationship between the so called Quality 3.0 approach (implemented as traditional well-known Quality Management Systems like ISO 9001) is shown based on [38]. Finally, Sader, Husti, and Daróczi expose several benefits of Industry 4.0 in quality assurance and quality control among other QMS principles. In [33] the authors highlight that an Industry 4.0 integrated production system can ensure high-quality products by defining and eliminating root causes of production defects, making instant early action to avoid defects and production failure, optimizing processes, and minimizing rework and scrap. It further notes that intelligent quality control systems are replacing traditional quality control techniques, leading to instant exclusion of defective products and minimizing the cost of quality. Furthermore, the text emphasizes that Industry 4.0 can aid evidence-based decision making by providing accurate data and information. It notes that Industry 4.0 can improve relationship management with business partners by optimizing the production supply chain and ensuring effective communication and collaboration tools between stakeholders.

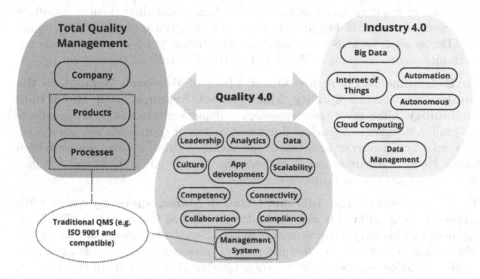

Fig. 4. Quality Management in the TQM-Quality 4.0-Industry 4.0 context

5   Conclusions

A number of articles related to the terms Blockchain, Industry 4.0, and Quality Management were identified and retrieved by conducting searches with different combinations of theme pairs. Once organized according to the theme in an order that allows moving from quality to Blockchain through coincidences in the Industry 4.0 dimension, points of contact between the three themes were established that were not evident at first glance or through the keywords. Quality is both a result and a requirement of digital industries, and at the same time, Blockchain technology (such as through Smart Contracts) is an increasingly present tool in Industry 4.0. Therefore, with regard to the objectives outlined, we can conclude the following:

To Find Relationships Between Publications to Determine if ISO 9001-Based Management Systems are compatible or adaptable to Industry 4.0 processes. Quality Management Systems are adaptable to Industry 4.0 but should go through a transformation to allow better resilience against changes driven by digital evolution. In this sense, Quality Management Systems could experience their own revolution in the context of the Fourth Industry Revolution.

To Analyze the Situation of Quality Management Systems in the Context of the Fourth Industrial Revolution. Quality Management Systems were conceived as tools that ensured the customer that the product supplied would meet their expectations even before evaluating it. To some extent, they worked as a commercial tool; in the context of the Fourth Industrial Revolution, Quality Management Systems are at risk of being relegated by the changes promoted by the digitization of industries, which would allow them to introduce improvements in other key aspects such as cost optimization. However, Quality Management Systems are compatible with Industry 4.0 because they do not introduce any restrictions to the object or the objectives of the system.

To Determine if There are Other Lines of Research Related to the Implementation of Quality Management Systems with Blockchain technology. Although there are research or implementations of some key aspects of Quality Management (such as document control or controlled evidence recording), no other authors or institutions specifically addressing this topic have been found. However, the relationship between the relevant publications makes it possible to categorize it as future research.

To Contextualize the ISO 9001-Based Management Systems with Respect to Quality 4.0 and Industry 4.0 It was found that Quality Management and Industry 4.0 are strongly linked through the concept of Quality 4.0, which aims to introduce key features such as interconnection, big data and integration to follow the principles of Total Quality Management. In this context, Quality Management Systems, based on ISO 9000 family and other compatible standards (such as ISO 14000, ISO/IEC 17025, etc.), take a set of TQM principles and define a way to certify the compliance to customer requirements, processes definition and quality policy. This principles correspond to the Management System axis of Quality 4.0.

References

1. A blockchain-based integrated document management framework for construction applications. Automation in Construction, **133** 104001, (2022). ISSN 0926–5805. https://doi.org/10.1016/j.autcon.2021.104001
2. Akhmatova, M.S., Deniskina, A., Akhmatova, D.M., Prykina, L.: Integrating quality management systems (tqm) in the digital age of intelligent transportation systems industry 4.0. volume 63, pp. 1512–1520 (2022). https://doi.org/10.1016/j.trpro.2022.06.163
3. Asif, M.: Are qm models aligned with industry 4.0? a perspective on current practices. J. Cleaner Prod. **258**, 120820 (2020). ISSN 0959–6526. https://doi.org/10.1016/j.jclepro.2020.120820
4. Baran, E., Korkusuz Polat, T.: Classification of industry 4.0 for total quality management: A review. Sustainability **14** (6), 2022. ISSN 2071–1050. https://doi.org/10.3390/su14063329.URL https://www.mdpi.com/2071-1050/14/6/3329
5. Burgess, P., Sunmola, F.,Wertheim-Heck, S.: Blockchain enabled quality management in short food supply chains. Procedia Comput. Sci. **200**, 904–913 (2022). https://doi.org/10.1016/j.procs.2022.01.288

6. Burgess, P., Sunmola, F., Wertheim-Heck, S.: Proposal for a maintenance management system in industrial environments based on iso 9001 and iso 14001 standards. Comput. Stand. Interfaces **73**, 904–913 (2021)
7. Chiarini, A., Kumar, M.: What is quality 4.0? an exploratory sequential mixed methods study of italian manufacturing companies. Int. J. Prod. Res. **60**(16), 4890–4910 (2022). https://doi.org/10.1080/00207543.2021.1942285
8. da Fonseca, L.M.C.M., Domingues, J.P., Machado, P.B., Harder, D.: Iso 9001:2015 adoption: A multi-country empirical research. J. Indust. Eng. Manage. **12**(1), 27–50 (2019)
9. Data quality certification using iso/iec 25012: Industrial experiences. J. Syst. Softw. **176**, 110938 (2021). ISSN 0164–1212. https://doi.org/10.1016/j.jss.2021.110938
10. Dubolazov, V., Tayushev, S., Gabdrakhmanova, I., Simakova, Z., Leicht, O.: Re-engineering of logistics business processes influenced by the digitalization. In: 14th International Scientific Conference on Precision Agriculture and Agricultural Machinery Industry, 246, pp. 539–547 (2021)
11. Durana, P., Kral, P., Stehel, V., Lazaroiu, G., Sroka, W.: Quality culture of manufacturing enterprises: A possible way to adaptation to industry 4.0. Social Sci. **8**(4), 124 2019. ISSN 2076–0760. https://doi.org/10.3390/socsci8040124. https://www.mdpi.com/2076-0760/8/4/124
12. ATCC Finance. Industry 4.0 challenges and solutions for the digital transformation and use of exponential technologies. Finance, audit tax consulting corporate: Zurich, Swiss, pp. 1–12 (2015)
13. Gaitero, D., Genero, M., Piattini, M.: System quality and security certification in seven weeks: a multi-case study in spanish smes. J. Syst. Softw. **178**(110960), 8 (2021)
14. Grochau, I.H., ten Caten, C.S.: A process approach to iso/iec 17025 in the implementation of a quality management system in testing laboratories. Accred. Qual. Assur. **17**, 519–527 (2012)
15. Gryna, F.M., Juran, J.M.: Quality Planning and Analysis: From Product Development Through Use. McGraw-Hill series in industrial engineering and management science. McGraw-Hill, 2001. ISBN 9780070393684. https://books.google.com.ar/books?id=xjUfAQAAIAAJ
16. AGunasekaran, A., Subramanian, N., Ngai, W.T.E.: Quality management in the 21st century enterprises: Research pathway towards industry 4.0. Int. J. Prod. Econ. **207**, 125–129 2019. ISSN 0925–5273. https://doi.org/10.1016/j.ijpe.2018.09.005.URL https://www.sciencedirect.com/science/article/pii/S092552731830375X
17. Jamulkar, S., Chandrakar, P., Ali, R., Agrawal, A., Tiwari, K.: Evidence management system using blockchain and distributed file system (ipfs). In: International Conference on Machine Learning and Big Data Analytics, pp. 337–359 (2021)
18. aradat, A., Ali, O., AlAhmad, A.: Blockchain Technology: A Fundamental Overview, pages 1–24. Springer Singapore, Singapore, 2022. ISBN 978-981-16-6301-7. https://doi.org/10.1007/978-981-16-6301-7_1
19. Khan, A.A. et al.: Eps-ledger: Blockchain hyperledger sawtooth-enabled distributed power systems chain of operation and control node privacy and security. Electronics (Switzerland), **10**(19), 2395 (2021)
20. Liu, Q.: Construction of Blockchain Technology Audit System. In: Macintyre, J., Zhao, J., Ma, X. (eds.) SPIoT 2021. LNDECT, vol. 97, pp. 523–529. Springer, Cham (2022). https://doi.org/10.1007/978-3-030-89508-2_67
21. Lodi, S., Shaikh, A., Wasif, M., Tufail, M., Butt, F.: A quality 4.0 assurance framework for the higher education institutes. vol. 2022-June, pp. 725–732, 2022. https://doi.org/10.4995/HEAd22.2022.14032

22. Loukil, F., Boukadi, K., Abed, M., Ghedira-Guegan, C.: Decentralized collaborative business process execution using blockchain. World Wide Web **24**(5), 1645–1663 (2021)
23. Marinez-Perales, S., Ortiz-Marcos, I., Ruiz, J.J.: A proposal of model for a quality management system in research testing laboratories. Accr. Qual. Assur. **26**, 237–248 (2021)
24. Midor, K., Wilkowski, G.: Recertification of a quality management system based on iso 9001 - is it a must for a modern manufacturing company? Prod. Eng. Archives **27**, 217–222 (2021). https://doi.org/10.30657/pea.2021.27.29
25. Narayanaswamy, T., Karthika, P., Balasubramanian, K.: Blockchain Enterprise: Use Cases on Multiple Industries, pp. 125–137. Springer International Publishing, Cham, 2022. ISBN 978-3-030-76216-2. https://doi.org/10.1007/978-3-030-76216-2_8
26. Lakshmi Patibandla, R.S.M., Vejendla, L.N.: Significance of Blockchain Technologies in Industry, chapter Signifcance of Blockchain Technologies in Industry, pp. 19–31. Springer Science and Business Media Deutschland GmbH (2022)
27. Petkoff Bankoff, K., Muñoz, R., Pasini, A.: Sistemas de Gestión de Calidad y Blockchain en la era de la Industria 4.0: una revisión de literatura, pp. 342–353. 2022. ISBN 978-987-1364-31-2
28. Velthuis, M.G.P., Rubio, F.O.G., Muñoz-Reja, I.C.: Calidad de Sistemas Informáticos, chapter 1. Alfaomega Grupo Editor, 2007. ISBN 84-7897-734-1
29. Preukschat, A., et al.: Blockchain. La revolución industrial de internet. Centro Libros PAPF, S. L. U., Barcelona, Spain, 2017. ISBN 978-84-9875-448-3
30. Procedure for Defining the System of Objectives in the Initial Phase of an Industry 4.0 Project Focusing on Intelligent Quality Control Systems, volume 52, pp. 262–267 (2016). https://doi.org/10.1016/j.procir.2016.07.067.The Sixth International Conference on Changeable, Agile, Reconfigurable and Virtual Production (CARV2016)
31. Puri, N., Garg, V., Agrawal, R.: Blockchain Technology Applications for Next Generation, chapter Blockchain Technology Applications for Next Generation, pp. 53–73. Springer Science and Business Media Deutschland GmbH (2022)
32. Rogala, P., Wawak, S.: Quality of the iso 9000 series of standards-perceptions of quality management experts. Int. J. Qual. Serv. Sci. 509–525 (2021)
33. Sader, S., Husti, I., Daróczi, M.: Industry 4.0 as a key enabler toward successful implementation of total quality management practices. Periodica Polytechnica Social and Management Sciences, **27**(2), 131–140, 2019. https://doi.org/10.3311/PPso.12675
34. Saha, P., Talapatra, S., Belal, B., Jackson, V.: Unleashing the potential of the tqm and industry 4.0 to achieve sustainability performance in the context of a developing country. Global Journal of Flexible Systems Management, **23**(4), 495–513 (2022). https://doi.org/10.1007/s40171-022-00316-x
35. Schwab, K.: The Fourth Industrial Revolution, chapter 1. World Economic Forum, 2016. ISBN 978-84-9992-699-5
36. da Silva, F.R., Grochau, I.H., Veit, H.M.: System proposal for implementation of risk management in the context of iso/iec 17025. Accr. Qual. Assur. **26**, 271–278 (2021)
37. Wienker, M., Henderson, K., Volkerts, J.: The computerized maintenance management system an essential tool for world class maintenance. Procedia Engineering, **138**, 413–420 (2016.) ISSN 1877-7058. https://doi.org/10.1016/j.proeng.2016.02.100. https://www.sciencedirect.com/science/article/pii/

S1877705816004641. SYMPHOS 2015 - 3rd International Symposium on Innovation and Technology in the Phosphate Industry
38. Zulqarnain, A., Wasif, M., Iqbal, S.A.: Developing a quality 4.0 implementation framework and evaluating the maturity levels of industries in developing countries. Sustainability **14**(18), 2022. ISSN 2071–1050. https://doi.org/10.3390/su141811298. https://www.mdpi.com/2071-1050/14/18/11298

Databases and Data Mining

Boosting the Permutation Index for Similarity Searching Using an Eclectic Approach

Karina Figueroa[1](✉)(iD), Antonio Camarena-Ibarrola[1](iD), Rodrigo Paredes[3](iD),
Nora Reyes[2](iD), and Braulio Ramses Hernández Martínez[1]

[1] Universidad Michoacana, Morelia, Mexico
{karina.figueroa,antonio.camarena,1578615h}@umich.mx
[2] Universidad de San Luis, San Luis, Argentina
nreyes@unsl.edu.ar
[3] Universidad de Talca, Talca, Chile
raparede@utalca.cl

Abstract. The permutation index is one of the best strategies for non-exact similarity searching. However, it is still possible to improve its remarkable performance. Hence, we propose boosting it by using an eclectic strategy that combines some interesting ideas from both pivot- and permutant-based indexes. We mix together (*i*) a convenient way of reducing the permutation length (where the clipped permutations might have different sizes), (*ii*) a permutation similarity measure adjusted for this permutation clipping, and (*iii*) the use of the closest permutant to each object as its pivot. This strategy allows us to both shrink the size and increase the discriminability of the permutation index in order to reduce even more the number of distance computations while maintaining the answer quality.

The performance of our proposal is tested using three well known real-world databases. As we experimentally show, the performance is improved by reducing more than 30% of the number of distance evaluations needed to solve approximate similarity queries on these real-world datasets.

Keywords: Similariy search · Permutant-based index · Pivot-based index · Permutation similarity measure

1 Introduction

Most database applications need to perform searches. Furthermore, today due to the high availability of multimedia data (such as, datasets of free text documents, images, audios, or videos, among others) many database applications must perform meaningful searches on these types of unstructured data. For this reason, similarity searches have become the more notable operation on these datasets

P. Pesado (Ed.): CACIC 2022, CCIS 1778, pp. 159–174, 2023.
https://doi.org/10.1007/978-3-031-34147-2_11

because for this kind of data two elements are never exactly the same, unless they were digital copies of each other. Two objects could be considered similar depending on the particular problem domain. In general, in order to capture the richness of the data, similarity is modeled and defined by domain experts as a function which is usually expensive to calculate, in terms of the number of operations (arithmetic, I/O, etc.) that are required to obtain it. The goal of any similarity search algorithm is to answer queries as quickly as possible, thus we try to reduce the amount of times we compute the similarity between two objects. Then, a direct way to achieve efficiency is by using an auxiliary index to reduce the number of distance computations needed for answering a query.

Any similarity search problem can be modeled as a metric space [6]. Formally, a metric space is a pair $(\mathbb{U}, d)$ which is composed of a universe of possible objects $\mathbb{U}$ and a distance function d, that allows us to compare any pair of objects from $\mathbb{U}$. Furthermore, the database will be any subset $\mathbb{X}$ of universe elements $(\mathbb{X} \subseteq \mathbb{U})$ whose elements are of interest. Let be n the cardinality of the database $\mathbb{X}$ ($n = |\mathbb{X}|$). As it is aforementioned, we assume that the function d is expensive to compute. Therefore, one of our goals is to minimize the use of d at answering queries.

The most known kinds of similarity searches are *range* and *K-nearest-neighbor* queries. On the one hand, Range queries retrieve all the dataset elements whose distance to a given query element q is lower than or equal to the given radius r. We denote this kind of query as $R(q, r)$. On the other hand, K-nearest-neighbor queries, denoted as $NN_K(q)$, retrieve K dataset elements that are the K most similar elements to the given query element q. Note that the answer set for a range query is unique, while it could vary in case of ties for the K-nearest neighbor query. Formally, these two kinds of queries can be defined as:

- $R(q, r) = \{x \in S \ , \ d(x, q) \leq r\}$.
- $NN_K(q) \subseteq \mathbb{U}$ and $|NN_K(q)| = k$ and $\forall x \in NN_K(q), y \in \mathbb{U} - NN_K(q), d(x, q) \leq d(y, q)$.

Since, it is not practical to sort a multimedia data according to any total order (because such an order is usually meaningless to solve a similarity query), it is necessary to build an index to organize the objects so as to solve queries efficiently. An index is a data structure that allows us to obtain a candidate set without sequentially scanning the entire database (unthinkable for huge datasets). There are three well-known index families, namely, the ones based on *pivots*, the ones based on *compact partitions*, and recently, the ones based on *permutations*. Pivot-based and compact-partition-based indexes are commonly used in *exact* proximity indexes, while permutation-based ones are *approximate* ones. In an approximate search we may lose a few relevant objects from the query answers, but accepting this loss allows us to improve searching time significantly.

In this paper, we propose a new hybrid method to enhance the performance of *permutation*-based indexes. Our proposal eclectically blends three main ideas: the first one is to conveniently reduce the length of the permutations stored within the index, the second one is adapting the permutation similarity measure for these clipped permutations, and the third one is to use the closest permutant of each object as a pivot for it. This novel strategy allows us to improve the already remarkable performance of the permutation-based index when solving approximate similarity queries.

The performance of our proposal is tested using three well known real-world databases: NASA and Colors, which are part of the SISAP project's metric space benchmark dataset available at [10], and SIFT image descriptors [12] from the TEXMEX website, available at `corpus-texmex.irisa.fr`. Using our eclectic blend, we reduce more than 30% of the number of distance evaluations needed to solve approximate similarity queries on these databases.

A preliminary version of this proposal appears in [9]. In this current version, we have extended and clarified the explanations of our proposal by adding more examples and several discussions about the ideas involved in this work. Besides, we extend the experimental evaluation to the SIFT image descriptors, a large dataset that allows us to verify that this proposal can effectively scale up.

The rest of this article is organized as follows: Sect. 2 describes the related work on metric spaces and similarity search, including a brief explanation of the Metric Inverted File index [1] and how to reduce and improve it [8,11]. In Sect. 3 we show our novel hybrid index, whose experimental evaluation is shown in Sect. 4. This evaluation considers two real-world datasets from the SISAP library [10] and the real-world dataset of SIFT image descriptors [12]. Finally, we expose conclusions and some possible extensions for this work in Sect. 5.

2   Related Work

Similarity searching in metric spaces has been studied in three leading families of algorithms: pivot-based algorithms [6,14], partition-based algorithms [5,7], and permutation-based algorithms [1,4]. As we aforementioned, the permutation-based approach is one of the best representative methods to solve approximate similarity searches.

Although general metric spaces do not have an explicit dimensionality, we can explain their *intrinsic dimensionality* following the same idea as in vector spaces. If we compute the histogram of distances between any object pairs in metric spaces of high intrinsic dimension, the probability distribution of distances would be narrow and peaked, making the work of any similarity search algorithm more difficult [2,6]. We say that a general metric space has high intrinsic dimensionality when its histogram of distances is concentrated and it is very difficult to solve any query on it.

Particularly, pivot-based algorithms work well on spaces with low intrinsic dimension, partition-based algorithms are adequate for medium to high intrinsic dimension, and permutation-based algorithms are useful on high intrinsic dimension in an approximate fashion. In the following we describe the pivot-based and permutation-based algorithms as they are relevant for this work.

2.1   Pivot-Based Algorithm

Pivot-based algorithms use a subset of objects $P = \{p_1, p_2, \ldots, p_k\} \subseteq \mathbb{U}$ to compute pseudo-coordinates in an auxiliary vector space. Each dataset object $x \in \mathbb{X}$ is represented by a vector containing its k distances to every pivot $p_i \in P$. Let $D(u, P) = (d(x, p_1), \ldots, d(x, p_k))$ be this vector. Given a query $R(q, r)$, we first represent q in the same auxiliary space as $D(q, P) = (d(q, p_1), \ldots, d(q, p_k))$. Thus, by virtue of the triangle inequality, any object $x \in \mathbb{X}$ can be discarded if $|d(p_i, x) - d(p_i, q)| > r$ for any pivot $p_i \in P$. Therefore, in this case, we do not need to explicitly evaluate $d(x, p)$ saving us one distance computation. Finally, to obtain the query answer, all the non-discarded database objects are directly compared with q and only the objects whose distance to q is within the threshold r are reported.

Since we want to discard objects, we need large values for $|d(p_i, x) - d(p_i, q)|$. Then, we would prefer pivots that are close to the objects or close to the query. We can obtain pivots close to the objects by selecting several pivots. However, we cannot anticipate the location of the query.

2.2   Permutation-Based Algorithm

Similar to pivot-based indexes, permutation-based indexes also use some distinguished elements from $\mathbb{U}$, but this time they are used as reference points and they are called *permutants*. The main idea of this method was introduced in [3]. Let $\mathbb{P}$ be the permutant set, formally, $\mathbb{P} = \{p_1, \ldots, p_k\} \subseteq \mathbb{U}$. For the sake of producing the index, each $u \in \mathbb{X}$ computes $D(u, \mathbb{P}) = \{d(u, p_1), \ldots, d(u, p_k)\}$, that is, u computes its distance to every permutant. Then, each object u sorts the set $\mathbb{P}$ using their distances computed in $D(u, \mathbb{P})$ in increasing order. This ordering is called the *permutation* of u, which is denoted by Π_u. Therefore, the permutant in the first position of Π_u is the closest one to u, and so on. Inversely, let Π_u^{-1} be the inverse of the permutation Π_u, so we can use Π_u^{-1} to identify the position of any permutant in Π_u.

As an example, Fig. 1 depicts a subset of points in $\mathbb{R}^2$, considering Euclidean distance. The set of permutants is $\mathbb{P} = \{p_1, p_2, p_3, p_4, p_5, p_6\}$; that is, $k = 6$. If we consider the object $u \in \mathbb{X}$, $D(u, \mathbb{P}) = (3, 4, 6, 3, 2, 5)$ where $d(u, p_1) = 3$ and so on. Then, sorting $D(u, \mathbb{P})$ by increasing distance, we can obtain the permutation of u as $\Pi_u = (5, 1, 4, 2, 6, 3)$, when we consider just the index of each permutant in such increasing order. It can be noticed that the closest permutant is p_5, because $d(u, p_5) = 2$. The inverse permutation Π_u^{-1} is $(2, 4, 6, 3, 1, 5)$. Then, $\Pi_u^{-1}(p_2) = 4$ means p_2 is in the 4th position in Π_u. It can be noticed that $O(nk)$ distance computations are needed to obtain the permutations of all the database objects, being $|\mathbb{X}| = n$ and $|\mathbb{P}| = k$.

As two identical elements must have exactly the same permutation, we expect the permutations of two similar elements to be also similar. Therefore, when we search for elements similar to a query q, the problem is translated to find objects whose permutations are similar to Π_q. An advantage of this approach is that

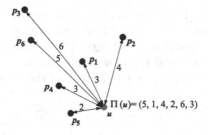

Fig. 1. Example of a permutation considering $\mathbb{P} \subset \mathbb{R}^2$ using Euclidean distance. In the plot, the distances between u and each permutant in the set $\mathbb{P} = \{p_1, p_2, p_3, p_4, p_5, p_6\}$ are represented by arrows labelled by the respective value of the distance.

computing the permutation similarity is usually cheaper than computing the *distance function d.*

There are different measures to compute similarity between permutations [13]. One of the most used is the *Spearman Footrule measure* F_k, defined as:

$$F(u,q)_k = F(\Pi_u, \Pi_q) = \sum_{i=1}^{k-|\mathbb{P}|} |\Pi_u^{-1}(p_i) - \Pi_q^{-1}(p_i)| \tag{1}$$

The basic permutation method stores the whole permutation of each dataset object. Hence, the index needs $O(nk)$ distance computations and also $O(nk)$ space.

An interesting member of this index family is the Metric Inverted File [1]. In the next section we describe it along with some of its improvements.

2.3   Metric Inverted File (MI-File)

Amato and Savino proposed to use an inverted file of permutations [1], where each permutant in $\mathbb{P}$ has its respective entry in the inverted file. We call this, the MI-File approach. To produce the index, they define a parameter $m_i < |\mathbb{P}|$ which is used during preprocessing time. For each permutant $p \in \mathbb{P}$ the MI-File index stores the list of elements $u \in X$ such that its permutation Π_u has the permutant p within the first m_i positions. The list for each permutant p stores pairs (u, pos), where u denotes an object in X and pos refers to the position of p within the permutation Π_u.

Given the query q, we need to determine Π_q. The MI-File index uses another parameter $m_s \ll m_i$ for searching. The MI-File search method only retrieves the posting lists of the first m_s permutants in Π_q and next, it joins all of them to obtain the candidate set. Finally, all the elements in the candidate set are directly compared with q using the distance d to produce the query answer. The authors in [1] proposed a variant of the Spearman Footrule permutation similarity measure, because each permutation was clipped by the parameter m_i.

In the works [8,11], the authors improved the performance of the MI-File index in two ways. On the one hand, each posting list stores only elements u

but not the positions *pos* [11] and each element maintains its short permutation. They also proposed a new way to compute the Spearman Footrule measure, considering that the permutations have changed. On the other hand, to reduce even more the candidate set cardinality, a new parameter m_{s_r} is selected according to the radius r of the similarity query [8] (instead of the fixed-parameter m_s from the MI-File index).

3   Our Proposal

In the state of the art, the works [8,11] show that the permutant-based index performance still allows room for improvement. We pick some ideas from these previous works, for instance, we also shorten the permutations, need to modify the similarity measure according to the shortening, and the use of additional parameters to control the permutation size. However, we still use a plain permutant index, that is, for each element we store its shorten permutation and some other additional information, but without using the auxiliary inverted index.

Now, we specific the three main aspects involved in our work. The first one is to introduce a new mechanism for shortening permutations in the index, the second one is to use one of the permutants as a pivot, and the third is to consider a modified permutation similarity measure adapted for our specific case. After explaining in detail these aspects, we show how to combine them in order to produce our novel index and its respective searching algorithm.

3.1   Clipped Permutations

Instead of having a maximum global length m_i, each permutation can be shortened with a different length, by considering for each object $u \in \mathbb{X}$ its appropriate permutation prefix. For this sake, we consider the distance to its closest permutant; that is, $d(u, p_{\Pi_u(1)}) = r_u$, and keep for u those permutants within a distance lower than or equal to $2r_u$. We ran preliminary experiments to determine that $2r_u$ performs well when solving queries. Our preliminary experimental results have shown that the value $2r_u$ has some dependence on the intrinsic dimension of the particular metric space; and as long as the intrinsic dimension increase, we could change the coefficient to a value lower than 2. However, this still deserves further study. We call Π'_u the u's clipped (or trimmed) permutation.

Let m_u denote the length of the trimmed permutation for element u; that is, $m_u = |\Pi'_u|$ is the length of the prefix selected. We note that if a permutant is very close to the object u then r_u will be small and consequently, it is possible that there is only one permutant within distance $2r_u$ from u. Therefore, we propose using a minimum global length $m_{\min}$ for all the permutations. On the other hand, since the distance histogram of spaces having high intrinsic dimension is concentrated, it is possible that some object could have all the permutants within distance $2r_u$ from u. Hence, we also propose a maximum global length $m_{\max}$ for all the permutations. As a by-product of this improvement, we can avoid adapting the coefficient 2 when the particular space has high intrinsic dimension.

In our example of Sect. 2.2, Fig. 1, for element u we obtained $r_u = 2$. So, its clipped permutation is $\Pi'_u = (5, 1, 4, 2)$ because $d(u, p_2) = 4 \leq 2r_u$. It can be noticed that, by this way of shortening the permutations, each clipped permutation would have a different length.

3.2   Including a Single Pivot

When we search for a query q, we have to compute Π_q by calculating all the distances between q and every permutant in $\mathbb{P}$. Besides, we know that if we keep the distances from the element $u \in \mathbb{X}$ to all the permutants in $\mathbb{P}$, we can use them to obtain lower bounds of the distance from u to q, as in a pivot-based algorithm. Hence, we can discard the elements whose lower bounds exceed the search threshold r. However, storing all the distances between the elements $u \in \mathbb{X}$ and the permutants $p \in \mathbb{P}$ is expensive.

We also know that a good pivot for estimating the distance from u to q is some element similar to u; so, we decided to use the permutant closest to u as its pivot. Then, we already have the pivot identifier and we only need to store the distance to it. Therefore, we only need one distance for each object $u \in \mathbb{X}$, which implies that we keep exactly n extra distances in the index, which is negligible for the index size.

Naturally, one can wonder whether storing more pivots for each object would be convenient. As we already mention, the closest permutant is a good pivot option. But, the question is which other permutant should be considered. There are two obvious choices, namely, the second closest permutant and the furthest one. The second closest permutant should be close to the first one; hence, there is a little chance that it could improve the lower bound of the distance to the query. Of course, adding another pivot also requires more space in the index for each object. Otherwise, the furthest permutant does have better chance of improving the lower bound, but as we only store the permutation prefix, we should need to store which is the furthest permutant and its respective distance, so we need even more space in the index. Clearly, this reasoning can be extended for including more pivots, and it involves even more space in the index with no significant chance of improving the query distance lower bound. Accordingly, we prefer to keep only one extra distance in the index; but, this deserves further study.

Continuing with our example in Fig. 1, the closest permutant of object u is p_5, so, we use it as pivot and store the distance 2.

3.3   Permutation Similarity Measure

As we have clipped permutations within the index, we have to reformulate the similarity measure. Moreover, since the permutation lengths can vary, we introduce two penalty strategies in order to cope with the lengths.

Given a query q, we first need to calculate all the distances between q and the permutants in $\mathbb{P}$ to obtain Π_q. At this point, we have the complete query permutation (with length k) and the distances $D(q, \mathbb{P})$. Thus, it should be possible to compare any clipped permutation Π'_u of any length with Π_q, using the same Eq. 2 proposed in [8]:

$$F^*(u, q)_{m_u} = F^*(\Pi'_u, \Pi_q) = \sum_{i=1}^{m_u} |i - \Pi_q^{-1}(\Pi_u(i))| \qquad (2)$$

If all clipped permutations had the same size, Eq. 2 should compute a fair value for the similarity measure. But, as we already said, we include a penalty system to compensate the case when we compare two clipped permutations of different size. In particular, we need to quantify penalties when we find a permutant that does not belong to Π'_u and, analogously, when we miss a permutant from the prefix of Π_q. Fortunately, these penalties also improve the discriminability of our proposal, as can be seen in Sect. 4.

Penalty When a Permutant does not Belong to Π'_u. The permutants not belonging in Π'_u (that is, the discarded ones) add a penalty that considers how big is the displacement of the remaining permutants in Π'_u with respect to their positions in Π_q. We call the maximum of all these displacements $maxi$. So, we add $maxi \cdot (k - m_u)$ to F^*.

Note that if permutants in Π'_u are placed in the prefix of Π_q, this penalty is very mild. Also, the penalty increases as long as displacements are bigger.

To illustrate this penalty we extend our running example of Fig. 1 as shown in Fig. 2, where we include the query q. The clipped permutation for u is $\Pi'_u = (5, 1, 4, 2)$, so $m_u = 4$. The permutation for q is $\Pi_q = (3, 6, 1, 2, 4, 5)$. The displacements of permutants in Π'_u are respectively $(5, 1, 2, 0)$, so $maxi = 5$, which corresponds to the displacement of permutant 5. Finally, k is $|\mathbb{P}| = 6$. Therefore, the penalty is $5 \cdot (6 - 4) = 10$.

Penalty When Missing a Permutant from the Prefix of Π_q. Two permutations starting with the same permutants give a strong suggestion that the respective objects could be similar. Likewise, if some of the permutants in the prefix of Π_q does not belong to Π'_u, we have a strong indicator that object u could be irrelevant to the query q.

So, we need to establish a criterion about what is this prefix. Analogously to Π'_u, considering the query radius r and using $D(q, \mathbb{P})$, we compute how many permutants have their distances from q within threshold $2r$. This value is called m_q, so the prefix of m_q permutants is called Π'_q. Notice that, if $m_q < m_{\min}$ then m_q is set to $m_{\min}$. Otherwise, if $m_q > m_{\max}$ then m_q is set to $m_{\max}$.

Therefore, we determine how many permutants in Π'_q are missing in Π'_u. We call this value c. Finally, as this is a strong indicator that u is not relevant to q, we strongly penalize the measure with $c \cdot F^*$. Of course, if all the permutants in Π'_q occur in Π'_u, this term is zero. But, the more the number of missing permutants in Π'_u, the greater the penalty (and each increment is also very strong).

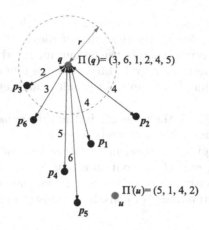

Fig. 2. Example of a permutation considering $\mathbb{P} \subset \mathbb{R}^2$ using Euclidean distance and a query.

Considering the example of Fig. 2, where the query radius $r = 2$, we obtain $\Pi'_q = (3, 6, 1, 2)$. Note that the missing permutants in Π'_u are 3 and 6, so $c = 2$ and $F^* = 5 + 2 + 2 + 0 = 9$. Therefore, this penalty is $c \cdot F^* = 18$.

Note that in the case of K-nearest-neighbor queries, as we do not know beforehand the final query radius that encloses the K nearest elements of q, we set the prefix of the query permutation as $m_{\max}$.

Resulting Permutation Similarity Measure. We use Eq. 2 and these two penalties in order to compute the permutation similarity measure. The obtained measure is depicted in Algorithm 1.

Algorithm 1 distanceBetweenPermutations($\Pi_q^{-1}, m_q, \Pi_u, m_u, k$)

1: OUTPUT: Reports modified Spearman Footrule.
2: $t \leftarrow 0, c \leftarrow m_q, maxi \leftarrow 0$
3: **for** $i \leftarrow 1$ to m_u **do**
4: $\quad \Delta_i \leftarrow |i - \Pi_q^{-1}(\Pi_u(i))|, \quad t \leftarrow t + \Delta_i$
5: $\quad maxi \leftarrow \max(\Delta_i, maxi)$
6: $\quad$ **if** $\Pi_q^{-1}(\Pi_u(i)) < m_q$ **then**
7: $\quad\quad c \leftarrow c - 1$
8: $\quad$ **end if**
9: **end for**
10: **return** $t \leftarrow t + maxi \cdot (k - m_u) + c \cdot t$

The variable t accumulates the similarity measure, c is initialized as m_q so we start by assuming that we miss all the permutant in Π'_q, and $maxi$ is initialized as zero. Then, we compute a **for** cycle to review all the permutants in Π'_u (Lines 3 to 9). Line 4 computes the displacement Δ_i for each permutant in Π'_u and accumulate it in t. Line 5 updates the value of $maxi$, when the displacement increases. In Line 6, we verify whether the permutant $\Pi_u(i)$ belongs to the prefix Π'_q, in whose case, we decrease c by 1 (Line 7), as we found another permutant within Π'_q. Finally, in Line 10 we apply the penalties and return the permutation similarity measure.

For the example of Fig. 2, the value of t is 9 and the penalties are respectively 10 and 18. Thus, the similarity measure between Π'_u and Π'_q reported by Algorithm 1 is 37. If we compute the Spearman Footrule measure (Eq. 1) between the whole permutations Π_u and Π_q, we obtain a value of 16. As it can be seen, the penalties tend to emphasize the differences between the clipped permutations, which diminishes the probability of considering this element as relevant to the query.

3.4 Solving Similarity Range Queries

Given dataset $\mathbb{X}$, we chose a subset $\mathbb{P}$ of k objects at random to compute the permutations. Then, for each object $u \in \mathbb{X}$ we compute its permutation Π_u and its clipped version Π'_u, and we store both Π'_u and the distance to the closest permutant in the index.

Given a range query $R(q, r)$, we compute its permutation Π_q and its prefix Π'_q, so $m_q = |\Pi'_q|$. Since, for each element $u \in \mathbb{X}$, the index stores the distance between u and its closest permutant and we already compute $D(q, \mathbb{P})$ at querying time, then, we can calculate a lower bound of $d(u, q)$. Thus, for each u, $d(u, q)$ is lower bounded by $|d(u, p^*) - d(p^*, q)|$, using the closest permutant p^* to u as a pivot. Then, if $|d(u, p^*) - d(p^*, q)| > r$ then u can be safely discarded from the candidate set as, by virtue of triangle inequality, it does not belong to the query answer. Therefore, only the non-discarded objects are included in the candidate set. We sort increasingly this set according to our adapted permutation similarity measure (computed by Algorithm 1) to obtain a candidate list. Next, since there is a good chance of having the relevant objects to the query q at the beginning of this sorted list, we can review just a small portion at its starting. Consequently, we would compare directly q with few elements using the distance function d.

The K-nearest-neighbor queries can be solved by using the range query procedure, starting from radius $r = \infty$ and then, reducing the query radius in order to enclose just the K current candidate objects to be the nearest neighbors of q, as we proceed.

4   Experimental Results

The performance of our proposal has been tested using three well known real-world databases: NASA, Colors, and SIFT. The two former datasets are available from SISAP project's metric space benchmark dataset [10]. The third one, SIFT image descriptors, belongs to the TEXMEX testbed, and this particular dataset was first introduced in [12]. Any quadratic form can be used as a distance on these spaces, so we chose Euclidean distance as the simplest meaningful alternative.

As NASA and Colors datasets are relatively small, we study the performance of our proposal when we have more space available for indexation; thus, we perform test varying the permutant set size (64, 128, and 256 permutants).

As SIFT is a large dataset, we study the behavior of our proposal considering space limitations that occurs in real-world scenarios, thus, we test only with 64 permutants. Hence, this allows us to study how much affect the other parameters to the performance of our proposal. Particularly, we are interested to experimentally evaluate what would happen if we force a value for radius r_u, instead of using the value that each object obtains to its closest permutant. As can be noticed, this selection should affect the index size.

4.1   NASA

NASA is a dataset where each object is represented as a 20-dimensional vector. They were generated from images downloaded from NASAand there are no duplicate vectors. The total number of vectors is 40,150. The first 39,650 are indexed and the remaining 500 vectors are used as queries.

In Fig. 3(a), we show the average performance of our proposal (ShP) along with those of the basic permutation idea (PP, with 64 permutants), the MI-File using m_i for the missing values during the Spearman Footrule computation (MIFI Pi, using similar space of our index), and the MI-File modified as in [8] (MIFI Pm, using similar space of our index). These experiments account for how many distances are needed to obtain the true $NN_K(q)$ answer, varing $K \in [1, 8]$. Notice that our proposal makes 30% fewer distance computations than the best technique proposed in [8] for NN_8. In Fig. 3(b), we show the histogram for different lengths of clipped permutations, considering that $m_{\min} = 8$ and $m_{\max} = 32$.

It is remarkable that using 64 permutants we can get clipped permutations with different m_u lengths and smaller than the original size (64), as shown in Fig. 3(b). The average length of the clipped permutation is 27. We note that our index having almost half the space of PP with 64 permutants, behaves better. Moreover, when using a more extensive set of permutants (128 concerning 64), the average searching cost is almost the same, since the clipped permutations have almost the same size. If we use more permutants, we increase the construction cost of the index. Therefore, it is not worth using more permutants because our proposal always leave only a few permutants that are good ones. In fact, in Fig. 3(a) we omit the plot for $k = 256$ as the results are similar to those of $k = 64$ and 128.

During searches, our proposal outperforms the other variants that build the index with the same number of permutants and construction costs. This behavior may be not only due to a good clipped permutation but also to the pruning ability that gives the stored distance to the nearest permutant of each element.

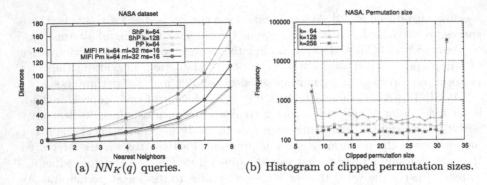

(a) $NN_K(q)$ queries.   (b) Histogram of clipped permutation sizes.

Fig. 3. Performance with NASA dataset.

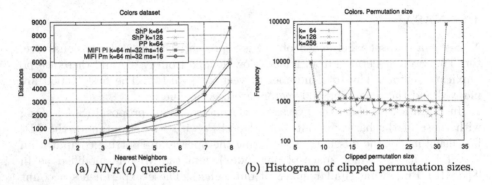

(a) $NN_K(q)$ queries.   (b) Histogram of clipped permutation sizes.

Fig. 4. Performance with Colors dataset.

4.2   Colors

This dataset consists of 112,682 color histograms represented as 112-dimensional feature vectors, from an image dataset[1] Similarly with the NASA dataset, the first elements are indexed and the last 500 color histograms are used as queries.

In Fig. 4(a), we show the performance of our proposal (ShP). Again, it is compared with the MI-File algorithms and the permutation-based algorithm (PP). In this dataset, our proposal needs 37% fewer distances than the best technique used in [8]. As it occurs in the NASA space, the number of permutants used does not significantly affect the search performance. On Fig. 4(b), we show the histogram for each length of clipped permutations, where $m_{min} = 8$ and $m_{max} = 32$. Please, note that all clipped permutations have almost the same length independently of the original permutation size. Surprisingly, the average length is again 27 permutants.

---

[1] Available at http://www.dbs.informatik.uni-muenchen.de/~seidl/DATA/histo112.112682.gz..

Newly, if we fix the number of permutants used to build the different alternatives of the indexes whose construction costs are the same, our proposal outperforms the others during searches.

4.3 SIFT

Nowadays, TEXMEX[2] offers four datasets to evaluate *approximate nearest neighbors* search algorithms. For each dataset, TEXMEX provides four sets. We only use the SIFT dataset [12] which contains a set of 1,000,000 image descriptors to build the index, a set of 10,000 elements as queries, and two other sets for other purposes. In the SIFT dataset, each element is represented as a 128-dimensional vector.

As can be noticed, the cardinality of this dataset is significantly larger than the two previous ones. Therefore, if we try to reproduce the test for NASA and Colors spaces we should require quite a lot of memory when we build the index, as we initially needs $O(nk)$ space to store the whole permutations which are later shortened with the described mechanism. Besides, we need $O(nk)$ distance computations to build the index, which involves an excessive time requirement. Therefore, we limit the number of permutants to 64 for this experimental series, while considering $m_{\min} = 8$ and $m_{\max} = 32$, as before.

Since we now have a fixed permutant set size, we cope the study of the parameter r_u, which affect the size of the clipped permutations. This time, instead of using r_u as the distance to the closest permutant, which implies that each object u has its own value for r_u, we set r_u to a fixed value for all $u \in \mathbb{X}$.

In Fig. 5(a), we show the average performance of our proposal, considering three fixed values for the parameter r_u chosen conveniently for this space ($r_u = 280, 350$ and 450). The average permutation size for these options are approximately 8, 10, and 19 permutants, respectively; hence, we include the performance of the plain permutant index with 8 and 16 permutants, as these alternatives use similar space for indexation. Besides, we include the performance of our non-fixed r_u option, whose average clipped permutation size is 30.

As can be seen, the fixed alternatives for $r_u = 280, 350$ and 450 overcome both plain variants while using less space for the index. On the other hand, the non-fixed r_u option obtains a similar performance but uses more permutants than the fixed ones. This reveals that our proposal improves over plain permutants, but add another parameter to be tuned. Clearly, it deserves more study.

Finally, Fig. 5(b) depicts the clipped permutation size histogram for the same values of r_u used before. As can be seen, using the smallest r_u value (280), the favorite clipped permutation size is the minimum value allowed in this case ($m_{\min} = 8$) and no clipped permutation reaches the maximum possible value ($m_{\max} = 32$); the average clipped permutation size is 8.02. When we increase the value of r_u, we appreciate that there is a more even distribution of the clipped permutation sizes; in fact, they can reach the maximum available value

---

[2] Available at http://corpus-texmex.irisa.fr/.

(32). The average clipped sizes are 9.90 and 18.65. This show that as we increase the value of r_u, more clipped permutations sizes reach the maximum value.

We note that we need a preliminar dataset study for fixing a specific value for r_u. However, having more information about the dataset compensates the needed effort to discover this knowing as it could minimize the searching cost.

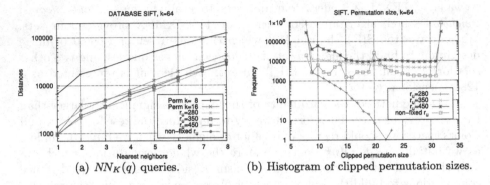

(a) $NN_K(q)$ queries.   (b) Histogram of clipped permutation sizes.

Fig. 5. Performance with SIFT dataset.

5   Conclusions and Future Work

In this paper, we propose a new strategy for reducing the permutation length, which we have called *clipped permutations*. We also propose a permutation similarity measure adapted for this clipping. Our approach also takes advantage of storing only one distance per database element to obtain a lower bound of the distance between the element and the query. For this sake, we store the distance from each object to its closest permutant. This stored distance allows for discarding many elements. This way we can use a smaller eclectic index which blends some good ideas from both pivots and permutant indexes, and at the same time it improves search performance.

We have tested the performance of our proposal with three well-known real-world databases: NASA and Colors, obtained from SISAP project's metric space benchmark set [10], and SIFT obtained from TEXMEX [12]. Our experimental results proved that our approach surpasses the other known permutation-based techniques. In fact, the eclectic combination of these good ideas significantly improves searching performance of the plain permutation-based index and overcomes the MI-File presented in [1], for approximate similarity searching. As it can be noticed, we reduced more than the 30% the distance evaluations needed to solve the queries on both databases.

As future work, even though we have already tested our proposal on a large dataset (SIFT images descriptors), we can consider even more large datasets. We continue analyzing the parameters of our proposal, that is verifying how the values of r_u, m_{min} and m_{max} affect the lengths of the permutations and their impact on storage and search performance. Besides, we plan to study the actual pruning ability of the stored distances to the nearest permutant of each database element. An appealing trend is to consider some synthetic databases of increasing dimension to evaluate how the dimensionality curse affects our proposal. Also, we consider investigating how the number of permutants used during the index construction affects the search performance considering other metric spaces.

References

1. Amato, G., Savino, P.: Approximate similarity search in metric spaces using inverted files. In: Proceedings of the 3rd International ICST Conference on Scalable Information Systems, INFOSCALE 2008, Vico Equense, Italy, June 4–6, 2008. p. 28 (2008)
2. Brin, S.: Near neighbor search in large metric spaces. In: Proceedings of the 21st Conference on Very Large Databases (VLDB'95), pp. 574–584 (1995)
3. Chávez, E., Figueroa, K., Navarro, G.: Proximity searching in high dimensional spaces with a proximity preserving order. In: Proceedings of the 4th Mexican Intl. Conf. in Artificial Intelligence (MICAI'05), pp. 405–414. LNAI 3789 (2005)
4. Chávez, E., Figueroa, K., Navarro, G.: Effective proximity retrieval by ordering permutations. IEEE Trans. on Pattern Analysis and Machine Intelligence (TPAMI) **30**(9), 1647–1658 (2009)
5. Chávez, E., Navarro, G.: A compact space decomposition for effective metric indexing. Pattern Recogn. Lett. **26**(9), 1363–1376 (2005)
6. Chávez, E., Navarro, G., Baeza-Yates, R., Marroquín, J.: Proximity searching in metric spaces. ACM Comput. Surv. **33**(3), 273–321 (2001)
7. Ciaccia, P., Patella, M., Zezula, P.: M-tree: an efficient access method for similarity search in metric spaces. In: Proceedings of the 23rd Conference on Very Large Databases (VLDB'97), pp. 426–435 (1997)
8. Figueroa, K., Camarena-Ibarrola, A., Reyes, N.: Shortening the candidate list for similarity searching using inverted index. In: Mexican Conf. on Pattern Recognition. vol. 12725, pp. 89–97. LNCS Springer (2021). https://doi.org/10.1007/978-3-030-77004-4_9
9. Figueroa, K., Camarena-Ibarrola, A., Reyes, N., Paredes, R., Martínez, B.R.H.: A hybrid approach to boost the permutation index for similarity searching. In: Actas del XXVIII Congreso Argentino de Ciencias de la Computación (CACIC 2022), pp. 458–467 (Oct 2022)
10. Figueroa, K., Navarro, G., Chávez, E.: Metric spaces library (2007), available at http://www.sisap.org/Metric_Space_Library.html
11. Figueroa, K., Reyes, N., Camarena-Ibarrola, A.: Candidate list obtained from metric inverted index for similarity searching. In: Martínez-Villaseñor, L., Herrera-Alcántara, O., Ponce, H., Castro-Espinoza, F.A. (eds.) Advances in Computational Intelligence, pp. 29–38. Springer International Publishing, Cham (2020)
12. Jégou, H., Douze, M., Schmid, C.: Product quantization for nearest neighbor search. IEEE Trans. Pattern Anal. Mach. Intell. **33**(1), 117–128 (2011). https://doi.org/10.1109/TPAMI.2010.57

13. Skala, M.: Counting distance permutations. J. Discrete Algorithms **7**(1), 49–61 (2009). https://doi.org/10.1016/j.jda.2008.09.011
14. Zezula, P., Amato, G., Dohnal, V., Batko, M.: Similarity Search: The Metric Space Approach, Advances in Database Systems, vol. 32. Springer (2006). https://doi.org/10.1007/0-387-29151-2

Dynamic Distal Spatial Approximation Trees

Edgar Chávez[1] , María E. Di Genaro[2] , and Nora Reyes[2]([☒])

[1] Centro de Investigación Científica y de Educación Superior de Ensenada, Ensenada, Mexico
elchavez@cicese.mx
[2] Departamento de Informática, Universidad Nacional de San Luis, San Luis, Argentina
{mdigena,nreyes}@unsl.edu.ar

Abstract. Metric space indexes are critical for efficient similarity searches across various applications. The *Distal Spatial Approximation Tree* (DiSAT) has demonstrated exceptional speed/memory trade-offs without requiring parameter tuning. However, since it operates solely on static databases, its application is limited in many exciting use cases.

This research has been dedicated to developing a dynamic version of DiSAT that allows for incremental construction. It is remarkable that the dynamic version is faster than its static counterpart. The outcome is a faster index with the same memory requirements as DiSAT. This development enhances the practicality of DiSAT, unlocking a wide range of proximity database applications.

Keywords: similarity search · dynamism · metric spaces · non-conventional databases

1 Introduction

In recent years, the metric space approach has become popular for handling complex and unstructured databases. These databases often require similarity searches to find objects similar to a given query object. Similarity searches have various applications in fields like text searching, information retrieval, machine learning, image processing, and computational biology.

In the metric space model, a distance function is defined between objects in a universe $\mathbb{U}$, and proximity searching involves finding objects in a dataset $\mathbb{X}$ that are similar enough to a given query object q. The database can be preprocessed to create a metric index, which accelerates query response times. Two common similarity queries are range queries and k-nearest neighbors queries.

There are numerous metric indexes available, with the Distal Spatial Approximation Tree (DiSAT) being a popular index that uses hyperplanes to divide the search space and approach the query spatially. However, the DiSAT is not well-suited for databases where data is obtained gradually over time. To address this issue, the Bentley-Saxe method (BS) can be used to create dynamic indexes that can be split or joined based on insertion/deletion rates. The Distal Spatial Approximation Forest (DiSAF) is a dynamic index based on the DiSAT, but it has limitations due to expensive rebuilds.

This paper presents a new dynamic version of the DiSAT called the dynamic DiSAT (DDiSAT). This version significantly reduces construction costs and improves search

P. Pesado (Ed.): CACIC 2022, CCIS 1778, pp. 175–189, 2023.
https://doi.org/10.1007/978-3-031-34147-2_12

performance. The approach allows for insertions and range searches, with deletions and k-NN searches left as future works. The paper also includes an analysis of how the similarity search and construction cost are affected by the number of pending elements to be inserted, providing insights into selecting the number of elements to decrease construction costs while maintaining search performance.

A preliminary version of this article appears in [2]. We extended the preliminary version with an in deep analysis of construction cost affected by the number of elements pending to be actually inserted into the tree, providing a guidance in selecting the number of the elements which will be effectively added as nodes into the tree, as a way to decrease construction costs while maintain the search performance.

The paper is organized as follows: Sect. 2 covers some basic concepts, Sect. 3 details the DiSAT, DiSAF, Spatial Approximation Trees, and Dynamic Spatial Approximation Trees, Sect. 4 introduces the DDiSAT, Sect. 5 evaluates the performance of the DDiSAT experimentally, Sect. 6 studies the impact of pending elements on similarity search and construction cost, and Sect. 7 presents conclusions and future works.

2   Some Notation

The metric space model can be defined as follows: Consider a set $\mathbb{X}$ of objects and a non-negative distance function $d : \mathbb{X} \times \mathbb{X} \longrightarrow \mathbb{R}^+$ defined on them. This function satisfies the three axioms of a metric, making the pair $(\mathbb{U}, d)$ a metric space: strict positivity $(d(x, y) \geq 0$ and $d(x, y) = 0 \Leftrightarrow x = y)$, symmetry $(d(x, y) = d(x, y))$, and triangle inequality $(d(x, z) \leq d(x, y) + d(y, z))$. We have a finite database $\mathbb{U} \subseteq \mathbb{X}$ with n elements, which can be preprocessed to build an index. Given a new object $q \in \mathbb{X}$ (a query), the goal is to retrieve all similar objects in $\mathbb{U}$. There are two common types of queries:

- Range query: retrieve all objects in $\mathbb{U}$ within a distance r of q. That is, $x \in \mathbb{U}, d(x, q) \leq r$.
- k-nearest neighbors query (k-NN): retrieve the k closest objects to q in $\mathbb{U}$. That is, a set $A \subseteq \mathbb{U}$ such that $|A| = k$ and $\forall x \in A, y \in \mathbb{U} - A, d(x, q) \leq d(y, q)$.

Since the distance function is expensive to compute, the complexity of the search is typically measured as the number of distance evaluations performed. The goal is to preprocess the dataset to minimize the number of distance evaluations needed to answer queries. This paper focuses on range queries, as k-NN queries can be obtained from range queries in an optimal way. There are many similarity search indexes available, and we will discuss some relevant ones in the next section [6,7,11,14].

3   Distal Spatial Approximation Trees

The *Distal Spatial Approximation Tree* (DiSAT) [4] is a type of the *Spatial Approxima-tion Tree* (*SAT*) [9]. These data structures use a spatial approximation approach to itera-tively approach a query by navigating the tree from the root. To construct the DiSAT, an element a is chosen as the root, and a set of *neighbors* $N(a)$ is identified. The neighbors are a subset of elements $x \in \mathbb{U}$ that are closer to a than any other element in $N(a)$. The remaining elements (not in $N(a) \cup a$) are assigned to their closest neighbor in $N(a)$. Each element in $N(a)$ recursively becomes the root of a new subtree that contains the assigned elements. For every node a, the covering radius, $R(a)$, which is the maximum distance between a and any element in the subtree rooted at a, is stored. The initial set of neighbors for the root a, $N(a)$, is empty, allowing for the selection of any database element as the first neighbor. Once the first neighbor is chosen, the database is split into two halves using the hyperplane defined by proximity to a and the selected neighbor, and any element on the a side can be selected as the second neighbor. The process of selecting subsequent neighbors continues until the root zone, which consists of database elements closer to the root than the previous neighbors, is empty.

The DiSAT aims to improve the performance of the original algorithm by selecting distal nodes instead of proximal ones. This approach increases the separation between hyperplanes, which in turn decreases the size of the covering radius, the two variables that govern the performance of these trees. The performance improvement depends on the root element selected, and different roots can lead to completely different DiSATs, each with different search costs. For instance, the DiSAT obtained by selecting p_6 as the tree root in a metric database is illustrated in Fig. 1(a) and Fig. 1(b), which depict the covering radii for the neighbors of the tree root.

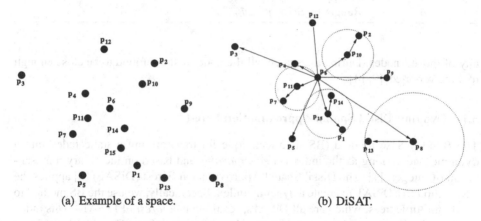

(a) Example of a space.   (b) DiSAT.

Fig. 1. Example of a metric database in $\mathbb{R}^2$, and DiSAT obtained if p_6 were the root.

The process for constructing the DiSAT is formally described in Algorithm 1. To perform a range search, Algorithm 2 is used and is called as RangeSearch$(a, q, r, d(a, q))$, where a is the root of the tree, q is the query object, and r is the search radius. One important feature of DiSAT is that a greedy search can be used to locate all the objects that have been inserted previously. For a range query with radius r and c being the closest element between the set $a \cup N(a) \cup A(a)$, where $A(a)$ is the set of ancestors of a, the same greedy search is used by traversing all the nodes $b \in N(a)$ such that $d(q, b) \leq d(q, c) + 2r$. This is because any element $x \in (q, r)_d$ can differ from q by at most r in any distance evaluation and could have been inserted into

---

Algorithm 1 Process to build a DiSAT for $\mathbb{U} \cup \{a\}$ with root a.

BuildTree(Node a, Set of nodes U)
1. $N(a) \leftarrow \emptyset$ /* neighbors of a */
2. $R(a) \leftarrow 0$ /* covering radius */
3. For $v \in U$ in increasing distance to a Do
4. $R(a) \leftarrow \max(R(a), d(v, a))$
5.   If $\forall b \in N(a),\ d(v, a) < d(v, b)$ Then
6. $N(a) \leftarrow N(a) \cup \{v\}$
7. For $b \in N(a)$ Do $S(b) \leftarrow \emptyset$
8. For $v \in U - N(a)$ Do
9. $c \leftarrow \text{argmin}_{b \in N(a)} d(v, b)$
10. $S(c) \leftarrow S(c) \cup \{v\}$
11. For $b \in N(a)$ Do **BuildTree**($b, S(b)$)

Algorithm 2 Searching of q with radius r in a DiSAT with root a.

RangeSearch(Node a, Query q, Radius r, Distance d_{min})
1. If $d(a, q) \leq R(a) + r$ Then
2.   If $d(a, q) \leq r$ Then Report a
3. $d_{min} \leftarrow \min\ \{d(c, q),\ c \in N(a)\} \cup \{d_{min}\}$
4.   For $b \in N(a)$ Do
5.   If $d(b, q) \leq d_{min} + 2r$ Then
6.   **RangeSearch**(b, q, r, d_{min})

---

any of those b nodes. During the search, all the nodes that are found to be close enough to q are reported. [9, 14].

3.1 Dynamic Distal Spatial Approximation Forest

The Bentley-Saxe method (BS) is a technique for transforming a static index into a dynamic one, as long as the index is *decomposable* and based on the binary representation of integers [1]. The Distal Spatial Approximation Forest (DiSAF) [3] applies the BS method to a DiSAT to create a dynamic index. Specifically, we use the BS method to create multiple trees, which are all DiSATs, resulting in a *forest* of DiSATs. This index is called the *Dynamic Distal Spatial Approximation Forest* (DiSAF), with each subtree T_i having 2^i elements.

To illustrate, consider the example shown in Fig. 1(a). Figure 2 illustrates the DiSAF obtained by inserting the objects $p_1, \cdots, p_{15}$ one by one in that order. This results in four DiSATs, T_0, T_1, T_2, and T_3, with T_0 containing only p_{15}, T_1 containing p_{13} and p_{14}, T_2 containing $p_9, \ldots, p_{12}$, and T_3 containing $p_1, \ldots p_8$. The covering radii of the tree roots' neighbors are depicted, with some having a radius of zero. It's worth noting that the DiSAF has no parameters, so the only way to get different forests is by considering different insertion orders.

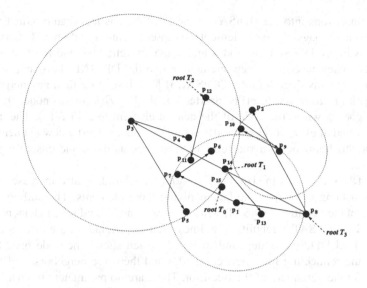

Fig. 2. Example of the DiSAF, inserting from p_1 to p_{15}.

Dynamic Spatial Approximation Tree

The *Dynamic Spatial Approximation Tree* (DSAT) [10] is an online version of the Static Approximation Tree (SAT) that enables dynamic insertions and deletions without increasing the construction cost. Although not intentionally designed as such, the DSAT has an impressive feature of enhancing the searching performance. The DSAT is faster in searching even when it has less information at construction than the static version of the index. The DSAT is designed for scenarios where the database is not known before-hand, and objects arrive at the index at random, along with queries. Since the DSAT is a dynamic data structure, it cannot make strong assumptions about the database and will not have statistics about all of the database.

4   Dynamic Distal Spatial Approximation Tree

The main cost of DSAT construction is the reconstruction required after insertion. To avoid this cost, the authors propose lazy insertions, where they delay the insertion of elements until the pool of objects is large enough to justify the insertion. This results in the Dynamic Distal Spatial Approximation Tree (DDiSAT), which significantly reduces construction costs compared to DiSAF and performs better in search performance than DiSAT.

Each DDiSAT node can store an element a, its covering radius $rc(a)$, its set of neighbors $N(a)$, and a bag $B(a)$ of pairs of (element, distance), that are new elements into the database, and the distance is its distance from a. The DDiSAT can store twice the number of elements compared to DiSAT inside its nodes. The authors rebuild the DDiSAT only when the number of elements in the node bags equals the number of nodes in the DDiSAT.

During insertions into the DDiSAT, if the DDiSAT has less than or equal to i elements in the node bags, the new element x is inserted into a node bag. Otherwise, all the elements in the DDiSAT (in nodes and bags) are retrieved, and the tree is rebuilt as a DiSAT. When inserting a new element x into the DDiSAT, the search begins at the tree root. For any node b in the DDiSAT, if b is closer to x than any neighbors in $N(b)$, the pair $(x, distance(b, x))$ is inserted into the bag $B(b)$ of this node. Otherwise, the search goes down to the node of the nearest element to x in $N(b)$. The covering radii are updated at every level while traversing the tree to insert a new element x. The authors use this heuristic to avoid rebuilding the tree as often and ensure top search performance.

As the DDiSAT grows in size, the threshold for rebuilding also increases, making the reconstructions more sporadic but involving more elements. The authors provide an example of the resulting DDiSAT, which has eight nodes and seven elements within their bags. The DDiSAT is rebuilt three times when p_2, p_4, and p_8 are inserted, respectively. The final DDiSAT is depicted in Fig. 3, which shows the node bags for lazy insertions, the connecting lines between nodes and their tree neighbors, and the covering radii for the neighbors of the tree root. There are no parameters in DDiSAT, and different trees can be obtained by considering different insertion orders.

Algorithm 3 illustrates the insertion process of a new element x into a DDiSAT T rooted at a. That means, when the first element x arrives to the database, we need to build the initial underlying DiSAT. Therefore, the first insertion will be done invoking **BuildTree** $(x, \emptyset)$. As it is possible to intuit, $\#nodes$ is the number of nodes into the underlying DiSAT tree, and $\#pendings$ is the number of elements into the bags; that is, elements pending to be actually inserted into the DiSAT. We follow the path from the tree root to the closest element to x in the underlying DiSAT, with a greedy spatial-approximation strategy, and then, we add the new element x in its bag B. Then, we need to verify whether this insertion produces that the number of pending elements ($\#pendings$) becomes equal to the number of nodes ($\#nodes$). In the case of $\#nodes = \#pendings$, we need to collect all the elements in a set S and rebuild

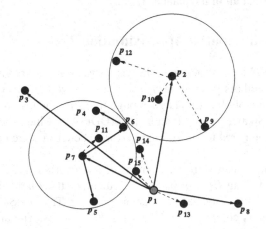

Fig. 3. Example of the DDiSAT, inserting from p_1 to p_{15}.

Algorithm 3 Insertion of a new element x in a DDiSAT T with root a.

Insert (Node a, Element x)
1. $c \leftarrow \text{argmin}_{b \in N(a)} d(b, x)$
2. $R(a) \leftarrow \max\{R(a), d(a, x)\}$ /* update the covering radius of a */
3. If $d(a, x) < d(c, x)$ Then
4. $B(a) \leftarrow B(a) \cup \{(x, d(a, x))\}$ /* add to the bag of a */
5. $\#pendings \leftarrow \#pendings + 1$
6.   If $(\#nodes = \#pendings)$ Then
7.   Collect in S the all the elements into the DDiSAT T
8. $\#nodes \leftarrow |S|, \quad \#pendings \leftarrow 0$
9.   Select randomly an element a from S /* a as tree root */
10.   **BuildTree** $(a, S - \{a\})$ /* rebuild the tree */
11. Else
12.   **Insert** (c, x)

Algorithm 4 Searching of q with radius r in a DDiSAT with root a.

RangeSearch (Node a, Query q, Radius r, Distance d_{min})
1. If $d(a, q) \le R(a) + r$ Then
2.   If $d(a, q) \le r$ Then Report a
3.   For any pair $(x, d_x) \in B(a)$
4.   If $|d(a, q) - d_x| \le r$ Then
5.   If $(d(x, q) \le r$ Then Report x
6. $d_{min} \leftarrow \min \{d(c, q), \ c \in N(a)\} \cup \{d_{min}\}$
7.   For $b \in N(a)$ Do
8.   If $d(b, q) \le d_{min} + 2r$ Then
9.   **RangeSearch** (b, q, r, d_{min})

---

with these objects the underlying DiSAT. Algorithm `BuildTree`(a, S), invoked at line 10, is that used for the static construction (Algorithm 1) The next rebuild will occur after $|S|$ new insertions.

During searches, we take advantage of all the information from the tree. As in a search on a DiSAT (Algorithm 2), we also use the distances stored in the buckets. The Algorithm 4 illustrates the new search process. This process is invoked as `RangeSearch`$(a, q, r, d(a, q))$, where a is the tree root, r is the radius of the search, and q is the query object.

5   Experimental Results

We conducted an empirical evaluation of various indexes in three different metric spaces from the SISAP Metric Library. These spaces include a dictionary of 69,069 English words where the distance is calculated using the edit distance, a set of 112,682 8-D color histograms with Euclidean distance, and a set of 40,700 20-dimensional feature vectors from NASA images with Euclidean distance.

To evaluate the construction costs of the indexes, we built the index using the entire database. For dynamic indexes, we inserted objects one by one, while for static indexes, all elements were known beforehand. To evaluate search performance, we used 90% of the database elements to build the index and the remaining 10% were randomly selected as queries. These query objects were not part of the index, and we averaged the search costs of all the queries over 10 index constructions with different datasets permutations.

We considered range queries retrieving on average 0.01%, 0.1%, and 1% of the dataset, which corresponded to specific radii for each metric space. For the dictionary, radii from 1 to 4 were used, which retrieved on average 0.00003%, 0.00037%, 0.00326%, and 0.01757% of the dataset, respectively. The same queries were used for all experiments on the same datasets, and we did not consider k-nearest neighbor searching experiments as range-optimal algorithms already exist for them.

We compared our dynamic DDiSAT to the static alternatives SAT and DiSAT, as well as to the DiSAF and DSAT indexes. The construction costs of all indexes on the three metric spaces are shown in Fig. 4. It is worth noting that DDiSAT outperformed DiSAF in terms of construction costs, while DSAT did not require any reconstruction during the index construction via insertions. The arity parameter of the DSAT, which is the maximum number of neighbors of each tree node, was tunable and set to 4 for the NASA images and color histograms and 32 for the dictionary, as suggested by the authors in [10]. The source code for the different SAT versions (SAT and DSAT) is available at www.sisap.org.

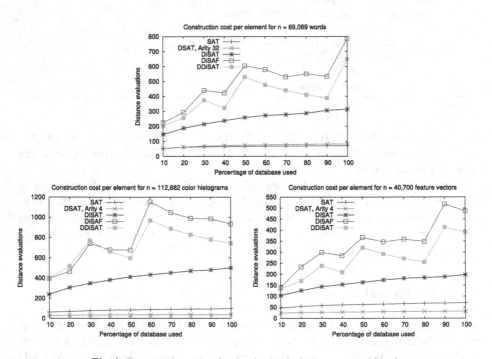

Fig. 4. Construction costs for the three metric spaces considered.

We analyze search costs in Fig. 5. As can be noticed, DDiSAT surpasses the dynamic indexes DiSAF and DSAT in all the spaces. Moreover, DDiSAT obtains the best search performance concerning the other four indexes (static and dynamic ones). Therefore, we can affirm that the heuristic of construction of DiSAT allows surpassing in searches the other strategies used in SAT and DSAT, and combining it with the bags into the nodes that store new elements near them, it is possible to obtain even better results. Besides, we have obtained a dynamic index with better search performance. Also notice that DDiSAT does not have tuning parameters, which is good for practitioners.

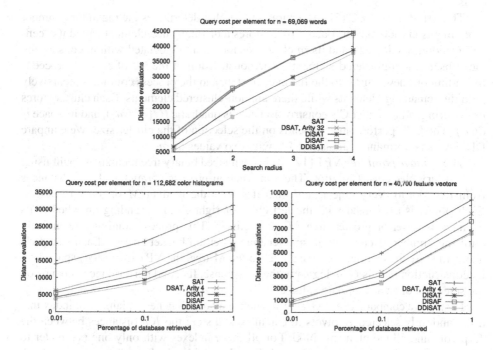

Fig. 5. Search costs for the three metric spaces considered.

5.1 Comparison with Other Representative Indexes

DDiSAT has shown outstanding performance compared to all the variants of the spatial approximation index. All of these indices use linear space, meaning that they require $O(N)$ distances to be stored. Specifically, in DDiSAT, each node of the underlying DiSAT only stores its covering radius, and each element in a bag only maintains its distance to the object in the DiSAT node that owns that bag.

To further understand DDiSAT's performance, we have selected several data structures from the literature whose source codes are available and whose space is also linear. Most of these data structures are static, but we also included the dynamic M-tree data structure, which is a crucial reference in the literature. We compare DDiSAT's performance against the M-tree, List of Clusters (LC), Vantage-point Tree (VPT), and a plain pivot-based index.

Although the M-tree [8] is designed for secondary memory, we only consider its construction and search costs regarding the number of distance computations. The M-tree[1] uses more memory than DDiSAT since it replies to its internal nodes with some elements as routing objects. Furthermore, all the database elements are in the tree's leaf-nodes, and each one stores one distance. It considers a minimum arity m for the internal nodes, where each node stores $2m$ distances and m pointers. We have experimented with different parameter settings and chosen the parameters that result in lower search costs.

The *list of clusters*LC [5] has a parameter m that determines the maximum number of elements in each cluster. Each cluster stores a distinguished element called its "center" (randomly selected), and its m closest elements are associated with it, considering the subset of non-clustered elements. The construction of the list of clusters proceeds by adding one new cluster to the list in each step, and the process continues recursively with the remaining elements while there are non-clustered elements. Each cluster stores its covering radius. The LC's construction cost is quadratic ($O(n^2/m)$), and its space is $O(n)$. The LC's performance depends on the selection of the cluster size. We compare DDiSAT's performance against the LC with two values of m.

The *vantage point tree* VPT [12, 13] is a balanced binary tree recursively built using an arbitrary element as its root. The construction process computes all the distances from the root to every object, and then it selects the median M of those distances. Each object is associated with the left child or right child depending on whether its distance is lower or greater than M, respectively. This process continues recursively until the number of elements is smaller than a certain bucket size m. Each tree node needs to store the median distance M. Like the M-tree, the VPT uses $O(n)$ space, and its construction time is $O(n \log n)$ in the worst case. Its good performance depends on the selection of an appropriate value of m.

Lastly, we compare DDiSAT's performance against a generic plain pivot index that uses randomly selected K pivots to calculate and store the Kn distances between the K pivots and all the elements in $\mathbb{U}$. For all these indexes with only one parameter to tune, we have chosen to display two of the values with which we have experimented. For LC, one value has a construction cost similar to that of DDiSAT, while the other achieves better search performance, but at a higher construction cost. As DDiSAT only stores one distance per element, it only requires linear space.

For all those indexes that only have one parameter to tune, we have chosen to display two of the values with which we have experimented. In LC one of those values achieves a construction cost similar to that of DDiSAT and the other, although it spends much more on construction, achieves better search performance. As our DDiSAT only stores one distance per element, the index needs only the space that is equivalent to store two distances per element [4]. Hence, for Pivot index we consider how is the behavior of this index when it only uses this space; that is only two pivots. Besides, we also show the behavior of this index when it uses 16 times the space of DDiSAT. For VPT index, we use two small values that appear with good search performance.

Figure 6 illustrates the comparison of construction costs of DDiSAT with the most of the indexes considered. In this case we do not show the construction costs of the pivot

---

[1] At http://www-db.deis.unibo.it/research/Mtree/.

index because it can be obtained as Kn. For the indexes that have only one parameter to set, we indicates between parentheses the value used of this parameter.

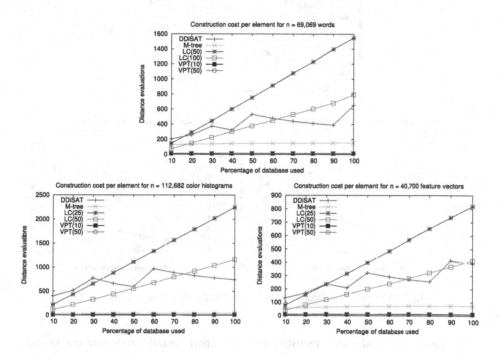

Fig. 6. Comparison of construction costs for the three metric spaces considered.

Figure 7 depicts the comparison of search costs of DDiSAT with the all the indexes considered. As it can be see, our proposal beats most of the other indexes in most of the metric spaces. Those options that surpass DDiSAT generally need much more construction time or much more space. The only option that have a better search performance than DDiSAT in all metric spaces is Pivot, considering $K = 32$; that is, more than 16 times more memory space than DDiSAT. However, when we have the memory space limited to the same space used for DDiSAT ($K = 2$), Pivot becomes as one of the worst alternatives for searches.

6   Analysis of Tree Partition Density

In the previous section we show that our proposal, the DDiSAT, improves simultaneosly in construction and search costs compared to DiSAT. Mind that the DiSAT tree has full knowledge of all the elements to build the index. As the DDiSAT is incrementally built, it only has knowledge of the elements inserted so far. An interesting question is about the partition induced for the DDiSAT, where some parts are denser because they also include pending close elements. We wanted to know how the relative density affects the search performance.

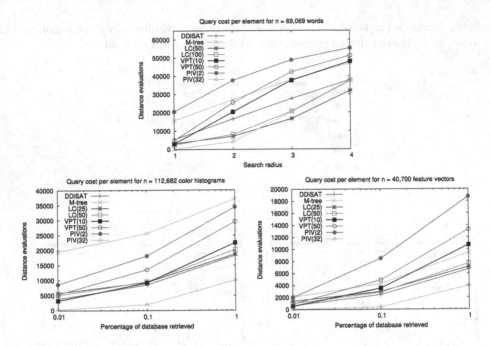

Fig. 7. Comparison of search costs for the three metric spaces considered.

To this end, using the same metric spaces, we experimentally study how the number of nodes into the DDiSAT affects the behavior of construction and search costs. Notice that the number of nodes is a proxy for the total number of objects indexed. In the experiment, as before, we build the DDiSAT with the 90% of the database elements and use the remaining 10% for searches. We randomly select the database elements used for building and for searching. We execute ten (10) times the experiments over different permutations of the database elements, and the results shown are the average of all obtained results.

To observe how the number of nodes and pending elements affects, we do not consider the restriction established to the DDiSAT previously: the DDiSAT will be rebuilt when a new insertion in a bag makes the number of elements in the bags (pending insertion in the DiSAT) equal to the number of nodes in the DDiSAT. Therefore, we build a DiSAT with a 10% (20%, 30%, ..., 80%) of the database elements, and the remaining 80% (70%, 60%, ..., 10%) is added into the bags of their closest node until we have the 90% of the database elements into the index. Then we query with the not yet used database elements (the remaining 10%). This way, the elements that are nodes into the DiSAT partition the space, and the remaining objects maintained into the node bags make the corresponding part denser.

Figure 8 depicts the analysis of the construction costs per element on the three metric space considered. As it can be observed, the costs increases slowly as the number of nodes into the DiSAT grows.

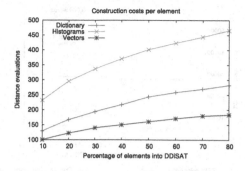

Fig. 8. Analysis on how the number of nodes affects the construction costs.

Figure 9 shows the analysis of the search costs on the tree metric space considered. We plot the behavior of each radii separately. Surprisingly, as it can be noticed, it is not necessary to do a more detailed partitioning of the space based on a large number of objects. Hence, few database objects are enough to define a good partition for the DiSAT. Moreover, relative to this space partition we locate the elements pending insertion are located to their closest representative object. Thereby, we can lower the construction cost of a static DiSAT, while maintaining a remarkable good search performance. Therefore, lazzy insertion has an added advantage for either an static index or a dynamic one.

7   Conclusions

We have introduced a new dynamic version of DiSAT that overcomes its previous limitations by incorporating insertion capability while improving search quality. The fact remains that there are only a few data structures that efficiently search metric spaces dynamically. Our proposed heuristic can further optimize the DiSAT by taking advantage of the compact subtrees produced by distal nodes, which create partitions over the metric space. This method assigns new elements to their nearest object in the tree, as they await insertion into the DiSAT node.

Previously, the DiSAT data structure was impractical due to its high construction cost and inability to accommodate insertions and deletions. However, we have addressed some of these weaknesses by obtaining reasonable construction costs, which can still be further improved. One possible approach is by providing a bulk-loading algorithm that initially creates the DDiSAT if we know a subset of elements beforehand, thus avoiding unnecessary rebuilding when we insert new elements. Additionally, using a combination of lazy insertion and tree rebuilding can further reduce insertion costs.

Our future work involves designing a fully dynamic DDiSAT data structure that can support deletions and an efficient bulk-loading algorithm to further decrease insertion costs. We also aim to develop a smart solution to k-NN search that uses all calculated distances to shrink the radius enclosing k elements as soon as possible. Moreover, we are currently pursuing in the direction of making the DDiSAT work efficiently in secondary memory. In that case we need to consider as relevant for index performance

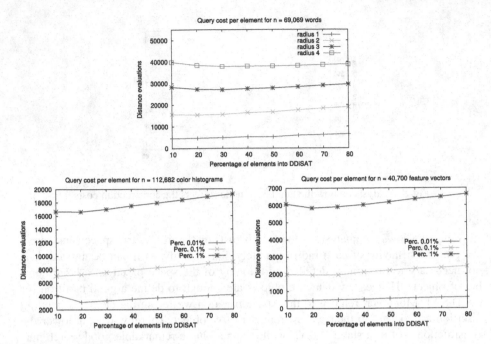

Fig. 9. Analysis on how the number of nodes affects the search costs.

both the number of distance computations and disk accesses. A simple solution could combine the DDiSAT with some ideas from the DiSAF; that is, we can consider a forest of DDiSAT, where each DDiSAT fit in a certain fixed number of disk pages.

References

1. Bentley, J.L., Saxe, J.B.: Decomposable searching problems I. Static-to-dynamic transformation. J. Algorithms **1**(4), 301–358 (1980)
2. Chávez, E., Di Genaro, M.E., Reyes, N.: An efficient dynamic version of the distal spatial approximation trees. In: Actas del XXVIII Congreso Argentino de Ciencias de la Computación (CACIC 2022), pp. 468–477, October 2022
3. Chávez, E., Di Genaro, M.E., Reyes, N., Roggero, P.: Decomposability of disat for index dynamization. J. Comput. Sci. Technol. 110–116 (2017)
4. Chávez, E., Ludeña, V., Reyes, N., Roggero, P.: Faster proximity searching with the distal sat. Inf. Syst. (2016)
5. Chávez, E., Navarro, G.: A compact space decomposition for effective metric indexing. Pattern Recogn. Lett. **26**(9), 1363–1376 (2005)
6. Chávez, E., Navarro, G., Baeza-Yates, R., Marroquín, J.L.: Searching in metric spaces. ACM Comput. Surv. **33**(3), 273–321 (2001)
7. Chen, L., et al.: Indexing metric spaces for exact similarity search. ACM Comput. Surv. **55**(6), 1–39 (2022)
8. Ciaccia, P., Patella, M., Zezula, P.: M-tree: an efficient access method for similarity search in metric spaces. In: Proceedings of the 23rd Conference on Very Large Databases (VLDB 1997), pp. 426–435 (1997)

9. Navarro, G.: Searching in metric spaces by spatial approximation. Very Large Databases J. (VLDBJ) **11**(1), 28–46 (2002)

10. Navarro, G., Reyes, N.: Dynamic spatial approximation trees. J. Exp. Algorithmics **12**, 1.5:1–1.5:68 (2008)

11. Samet, H.: Foundations of Multidimensional and Metric Data Structures (The Morgan Kaufmann Series in Computer Graphics and Geometric Modeling). Morgan Kaufmann Publishers Inc., San Francisco (2005)

12. Uhlmann, J.K.: Satisfying general proximity/similarity queries with metric trees. Inf. Process. Lett. **40**, 175–179 (1991)

13. Yianilos, P.N.: Data structures and algorithms for nearest neighbor search in general metric spaces. In: Proceedings of the 4th ACM-SIAM Symposium on Discrete Algorithms (SODA 1993), pp. 311–321 (1993)

14. Zezula, P., Amato, G., Dohnal, V., Batko, M.: Similarity Search: The Metric Space Approach. Advances in Database Systems, vol. 32. Springer, New York (2006). https://doi.org/10.1007/0-387-29151-2

Hardware Architectures, Networks, and Operating Systems

Analysis of QoS and QoE Metrics of IPTV Multicast Video Traffic on a LAN TestBed

Santiago Pérez(✉) [ID], Higinio Facchini [ID], Alejandro Dantiacq, Pablo Varela [ID], Fabián Hidalgo, Bruno Roberti [ID], María Stefanoni [ID], and Matilde Césari [ID]

CeReCoN – Department of Electronics – Regional Mendoza, National Technological University, Rodríguez 273, M5502AJE Mendoza, Argentina
santiagocp@frm.utn.edu.ar

Abstract. Analog television systems have been around for over 70 years now. Over this period, viewers have witnessed several improvements, including the transition from black and white to color television. In the last few years, the industry has undergone a profound transition, migrating from conventional television to a new digital era. Indeed, digital television has become the most significant advance in television technology, providing users with multiple options, increased flexibility and an enhanced interactive visual experience. Internet Protocol television (IPTV) constitutes a means to carry a stream of video content over a network using an Internet protocol (IP). The ultimate goal of IPTV is offering a completely personalized experience, ensuring Quality of Service (QoS) and QoE (Quality of Experience) within the organization, including LAN networks of a television channel or traditional LAN networks. This research study analyzes the behavior of IPTV traffic in an experimental LAN with controlled traffic, and is the continuation of a previous experimental study discussed in a paper presented at CACIC 2022. Different codecs are used for comparison purposes, using detailed quantitative results of QoS metrics as well as a basis to establish indicative QoE values. The findings reported in this paper offer guidance on suitable software and network topology configurations for managing similar networks, in addition to providing detailed values for simulation analysts.

Keywords: IPTV · Multicast traffic · Codecs · QoS · QoE

1 Introduction

In general, IPTV is a term applicable to the delivery of traditional television content, such as movies and on-demand video, over a private network. From a service provider perspective, IPTV covers the acquisition, processing and safe delivery of video content over an IP-based network infrastructure. From a user perspective, IPTV looks and operates like a standard pay-per-view TV subscription service. For these reasons, most TV operators have upgraded their existing networks and implemented advanced digital platforms, in an attempt to migrate their traditional analog service subscribers to more sophisticated digital services.

P. Pesado (Ed.): CACIC 2022, CCIS 1778, pp. 193–208, 2023.
https://doi.org/10.1007/978-3-031-34147-2_13

The official definition of IPTV, as approved by the International Telecommunication Union IPTV Focus Group (ITU-T FG IPTV) is as follows: IPTV is defined as "multimedia services such as television/video/audio/text/graphics/data delivered over IP based networks managed to provide the required level of quality of service and experience, security, interactivity and reliability." When discussing IPTV audiovisual format transmission, receiving devices include tablets, notebooks, smartphones, PCs, TV sets, etc. At this point, it is worth differentiating this service from other online options, such as free Internet channels or YouTube-like channels, where videos can be downloaded and played with no quality guarantee.

This paper describes an experimental study on multicast IPTV video traffic on an actual laboratory LAN network used as a testbed, emulating an IPTV LAN network in a TV channel or LAN campus. An experimental, controlled traffic, wired-client network topology was used, utilizing FFmpeg Server software as video server and WireShark as traffic analyzer. IPTV video traffic was encoded in H.264, H.265, VP8 and Theora, so as to compare and understand the impact of different codecs on network traffic QoS and QoE. The experiments were run using a video trailer of the movie *Star Trek*. This paper builds upon previous experimental studies performed on wired Ethernet and Wi-Fi networks for general video (non-IPTV) traffic using H261, H263 and H264 codecs in IPv4.

The main contributions of this study include: i)Quantitative results emerging from experimental studies on an actual laboratory LAN network, so as to assess QoS and QoE behavior for IPTV traffic and different codecs; ii) The conclusions emerging from the experimental setup, which can serve as reference to simulation analysts when determining IPTV traffic simulator settings; and iii) The definition of a new topology, methodology and a variety of experimental sub-scenarios —depending on the codec— applicable when assessing such elements or other complementary aspects of IPTV video streaming and the relevant QoS and QoE.

The rest of this paper is structured as follows: Sect. 2 (Protocols and Codecs) describes the main features of these components as per this experimental study, Sect. 3 (Scenarios and Experimental Resources) offers a description of the topology and hardware and software devices, Sect. 4 (Results) provides the quantitative data obtained from the QoS and QoE metrics. Finally, Sect. 5 discusses the main conclusions emerging from this work.

2   Protocols and Codecs

Research groups continue working towards understanding traffic behavior in data networks and the behavior of traffic generated or received by network nodes (servers, end workstations and active devices), in an attempt to improve their performance and throughput.

Insufficient knowledge about this topic may lead to oversimplified conclusions or interpretations, planning errors and poor simulations, ultimately resulting in lack of stability in the infrastructure. This study on IPTV traffic is part of the Data Network Traffic Engineering Theory. Network Traffic Theory applies probability theory to the solution of issues related to planning, service assessment, operation and maintenance of communication systems.

A number of earlier research papers and publications have been taken into account for this study. Unfortunately, experimental studies on IPTV have often failed to exhibit topologies that are standardized or harmonized for the scenarios under study, resulting in discrepancies in the methodology, video(s), or video codecs being used. This situation hinders the comparison and contrast of measurements and conclusions of contemporary studies and/or studies conducted over time by the same or different authors.

The rest of this section briefly describes the main features of the tools, protocols and codecs used.

2.1 Video Streaming

A broad range of video streaming options are available in networks, each of which may display different sets of behavior. Video traffic may be point-to-point, multicast or broadcast. Additionally, videos may be precoded (stored) or they may be coded in real time (for example, while an interactive videophone communication or video conference ensues). Video channels may be static or dynamic, and require a packet-based or a circuit-based switching system. Additionally, channels may withstand a constant or a variable bit rate speed. They may have also reserved a number of resources in advance or they may simply be offering best-effort capacity.

Clearly, a few basic issues are at play here, since only best-effort delivery is generally offered, which means there are no guarantees regarding bandwidth, jitter or potential packet losses. Therefore, a key goal in IPTV video streaming involves designing a reliable system that delivers high quality video and takes into account Traffic Engineering, QoS and QoE.

2.2 IP Multicast

IP multicast is defined as "a bandwidth-conserving technology that reduces traffic by delivering a single stream of information simultaneously" to dozens, hundreds or thousands of businesses and homes.

Some of the advantages of multicast content streaming solutions include:

- Scalability: Bandwidth requirements are no longer proportional to the number of receivers.
- Performance: Having each source process a single flow of data will be always more efficient than having one receiver process each flow.
- Lower capital expenditure: Due to the less tight specs of the network elements necessary to provide the service.

Routers rely on multicast protocols that form distribution trees to deliver multicast content, ensuring highly efficient delivery of data to multiple receivers. They are responsible for replicating and distributing the multicast content to all the receivers within a multicast group. IP uses PIM-SM, PIM-SSM or other protocols. For this study in particular, PIM-SM (Protocol Independent Multicast – Sparse Mode) was used.

2.3 Video Codec

Figure 1 shows a simplified visual representation of the TCP/IP stack, describing the suite of protocols that enables IPTV traffic transfer. The communication process begins at the encoding layer, where the uncompressed analog or digital signal becomes compressed, and an elementary stream is output from the encoder. An elementary stream can be defined as a continuous digital signal in real time.

Video encoding refers to the process of converting a video with no format into a digital format that is compatible with multiple devices. In order to reduce the size of a video to a more manageable one, content distributors use video compression technology known as codec. This is done by means of sophisticated lossy compression methods that do away with unnecessary data. A codec operates on the video twice: at the source, to compress it, and prior to playing the video, to decompress it.

In this case, for the IPTV experimentation, a balanced mix of established and newer standards was selected. The video codecs that were used in this study are listed and described below:

- H.264/MPEG-4 AVC: A video compression standard promoted jointly by the ITU and the ISO, offering significant advances in terms of compression efficiency, which result in half or lower bit rate when compared to MPEG-2 and MPEG-4 Simple Profile.
- H.265/ MPEG-H Part 2/ High Efficiency Video Coding (HEVC): A video compression format following H.264/MPEG-4 AVC, developed jointly by the ISO/IEC Moving Picture Experts Group (MPEG) and ITU-T Video Coding Experts Group (VCEG), corresponding to ISO/IEC CD 23008-2 High Efficiency Video Coding.

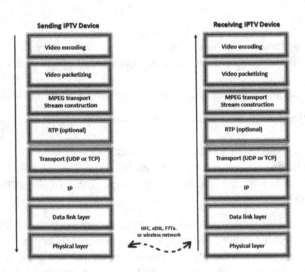

Fig. 1. IPTV protocol stack.

This standard may be used to deliver higher quality, low bit-rate video while requiring the same bit rate. It is compatible with ultra-high-definition television and 8192 × 4320 display resolution.

- VP8: A video codec by On2 Technologies, released on September 13, 2008. On May 19, 2010, Google, having acquired On2 Technologies back in 2009, released VP8 as an open-source codec (under a BSD-like license).
- Theora: A free video compression format developed by the Xiph.Org Foundation as part of the Ogg project. It derives from VP3 codec. In 2010, Google began funding part of the Ogg Theora Vorbis project. Theora stands for a general-purpose video codec requiring low CPU usage.

3 Scenarios and Experimental Resources

Within the scientific/technology community, different lines of research are devoted to studying IPTV and non-IPTV video traffic based on experimental studies on actual networks showing their behavior in each case [1–14]. Among them, our own contributions from previous studies on video traffic in various networks [9–14] and IPTV networks [12], which is now enhanced with new results and a more detailed discussion.

These studies involve capturing traffic in current and/or synthetic video traffic scenarios. Unfortunately, research studies covering IPTV LAN for TV channels, or traditional LAN networks in particular, often fail to exhibit harmonized, standardized experimental scenarios in terms of the number and type of codecs used, the videos analyzed, etc. This situation, combined with other aspects, makes it difficult to compare across contemporary studies and/or studies conducted in the past. This has been the main motivation to propose a new scenario and, consequently, a new experimental methodology for capturing IPTV video traffic.

3.1 Network Topology

The selected topology entails having one computer functioning as video streaming server, and desktop computers (PCs) as clients, all connected at the endpoints of a mixed network made up of routers and switches with different types of links interconnecting them. Links are of the FastEthernet type, with a data transmission rate of 100 Mbps. For data transmission between routers R1 to R6, the OSPFv2 routing protocol was configured. Additionally, PIM Sparse Mode (PIM-SM) was set up for these routers. Existing redundant links were used to arrive at an approximation of an actual network, but the routing protocol was configured so that the traffic between the server and each client would always follow a single path. The network topology has been represented in Fig. 2: i) As server: One desktop computer feauturing Intel Core I5 processor, 8 GB RAM and Linux Ubuntu; ii) As clients: Desktop computers featuring AMD Athlon(tm) II X2 250 3 GHz processor, 4 GB RAM and 64-bit Windows 10; iii) Routers R1, R2, R3 and R4 were Cisco 2811 models, while R5 and R6 were resolved with Cisco WS-CS3750 multilayer switches; and iv) Finally, the routers were connected to the PCs by means of Cisco Layer 2 Catalyst Model WS-2950–24 switches.

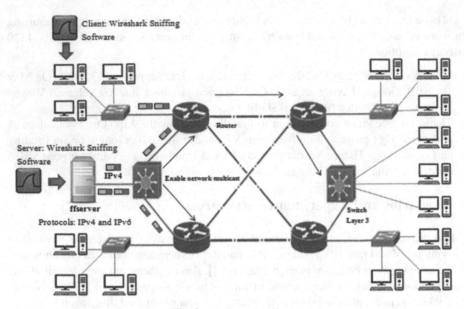

Fig. 2. Network topology.

FFmpeg software was used as a streaming server [15]. FFmpeg is a cross-platform tool to record, convert and edit audio and video. The framework consists of a component library, the elements of which interact with the application using ffmpeg commands in order to complete streaming processes properly.

3.2 Video and Video Sniffer

At this stage, a video was used, which had been encoded using alternatively the codecs listed above. The video material was a trailer of the movie *Star Trek* [16], 2 min and 11 s long (Fig. 3). Table 1 compares the features of each codec for this video.

Fig. 3. Screenshot of the *Star Trek* movie trailer 1.

Wireshark [17] was used to measure and capture traffic. This software includes several features intended to analyze each data packet while also evaluating as a whole the set of packets of the video transmission. For the purposes of this experimental study, several network traffic parameters were evaluated, such as delay, the number of packets transmitted, etc.

Based on this experimental scenario, a series of tests were performed, taking into consideration the following:

a) The video file encoded in each of the 4 formats listed above was configured alternatively on the streaming server.
b) Prior to being measured, all equipment items in the topology were synchronized by means of an NTP local server.
c) From the server, the video file was then sent in its specific codec to the network, using a multicast configuration.
d) Afterwards, the video format was rotated to the other three video codecs, as described in step c) above.

During each test, traffic captures were performed on the server and on each client node using the Wireshark sniffer software. The packets were filtered by RTCP or UDP packet type (Fig. 4). For video transfer purposes, 59,644, 54,202, 46,502 and 61,986 frames were needed for H.264, H.265, Theora and VP8 codecs, respectively.

Captures were exported from Wireshark.pcap files to.csv files (Fig. 5). A.csv file is basically a text file that stores captures as frame vectors, which are then analyzed in Excel or using a special-purpose program (in this case, using the Python programming language).

Table 1. Video Properties – *Star Trek* movie trailer.

Video 1	H.264	H.265	Theora	VP8
Format	MPEG-4	MPEG-4	Ogg	WebM v2
File size	79.9 MiB	72.3 MiB	83.3 MiB	78.6 MiB
Length	2 min 11 s	2 min 11 s	2 min 11 s	2 min 11 s
Bit rate mode	Variable	Variable	Variable	Variable
Bit rate	5,109 kb/s	4,620 kb/s	5,329 kb/s	5,028 kb/s
Video				
Format	AVC	HEVC	Theora	VP8
Bit rate	5,011 kb/s	4,514 kb/s	5,010 kb/s	4,721 kb/s
Width [in pixels]	1,280 pixels	1,280 pixels	1,280 pixels	1,280 pixels
Height [in pixels]	528 pixels	528 pixels	528 pixels	528 pixels
Aspect ratio	2.4:1	2.4:1	2.4:1	2.4:1
Frame rate mode	constant	constant	constant	constant

(continued)

Table 1. (*continued*)

Video 1	H.264	H.265	Theora	VP8
Frame rate [in fps]	23.976 fps	23.976 fps	23.976 fps	23.976 fps
*Bits/(pixel*frame)*	0.309	0.279	0.309	0.291
Audio				
Format	AAC LC	AAC LC	Vorbis	Vorbis
Bit rate mode	Variable	constant	Variable	Variable
Bit rate	98.7 kb/s	99.7 kb/s	98.7 kb/s	98.7 kb/s
Maximum bit rate	167 kb/s	167 kb/s	167 kb/s	167 kb/s
Channel	2 channels	2 channels	2 channels	2 channels
Sampling rate	44.1 kHz	44.1 kHz	44.1 kHz	44.1 kHz
Track size	1.54 MiB (2%)	1.56 MiB (2%)	1.54 MiB (2%)	1.54 MiB (2%)

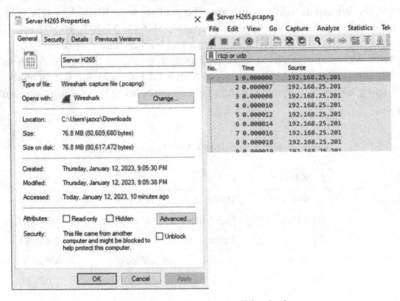

Fig. 4. Packet filtering on Wireshark.

4 Test Results

4.1 QoS Analysis

The QoS of specific network traffic in a given network topology and architecture can be considered based on the behavior of certain characteristic network parameters. Standardized QoS parameters are delay, jitter and packet loss. Reference values for these network metrics are 100 ms, 30 ms and 0.1%, respectively.

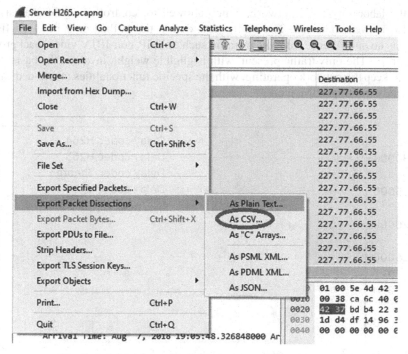

Fig. 5. Wireshark capture file being converted to a CSV file.

When suggesting instances of comparison in the sub-scenarios under study, the following QoS critical or verification points were established:

- Average delay,
- Maximum delay,
- Minimum delay,
- Average jitter,
- Maximum jitter,
- Minimum jitter.

The delay metrics for each codec have been depicted for comparison purposes in Fig. 6. As made evident by the chart, the values meet QoS requirements by a wide margin. Additionally, within the 1 to 2 ms range, the codecs behave clearly different from one another, except for H.264 and H.265. These two codecs have an average delay of around 2 ms, while Theora's is close to 1.5 ms.

Finally, VP8 delays are around 1 ms. Similarly, Fig. 7 shows the behavior of the different codecs under study with respect to jitter metrics. The values meet QoS requirements by a wide margin. Within the -0.010 to + 0.020 ms range, the codecs reveal clearly different behaviors for this measurement.

Each codec creates a response in the Cartesian coordinate system which can be represented as a triangle. However, the codecs vary in the base width and height of each triangle, thus implying different responses in the bandwidth of possible jitter values and the level of repetition at which most of these values are concentrated.

In the laboratory LAN network, which allowed for controlled traffic analysis, no frame losses were detected. The traffic flow during the testbed only involved IPTV. There was no interference from other traffic such as VoIP, non-IPTV video, background or best effort. The only traffic present, with negligible weight, involved the basic flows needed to keep the network operating, with the specific functionalities mentioned earlier in this study (routing, PIM, etc.).

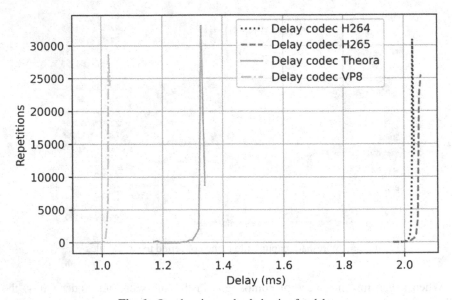

Fig. 6. Overlapping codec behavior for delay.

4.2 QoE Analysis

On their own, QoS processes are not entirely adequate to deliver guaranteed performance, since they fail to consider user perception about network behavior. This is how Quality of Experience (QoE) emerged as a discipline. From a theoretical standpoint, QoE is the user's degree of satisfaction or dissatisfaction with an application or service. It results from the ability to comply with user expectations with regards to the use/enjoyment of an application or service, in light of the user's personality and current mood.

In practical terms, key findings from QoE-related projects show that, for many services, there are multiple QoS parameters contributing to users' overall perception of quality. This situation has resulted in the emergence of a layered approach to QoE/QoS, in which network sizing strategies are governed by user requirements. This layered approach to QoE/QoS does not ignore the QoS aspect of the network: on the contrary, it complements the perspectives at the user and service levels, as shown in Fig. 8.

It should be noticed that because the domains of QoE and QoS overlap somewhat, there is a considerable volume of information exchange/feedback between the frameworks.

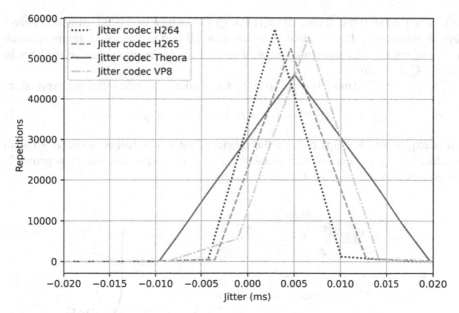

Fig. 7. Overlapping codec behavior for jitter.

This discussion suggests that the effect of QoE might be attributable to the application layer or to a combination of the network and application layers only. Even though trade-offs between network quality and network capacity could start by QoS (at the level of the application layer, given network capacity considerations), it is an understanding of user requirements at the service level (i.e., in terms of QoE measurements) that will help better select the QoS parameters at the application level which will then be assigned to the QoS parameters at the network level. Some working scenarios aim at controlling QoE by relying on QoS parameters as actuators.

In order to evaluate or measure QoE as perceived by the user, three methods have been proposed: (i) subjective methods, (ii) objective methods and (iii) indirect methods. Subjective methods involve having people evaluate video quality in a controlled environment, by means of polling mechanisms. Objective mechanisms are algorithms which rely on a full, partial or unused reference signal to measure video quality. Finally, indirect methods resort to mathematical modeling to evaluate the experience associated to the video. Such mathematical model is generated taking into account the variation in QoS measurements.

Bearing in mind the above, the network QoE was then evaluated using an indirect method, which served as an initial approximation. (Based on these data, future research work will resume this study and enhance its findings by using subjective methods to arrive at QoE results.)

The mathematical model proposed in [8] was applied, using the following expression:

$$QoE = 1/(Delay + K * Jitter) * e^{\wedge}(Lost\ of\ packets) \tag{1}$$

In this expression, K helps balance the impact of jitter with respect to delay so as to calculate user QoE. None of the parameters used in this expression can be negative. K was assigned a value of 2 during the evaluation.

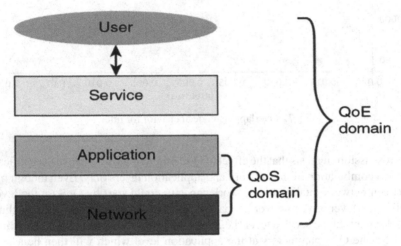

Fig. 8. Relationship between QoS and QoE domains for a QoE/QoS approach.

Figure 9 shows a comparison of QoE for each of the codecs under study, based on delay and using average and maximum jitter values as parameters, in each case. As made evident by the figure, within the 1 to 2 ms range, the codecs behave clearly different from one another, except for H.264 and H.265. The response of these two codecs is worse in terms of QoE. VP8 reveals better behavior, while the response by Theora can be described as intermediate.

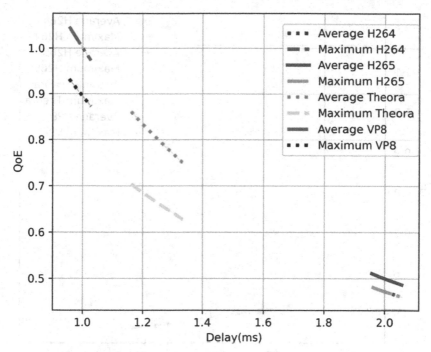

Fig. 9. Comparison of QoE based on delay, for average and maximum jitter values applicable to all 4 codecs.

Conversely, Fig. 10 shows QoE for each of the codecs analyzed, based on jitter and using average and maximum delay values as parameters, in each case. Within the -0.10 to +0.15 ms range, the codecs display different behaviors, except for H.264 and H.265. The response of these two codecs is worse in terms of QoE. Once again, VP8 reveals better behavior, while the response by Theora can be described as intermediate in all cases.

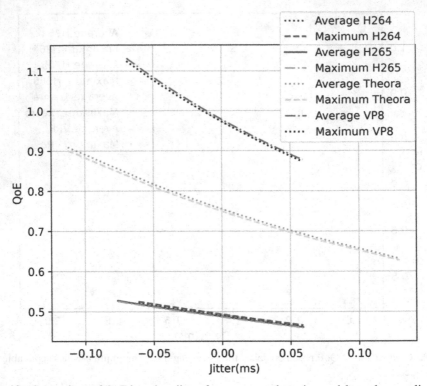

Fig. 10. Comparison of QoE based on jitter, for average and maximum delay values applicable to all 4 codecs.

5 Conclusions

The scopes of the QoS and QoE of IPTV traffic were analyzed thoroughly on an experimental network. To that end, an actual network topology of controlled traffic was used, which included a server and IPTV video clients, a *Star Trek* movie trailer, and 4 sub-scenarios or specific cases for each of the following 4 codecs: H.264, H.265, Theora and VP8. In all cases, a sniffer software was used to capture IPTV traffic.

The experiment revealed the following:

- In the experimental network intended for IPTV traffic, delay metrics meet QoS requirements by a wide margin, while delay shows clearly differentiated behavior among the codecs, except for that of H.264 and H.265. These two codecs have an average delay of around 2 ms, while Theora's is close to 1.5 ms. Finally, VP8 delays are around 1 ms.
- Jitter metrics also meet QoS requirements with ease, behaving differently depending on the codec being used. When values are represented, in repetition, based on jitter data, each codec creates a specific response, the graphic representation of which forms a triangle. Codec response varies in the base width and height of these triangles. Codec H.264 (Theora) shows the best (worst) overall response.

- When representing the adopted QoE expression, using delay (jitter) as independent variable, and jitter (delay) as parameter, codecs H.264 and H.265 have the worst behavior. VP8, however, has the best behavior, while the response by Theora can be described as intermediate.
- Neither the network topology nor the equipment type exercise significant impact, since their behavior is virtually identical for clients located at different network nodes.

The experience harnessed by the studies conducted on QoS and QoE of IPTV traffic on a LAN network using different codecs has opened the door to a series of alternative mechanisms to further explore this line of research, in order to continue making progress in refining QoE results, including a few considerations about user subjectivity.

QoE for multimedia content such as IPTV has also been defined in the ETSI (European Telecommunications Standards Institute) Standard TR 102 479.2 by the Telecommunications and Internet converged Services and Protocols for Advanced Networking (TISPAN). The MOS (Mean Opinion Score) refers to a measure that has been used in telephone networks for decades to obtain network quality information from a user perspective. Initially, and according to Recommendation T P.800 by the ITU, MOS was a subjective measurement, as audience members would sit in a "quiet" room and rate the quality of a phone call based on their own perception. It should be noted that MOS provides a numerical indication of the quality perceived by the user, which is issued after the multimedia content has been compressed and/or transmitted. In the future, the goal is to include an evaluation of user expectations in terms of QoE, using the same methodology and experimental scenario as applied in this paper. Of course, the subjective component may vary among users.

These conclusions may serve as reference material for following research analyzing similar contexts. Furthermore, IPTV traffic designers, analysts, planners and simulators may rely on the results from this case study to improve the implementation of their own tests and projects. Naturally, it is not possible to ensure the same type of behavior when using other video types or codec types different from those used in this experiment, or when traffic is carried over a network different from IEEE 802.3. Nevertheless, simulation analysts may use the metrics obtained experimentally in this paper as a guide to the network demands exercised by video conferences, movies, and so on, as well as their characteristics and features. Designers, planners and network administrators, on their part, with a keener interest in bandwidth data, may use the *Star Trek* movie trailer as reference data.

References

1. Driscoll, G.: Next Generation IPTV Services and Technologies, 1st edn. Publishing House: Wiley-Interscience, Canada (2018)
2. Lloret, J., Canovas, A., Rodrigues, J.J.P.C., Lin, K.: A network algorithm for 3D/2D IPTV distribution using WIMAX and WLAN technologies. Multimed. Tools Appl. **67**, 7–30 (2013)
3. Valencia, J., Muñoz, W., Golondrino, G.: Análisis de QoS para IPTV en un entorno de redes definidas por software. Revista Ingenierías Univer, Medellín, Colombia (2019)
4. Cuellar, J., Arciniegas, J., Ortiz, J.: Modelo para la medición de QoE en IPTV. Publishing House: Universidad Ecesi, Colombia (2018)

5. Herranz, J., Mauri, L.: Estudio de la variación de QoE en Televisión IP cuando varían los parámetros de QoS, Master's Thesis, Universidad Politecnica de Valencia, Gandia, Spain (2014)
6. Cuellar, J., Acosta, S., Arciniegas, J.: QoE/QoS Mapping Models to measure Quality of Experience to IPTV Service, Conference Paper, Publication: ResearchGate, Oct 2018
7. Baltoglou, G., Karapistoli, E., Chatzimisios, P.: IPTV QoS and QoE Measurements in Wired and Networks, Publication: Globecom. IEEE, Apr 2013
8. Solbes, A., Mauri, D., Gironés, D.: Diseño y Desarrollo de un Sistema de Gestión Inteligente integrado de servicios de IPTV estándar, estereoscópico y HD basado en QoE, Thesis work, Universidad Politecnica de Valencia, Gandia, Spain, Sep 2013
9. Pérez, S., et al.: Estudio experimental de tráfico de video en redes IPv6 multicast IEEE 802.11ac, In: Congreso Argentino de Ciencias de la Computación, CACIC 2019, Minutes Book, pp. 847–856. Rio Cuarto, Córdoba, Argentina (2019). ISBN: 978-987-688-377-1
10. Facchini, H., Perez, S., Hidalgo, F., Varela, P.: Análisis, simulación y estudio experimental del comportamiento de métricas de QoS y QoE de streamings de video multicast IPTV, WICC 2020, Santa Cruz, Argentina, May 2020
11. Perez, S., Salomón, G., Facchini, H.: Comparación del comportamiento de los códecs de video en el entorno WI-FI IEEE 802.11ac, Argencon 2020, Chaco, Argentina, Dec 2020
12. Pérez, S., et al.: Estudio Experimental del Comportamiento de Métricas de QoS y QoE de Streamings de Video Multicast IPTV, In: Congreso Argentino de Ciencias de la Computación, CACIC 2022, Editorial de la Universidad Nacional de La Rioja, pp. 479–488. La Rioja, Argentina (2022). ISBN: 978-987-1364-31-2
13. Pérez, S., Campos, J., Facchini, H., Dantiacq, A.: Experimental study of unicast and multicast video traffic using WAN test bed. https://ieeexplore.ieee.org/document/7585260. Last accessed 18 Jan 2020
14. Pérez, S., Marrone, L., Facchini, H., Hidalgo, F.: Experimental study of multicast and unicast video traffic in WAN links. IEEE Latin Am. Trans. **15**(10), 1847–1855 (2017). ISSN: 1548-0992
15. FFmpeg: https://www.ffmpeg.org/. Last accessed 18 Jan 2023
16. *Star Trek* Video: https://www.youtube.com/watch?v=g5lWao2gVpc. Last accessed 18 Jan 2023
17. Wireshark Foundation: https://www.wireshark.org/. Last accessed 18 Jan 2023

Innovation in Software Systems

A Query-By-Example Approach to Compose SPARQL Queries in the GF Framework for Ontology-Based Data Access

Sergio Alejandro Gómez[1,2(✉)] and Pablo Rubén Fillottrani[1,2]

[1] Laboratorio de I+D en Ingeniería de Software y Sistemas de Información (LISSI), Departamento de Ciencias e Ingeniería de la Computación, Universidad Nacional del Sur, San Andrés 800, Bahía Blanca, Argentina
{sag,prf}@cs.uns.edu.ar
[2] Comisión de Investigaciones Científicas de la Provincia de Buenos Aires (CIC-PBA), Calle 526 entre 10 y 11, La Plata, Argentina
https://lissi.cs.uns.edu.ar/

Abstract. The gap between legacy data sources and semantic web technologies can be bridged with the Ontology-Based Data Access (OBDA) methodology by providing protocols and tools for translating old data into ontologies. Querying modern ontologies in OWL/RDF files and understood as networks of objects having describing properties and interlinked by relations requires writing SPARQL queries, where it is essential to have a technical proficiency not usually in the hands of lay users. For studying this problem, we developed a prototype tool called GF to capable of executing arbitrary SPARQL queries posed against OWL/RDF ontologies obtained by OBDA from H2 relational databases as well as Excel and CSV spreadsheets. The tool allows to visually specify a subset of SPARQL selection and construction queries using a Query-By-Example approach. Our research shows that, given an OWL/RDF ontology obtained from any suitable data source, our implementation can express an important proper subset of queries and translate them into executable SPARQL queries.

Keywords: Ontologies · Ontology-Based Data Access · SPARQL · Knowledge Representation

1 Introduction

The Semantic Web (SW) is an interpretation of the web whose data resources have precise meaning defined in terms of conceptualizations known as ontologies allowing software agents to reason about such data thus permitting to elicit implicit knowledge hidden in the data [3]. Ontology-Based Data Access (OBDA) is a discipline concerned with bridging the gap between legacy data

© The Author(s), under exclusive license to Springer Nature Switzerland AG 2023
P. Pesado (Ed.): CACIC 2022, CCIS 1778, pp. 211–226, 2023.
https://doi.org/10.1007/978-3-031-34147-2_14

sources and SW technologies by providing protocols and tools for expressing old data into ontologies [4,11]. Querying ontologies provides many additional benefits to those offered by querying relational data such as allowing the usage of open-world semantics in contrast to closed-world semantics. Automated reasoning with ontologies allows to make explicit implicit conclusions hidden in the non-trivial subclass and composition relations that describe the underlying application domain modeled by the queried ontologies.

One of the advantages of OBDA is that old, legacy data can be then combined with new more modern ontological data. Legacy data include tabular data as relational database, Excel spreadsheets and CSV text files. Modern ontological data in contrast is represented as networks of objects interlinked by relations and properties and stored as OWL/RDF text files distributed in the SW. Querying modern ontologies requires writing SPARQL queries [9], an activity that have as requisite a user with technical proficiency that quite normally is not possessed by lay users.

In this work, we extend a prototype for OBDA called GF [7] that we have been developing in the last years to include the functionality of executing arbitrary SPARQL queries posed against OWL/RDF ontologies obtained by OBDA from H2 relational databases as well as Excel and CSV spreadsheets. Also to help naive users with less technical programming skills to perform queries on such ontologies, we introduce a wizard for expressing a subset of SPARQL queries visually based on a Query-By-Example (QBE) approach [12]. Our solution provides a concrete way of writing SPARQL queries over legacy data without requiring the user to know explicitly SPARQL syntax. For reproducibility of the results reported here, an executable file along with the files of the examples presented in this paper and its results can be checked online (see http://cs.uns.edu.ar/~sag/gf-v4.3.2).

This article consolidates and extends the results presented in [6]. We extend the discussion about SPARQL selection queries including additional operators, its relation with knowledge graphs and, additionally, we introduce the feature of how to build construction queries within the system. In [6], we presented how to visually codify a very specific subset of queries and categorize its cases as selection queries as queries over a single class, queries over a simple hierarchy of classes, totalization queries, and queries over associations Here we discuss more in detail optional queries and besides we present how to codify selection queries using the *IN* and *NOT IN* operators. Additionally, we explain the feature of building construction queries, where, besides specifying a graph pattern for the conditions the input data have to comply to, the user has to define the structure of the triples to be constructed. We explain how this is done in our system.

The rest of the work is structured as follows. In Sect. 2, we review the subset of SPARQL selection queries that our wizard can generate visually. In Sect. 3, we present the wizard to build the selection queries discussed previously. In Sect. 4, we extend the wizard to be able to build SPARQL construction queries in a visual manner. In Sect. 5, we review related work. Finally, in Sect. 6, we conclude and foresee future work.

2   Selection Queries in SPARQL

SPARQL [9] is the standard query language and protocol for Linked Open Data and RDF databases that can efficiently extract information hidden in non-uniform data and stored in various formats and sources, such as the web or RDF triple-stores. The distributed nature of SW data, unlike relational databases, helps users to write queries based on what they want to know instead of how the data is organized. In contrast to the SQL query language for relational databases, SPARQL queries are not constrained to working within one database – federated queries can access multiple data stores (or endpoints) because SPARQL is also an HTTP-based transport protocol, where any endpoint can be accessed via a standardized transport layer. RDF results can be returned in several data-interchange formats and RDF entities, classes, and properties are identified by IRIs such as <http://example.org/Person/name>, which are difficult to remember even knowing SPARQL and the underlying structure of the data source.

As mentioned in the introduction, we propose a wizard for visually composing SPARQL queries posed against a data source expressed as an OWL/RDF ontology. We now present the subset of queries that we solve with our implementation. We present a running example with which we present some prototypical queries and in Sect. 3 we show how these queries can be solved by using the wizard that we defined. We present a relational database schema for which the GF system produces an ontology automatically. Then we show some SPARQL queries posed against the ontology. We will see that writing those queries from scratch present an important challenge even for experienced users and that the proposed wizard can help in easing such task by allowing the composition of queries by a Query-By-Example methodology (i.e., visually and abstracting from some of the inner details of the query structure and the queried dataset).

Example 1. In Fig. 1, we define the schema of a very simple relational database and show how its translation to an OWL Description Logic (DL)[1] ontology should be and then propose some iconic SPARQL queries. There are two tables: *Person* and *Phone*. A person has a unique identifier, a name, a weight in kilograms, a sex that is false if the person is female and true if the person is male, also a person has a birth date. A phone has a unique identifier, a number, a price, and its owner. There is an implicit one-to-many relation from Person to Phone, meaning that a person can have 0, 1, or more phones and a phone can belong to 0 or at most 1 person.

Notice that in this work, we have added extra functionality to the direct mapping specification programmed in previous versions of GF (see [7] and references therein for details) in order to simulate the natural joins between tables and be able to retrieve that characteristic from SPARQL. Thus, the person now knows his phones and vice versa.

Person (personID, name, weight, sex, birthDate)
Phone (phoneID, number, price, owner)

Person					Phone			
personID	name	weight	sex	birthDate	phoneID	number	price	owner
1	John	120.0	true	2001-01-01	1	555-1234	200.00	1
2	Paul	110.0	true	2002-01-01	2	555-1235	220.00	1
3	Mary	60.0	false	2001-01-01	3	555-1236	230.00	2

Fig. 1. Relational schema and instance for tables *Person* and *Phone*

---

[1] We see a DL ontology as a mathematical conceptualization of an equivalent OWL/RDF file, which is understood as the serialization of such ontology [2].

Example 2 (Continues Example 1). In Fig. 2, the UML design of the classes Person and Phone can be seen. In Fig. 3, the instances of classes Person and Phone are shown. There are three people, two males named John and Paul, and one female of name Mary. John has two phones (viz., 1 and 2), Paul has only one (viz., 3) but Mary has none. The class HeavyYoungMan is defined as a subclass of Person according to the SQL filter: `select "personID" from "Person" where "sex"=true and "birthDate">='2001-01-01' and "weight">=100.0`.

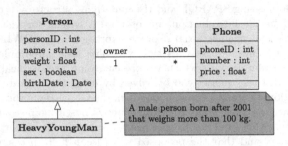

Fig. 2. UML class diagram for people and their phones obtained via OBDA from Fig. 1

```
Person(p1).                personID(p1,1).      name(p1, john).      weight(p1,120.0).      sex(p1,true).
birthDate(p1,2001-01-01).  phone(p1,t1)         phone(p1,t2).        HeavyYoungMan(p1).
Person(p2).                personID(p2,2).       name(p2, paul).      weight(p2,110.0).      sex(p2,true).
birthDate(p2,2002-01-01).  phone(p2,t3).        HeavyYoungMan(p2).
Person(p3).                personID(p3,2).       name(p3, mary).      weight(p3,60.0).       sex(p3,false).
birthDate(p3,2001-01-01).
Phone(t1).                 number(t1, 555-1234). price(t1, 200.0).    owner(t1, p1).
Phone(t2).                 number(t2, 555-1235). price(t2, 220.0).    owner(t2, p1).
Phone(t3).                 number(t3, 555-1236). price(t3, 230.0).    owner(t3, p2).
```

Fig. 3. Assertional knowledge about people and their phones for UML diagram in Fig. 2 obtained from the relational instance in Fig. 1

We now explore several paradigmatic query cases in SPARQL. The choice of the particular syntax of some queries is due to that they are presented in the exact way that they are composed by our tool employing the visual specification that we present in Sect. 3. We solve a very specific subset of queries and categorize its cases as selection queries and then construction queries. In the class of selection queries we deal with queries over a single class, queries over a simple hierarchy of classes, totalization queruies, queries over associations, queries using the *IN* and *NOT IN* operators, and queries with optional data.

Example 3 (Continues Example 2). We start with a *selection query having several conditions over a single class*: Select the portion of the data that comprise all the females that were born in 2001 that weigh less than 70 kilos, and her name starts with an M, contains an r, and ends with a y. When it is relevant, in all queries, we ask the query processor to show at most 10 results starting with the first result. The graph pattern that a user have to devise is shown in Fig. 5. We have to search for the x that are members of the class *Person* and have a sex called *isMale* that equals to false, a *weight* less than 70, and a birth date *bd* whose year is 2001. The text of the SPARQL

```
PREFIX  rdf :  <http :// www. w3 . org /1999/02/22 − rdf −syntax −ns#>
PREFIX  xsd :  <http :// www. w3 . org /2001/XMLSchema#>

SELECT  ?id  ?name  ?isMale  ?bd  ?weight
WHERE
{
        ?x  rdf : type  <http :// example . org /Person>  .
        ?x  <http :// example . org /Person/personID>  ?id  .
        ?x  <http :// example . org /Person/name>  ?name  .
        ?x  <http :// example . org /Person/sex>  ?isMale  .
        ?x  <http :// example . org /Person/birthDate>  ?bd  .
        ?x  <http :// example . org /Person/birthDate>  ?bd  .
        ?x  <http :// example . org /Person/weight>  ?weight  .
        ?x  <http :// example . org /Person/name>  ?name  .
        ?x  <http :// example . org /Person/name>  ?name  .
        FILTER  (  strstarts ( str (?name) ,  'M' )  &&  ?isMale  =  false
        &&  ?bd  >=  '2001−01−01T00:00:00'^^xsd : dateTime
        &&  ?bd  <=  '2001−12−31T00:00:00'^^xsd : dateTime  &&  ?weight  < 70
        &&  regex ( str (?name) ,  'r' ,  "i" )  &&  strends ( str (?name) ,  'y' )  )
}
ORDER BY DESC(?name)
LIMIT 10
OFFSET 0
```

Listing 1.1. SPARQL query for all the females that were born in 2001 that weigh less than 70 kilos, and her name starts with an M, contains an r and ends with a y

```
PREFIX  rdf :  <http :// www. w3 . org /1999/02/22 − rdf −syntax −ns#>
PREFIX  xsd :  <http :// www. w3 . org /2001/XMLSchema#>

SELECT  (AVG(?weight)  AS  ?averageWeight)
WHERE
{
        ?x  rdf : type  <http :// example . org /Person>  .
        ?x  <http :// example . org /Person/weight>  ?weight  .
        ?x  <http :// example . org /Person/sex>  ?isMale  .
        FILTER  (  ?isMale  =  true  )
}
```

Listing 1.2. SPARQL query for the average weight of the men

query can be seen in Listing 1.1. The result of the query computed in tabular form is shown in Fig. (4.a). In Fig. 10, we will show how this query can be visually expressed without worrying about implementation details.

id	name	isMale	bd	weight	averageWeight
3	Mary	false	2001-01-01	60.0	115.0

(a)   (b)

Fig. 4. Result of queries from Example 3 in (a) and from Example 4 in (b)

Example 4 (Continues Example 2). We now show a *totalization query*: select the average weight of the men. The source code for the query is shown in Listing 1.2. The result of the query is shown in Fig. (4.b).

Example 5 (Continues Example 2). We now show a query that works by *grouping similar data according to the value of a property*: Categorize people by sex and compute the average and maximum weight, least birthdate, person count, and sum of weights. The code of the query can be read in Listing 1.3. The result of the query is shown in Fig. (6.a).

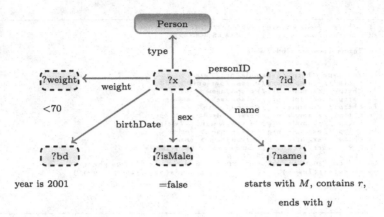

Fig. 5. Graph pattern for finding all the females that were born in 2001 that weigh less than 70 kilos, and her name starts with an *M*, contains an *r* and ends with a *y*

isMale	averageWeight	maximumWeight	leastBirthDate	personCount	weightSum
false	60.0	60.0	2001-01-01T00:00:00	1	60.0
true	115.0	120.0	2001-01-01T00:00:00	2	230.0

(a)

personID	name
1	John
2	Paul

(b)

Fig. 6. Result of queries from Example 5 in (a) and from Example 6 in (b)

Example 6 (Continues Example 2). We now show a *query over a simple hierarchy of classes*, in particular showing the case of inheritance of attributes in sub-classing: Find the name of all the young heavy weighted men. The source code is in Listing 1.4. The result of the query reads as shown in Fig. (6.b).

Example 7 (Continues Example 2). We now show a *query over an association*: Find all the heavy men named John that have a phone containing 555 in its number and with a price of at least 200 dollars. The source code of the query is presented in Listing 1.5 and its result is in Fig. (7.a).

personID	name	p	phoneID	phoneNumber	phonePrice
1	John	http://example.org/Phone/phoneID=1	1	555-1234	200.0
1	John	http://example.org/Phone/phoneID=2	2	555-1235	220.0

(a)

averagePrice
216.6

(b)

Fig. 7. Result of queries from Example 7 in (a) and from Example 8 in (b)

Example 8 (Continues Example 2). Now we present a *totalization query over a composition*: Find the average price of phones whose owner weighs between 110 and 120 kg. The source code of the query is in Listing 1.6. The result of the query is in Fig. (7.b).

```
PREFIX rdf: <http://www.w3.org/1999/02/22-rdf-syntax-ns#>
PREFIX xsd: <http://www.w3.org/2001/XMLSchema#>

SELECT ?isMale (AVG(?weight) AS ?averageWeight) (MAX(?weight) AS ?maximumWeight)
(MIN(?bd) AS ?leastBirthDate)
(COUNT(?id) AS ?personCount) (SUM(?weight) AS ?weightSum)
WHERE
{
        ?x rdf:type <http://example.org/Person> .
        ?x <http://example.org/Person/sex> ?isMale .
        ?x <http://example.org/Person/weight> ?weight .
        ?x <http://example.org/Person/weight> ?weight .
        ?x <http://example.org/Person/birthDate> ?bd .
        ?x <http://example.org/Person/personID> ?id .
        ?x <http://example.org/Person/weight> ?weight .
}
GROUP BY ?isMale
```

Listing 1.3. SPARQL query for categorizing people by sex and computing the average and maximum weight, least birthdate, person count, and sum of weights

```
PREFIX rdf: <http://www.w3.org/1999/02/22-rdf-syntax-ns#>
PREFIX xsd: <http://www.w3.org/2001/XMLSchema#>

SELECT ?personID ?name
WHERE
{
        ?x rdf:type <http://example.org/HeavyYoungMan> .
        ?x <http://example.org/Person/personID> ?personID .
        ?x <http://example.org/Person/name> ?name .
}
LIMIT 10
OFFSET 0
```

Listing 1.4. SPARQL query for finding the name of all the young heavy weighted men

```
PREFIX rdf: <http://www.w3.org/1999/02/22-rdf-syntax-ns#>
PREFIX xsd: <http://www.w3.org/2001/XMLSchema#>

SELECT ?personID ?name ?p ?phoneID ?phoneNumber ?phonePrice
WHERE
{
        ?x rdf:type <http://example.org/HeavyYoungMan> .
        ?x <http://example.org/Person/personID> ?personID .
        ?x <http://example.org/Person/name> ?name .
        ?x <http://example.org/Person/ref-phone> ?p .
        ?p rdf:type <http://example.org/Phone> .
        ?p <http://example.org/Phone/phoneID> ?phoneID .
        ?p <http://example.org/Phone/number> ?phoneNumber .
        ?p <http://example.org/Phone/price> ?phonePrice .
        FILTER (strstarts(str(?name), 'John') && regex(str(?phoneNumber), '555', "i")
        && ?phonePrice >= 100)
}
LIMIT 10
OFFSET 0
```

Listing 1.5. SPARQL query for finding all the heavy men named John that have a phone containing 555 in its number and with a price of at least 200 dollars

```
PREFIX rdf: <http://www.w3.org/1999/02/22-rdf-syntax-ns#>
PREFIX xsd: <http://www.w3.org/2001/XMLSchema#>

SELECT (AVG(?phonePrice) AS ?averagePrice)
WHERE
{
        ?phone rdf:type <http://example.org/Phone> .
        ?phone <http://example.org/Phone/price> ?phonePrice .
        ?phone <http://example.org/Phone/ref-owner> ?phoneOwner .
        ?phoneOwner rdf:type <http://example.org/Person> .
        ?phoneOwner <http://example.org/Person/weight> ?ownersWeight .
        ?phoneOwner <http://example.org/Person/weight> ?ownersWeight .
        FILTER (?ownersWeight >= 110 && ?ownersWeight <= 120)
}
```

Listing 1.6. SPARQL query to find the average price of phones whose owner weighs between 110 and 120 kg

```
PREFIX rdf: <http://www.w3.org/1999/02/22-rdf-syntax-ns#>
PREFIX xsd: <http://www.w3.org/2001/XMLSchema#>

SELECT ?id ?name ?weight
WHERE
{
    ?x rdf:type <http://example.org/Person> .
    ?x <http://example.org/Person/personID> ?id .
    ?x <http://example.org/Person/name> ?name .
    ?x <http://example.org/Person/weight> ?weight .
    FILTER ( ?weight IN (60.0, 120.0) )
}
```

Listing 1.7. SPARQL query to find persons with his or her weight in the set {60, 120}

Example 9. We present a query using the *IN operator*: Find all the people whose weight is in the list 60.0, 120.0. The SPARQL code of the query is shown in Listing 1.7. The result of the query is in Fig. (8.a).

Example 10. We present a query using the *NOT-IN operator*: Find all the people whose weight is not in the list 60.0, 120.0. The SPARQL code of the query is shown in Listing 1.8. The result of the query is in Fig. (8.b).

Example 11. We now introduce a query of people who *optionally* have a phone. Notice that optional triple patterns are signaled with the OPTIONAL keyword. The code of the query can be seen in Listing 1.9. The result of the query can be seen in Fig. (8.c); notice that Mary's phone is empty.

```
PREFIX rdf: <http://www.w3.org/1999/02/22-rdf-syntax-ns#>
PREFIX xsd: <http://www.w3.org/2001/XMLSchema#>

SELECT ?id ?name ?weight
WHERE
{
    ?x rdf:type <http://example.org/Person> .
    ?x <http://example.org/Person/personID> ?id .
    ?x <http://example.org/Person/name> ?name .
    ?x <http://example.org/Person/weight> ?weight .
    FILTER ( ?weight NOT IN (60.0, 120.0) )
}
```

Listing 1.8. SPARQL query to find persons whose weight is not in the set {60, 120}

id	name	weight
1	John	120.0
3	Mary	60.0

(a)

id	name	weight
2	Paul	110.0

(b)

id	name	phone
1	John	http://example.org/Phone/phoneID=1
1	John	http://example.org/Phone/phoneID=2
2	Paul	http://example.org/Phone/phoneID=3
3	Mary	

(c)

Fig. 8. Results of queries from Example 9 in (a), from Example 10 in (b) and from Example 11 in (c)

```
PREFIX  rdf :  <http ://www.w3 . org/1999/02/22 − rdf −syntax−ns#>
PREFIX  xsd :  <http ://www.w3 . org/2001/XMLSchema#>

SELECT  ?id  ?name  ?phone
WHERE
{
    ?person  rdf:type  <http :// example.org/Person> .
    ?person  <http :// example.org/Person/personID>  ?id .
    ?person  <http :// example.org/Person/name>  ?name .
    OPTIONAL  {  ?person  <http :// example.org/Person/ref−phone>  ?phone .  }
}
```

Listing 1.9. SPARQL query to find people who optionally have a phone

Example 12. We now show an example of how to use the *DISTINCT* keyword to avoid repetition of results. Suppose that we want to find up to a hundred people that has a phone ordered alphabetically. The SPARQL code is presented in Listing 1.10. Naturally, only John and Paul will appear in the result of the query under the column *personName*. In Fig. 9, we present the user interface where this query is composed visually. We will explore this interface in detail in the following section showing how to compose all the queries of the preceding examples.

3   A Wizard for Composing SPARQL Selection Queries

Now we present a wizard for composing the queries presented previously in a visual way. We based our approach on the Query-By-Example (QBE) paradigm where queries are specified by giving symbolic examples of the information to be retrieved. As in most QBE solutions, such us commercial front-ends for relational database management systems intended for naive users as MS Access or OO Base, or QBE approaches to SPARQL such as Swipe (see Sect. 5), our program uses the usual form called QBE grid to indicate the subject, predicate, and object of the triples involved in the query, the conditions they have to satisfy if a totalization or grouping is involved and aliases for

```
PREFIX  rdf :  <http ://www.w3 . org/1999/02/22 − rdf −syntax−ns#>
PREFIX  xsd :  <http ://www.w3 . org/2001/XMLSchema#>

SELECT  DISTINCT  ?personName
WHERE
{
    ?person  rdf:type  <http :// example.org/Person> .
    ?person  <http :// example.org/Person/name>  ?personName .
    ?person  <http :// example.org/Person/ref−phone>  ?phone .
}
ORDER BY  ?personName
LIMIT  100
```

Listing 1.10. SPARQL query to find people who has a phone without repetitions

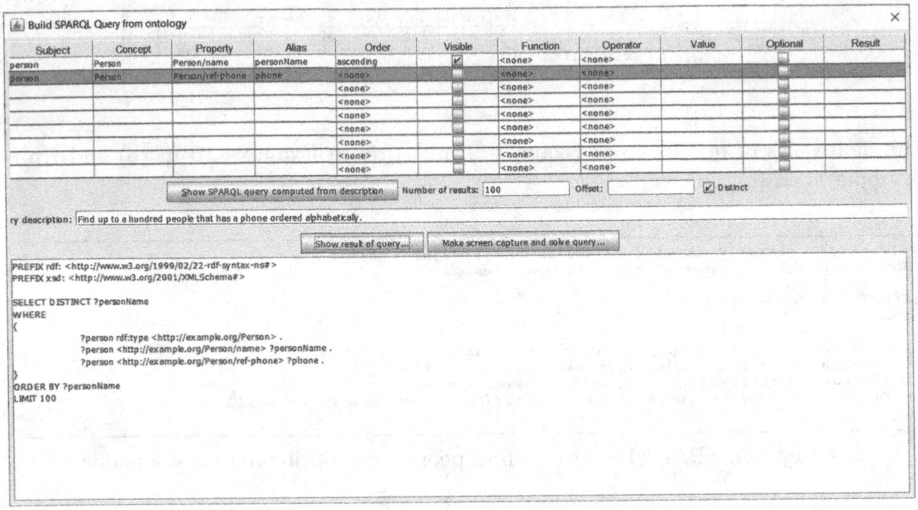

Fig. 9. User interface for composing SPARQL selection queries

results. The names of properties and concepts are presented synthetically to avoid the information overload associated with full IRIs. As in all QBE environments, there is a parser that can convert the user's actions into statements expressed in a manipulation language, in this case, SPARQL. Behind the scenes, it is this statement that is executed. A suitably comprehensive front-end can minimize the burden on the user to remember the finer details of SPARQL, and it is easier and more productive for end-users (and even programmers) to select concepts and properties by selecting them rather than typing in their names.

We now address a brief description of the wizard. The ontology to be queried has to be loaded into the system. The limitations of the current status of the system include that only one ontology can be queried at a time. The ontology that is queried cannot reference other ontologies except the one that defines the basic datatypes. Our implementation addresses the visual specification employing a form, then generates automatically the source code of the equivalent SPARQL query and this query is evaluated against the ontology using the RDF4J library (see https://rdf4j.org/) and then generates a web page showing the result of the query (see accompanying online documentation).

Here we will only discuss how the queries of Sect. 2 are expressed in our tool. In Fig. 10, we can see how the SPARQL query presented in Listing 1.1 is visually codified. The user has to name the subject of the triples (viz., x), then establish the concept the subject belongs to (viz., Person), and then for each property that the user desires a column in the result, has to assign an alias and establish a condition, that can be deemed as invisible and/or optional if desired (viz., property sex with alias *isMale* and value equal to `false`). Notice how the user interface hides the low-level details of IRIs from the user.

In Fig. 11, we can see visual specification of the SPARQL query of Listing 1.2. In this case, as this totalization query must compute a single number (i.e., the average weight of the men), only one field has to be made visible and the result column for

Subject	Concept	Property	Alias	Order	Visible	Function	Operator	Value	Optional	Result
x	Person	Person/personID	id	\<none\>	✓	\<none\>	\<none\>		▢	
x	Person	Person/name	name	descending	✓	\<none\>	starts with	M	▢	
x	Person	Person/sex	isMale	\<none\>	✓	\<none\>	=	false	▢	
x	Person	Person/birthDate	bd	\<none\>	✓	\<none\>	\>=	2001-01-01	▢	
x	Person	Person/birthDate	bd	\<none\>	▢	\<none\>	\<=	2001-12-31	▢	
x	Person	Person/weight	weight	\<none\>	✓	\<none\>	\<	70	▢	
x	Person	Person/name	name	\<none\>	▢	\<none\>	contains	r	▢	
x	Person	Person/name	name	\<none\>	▢	\<none\>	ends with	y	▢	

Fig. 10. Querying people with several conditions

this property has to be named (viz., *averageWeight*). More importantly, in this kind of query a totalization function has to be selected (viz., *Average*).

Subject	Concept	Property	Alias	Order	Visible	Function	Operator	Value	Optional	Result
x	Person	Person/weight	weight	\<none\>	✓	Average	\<none\>		▢	averageWeight
x	Person	Person/sex	isMale	\<none\>	▢	\<none\>	=	true	▢	

Fig. 11. Finding the average weight of the men

In Fig. 12, we can see the visual specification of the SPARQL query of Listing 1.3. This kind of query shows how to partition a set of individuals using the values of a property (in this case *sex*). As the *sex* property is of Boolean type, the set of people is partitioned into two disjoint subsets (assuming that the sex for all people is determined), this is done by using the *Group* function. For each sex, the usage of several totalization functions are shown: *Average*, *Max*, *Min*, *Count*, and *Sum* for computing the average and maximum weight, least date of birth, the number of people and the sum of their weights. Notice that variables for the results must be defined (viz., *averageWeight*, *maximumWeight*, *leastBirthDate*, *personCount*, and *weightSum*).

Subject	Concept	Property	Alias	Order	Visible	Function	Operator	Value	Optional	Result
x	Person	Person/sex	isMale	\<none\>	✓	Group by	\<none\>		▢	
x	Person	Person/weight	weight	\<none\>	✓	Average	\<none\>		▢	averageWeight
x	Person	Person/weight	weight	\<none\>	✓	Max	\<none\>		▢	maximumWeight
x	Person	Person/birthDate	bd	\<none\>	✓	Min	\<none\>		▢	leastBirthDate
x	Person	Person/personID	id	\<none\>	✓	Count	\<none\>		▢	personCount
x	Person	Person/weight	weight	\<none\>	✓	Sum	\<none\>		▢	weightSum

Fig. 12. Totalizing functions according to sex

In Fig. 13, we see that querying a hierarchy of classes is straightforward as the inheritance of properties (attributes) is computed seamlessly. In this case, it is shown how the names and identifiers of people can be used for the class HeavyYoungMan which is a subclass (sub-concept) of Person. Notice that in particular, this is the visual presentation of the SPARQL query of Listing 1.4.

In Fig. 14, we see how an association between classes can be queried (this is the visualization of the SPARQL query in Listing 1.5). In particular, two variables for the subjects have to be defined: x for people and p for phones. Notice in the third row how x is associated with p by means of the Person/ref-phone property.

Subject	Concept	Property	Alias	Order	Visible	Function	Operator	Value	Optional	Result
x	HeavyYoungMan	Person/personID	personID	<none>	✓	<none>	<none>		☐	
x	HeavyYoungMan	Person/name	name	<none>	✓	<none>	<none>		☐	

Fig. 13. Querying a hierarchy: Find the name of heavy men'

Subject	Concept	Property	Alias	Order	Visible	Function	Operator	Value	Optional	Result
x	HeavyYoungMan	Person/personID	personID	<none>	✓	<none>	<none>		☐	
x	HeavyYoungMan	Person/name	name	<none>	✓	<none>	starts with	John	☐	
x	HeavyYoungMan	Person/ref-phone	p	<none>	✓	<none>	<none>		☐	
p	Phone	Phone/phoneID	phoneID	<none>	✓	<none>	<none>		☐	
p	Phone	Phone/number	phoneNumber	<none>	✓	<none>	contains	555	☐	
p	Phone	Phone/price	phonePrice	<none>	✓	<none>	>=	100	☐	

Fig. 14. Querying an association: Find the heavy men with their phones

In Fig. 15, we can observe the visual expression of the SPARQL query in Listing. 1.6 showing how to perform a totalization over an association. Notice how again two different variables for the subject have to be defined for indicating the association between subject and objects in RDF triples and also how the *averagePrice* variable in the result column has to be declared.

Subject	Concept	Property	Alias	Order	Visible	Function	Operator	Val.	Optional	Result
phone	Phone	Phone/price	phonePrice	<none>	✓	Average	<none>		☐	averagePrice
phone	Phone	Phone/ref-owner	phoneOwner	<none>	☐	<none>	<none>		☐	
phoneOwner	Person	Person/weight	ownersWeight	<none>	☐	<none>	>=	110	☐	
phoneOwner	Person	Person/weight	ownersWeight	<none>	☐	<none>	<=	120	☐	

Fig. 15. Querying an association: Find the average price of phones of people weighing between 110 and 120 kg

In Fig. 16 and 17, we show how to use the tool for expressing the queries of Example 9 and 10, resp., using the IN and NOT IN operators for expressing membership to sets of values. In Fig. 18, we show how to express the query from Example 11 regarding the use of the OPTIONAL keyword.

4   Extending the Wizard for Building SPARQL Construct Queries

In Sect. 2, we saw how to write selection queries, that basically pull triples out of a RDF graph database that comply to a certain graph pattern. But this is not enough because the user might need to retrieve the triples to store them in a different database. Some other times, the user needs to create new triples out of some data to allow applications to retrieve those triples more efficiently. These situations lead into *SPARQL construction queries*. Thus, here we briefly discuss how our tool can be used to compose these kind of queries as well by a naive user.

The similarities of building SPARQL construction queries w.r.t. building selection queries stand in that the user still has to specify the graph pattern in terms of triples in the underlying RDF graph to be queried. In contrast to selection queries, construction

Subject	Concept	Property	Alias	Order	Visible	Function	Operator	Value	Optional	Result
x	Person	Person/personID	id	<none>	✔	<none>	<none>		☐	
x	Person	Person/name	name	<none>	✔	<none>	<none>		☐	
x	Person	Person/weight	weight	<none>	✔	<none>	in	60.0, 120.0	☐	

Fig. 16. Find all people whose weight is in the list [60, 120]

Subject	Concept	Property	Alias	Order	Visible	Function	Operator	Value	Optional	Result
x	Person	Person/personID	id	<none>	✔	<none>	<none>		☐	
x	Person	Person/name	name	<none>	✔	<none>	<none>		☐	
x	Person	Person/weight	weight	<none>	✔	<none>	not in	60.0, 120.0	☐	

Fig. 17. Find all people whose weight is not in the list [60, 120]

queries also require the user to specify the triples to be constructed. We address this as shown in Fig. 19. The system uses the variables from the condition part as well as the names of the individuals of the ontology to help the user to build the pattern for the triples. We show some paradigmatic examples next.

Example 13. Consider a simple example where we need to retrieve the set of triples whose subject has name John and export them to another file called john.owl. The SPARQL code for this query can be seen in Listing 1.11. In Fig. 19, we can see that in the GUI, besides specifying the triple patterns for retrieving results, the triples that comprise the result must be specified, viz. *(?person, ?p, ?o)*. In the example shown, the system will ask the user to establish a file path where to save the newly created triples; in this case, it is john.owl.

Example 14. In this example, we see how to create a new individual named JCVD with ID 999. In Listing 1.12, we see the SPARQL code that will ultimately be generated by our tool to perform this task. In Fig. 20, we can see how the pattern for the new triples is specified in the system. In this case, the triples involve values taken directly from the ontology and no variables from the condition part are referred to in the CONSTRUCT part of the query.

5   Related Work

Swipe [1] implements a search-by-example approach to query Wikipedia where naive users can enter query conditions directly on the Infobox of a Wikipedia page, and then Swipe uses these conditions to generate equivalent SPARQL queries and execute them on DBPedia. As Swipe, our system makes querying ontologies user-friendly but our system is more general as it is not limited to DBPedia. Our system could do something

Subject	Concept	Property	Alias	Order	Visible	Function	Operator	Value	Optional	Result
person	Person	Person/personID	id	<none>	✔	<none>	<none>		☐	
person	Person	Person/name	name	<none>	✔	<none>	<none>		☐	
person	Person	Person/ref-phone	phone	<none>	✔	<none>	<none>		✔	

Fig. 18. Find people with optional phone

```
PREFIX rdf: <http://www.w3.org/1999/02/22-rdf-syntax-ns#>
PREFIX xsd: <http://www.w3.org/2001/XMLSchema#>

CONSTRUCT {
    ?person ?p ?o .
} WHERE {
    ?person rdf:type <http://example.org/Person> .
    ?person <http://example.org/Person/name> ?name .
    FILTER ( ?name = 'John' ) .
    ?person ?p ?o .
}
```

Listing 1.11. Retrieve the set of triples whose subject has name John and export them to another file called john.owl from Ex. 13

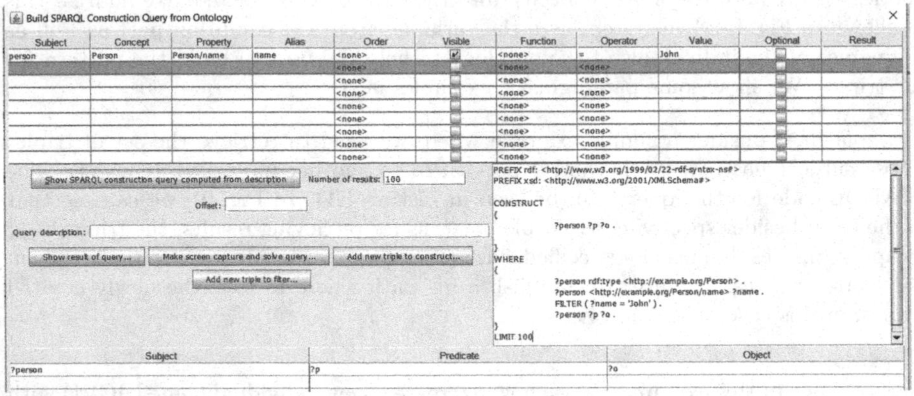

Fig. 19. Constructing the triples of John from Example 13

```
PREFIX rdf: <http://www.w3.org/1999/02/22-rdf-syntax-ns#>
PREFIX xsd: <http://www.w3.org/2001/XMLSchema#>

CONSTRUCT {
    <http://example.org/Person/personID=999>
    <http://example.org/Person/personID> 999 .
    <http://example.org/Person/personID=999>
    <http://example.org/Person/name> "JCVD" .
} WHERE {
}
```

Listing 1.12. SPARQL code for creating new RDF triples for JCVD from Ex. 14

Subject	Predicate	Object
<http://example.org/Person/personID=999>	<http://example.org/Person/personID>	999
<http://example.org/Person/personID=999>	<http://example.org/Person/name>	"JCVD"

Fig. 20. Creating a new individual named JCVD with ID 999 from Example 14

similar by, given a Wikipedia page, first downloading the associated DBPedia OWL ontology and loading it in GF, then expressing the query on the GF wizard and executing it. Like DBPedia, iSparQL end-point [8], our system allows also us to enter a SPARQL query in text form to be submitted against the current ontology loaded in the program. Diaz et al. [5] present SPARQLByE (for SPARQL by Example) which is a front-end for DBPedia where a naive user can input positive and negative examples of what he desires, and then the system uses a reverse engineering heuristic to induce a SPARQL query. As our system, SPARQLByE abstracts full IRIs and works with joins and optional statements. Horridge and Musen [10] present Snap-SPARQL, a Java framework for working with SPARQL and OWL, that includes a parser, axiom template API, SPARQL algebra implementation, and graphical user interface components for reading, processing, and executing SPARQL queries. Our system does this by using an auxiliary library and provides a visual interface for the composition of queries.

In brief, our solution provides a concrete way of writing SPARQL queries over legacy data from H2 databases, Excel spreadsheets and CSV tabular data, all expressed as an OWL ontology without requiring the user to know explicitly SPARQL syntax and it is available as a downloadable standalone application unlike many of the solutions reviewed here that are custom built for specific ontologies. However, referring to external ontologies in the data except for the usual OWL/RDF data type is not supported in the current version of GF's implementation. Other limitations include that the current status of the tool does not support any describe and ask queries.

6   Conclusions and Future Work

We presented an extension for the GF framework for ontology integration to allow a naive user to visually build a restricted set of SPARQL selection and construction queries by using a Query-By-Example approach. A prototype implementation of the approach was introduced along with examples of its intended use for dealing with an ontology obtained from a relational database with added classes and relations. We showed how our tool is capable of producing selection queries including one with several conditions over a single class, totalization, grouping of similar data according to the value of a property, over a simple hierarchy of classes, over an association, totalization over compositions, using the IN and NOT-IN operators, with optional data, and distinct results. The composition queries discussed shown that our approach is capable of summarizing data and exporting it an RDF triple file. The limitations of our approach include that in its current state it is only capable of working with a single data source comprised of an OWL ontology loaded into memory. Then it does not allow to make use of several data sources at the same time nor make the query refer to other data sources. Describe and ask queries are not supported yet because the part of our tool that solves SPARL queries relies on RDF4J, that currently does not implement those features. We have not tested our implementation with naive users to account for its usability in real cases. Part of our current research is focused on solving these matters.

Acknowledgments. This work was supported by Secretaría General de Ciencia y Técnica, Universidad Nacional del Sur, Argentina, and by Comisión de Investigaciones Científicas de la Provincia de Buenos Aires (CIC-PBA).

References

1. Atzori, M., Zaniolo, C.: Swipe: searching wikipedia by example. In: Proceedings of the 21st International Conference on World Wide Web, pp. 309–312 (2012)
2. Baader, F., Horrocks, I., Lutz, C., Sattler, U.: An Introduction to Description Logic. Cambridge University Press (2017)
3. Berners-Lee, T., Hendler, J., Lassila, O.: The Semantic Web. Sci. Am. **284**(5), 34–43 (2001)
4. Calvanese, D., Giacomo, G.D., Lembo, D., Savo, D.F.: The MASTRO system for ontology-based data access. Semantic Web **2**(1), 43–53 (2011)
5. Diaz, G., Arenas, M., Benedikt, M.: SPARQLByE: querying RDF data by example. Proc. VLDB Endowment **9**, 1533–1536 (2016). https://doi.org/10.14778/3007263.3007302
6. Gómez, S., Fillottrani, P.R.: A wizard for composing SPARQL queries in the GF framework for ontology-based data access. In: Rodríguez, S.I., Giménez, M.N., Molina, M.Á. (eds.) Libro de Actas: XXVIII Congreso Argentino de Ciencias de la Computación (CACIC 2022), pp. 516–525. Universidad Nacional de La Rioja - EUDELAR (jan 2023)
7. Gómez, S.A., Fillottrani, P.R.: Ontology metrics and evolution in the GF framework for ontology-based data access. In: Computer Science - CACIC 2021. Springer International (2022)
8. Grobe, M.: RDF, Jena, SparQL and the semantic web. In: SIGUCCS '09: Proceedings of the 37th Annual ACM SIGUCCS fall Conference: Communication and Collaboration, pp. 131–138 (oct 2009)
9. Harris, S., Seaborne, A.: SPARQL 1.1 Query Language for RDF W3C recommendation 21 March 2013 (2013). https://www.w3.org/TR/sparql11-query/
10. Horridge, M., Musen, M.: Snap-SPARQL: a Java framework for working with SPARQL and OWL. In: International Experiences and Directions Workshop on OWL, pp. 154–165 (04 2016). https://doi.org/10.1007/978-3-319-33245-1_16
11. Xiao, G., et al.: Ontology-based data access - a survey. In: Proceedings of the Twenty-Seventh International Joint Conference on Artificial Intelligence (IJCAI-18), pp. 5511–5519 (2018)
12. Zloof, M.M.: Query by Example. In: NCC (proceedings), vol. 44. Anaheim, California: AFIPS (May 1975)

Systematic Mapping of the Literature on the Conceptual Modeling of Industry 4.0

Ayelén Zapata, Marcelo Fransoy, Salvador Soto, Martín Di Felice, and Marisa Panizzi

Master's Program in Information Systems Engineering, Graduate School, Universidad Tecnológica Nacional Regional Buenos Aires (UTN-FRBA), CABA Autonomous City of Buenos Aires, Medrano 951. (C1179AAQ), Buenos Aires, Argentina
mdifelice@live.com.ar, marisapanizzi@outlook.com

Abstract. The Industry 4.0 concept refers to a new way of producing through the adoption of 4.0 technologies based on solutions focused on interconnectivity, automation, and real-time data. Given the importance of conceptualizing the problem domain and its solution, this paper presents the results of a systematic mapping to identify the state of the art and discover the existing contributions to the conceptual modeling of industry 4.0. A search was carried out in the Scopus, IEEE Xplore, and ACM DL digital libraries from January 2017 to May 2022. It was found that no article describes the model through a language known for this purpose, except for two articles that use Domain Specific Modeling Languages (DSML) and Unified Modeling Language (UML). Of the total number of primary studies, 63.33% propose a model-based solution, while 13.34% propose the use of tools, methods, and processes. Finally, 23.33% present the state of the art.

Keywords: Conceptual modeling · industry 4.0 · systematic mapping of the literature

1 Introduction

According to Zenón [1], in problem solving, the elaboration of the conceptual model is the graphic, written or mental representation elaborated by the analyst as a support framework to situate and organize their perceptions, in order to fix the structure of the problem, define the area of interest and decide which aspects are relevant and which are not.

According to Sokolowski *et al.* [2], a system is a general idea of one or a group of interacting components whose desired functionality is articulated through graphic and textual means. The level of generalization is what distinguishes one conceptual model from other models, typically being more informal in terms of details and certainty, focusing on rapid communication of the main features of the target system. Consequently, a conceptual model should express, in no more than a couple of paragraphs, what the system is about, what it does and does not do.

P. Pesado (Ed.): CACIC 2022, CCIS 1778, pp. 227–240, 2023.
https://doi.org/10.1007/978-3-031-34147-2_15

According to the Ministry of Productive Development [3], industry 4.0 refers to a new way of producing through the adoption of 4.0 technologies, that is, solutions focused on interconnectivity, automation and real-time data.

Its first formal mention with this connotation dates back to 2011, at the Hannover Fair, Germany, in the presentation of the article entitled Industry 4.0: *With the Internet of Things on the way to the 4th industrial revolution* [4], which discussed how Germany could be the next leader and provider of the new market in 2020 thanks to the internet of things in the industrial environment.

According to Rainer Drath and Alexander Horch [5], the hypotheses or foundations that must exist in order for the conditions for the development of industry 4.0 to arise state that the communication infrastructure in production systems will be more affordable and, therefore, it will be part of everything; devices in the field, machines, plants, and factories (even individual products) will be more connected to a network (the Internet or a manufacturer's private network); and that the devices in the countryside, machines, plants and factories will be able to store documents and knowledge about themselves outside their corporeality in the network.

The systematic mapping of literature (*Systematic Mapping Study* or *SMS*) originates in the field of software engineering research as evidence-based software engineering [6], which aims at an evidence-based approach to theoretical research and software engineering practice. This evidence-based approach arises in turn from medicine since the investigations used to reflect the opinions of experts to give medical advice and these were not reliable given the non-accumulation of scientific evidence to support them.

The purpose of the search for evidence is to provide the means by which the best current research evidence can be integrated with practical experience and human values in the decision-making process related to software development and maintenance [6]. That is why, in this context, evidence is defined as the synthesis of studies of the highest scientific quality on a specific topic or research question. The primary method for synthesizing is a systematic literature review, as opposed to peer review using literature on demand, the former being a methodologically rigorous review of research results. Its purpose is not just to collect all the existing evidence, but to support the development of evidence-based rules and guidelines for practitioners. The main purpose is for professionals to use these guidelines to develop appropriate software engineering solutions in a specific context.

Among the related works, we can mention the Systematic Mapping Study (SMS), described in CACIC 2022 [7]. The main differences between this article and that of CACIC are: 1) In the planning stage, the incorporation of elements of the SMS review protocol: classification scheme, the data extraction form, 2) In the execution stage: the list of primary studies analyzed is presented and 3) In the results reporting stage: they are presented in a more developed way.

Research by Dreyfus *et al.* [8] in which they carry out a Systematic Literature Review (SLR), with the aim of presenting a detailed analysis of the 199 articles that it identifies and generating a conceptual model for it. They then assign these documents to categories and highlight deficiencies. Finally, they discuss the use of Virtual Metrology in various industrial fields, underlining its potential for all manufacturing industries.

In turn, in their study, Dornelles *et al.* [9] also carried out an SLR to build a conceptual framework to consolidate a common vision on this growing but fragmented topic by integrating a wide range of findings from the literature. The study systematized this knowledge in a unique and consolidated perspective on the technologies and work of Industry 4.0.

Wankhede *et al.* [10] also conducted an SLR to generate a conceptual framework with the guidelines and strategy to implement industry 4.0 technologies in the automotive industry.

In addition, Ding *et al.* [11] performed the first systematic review of the literature linking Industry 4.0 with agile and lean manufacturing, proposing a conceptual framework for their relationships. Finally, Machado *et al.* [12] carried out a systematic review of the literature taking into account sustainable manufacturing.

This article is developed within the framework of the Conceptual Modeling Seminar of the Master's Program in Information Systems Engineering of Universidad Tecnológica Nacional, Regional Buenos Aires, with the purpose of internalizing the importance of conceptualization to understand the part of the world that we want to represent in a computer, as well as to share, communicate and establish that knowledge and to understand that only by starting from a conceptual model is it possible to design and implement a correct, effective and efficient process of data analysis.

This article presents a systematic mapping of the literature (SMS) to analyze the state of the art regarding conceptual modeling for industry 4.0. To carry out the SMS, the guidelines proposed by Kitchenham *et al.* [13] were followed.

The article is structured as follows: Sect. 2 describes the planning of the SMS; Sect. 3 describes its execution. The results are presented in Sect. 4. In Sect. 5 presents an analysis of the threats to validity and, finally, Sect. 6 presents the conclusions and future work.

2 Planning of the SMS

This section presents the definition of the SMS review protocol, consisting of the research questions (RQ), search strategy, study selection, selection process and criteria, extraction form, and the data synthesis process.

The objective of this SMS is to answer the following research question (RQ): *What is the state of the art regarding the conceptual modeling of industry 4.0 in factories today?*

This main question is broken down into a set of sub-questions (RQ1–6), which are presented in Table 1 along with their motivation.

An automatic search was carried out in the *Scopus* and *IEEE Xplore* and the ACM DL digital libraries and platforms as they are the most widely used libraries in the field of computer science. Conference articles and journal articles published in the period from January 2017 to May 2022 are considered.

For the creation of the search chain, "Industry 4.0", "Conceptual modeling" and "Factory" were considered as main terms, including their alternative terms. The resulting search string is:

("industry 4.0" AND "conceptual model*" AND "factory") OR ("industry 4.0" AND "conceptual model*" AND "manufactur*") OR ("industry 4.0" AND

Table 1. Research questions (RQ) and motivation.

Research Question (RQ)	Motivation
RQ1: What contributions exist regarding conceptual modeling in factories in the context of Industry 4.0?	To know the contributions of conceptual modeling in the context of industry 4.0
RQ2: What modeling language is used in Industry 4.0?	To determine the language used for modeling in industry 4.0
RQ3: What diagrams are considered for modeling in Industry 4.0?	To identify which diagrams are used in industry 4.0 modeling
RQ4: In what types of industries are the studies carried out?	To identify whether they correspond to the automotive, aerospace, financial, pharmaceutical industry, etc
RQ5: which pillar of industry 4.0 does it contribute to?	To identify what kind of technologies, the model focuses on
RQ6: What is the type of investigation?	To identify the types of research studies according to the classification proposed by Wieringa *et al.* [14]

"conceptual framework" AND "factory") OR ("industry 4.0" AND "conceptual framework" AND "manufactur*").

The inclusion and exclusion criteria used for the article selection process are presented in Table 2.

Table 2. Inclusion and exclusion criteria.

Inclusion Criteria	Exclusion Criteria
I1. Articles in English	E1. Systematic Literature Mappings (SMS) and Systematic Literature Reviews (SLR)
I2. For articles written by the same author and focused on the same research, the most recent and complete one is selected	E2. Not accessible
I3. Articles published between January 2017 and May 2022	E3. Grey literature
I4. Articles containing candidate strings in the title, keywords and/or in the abstract	E4. Articles whose content does not focus on conceptual modeling

The study selection process consists of the following steps: 1) carry out the search in the defined sources applying the string in the title, keywords and/or in the abstract, 2) eliminate duplicate articles, 3) apply the inclusion and exclusion criteria in the title, abstract and keywords, 4) apply the inclusion and exclusion criteria to the full text. This process allowed the selection of the primary studies (PS) that were analyzed to answer the research questions (RQ) formulated.

To answer each of the research questions (RQ), a classification scheme was defined that is presented in Table 3, together with the data extraction form that is presented in Table 4.

Table 3. Classification scheme of the primary studies.

Dimension	Categories
Contribution	Model, Method, Metrics, Process, Tool, Good practices, Does not contribute
Modeling language	UML, UP4EG, DSML, Does not specify, Others
Diagrams	Domain diagram, Communication diagram, State diagram, Sequence diagram, Activity diagram, Component diagram, Class diagram, Object diagram, Does not specify, Others
Industry	Agriculture, Livestock, Food, Beverages, Tobacco, Commerce, Construction, Education, Transport equipment manufacturing, Public service, Tourism and hospitality, Chemical industries, Mechanical and electrical engineering, Media, culture, Mining (coal, other mining), Oil and gas production; Oil refining, Base metal production, Parcel delivery service, Telecommunications, Healthcare services, Pharmaceutical, Financial services, Professional services, Utilities: water, gas, electricity, Forestry, wood, pulp, paper, Textiles, clothing, leather, footwear, Land transport, Air transport, Maritime transport, Fishing, Manufacturing
I4.0 pillar	AI: Artificial Intelligence, AR: Autonomous Robots, BD: Big Data, CC: Cloud Computing, CS: Cobotic Systems, IoT: Internet of Things, RFID: Radio-Frequency Identification, SA: Sensors and Actuators, AM: Additive manufacturing, VR: Augmented & Virtual reality, CB: Cibersecurity
Type of Research	Evaluation, solution proposal, validation, philosophical articles, personal experience, opinion [14]

Table 4. Data extraction form.

Metadata	Paper ID, year, title, authors, source, type of publication (journal or conference), keywords
RQ/Dimension	**Categories**
RQ1/Contribution	Model, Method, Metrics, Process, Tool, Good practices, Does not contribute
RQ2/Modeling Language	UML, UP4EG, DSML, Does not specify, Others

(continued)

Table 4. (*continued*)

RQ3/Diagrams	Domain Diagram, Communication Diagram, State Diagram, Sequence Diagram, Activity Diagram, Component Diagram, Class Diagram, Object Diagram, Does not specify, Others
RQ4/Industry	Agriculture, Livestock, Food, Beverages, Tobacco, Commerce, Construction, Education, Transport equipment manufacturing, Public service, Tourism and hospitality, Chemical industries, Mechanical and electrical engineering, Media, culture, Mining (coal, other mining), Oil and gas production; Oil refining, Base metal production, Parcel delivery service, Telecommunications, Healthcare services, Pharmaceutical, Financial services, Professional services,
	Utilities: water, gas, electricity, Forestry, wood, pulp, paper, Textiles, clothing, leather, footwear, Land transport, Air transport, Maritime transport, Fishing, Manufacturing
RQ5/ I4.0 pillar	AI: Artificial Intelligence, AR: Autonomous Robots, BD: Big Data, CB: Cybersecurity, CC: Cloud Computing, CS: Cobotic Systems, IoT: Internet of Things, RFID: Radio-Frequency Identification, SA: Sensors and Actuators, AM: Additive manufacturing, VR: Augmented & Virtual reality
RQ 6 /Type of research	Evaluation, solution proposal, validation, philosophical articles. Personal experience, opinion [14]

3 SMS Execution

This section presents the search carried out in libraries and digital platforms and the selection of primary studies in accordance with what is defined in the SMS review protocol. The first search returned a total of 58 articles belonging to *Scopus*, 2 belonging to *IEEE Xplore* (one of which had already been found within *Scopus*) and 2 from *ACM DL*, giving a total of 61 articles. After applying the exclusion criteria, a total of 30 primary studies remained, which are detailed in Table 5.

Table 5. Primary studies analyzed.

Id	Primary Study
[PS1]	Elnagar S. *et al.*, Federated deep learning: A conceptual model and applied framework for industry 4.0 (2020)
[PS2]	Bennulf M. *et al.*, A conceptual model for multi-agent communication applied on a plug & produce system (2020)

(*continued*)

Table 5. (*continued*)

Id	Primary Study
[PS3]	Thomas Polacsek *et al.*, Design for Efficient Production, A Model-Based Approach (2019)
[PS4]	Serrano-Ruiz J.C. *et al.*, Development of a multidimensional conceptual model for job shop smart manufacturing scheduling from the Industry 4.0 perspective (2022)
[PS5]	Gupta S. *et al.*, Big data and firm marketing performance: Findings from knowledge-based view (2021)
[PS6]	Reyes J. *et al.*, Development of a conceptual model for lean supply chain planning in industry 4.0: multidimensional analysis for operations management (2021)
[PS7]	Saboor A. *et al.*, Flexible cell formation and scheduling of robotics coordinated dynamic cellular manufacturing system: A gateway to industry 4.0 (2019)
[PS8]	Kim T.H. *et al.*, A conceptual model of smart manufacturing execution system for rolling stock manufacturer (2019)
[PS9]	Rahamaddulla S.R.B. *et al.*, Conceptualizing smart manufacturing readiness-maturity model for small and medium enterprise (Sme) in malaysia (2021)
[PS10]	Cañas H. *et al.*, Implementing Industry 4.0 principles (2021)
[PS11]	Le C.H. *et al.*, Challenges and conceptual framework to develop heavy-load manipulators for smart factories (2020)
[PS12]	Onaji I. *et al.*, Digital twin in manufacturing: conceptual framework and case studies (2022)
[PS13]	Eirinakis P. *et al.*, Cognitive Digital Twins for Resilience in Production: A Conceptual Framework (2022)
[PS14]	Doyle-Kent M. *et al.*, Adoption of collaborative robotics in industry 5.0. An Irish industry case study (2021)
[PS15]	Culot G. *et al.*, Behind the definition of Industry 4.0: Analysis and open questions (2020)
[PS16]	Taifa I.W.R. *et al.*, Computer modelling and simulation of an equitable order distribution in manufacturing through the Industry 4.0 framework (2020)
[PS17]	Oluyisola O.E. *et al.*, Smart production planning and control: Concept, use-cases and sustainability implications (2020)
[PS18]	Nick G. *et al.*, Industry 4.0 readiness in manufacturing: Company Compass 2.0, a renewed framework and solution for Industry 4.0 maturity assessment (2020)
[PS19]	Peres R.S. *et al.*, Industrial Artificial Intelligence in Industry 4.0 -Systematic Review, Challenges and Outlook (2020)
[PS20]	Rojas R.A. *et al.*, From a literature review to a conceptual framework of enablers for smart manufacturing control (2019)

(*continued*)

Table 5. (*continued*)

Id	Primary Study
[PS21]	Frank A.G. *et al.*, Industry 4.0 technologies: Implementation patterns in manufacturing companies (2019)
[PS22]	Frank A. *et al.*, Servitization and Industry 4.0 convergence in the digital transformation of product firms: A business model innovation perspective (2019)
[PS23]	Raharno S. *et al.*, Jumping to industry 4.0 through process design and managing information for smart manufacturing: Configurable virtual workstation (2019)
[PS24]	Boukerika A. *et al.*, Key factors of customer-supplier of smart manufacturing implementation (2019)
[PS25]	Hubert Backhaus S. *et al.*, Investigating the relationship between industry 4.0 and productivity: A conceptual framework for Malaysian manufacturing firms (2019)
[PS26]	Chen Y. *et al.*, Intelligent autonomous pollination for future farming - A micro air vehicle conceptual framework with artificial intelligence and human-in-the-loop (2019)
[PS27]	Boucher X. *et al.*, Towards Reconfigurable Digitalized and Servitized Manufacturing Systems: Conceptual Framework (2019)
[PS28]	Manavalan E. *et al.*, A review of Internet of Things (IoT) embedded sustainable supply chain for industry 4.0 requirements (2019)
[PS29]	Kunath M. *et al.*, Integrating the Digital Twin of the manufacturing system into a decision support system for improving the order management process (2018)
[PS30]	Zhong R. *et al.*, Smart manufacturing systems for industry 4.0: A conceptual framework (2017)

4   SMS Results

Table 6 presents a summary of the results of the analysis of the primary studies based on the classification scheme defined in the review protocol.

Below, we seek to answer the research questions (RQ) considering the material analyzed.

Table 6. Summary of the results obtained.

Study	[RQ1] Contribution	[RQ2] Language	[RQ3] Diagrams	[RQ4] Industry	[RQ5] Pillar	[RQ6] Type
[PS1]	Model	Does not specify	Activity diagram	Transport equipment manufacturing	IoT CC	Solution proposal
[PS2]	Model	Does not specify	Others	Manufacturing	AI AR	Solution proposal

(*continued*)

Table 6. (*continued*)

Study	[RQ1] Contribution	[RQ2] Language	[RQ3] Diagrams	[RQ4] Industry	[RQ5] Pillar	[RQ6] Type
[PS3]	Method	UML	Class diagram	Transport equipment manufacturing	Does not specify	Solution proposal
[PS4]	Model	Does not specify	Activity diagram	Manufacturing	AI IoT SA	Solution proposal
[PS5]	Model	Does not specify	Others	Does not specify	BD	Solution proposal
[PS6]	Model	Does not specify	Others	Manufacturing	Does not specify	Solution proposal
[PS7]	Model	Does not specify	Activity diagram	Manufacturing	AR	Solution proposal
[PS8]	Model	Does not specify	Others	Transport equipment manufacturing	SA AR IoT	Solution proposal
[PS9]	Model	Does not specify	Others	Manufacturing	AM, CB, VR, AR, IoT, BD, CC	Solution proposal
[PS10]	Good practices	Does not specify	Others	Manufacturing	IoT CS BD	Evaluation
[PS11]	Model	Does not specify	Others	Manufacturing	IoT BD AI CC SA	Solution proposal
[PS12]	Model	Does not specify	Others	Manufacturing	SA	Solution proposal
[PS13]	Model	Does not specify	Others	Manufacturing	SA	Solution proposal
[PS14]	Model	Does not specify	Others	Manufacturing	CS	Evaluation
[PS15]	Model	Does not specify	Does not specify	Manufacturing	IoT CC CS	Opinion
[PS16]	Model	Does not specify	Does not specify	Manufacturing	SA	Solution proposal

(*continued*)

Table 6. (*continued*)

Study	[RQ1] Contribution	[RQ2] Language	[RQ3] Diagrams	[RQ4] Industry	[RQ5] Pillar	[RQ6] Type
[PS17]	Model	Does not specify	Does not specify	Manufacturing	IoT AI CC	Validation
[PS18]	Model	Does not specify	Does not specify	Manufacturing	AR SA	Solution proposal
[PS19]	Model	Does not specify	Does not specify	Does not specify	AI	Evaluation
[PS20]	Model	Does not specify	Does not specify	Does not specify	CS	Evaluation
[PS21]	Process	Does not specify	Does not specify	Manufacturing	IoT CC BD	Solution proposal
[PS22]	Model	Does not specify	Does not specify	Does not specify	Does not specify	Solution proposal
[PS23]	Process	Does not specify	Does not specify	Transport equipment manufacturing	RFID SA	Solution proposal
[PS24]	Model	Does not specify	Does not specify	Does not specify	Does not specify	Evaluation
[PS25]	Model	Does not specify	Does not specify	Manufacturing	IoT CS BD	Evaluation
[PS26]	Tool	DSML	Sequence diagram	Agriculture	AR AI	Solution proposal
[PS27]	Model	Does not specify	Does not specify	Manufacturing	Does not specify	Solution proposal
[PS28]	Model	Does not specify	Does not specify	Parcel delivery service	IoT	Evaluation
[PS29]	Model	Does not specify	Does not specify	Manufacturing	CS	Solution proposal
[PS30]	Model	Does not specify	Does not specify	Manufacturing	IoT CS BD	Evaluation

RQ1: What contributions exist regarding conceptual modeling in factories in the context of Industry 4.0?

Elnagar *et al.* [PS1] propose a conceptual model for companies to adopt deep learning for IoT, applying the federated deep learning (FDL) approach and presenting a framework for its application in an industry 4.0 automotive manufacturing plant.

Bennulf M. *et al.* [PS2] presents a conceptual model of communication and negotiation between agents for a Plug&Produce system in the manufacturing industry, which is more flexible and increases the speed of adaptation to incorporate new products and resources.

Polacsek T. *et al.* [PS3] proposes a model-based method to jointly develop the design and production of a product, making it possible to evaluate its manufacturing feasibility, applied to industry 4.0.

In turn, Serrano-Ruiz J.C. *et al.* [PS4], Gupta S. *et al.* [PS5], Saboor A. *et al.* [PS7], Kim T.H. *et al.* [PS8], Rahamaddulla *et al.* [PS9], Le *et al.* [PS11], Onaji *et al.* [PS12], Eirinakis *et al.* [PS13], Taifa *et al.* [PS16], Oluyisola *et al.* [PS17], Nick *et al.* [PS18], Frank *et al.* [PS22], Boucher *et al.* [PS27], Manavalan *et al.* [PS28], Kunath *et al.* [PS29] and Zhong *et al.* [PS30] propose a solution for the incorporation of Industry 4.0 technologies within organizations, also in the form of a model or conceptual framework.

Reyes J. *et al.* [PS6] proposes a conceptual model that merges industry 4.0 technologies with lean manufacturing tools to reduce waste and minimize costs, in the context of lean supply chain planning.

Doyle-Kent *et al.* [PS14], Culot *et al.* [PS15], Peres *et al.* [PS19], Rojas *et al.* [PS20], Boukerika *et al.* [PS24] and Hubert Backhaus *et al.* [PS25] seek to present a state of the art regarding conceptual modeling and industry 4.0 and, for this purpose, they present a conceptual framework.

In turn, Frank *et al.* [PS21] and Raharno *et al.* [PS23] also propose solutions but in the form of processes, while Chen *et al.* [PS26] does so in the form of a tool.

Finally, Cañas *et al.* [PS10] presents the state of the art, highlighting good practices and principles when implementing a transformation towards industry 4.0.

RQ2: What Modeling Language is Used in Industry 4.0?

Chen *et al.* [PS26] proposes a tool for the application of a specific solution with Industry 4.0 technologies by means of a specific domain modeling language (DSML), while Polacsek T. *et al.* [PS3] uses UML.

The rest of the studies do not refer to any specific modeling language.

RQ3: What Diagrams Are Considered for Modeling in Industry 4.0?

Elnagar *et al.* [PS1] presents an activity diagram to represent the operation of the federated deep learning (FDL) approach presented in his model, as does Serrano-Ruiz J.C. *et al.* [PS4] to represent their smart production scheduling model and Saboor A. *et al.* [PS7] for his manufacturing system model without human intervention.

Bennulf M. *et al.* [PS2], Gupta S. *et al.* [PS5], Reyes J. *et al.* [PS6], Kim T.H. *et al.* [PS8], Rahamaddulla *et al.* [PS9], Cañas *et al.* [PS10], Le *et al.* [PS11], Onaji *et al.* [PS12], Eirinakis *et al.* [PS13] and Doyle-Kent *et al.* [PS14] use a diagram to represent their model, but it does not correspond to any of the diagram categories defined in the review protocol.

Polacsek T. *et al.* [PS3] uses a class diagram to represent his model and the connections between product and production.

Chen *et al.* [PS26] uses a sequence diagram for his tool in order to specify its operation.

The rest of the studies do not include any diagrams for the specification of their models.

RQ4: In What Types of Industries Are the Studies Carried Out?

Elnagar *et al.* [PS1], Bennulf M. *et al.* [PS2], Serrano-Ruiz J.C. *et al.* [PS4], Reyes J. et al. [PS6], Saboor A. *et al.* [PS7], Kim T.H. *et al.* [PS8], Rahamaddulla *et al.* [PS9],

Cañas *et al.* [PS10], Le *et al.* [PS11], Onaji *et al.* [PS12], Eirinakis *et al.* [PS13], Doyle-Kent *et al.* [PS14], Culot *et al.* [PS15], Taifa *et al.* [PS16], Oluyisola *et al.* [PS17], Nick *et al.* [PS18], Frank *et al.* [PS21], Hubert Backhaus *et al.* [PS25], Boucher *et al.* [PS27], Kunath *et al.* [PS29] and Zhong *et al.* [PS30] focus their works on the manufacturing industry, while Elnagar *et al.* [PS1], Polacsek T. *et al.* [PS3] and Raharno *et al.* [PS23] focus on the transport equipment manufacturing industry. Chen *et al.* [PS26] proposes a solution within the agricultural sector. Finally, Manavalan *et al.* [PS28] does so within the parcel delivery service industry.

The remaining studies do not refer to any specific industry.

RQ5: Which Pillar of Industry 4.0 Does It Contribute to?

Bennulf M. *et al.* [PS2], Serrano-Ruiz J.C. *et al.* [PS4], Le *et al.* [PS11], Oluyisola et al. [PS17], Peres *et al.* [PS19] and Chen *et al.* [PS26] focus on the implementation of artificial intelligence. Cañas *et al.* [PS10], Doyle-Kent *et al.* [PS14], Culot *et al.* [PS15]; Rojas *et al.* [PS20], Hubert Backhaus *et al.* [PS25], Kunath *et al.* [PS29] and Zhong *et al.* [PS30] mention the application of cobotic systems.

Elnagar *et al.* [PS1], Rahamaddulla *et al.* [PS9], Cañas *et al.* [PS10], Le *et al.* [PS11], Culot G. *et al.* [PS15], Oluyisola et al. [PS17], Frank *et al.* [PS21], Manavalan *et al.* [PS28] and Zhong *et al.* [PS30] mention the Internet of Things.

In turn, cloud computing is addressed by Elnagar *et al.* [PS1], Rahamaddulla *et al.* [PS9], Le *et al.* [PS11], Culot *et al.* [PS15], Oluyisola et al. [PS17], and Frank *et al.* [PS21], while Big Data and analytics is also mentioned by Gupta S. *et al.* [PS5], Rahamaddulla *et al.* [PS9], Cañas *et al.* [PS10], Le *et al.* [PS11], Frank *et al.* [PS21], Hubert Backhaus *et al.* [PS25] and Zhong *et al.* [PS30].

RFID is included by Kim T.H. *et al.* [PS8] as well as Raharno *et al.* [PS23], who additionally addresses sensors and actuators, as do Le *et al.* [PS11], Onaji *et al.* [PS12], Eirinakis *et al.* [PS13], Taifa *et al.* [PS16] and Nick *et al.* [PS18].

Finally, Bennulf M. *et al.* [PS2], Saboor A. *et al.* [PS7], Nick *et al.* [PS18] and Chen *et al.* [PS26] deal with autonomous robots in their proposals.

There are studies which do not refer to any pillar in particular and it is also common to find research studies which mention several of them.

RQ6: What is the Type of Investigation?

Following the criteria proposed by Wieringa *et al.*[12] for the classification of articles, we found evaluation research in the articles by Cañas *et al.* [PS10], Doyle-Kent *et al.* [PS14], Peres *et al.* [PS19], Rojas *et al.* [PS20], Boukerika *et al.* [PS24], Hubert Backhaus *et al.* [PS25], Manavalan *et al.* [PS28] and Zhong *et al.* [PS30].

The studies conducted by Elnagar *et al.* [PS1], Bennulf M. *et al.* [PS2], Polacsek T. et al. [PS3], Serrano-Ruiz J.C. *et al.* [PS4], Gupta S. *et al.* [PS5], Reyes J. *et al.* [PS6], Saboor A. *et al.* [PS7], Kim T.H. *et al.* [PS8], Rahamaddulla *et al.* [PS9], Le *et al.* [PS11], Onaji *et al.* [PS12], Eirinakis *et al.* [PS13], Taifa *et al.* [PS16], Nick *et al.* [PS18], Frank *et al.* [PS21], Frank *et al.* [PS22], Raharno *et al.* [PS23], Chen *et al.* [PS26], Boucher *et al.* [PS27] and Kunath *et al.* [PS29] are considered solution proposals.

The study by Culot *et al.* [PS15] is the only one considered an opinion article while the one by Oluyisola *et al.* [PS17] is the only one classified as validation article.

5 Threats to Validity

The actions taken to mitigate the threats to validity categorized by Petersen *et al.* [15] are presented below:

- Descriptive: it seeks to ensure that observations are described objectively and accurately. The information to be collected has been structured by means of a data extraction form, presented in Table 4, to answer the RQs, in order to support a uniform data record and objectify the data extraction process.
- Theoretical: it depends on the ability to obtain the information that is intended to be captured. We started with a search string (Sect. 2) tailored to the three most popular computer science digital libraries. A set of inclusion and exclusion criteria was defined (Sect. 2, Table 2) to objectify the selection process.
- Generalization: it is the ability to generalize the results to the entire domain. The set of RQs is general enough to identify and classify the findings on conceptual models of Industry 4.0, regardless of the specific cases, the type of industry, etc.
- Interpretive: it is achieved when the conclusions are reasonable, given the data. The process has been carried out by two groups in parallel and validated with the seminar teacher (last author) to resolve discrepancies at the time of deciding on the inclusion and exclusion of articles. All the members of the group validated the conclusions.
- Repeatability: the investigation process must be detailed enough to ensure that it can be replicated exhaustively. A review protocol for the SMS has been designed that is detailed enough to allow other researchers to repeat the process.

6 Conclusions

- Most of the papers present a model whose contribution is a solution proposal, generally for the introduction of industry 4.0 technologies within organizations.
- There is no formal use of languages or diagrams for the application of these models.
- The industry most addressed by the different studies is the manufacturing industry.
- Most of the studies mention various pillars in their research, the most frequently mentioned being: the Internet of Things (21.4%), Sensors and Actuators (14.3%), Big Data and Analytics (12.5%) and Cobotic Systems (12.5%).
- Regarding the type of research, most of the articles fall into proposed solutions and evaluation research, the former being the most frequently found type.

Future works to be developed are: a) to fill the conceptual modeling gap for the different types of industry 4.0 and b) to carry out the conceptual modeling with the existing diagrams, contrast the results and evaluate which is the most accurate.

References

1. Fuentes-Zenón: 4 El enfoque de Sistemas en la Solucion de Problemas La Elaboracion del Modelo Conceptual. Consultado: el 20 de junio de 2022. https://www.academia.edu/409 0548/4_El_enfoque_de_Sistemas_en_la_Solucion_de_Problemas_La_Elaboracion_del_ Modelo_Conceptual

2. Banks, M., Sokolowski, J.A.: Modeling and Simulation Fundamentals: Theoretical Underpinnings and Practical Domains. Hoboken, N.J. (2010)

3. "¿Qué es la Industria 4.0?", *Argentina.gob.ar*, el 7 de abril de 2021. https://www.argentina.gob.ar/produccion/planargentina40/industria-4-0 (consultado el 28 de junio de 2022)

4. "Industrie 4.0: Mit dem Internet der Dinge auf dem Weg zur 4. industriellen Revolution – ingenieur.de", *ingenieur.de – Jobbörse und Nachrichtenportal für Ingenieure*, el 1 de abril de 2011. https://www.ingenieur.de/technik/fachbereiche/produktion/industrie-40-mit-internet-dinge-weg-4-industriellen-revolution/ (consultado el 20 de junio de 2022)

5. Drath, R., Horch, A.: Industrie 4.0: hit or hype? [industry forum]. IEEE Ind. Electron. Mag. **8**(2), 56–58 (2014)

6. Kitchenham, B., Dybå, T., Jørgensen, M.: Evidence-based software engineering. Perspect. Data Sci. Softw. Eng. **2016**, 273–281 (2004)

7. Zapata, A., Fransoy, M., Soto, S., Di Felice, M., Panizzi, M.: Modelado Conceptual en Industria 4.0: *Mapeo sistemático de la literatura*. En las Actas del XXVIII Congreso Argentino en Ciencias de la Computación (CACIC 2022), La Rioja, Argentina, pp. 526–535 (2022). ISBN 978-987-1364-31-2

8. Dreyfus, P.-A., Psarommatis, F., May, G., Kiritsis, D.: Virtual metrology as an approach for product quality estimation in Industry 4.0: a systematic review and integrative conceptual framework. Int. J. Prod. Res. **60**, 742–765 (2022)

9. de Assis, D.J., Ayala, N.F., Frank, A.G.: Smart working in industry 4.0: How digital technologies enhance manufacturing workers' activities. Comput. Ind. Eng. **163**, 107804 (2022)

10. Wankhede, V.A., Vinodh, S.: State of the art review on Industry 4.0 in manufacturing with the focus on automotive sector. Int. J. Lean Six Sigma **13**(3), 692–732 (2021)

11. Ding, B., Ferràs Hernández, X., Agell Jané, N.: Combining lean and agile manufacturing competitive advantages through Industry 4.0 technologies: an integrative approach. Prod. Plann. Control **34**(5), 442–458 (2021). https://doi.org/10.1080/09537287.2021.1934587

12. Machado, G., Winroth, M.P., Ribeiro da Silva, E.H.D.: Sustainable manufacturing in Industry 4.0: an emerging research agenda. Int. J. Prod. Res. **58**(5), 1462–1484 (2020)

13. Kitchenham, B., Charters, S.: Guidelines for Performing Systematic Literature Reviews in Software Engineering. Citeseer (2007)

14. Wieringa, R., Maiden, N., Mead, N., Rolland, C.: Requirements engineering paper classification and evaluation criteria: a proposal and a discussion. Requirements Eng. **11**(1), 102–107 (2006)

15. Petersen, K., Vakkalanka, S., Kuzniarz, L.: Guidelines for conducting systematic mapping studies in software engineering: an update. Inform. Softw. Technol. **64**, 1–18 (2015). https://doi.org/10.1016/j.infsof.2015.03.007

SIBDaCAr: A Chronotanatodiagnostic System Prototype for the Republic of Argentina

Paola Azar[1,3], Darío Ruano[1,3], Andrea Maldonado[1], Norma Herrera[1,3(✉)], Daniel A. Jaume[2,3], and Marcelo Martínez[4]

[1] Departamento de Informática, Universidad Nacional de San Luis, San Luis, Argentina
{epazar18,dmruano,nherrera}@unsl.edu.ar
[2] Departamento de Matemática, Universidad Nacional de San Luis, San Luis, Argentina
djaume@unsl.edu.ar
[3] Laboratorio de Investigación y Desarrollo en Base de Datos, Universidad Nacional de San Luis, San Luis, Argentina
[4] Cuerpo Médico Forense y Criminalístico de la Tercera Circunscripción Judicial de la Provincia de Mendoza, Mendoza, Argentina

Abstract. Chronotanatodiagnosis is the set of observations and techniques that allow indicating the time interval in which the death process has most likely occurred. The estimation of this interval, known as PMI (post-mortem interval), is perhaps one of the most complicated tasks in forensic medicine.

The support of computer tools available to a forensic pathologist in our country to date death is scarce or null in some cases. In this article, we present the development of a prototype of a comprehensive database system (SIBDaCAr) that could help establishing the PMI and that can be used in the context of our country.

Keywords: Database System · Prototype · Chronotanatodiagnosis · PMI

1 Introduction

In the current era, characterized by the evolution of information and communication technologies, computer science is transversal to most of our daily activities, providing the necessary tools to address complex problems and contributing to the search for efficient solutions to problems of interest. Legal and forensic medicine is not exempt from this reality. A topic of particular interest in this field is the determination of the time of death. Determining the time of death is perhaps one of the most complex problems in forensic medicine.

Chronotanatodiagnosis (or dating of death) is the set of observations and techniques that allow indicating the time interval in which the death process has most likely occurred [1]. This interval, known as PMI (post-mortem interval), indicates a period of time circumscribed by the moment of death and the discovery of the body. Obtaining an accurate estimate of this interval is of utmost importance both in the criminal and civil context. The time of death can, for example, allow accepting or rejecting alibis during the investigation of a crime, and it can also have economic consequences related

P. Pesado (Ed.): CACIC 2022, CCIS 1778, pp. 241–256, 2023.
https://doi.org/10.1007/978-3-031-34147-2_16

to inheritance. Estimating the PMI is one of the most complicated tasks in forensic medicine, and there is no method that is completely accurate for this purpose. The longer the PMI, the less accurate the estimate becomes.

The support of computer tools available to a forensic pathologist in our country to date death is scarce or non-existent in some cases. The existing software is based on other realities: they request data that are not viable in our country and/or use formulas based on climatic conditions that are unlikely to occur in our country. To further complicate the situation, there is no common core of data that is used in all provinces to date death.

On the other hand, classical mathematical models used for dating death have been shown to be limited [1,3] and [4]. For this reason, it is also necessary to adapt and validate them to the different geographies of Argentina [5].

In this work, we are focused on the study and development of analytical and computational tools to support and assist the tasks of chronotanathology of recent corpses for national forensic systems. Dating the death of non-recent corpses is an extremely complex matter and will be addressed at a later stage. We present the work carried out, which includes the design and implementation of a database system prototype that allows establishment the PMI and that can be used in the scope of our country.

This document is an updated and expanded version of the previous paper that was presented in [7]. In this version, we have included a more detailed description of the development process of the prototype and the progress achieved in cluster analysis.

The remaining part of the article is organized as follows: in Sect. 2 we provide a brief overview of chronotanatodiagnosis, where we introduce the basic concepts of the problem, and then in Sect. 3 we analyze the situation in Argentina. In Sect. 4 y 5 we present our contribution: the design and implementation of a prototype system and the advancements made in cluster analysis. Finally, in Sect. 6, we conclude with the conclusions and future work.

2   Chronotanatodiagnosis: An Open Problem

Chronotanatodiagnosis can be defined as a set of observations, techniques, and methods that allow establishing a temporal interval (PMI) in which a death has most likely occurred. It is one of the three questions that arise in criminalistics (place, date, and cause of death) and perhaps one of the most difficult problems in legal medicine.

The precision and applicability of existing procedures depend on the characteristics and circumstances of the death and the time elapsed since death. Additionally, the type of technique used depends on the state of the body. There are two cases: a recent corpse, which does not have obvious signs of decomposition, and a non-recent corpse, which has obvious signs of decomposition [2]. As we mentioned earlier, this work focuses on dating recent corpses.

Despite the fact that determining the time of death is never an entirely exact science, there are a large number of factors that help to have a more precise idea of the time that has elapsed since the death. These factors, called cadaveric phenomena, can be classified as immediate, intermediate, or late depending on the time it takes for them to appear. In the case of recent corpses, data should be taken into account are:

- Signs of molecular death: changes that occur in the body depending on environmental circumstances, which can be known and measured (abiotic phenomena) and those of a physical-chemical nature that occur in the body after death (biotic phenomena). Within the abiotic phenomena we find: cooling, dehydration, livor mortis, visceral hypostasis. Within the biotic phenomena we can mention rigor mortis, spasms, physical-chemical changes, thanatochemistry, and microbiology.
- Paramedic signs: elements that surround the corpse and the situation in which it is found, characteristics of the crime scene (if it has rained, for example), objects belonging to the victim (for example, electronic devices with batteries that have not yet been depleted), etc.
- Signs of residual life: pupil reaction to light, pupil reaction to atropine and pilocarpine, muscle contraction, mortality of sperm cells, among others.
- Signs derived from the cessation of vital functions: here the data comes from observing the state in which physiological functions have been stopped after death.

As can be seen, the volume of data handled by a forensic pathologist and the variability of the data depending on factors that are unique to each case, makes the estimation of time of death extremely non-linear. Classical mathematical models that provide indicators for establishing the time of death are fundamentally based on linear, logarithmic, and sigmoidal models (depending on the case) of a few variables, typically one or two. This approach has proven to be limited [1,3,4].

To understand the complexity of the dating process, let's take an example. Body temperature is one of the most used data in determining PMI. Once death has occurred, the temperature gradually and progressively decreases until it becomes equal to the environment. To calculate the post-mortem interval using temperature, a double exponential model proposed by Marshal and Hoare in 1962 is followed. This model establishes that it is possible to differentiate a double cooling phase: a plateau where there is practically no cooling, and a progressive final phase. But there are multiple factors that affect the cooling process of a corpse: ambient temperature, weight of the person since fat acts as a thermal insulator, layers of clothing, air currents, humidity, hyperthermia, and some diseases and situations prior to death (intoxications, sepsis, hemorrhages) that alter the cooling curve. In addition, since temperature-based dating methods depend on the difference between body temperature and ambient temperature, their effectiveness is significantly reduced in places with high temperatures or abrupt temperature changes.

The complexity and difficulties posed by determining PMI are categorical and that is why it constitutes one of the most complex problems faced by the forensic pathologist.

3   Chronotanatodiagnosis: Software and Argentine Reality

At present, establishing the post-mortem interval (PMI) accurately remains a challenge. Argentina is not exempt from this reality. As we explained in the previous section, calculating the PMI is a nonlinear problem with multiple variables whose values are affected by multiple factors. Perhaps this is one of the main reasons why support software for chronotanatodiagnosis is scarce or not widely used, as is the case in other sciences. For example, the software AMAsoft (www.amasoft.de/index_e.html) uses two methods to perform the dating process: Henssge's Nomogram [3] and non-temperature-based methods. In the case of Henssge's Nomogram, it is not suitable for the usual climatic conditions in most of our country because it requires smooth temperature variations of less than 5 °C throughout the day, with a range of between 16 to 24 °C. This implies that the Nomogram Method is only usable in the southern region of the country.

The model proposed in [6] represents an improvement over the Henssge's model, as the authors propose a thermodynamic model based on finite differences, whose initialization (boundary initial conditions) is a thermometric reading of the corpse's skin. Unfortunately, this approach is not applicable to the forensic reality in Argentina due to the type of equipment required for taking readings and the training that would be required for personnel: training in space discretization and elementary knowledge of the theory of finite difference equations.

Regarding the non-temperature-based methods used in AMAsoft, they require as input data: stiffness, lividity, mechanical excitability of skeletal muscles, electric excitement of mimic muscles, and chemical excitability of the iris (atropine, tropicamide/cyclopent, acetylcholine). And this is where we face the second problem: not all of this data is always available. Furthermore, there is no common core of data used by all forensic pathologist in the country to carry out the dating process. Although there is a general consensus on what data should be used to date death, the data that is actually used is determined by the circumstances of death, the availability of resources, and in some cases, also by the experience of the forensic pathologist involved.

All of the above justifies the survey conducted on existing software in our country for chronothanatodiagnosis (see Sect. 4.1) revealing that the computer tools available to a forensic physician for dating death are scarce or nonexistent in most cases. It is essential, therefore, to provide technological tools to support chronothanatodiagnosis, which should arise from a multidisciplinary approach to the problem, ensuring their robustness.

In this work, we address the problem of chronotanatodiagnosis in Argentina by proposing a paradigm shift: starting from the design of a specific database, we apply clustering algorithms to find relevant clusters of cases grouped according to multiple extrinsic and intrinsic factors. In a second stage, we will address the problem of developing specific mathematical models of chronotanatodiagnosis for the different clusters of cases found.

4   A Prototype for a Dating System

The ultimate goal of this work is to design a suitable database system for the Argentine thanatological community, which we have called "SIBDaCAr" (comprehensive system of Argentine chronotanatological database). In this section, we present the process of developing of the prototype for the SIBDaCAr system. Given the complexity of the problem, we decided to use the technique of evolutionary prototyping.

For reasons of space we do not show the complete documentation but it is available for those who require it.

4.1   Requirements Analysis

Like any software project, we began with requirements analysis to identify functional and non-functional requirements of the system using elicitation techniques such as interviews, observation, and surveys.

The interviews were initially conducted with forensic pathologists from Mendoza, Córdoba, Tierra del Fuego, and Corrientes (provinces of Argentina). After each interview, a brainstorming session was held with the team responsible for developing the prototype.

In regards to observation, given that direct observation of the activities carried out in the process of dating is impossible due to the involved topic, a seminar of 4 meetings was organized where forensic pathologists presented cases of dating from different regions of the country and under different circumstances.

As explained in the previous section, an important point was to establish a common core of data. To achieve this, a survey was developed and distributed among forensic pathologist throughout the country. This survey presented data used in chronotanatodiagnosis organized into two categories:

Data taken at the scene of the event: body temperature, body position, ambient temperature, pupillary light reflex, evaluation/description of clothing under circumstances of clothed cadaver, evaluation of environmental context at the place of discovery.

Data taken at the Forensic Institute: hepatic temperature, rectal temperature, auricular temperature, livor mortis, rigor mortis, opacity of the cornea, concentration of potassium in vitreous humor, degree of putrefaction, mechanical excitability of skeletal muscles, electric excitation of mimic muscles, evaluation of gastric contents, evaluation of intestinal contents, state of the bladder, pupillary reaction to light stimulation, pupillary reaction to chemical stimulation, mobility of respiratory epithelium, mobility of sperm, maintenance of the corpse between the time of discovery and the autopsy.

For each data, two assessments were requested: the degree of importance that the respondent assigns to that data on a scale of 0 to 5, where 0 means not important at all and 5 means very important, and the *frequency of use* that the respondent makes of that data, using the scale of values: never, 20%, 40%, 60%, 80%, always.

4.2   Results Obtained

Regarding the survey, a total of 35 responses were received, which were analyzed using the data studio platform. Perhaps the most It was surprising to see that there is no direct relationship between the degree of importance and frequency of use. Figure 1 shows the result for the *pupil reaction to light* data as an example. As can be observed is a data considered important by approximately 72% of those surveyed (areas corresponding to the values 3, 4 and 5) but 75% of those surveyed state that they never use it.

The survey also asked about the support software used, obtaining as response that, of the 35 respondents, only one refers to using the SWISSWUFF software (https://www.swisswuff.ch).

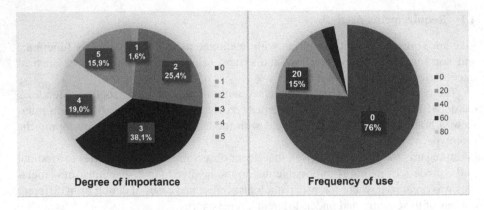

Fig. 1. Result of the survey for the data *reaction of the pupil to light.*

These results were also used to establish the data core: those data that were considered important by at least 40% of the surveyed users and that had a frequency of use from medium to high was included.

Regarding the requirements, they were documented specifying: objective of the system, scopes and limitations, functional requirements and non-functional requirements.

The functional requirements of the system have been organized by the functionalities provided by it. Below is a summary of the functionalities and the requirements associated with each of them

Functionality 1: User Registration and Access Control

In order to use the system, users must be properly registered. Each registered user will have a category assigned with access restrictions associated with that category. The system must perform strict control about who access it, where they access from and which data from the database they access.

Requirements:

R1. User registration.
R2. Access control.
R3. Generation of access reports.

Functionality 2: Estimation of Deadth Date

The system should allow for the estimation of the time of death for the cases entered into it.

Requirements:

R4. Input of data core.
R5. Detection of possible inconsistencies between the entered data.
R6. Determination of the postmortem interval (PMI).
R7. Generation of a dating report.

Functionality 3: Clustering

The system should allow for finding cases similar to a given one

    Requirements:

R8. Cluster detection.

R9. Report generation.

Each of the requirements was documented with a table specifying details such as functionality, development priority, input and output data, etc. As an example, Fig. 2 shows the description of R5 requirement.

ID: R5	Title : Detection of inconsistencies between the entered data.
Type (necessary/desirable): desirable	**Funcionality:** Estimation of deadth date.
Critical: NO	**Development priority:** Medium
Input: Data core.	**Output:** Inconsistencies found (if any exist)
Description Perform data correlation to detect possible inconsistencies among them.	
Handling of exception situations: The user is not authorized to access this module: record the user's information and issue an alert.	
Acceptance criteria: The user must confirm the entered data.	

Fig. 2. Documentation of the R5 requirement - Functionality 2.

Similar work was done with non-functional requirements.

4.3 Elaboration of Models

In the second stage, the following models were developed for SIBDaCAr:

– The entity-relationship model and the relational model of the database
– UML[1] component diagram of the system
– UML use case diagram

Figure 3 shows the relational model, which was generated using MySQL Workbench. The data considered there are those that were established as the core but without discard those that are considered important even though they are infrequently used. The goal is that the process of dating uses at least the data belonging to the nucleus, but that the estimate can be improved in those cases in which there are other additional data to the kernel.

---

[1] Unified Modeling Language.

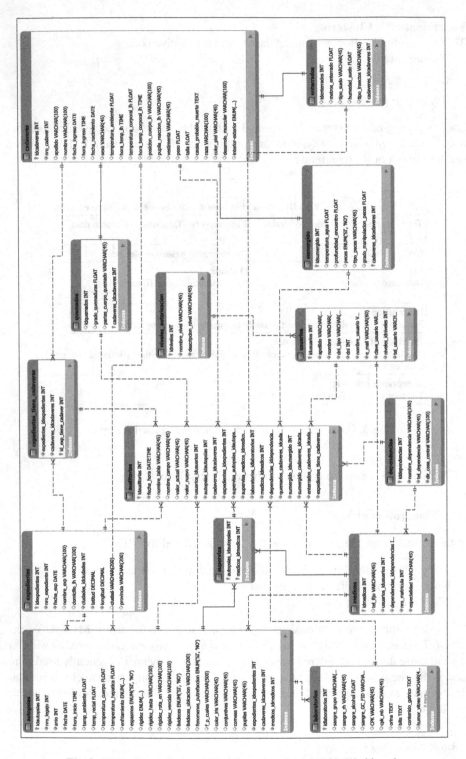

Fig. 3. SIBDaCAr Relational Model, made using MySQL Workbench

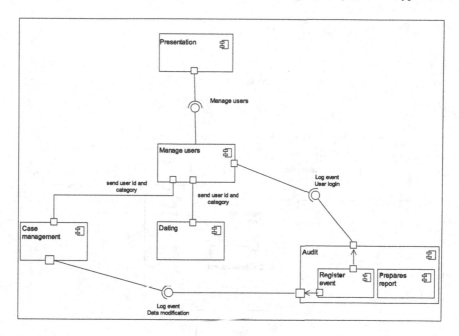

Fig. 4. UML componente diagram for SIBDaCAr system.

Figure 4 shows the main UML component diagram of SIBDaCAr, specifying internal parts, connectors, and ports that implement this component. As can be seen, the system is organized around four main components: *user management, case management, dating* and *auditing*. A diagram was created for each of these components, adding to each one of them the databases access.

The UML component diagram for the *user management* component is depicted in Fig. 5. As discussed in Sect. 4.1, it is necessary to perform strict control over user registration and access to the system due to the sensitive information stored in the database. To address this requirement, the diagram includes a module that manages registration permissions and, furthermore, all the access information is transmitted to the *auditing* component.

Figures 6 and 7 shows de UML diagrams for *case management* and *dating* components respectively. The *case management* component is responsible for entering data related to files, corpses, autopsies, and laboratory results. It also enables users to modify previously entered data while maintaining a record of the changes made through the *auditing* component. The *dating* module, on the other hand, allows dating using Henssge's Nomogram, dating using the data core and searching for similar cases through a clustering algorithm. In the case of Henssge's Nomogram, the system verifies that exists the necessary conditions to ensure an acceptable level of confidence in the result.

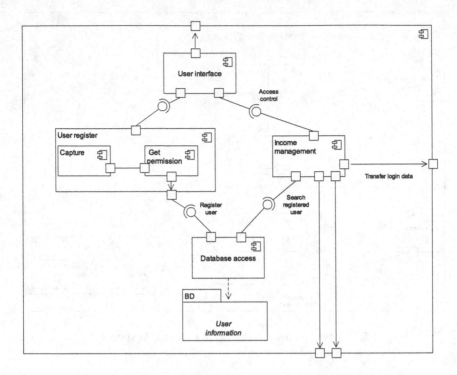

Fig. 5. UML diagram for *user management* component

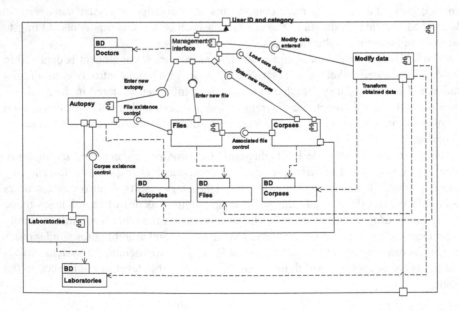

Fig. 6. UML diagram for *case management* component.

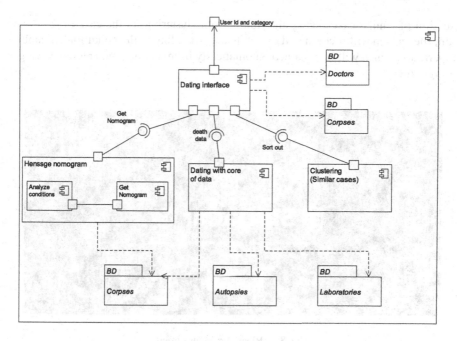

Fig. 7. UML diagram for *dating* component.

4.4   Prototype Implementation

In the programming of the prototype, Python was used as the main language and CSS, Javascripts and HTML for the graphic part. We choice Python because that it is free software licensed under the Python Software Foundation License, a license very similar to that of the GPL, with the ease of distributing the code binaries without having to attach the sources; It is multiparadigm and multiplatform and offers frameworks for the development of web applications.

The implementation of the prototype included the generation of the databases. For this, we use the engine MySQL databases since it is free software under the open source GPL license, it is customizable because the GPL license allows to adapt it to the specific needs of the application, it is multiplatform, it allows several layers of security and supports large databases.

Obviously, this prototype is based on the architecture proposed in the component diagrams and with the data organized according to the given relational model. As this prototype evolves into the final SIBDaCAr system, the diagrams and models provided in the previous section should be refined and possibly modified. Feedback received from the forensic community when testing the prototype will be important for this task.

Figures 8 and 9 show the screens corresponding to the entry and main menu. The main menu consists of 4 options: files, corpses, autopsies and estimation (PMI). Figures 10, 11 and 12 show the screens corresponding to the input modulesSIBDaCAr: input screen file data entry and dating module. In the case of the dating module, they are considered three possibilities: Henssge's Nomogram, dating using data core and detection of similar cases using algorithms from clustering. In the case of the Nomogram, the system will recommend or not its use according to the conditions of ambient temperature, which will be obtained automatically from the location entered when generating a file.

Fig. 8. SIBDaCAr: input screen

Fig. 9. SIBDaCAr: main menu

Fig. 10. SIBDaCAr: cadaver data entry

Fig. 11. SIBDaCAr: file data entry

Fig. 12. SIBDaCAr: dating module

5 Clustering Analysis

To overcome the theoretical limitations of the Henssge model and the practical limitations of the model presented in [6] we started developing a prediction model based on clustering. The objective is to find corpses that have comparable features and, consequently, could be valuable in determining the time of death.

Cluster analysis is the process of detecting groups by reducing the inter-group similarity (compactness property) while simultaneously increasing the intra-group similarity (separateness property). Typically, the criteria involved in the clustering process are based on a measure of (dis)similarity between objects. Data clustering is an unsupervised learning technique because it does not require any a priori labeling of training objects, and there is no need to know in advance the number or nature of the clusters.

We briefly describe the work done so far:

Data Processing. Relational databases store tuples in relationships, therefore, a clustering algorithm can be used to identify meaningful subgroups of tuples. However, it is not possible to directly apply a clustering algorithm to a relational database, first it is necessary to decide which tuples and which attributes to use. In our case, for each cadaver, we generate a feature vector that only contains the data that is relevant to establish the PMI. Data that are not numerical are transformed into numbers that reflect the degree of similarity between the considered values.

Similarity Function. To measure the distance between the vectors, in the first stage we will use the cosine function [8]. If $d_i = (w_{i1}, ..., w_{it})$ and $d_j = (w_{j1}, ..., w_{jt})$ are the feature vectors of two cadavers registered in the database, then the degree of similarity between them is determined by:

$$sim(d_i, d_j) = \frac{d_i.d_j}{|d_i| \times |d_j|} = \frac{\sum_{l=1}^{t} w_{il} \times w_{jl}}{\sqrt{\sum_{l=1}^{t} w_{il}^2 \times \sum_{l=1}^{t} w_{jl}^2}} \tag{1}$$

6 Conclusions and Future Work

In this article, we present the development of a prototype of an integral system of databases (SIBDaCAr) that allows establishing the PMI and that can be used in the scope of our country. The work included the analysis of requirements, the elaboration of model and the programming of the prototype of the system, using the idea of prototyping evolutionary. The work done so far has allowed us to understand the enormous complexity of the problem and visualize the shortcomings computer tools appropriate to the conditions of our country for chronotanatodiagnosis. As future work, we propose to study clustering methods.

Acknowledgments. We would like to thank Dr. Inés Aparici (Poder Judicial de Tierra del Fuego), to Dr. José Gálvez (Instituto Médico Forense del Poder Judicial de Corrientes) and to Dr. Moisés Dib (Instituto de Medicina Forense de Córdoba) for the collaboration received for the development of this work.

This work was partially supported by the Universidad Nacional de San Luis, Argentina, grant ROICO 03-0918, MATH AmSud, grant 21-MATH-05, Agencia I+D+T+i, Argentina, grant PICT 2020-Serie A-00549, and Facultad de Ciencias Físico Matemáticas y Naturales, UNSL, Argentina, Proy D+i, Estudio Analítico y Computacional de la Cronotanatología, Res 087-21.

References

1. Maldonado, A.L.: La data de la muerte, un desafío no resuelto. Revista Española de Medicina Legal (2010)
2. Trezza, F.C.: La data de la muerte. Las trasformaciones cadavéricas. Ediciones Argentinas, Buenos Aires (2006)
3. Henssge, C., Madea, B.: Estimation of the time since death. Forensic Sci. Int. **165**(2–3), 182–184 (2007)
4. Vidoli, G.M., Beasley, M.M., Jantz, L.M., Devlin, J.B., Steadman, D.W.: The future of taphonomic research. In: Estimation of the Time since Death: Current Research and Future Trends, pp. 251–261 (2020)
5. Hayman, J., Oxenham, M.: Estimation of the time since death in decomposed bodies found in Australian conditions. Aust. J. Forensic Sci. **49**(1), 31–44 (2017)
6. Wilk, L., et al.: Reconstructing the time since death using noninvasive thermometry and numerical analysis. Sci. Adv. **6**(22), eaba4243 (2020)
7. Azar, P., Ruano, D., Maldonado, A., Herrera, N., Jaume, D., Martínez, M.: SIBDaCAr: Un Prototipo de Sistema de Cronotanatodiagnóstico para la República Argentina. XXVIII Congreso Argentino de Ciencias de la Computación, 588–597 (2022). ISBN 978-987-1364-31-2
8. Baeza-Yates, R., Ribeiro-Neto, B.: Modern Information Retrieval. Addison-Wesley (1999)

Signal Processing and Real-Time Systems

A New Academic RTOS: Xinu Port to the AVR Architecture

Rafael Ignacio Zurita[1]([⊠]), Candelaria Alvarez[2], Miriam Lechner[1], Alejandro Mora[1], and Mariana Zárate[1]

[1] Departmento de Ingeniería de Computadoras, Facultad de Informática, Universidad Nacional del Comahue, Neuquén, Argentine
{rafa,mtl,alejandro.mora,mariana.zarate}@fi.uncoma.edu.ar
[2] Departamento de Arquitectura de Computadoras y Sistemas Operativos, Escuela de Ingeniería, Universidad Autónoma de Barcelona, Barcelona, Spain
anacandelaria.alvarez@uab.cat

Abstract. The software development tools used in the industry for automation and control do not always have desirable characteristics to be used in the process of learning the concepts associated with them. For example, most real-time operating systems (RTOS), which are the main commonly low-level software used in automation and control, usually present a complex API, designed mainly to support tens or hundreds of different microcontrollers existing in the industry. By contrast, the general-purpose Xinu operating system, originally developed by Douglas Comer at Purdue University, was developed from its first versions for instructional purposes. This article reports the work carried out to port Xinu to the Harvard-type 8-bit AVR microcontroller architecture, in order to be used as an academic RTOS. Qualitative and quantitative evaluations of this new port are presented. The results show that XINU has the potential to be ported to other low-resource microcontroller families, and to be used as an academic RTOS on those platforms as well.

Keywords: Real-time Operating System · RTOS · Embedded System · Xinu · AVR · Operating System · Arduino · atmega328p · Microcontroller

1 Introduction

Usually the teaching of real-time embedded systems programming, at universities, is supported by the use of a real-time operating system (RTOS), as a practical tool [1]. It runs mainly on low complexity microprocessors, and mostly on microcontrollers.

Real-time operating systems (RTOS) are not complete operating systems. They are basically composed by a preemptive task manager, and mechanisms for synchronization and communication between tasks [2]. Its main characteristic is that it allows the concurrent execution of tasks or processes in a predictable manner, therefore, the CPU scheduler usually works using priorities, and in a round-robin manner in case the priorities are the same.

© The Author(s), under exclusive license to Springer Nature Switzerland AG 2023
P. Pesado (Ed.): CACIC 2022, CCIS 1778, pp. 259–271, 2023.
https://doi.org/10.1007/978-3-031-34147-2_17

This reduced set of features is directly related to the hardware on which it is run. RTOS are mostly used in low-resource microcontroller-based computing platforms for automation and control. In recent years, with the exponential growth in the development of IOT devices, its use has multiplied in environments of sensors connected to the Internet, also generally controlled by microcontrollers [3].

Unfortunately, there is not a wide variety of academic RTOS. Generally, in specialized university courses related to real-time embedded systems, some industrial kind of RTOS is used for the hands-on practice part of the course. There is a variety of industrial RTOS, some of them that are widely used are FreeRTOS, ChibiOS/RT, Cesium RTOS, or VxWorks [4–7]. The first two RTOS are open source systems, and the latter ones are proprietary. All these RTOS provide an API oriented to the professional programmer of real-time systems, and not to the average university student. Besides, its internal structure is not usually easy to understand during only one semester (average duration of university courses). This restricts the academic possibilities, and usually, most of the available weeks for the laboratory work on RTOS, during the semester, is employed to learn about its API, and also to know how to use it. If there were more time available, extra topics could be developed. For example, it might be very productive to analyze and learn about its internal data structures and algorithms; or how the expansion and/or modification of its functionalities and services would be possible. The knowledge of these topics are usually necessary for research. In order to improve this situation, the modification of an academic operating system is proposed in this work, to be used in microcontroller environments, and also as a real-time operating system. The Xinu operating system was chosen because of its elegant internal data structure, its easy to learn API, and its current CPU scheduler, which is suitable for using Xinu as RTOS. As the target hardware platform, the AVR architecture atmega328p microcontroller was selected, since it is the original microcontroller of the Arduino hardware boards, widely available in the regional market.

This work extends and consolidates results in the article presented previously in October, 2022 at the XXVIII Argentine Congress of Computer Science (CACIC 2022) [8]. One concern in using an RTOS on small microcontrollers is memory, both RAM and ROM. In order to exhibit that there are available resources for the real-time application to be developed on top of the RTOS, we have included a quantitative analysis of the resources used by this new port. We also include a qualitative example of API comparison, which shows the readability of this new Xinu version for AVR as RTOS.

The rest of the paper is structured as follows. In Sect. 2, we define all the concepts associated with this work, and present some previous work related to porting a RTOS. In Sect. 3, we detail the method and work made during all the stages of the port. In Sect. 4, we present a qualitative and quantitative evaluation, detailing the resources available after the port, and an API comparison between Xinu and FreeRTOS. In Sect. 5, we conclude and foresee future work.

2 Background and Related Work

2.1 Real-Time Embedded Systems and RTOS

A real-time system is that type of computing where the correctness of the system depends not only on the logical result of the computation, but also on the time at which the results are produced [2, 9]. When a system does not produce the correct output before the maximum time imposed by the requirements, a failure happens, and the system is defined as a non real-time system.

The document of requirements of a real-time system specifies events and actions, and for specific events, a maximum time is defined for each of such events. Usually, the design consists of independent tasks, which will be concurrent tasks on run time. Also, an extra layer of software is used, mostly a real-time operating system. This extra support software is able to execute the tasks concurrently, and also provides support to accomplish the deadlines for each event. Anyway, this is not an automatic process. That is, using a real-time operating system does not imply that the system will be real-time. In order to achieve the proper operation of the system, developers must specify a priority for each task, relate tasks to events, and define how these tasks must synchronize and communicate. At run time, the real-time operating system will be in charge of assuring that the task with the highest priority is being executed. The previous model and tools allow developers to evaluate the design and software code in all possible situations, in order to verify that the time to produce a result for an event and/or task is always less than the defined time in the requirements. If the number of system states and possible situations are unmanageable, developers can run simulations to estimate whether the designed model will meet the required deadlines.

Generally, the CPU scheduler (scheduler) of a real-time operating system is fixed-priority (the priority of each task is defined at the design stage) and preemptive. When the system is running, every time the RTOS activates a task, that is, it places the task in the "ready to run" state, it verifies its priority. If this priority is higher than the current task in "running" state, then the RTOS performs a context switch and places the new, higher priority task to execute. If there are multiple tasks "ready to run" with the same priority as the task currently using the CPU, then the RTOS preempts the CPU at regular intervals, using round-robin to allocate it to another task.

There are other means and methods for developing a real-time system, but the use of an RTOS with these characteristics and running model is the most common situation. In summary, an RTOS must have the following features:

- An RTOS (Real-Time Operating System) must be able to schedule different tasks[1] (multiprogramming/multithreading), and be preemptive.
- Each task must have a priority, and the RTOS always executes the highest priority task in the "ready to run" state.
- The RTOS must have task synchronization and communication mechanisms.
- There must be a priority inheritance system.

---

[1] An RTOS would be useless if the available memory is only enough to run one or two tasks.

- The RTOS must allow asynchronous events, such as I/O interruptions.

The previous characteristics allow the developers to build a system whose operation is predictable, which is a prerequisite to evaluate the design, and to know if the resulting system meets the defined deadlines, and therefore, to be real-time.

2.2 Xinu

Xinu is a small and easy to understand operating system, originally developed by Douglas Comer for instructional purposes at Purdue University in the 1980s [10]. Since then it has been ported to many architectures and hardware platforms. The current versions of Xinu (2015) are for x86(PC), ARM, MIPS y x86 virtual machines. Although Xinu shares some ideas and terminology with UNIX, it is not a member of the Unix systems family. Their internal structures differ completely. Applications written for one system will not run on the other without modification.

Xinu is an operating system with an elegant design, whose internal structure is made up of a multilevel hierarchy of essential components. Other more complex levels can be later added over the multilevel hierarchy. Xinu has support for dynamic process creation, dynamic memory allocation, file systems, network support, and device-independent I/O functions. It also provides communication and synchronization services between processes. Xinu does not implement virtual memory, nor does it have support for hardware paging. At runtime, the Xinu image with a series of applications is fully loaded into RAM, using a single address space for all processes. This means that the processes share memory, although Xinu manages one different stack for each process.

The existing Xinu versions are for 32-bit processors. However, the system was selected for this work because it is also suitable for embedded environments. Xinu's source code is small in comparison with other academic operating systems (such as MINIX). The x86 version of Xinu contains approximately ten thousand lines of C language source code. 75% of these belong to the source code of drivers, network support, and.h headers; so the kernel was written in approximately 2500 lines of C code.

2.3 Previous Work

The port of an operating system or RTOS to a new architecture involves several technical stages. Some of them are essential, like knowing the basic features of the new architecture -processor registers, ISA, and addresses modes-, the toolchain to use, and the system boot process. Then, it will be necessary to follow some already validated methodology.

In [11] and [12] the port of the uC/OS-II real-time operating system to two different architectures, both 16-bit, is detailed. These papers describe ports that followed the methodology proposed by the official RTOS documentation in [13]. uC/OS-II is an open source RTOS, developed by Micrium Inc. It offers an industry-oriented API, and Micrium offers commercial support and non-free licenses for companies that require it. In [14] and [15] the processes accomplished to port FreeRTOS and VxWorks to new platforms are detailed (for x86 in the case of the FreeRTOS article, and MPC8313E in the case of VxWorks).

Both works expose examples of how to port a real-time operating system to ne~
architectures, for readers who have no previous experience in this type of work. In [16,
the IEEE documents a standard that describes the necessary characteristics of a real-time
operating system for embedded systems composed of 16-bit processors, without MMUs.
In [17] a model for the design of hardware-independent RTOS is described. The focus
is on separating the general RTOS kernel code from the particular hardware features.
With a final hardware description it will be possible, at compile time, to generate specific
missing code, for example, the task context switching for a specific microcontroller.

We have not found recent work on how to port a conventional academic operating
system to be executed in microcontroller embedded environments as RTOS. However,
the previously mentioned work provided us with design principles and methodologies,
which we were able to use to achieve the version of Xinu presented in this article.

3 Porting Xinu to the AVR Architecture

The port of Xinu to the AVR atmega328p microcontroller was carried out mostly using
the methodology described in [10].

The steps of this methodology can be observed in Fig. 1 (b) and are directly related
to the internal structure of Xinu. Figure 1 (a) shows a diagram of this structure, where the
software components of Xinu are organized in a multilevel hierarchy. When software is
designed using that hierarchy, the interconnections between the components are clear,
and the internal design is easy to understand. Both figures were extracted from [10].

Not all the steps were necessary in tis work, since an RTOS does not contain all the
components of a traditional operating system. Additionally, steps 13 to 17 from the list
in Fig. 1 (b) were not necessary because the target microcontroller does not have the
necessary hardware for those components.

Step 1. The first task is learning about the target hardware. This task was of great
relevance in this work because the hardware organization of the selected microcontroller
differs greatly from the processors where Xinu runs. The x86, ARM, and MIPS processors supported by Xinu present a Von Neumann model. This means a single memory for
programs and data (even if some of these contain internal memory caches in the processor, different for data and code, as this is transparent to the program's binary code).
In contrast, the AVR target microcontroller has a Harvard architecture. This architecture presents at least two memories accessed by different buses and addresses, one for
instructions and another for data.

The memory for the code (instructions), in the Atmega328p, consists of a 32 KB
FLASH memory, and usually, its name is program memory. The memory for dynamic
data is a small 2 KB of RAM.

Additionally, there is a third general-purpose 1 KB memory for non-volatile data,
which is an EEPROM memory. Furthermore, the AVR architecture has an improvement
over the theoretical Harvard architecture. The AVR processors can store read-only data
in the program memory (which is usually larger than the RAM). This means that constant
variables can be stored in FLASH, thus saving space in RAM. This is useful because
constant variables will not be modified on program runtime. Another important characteristic of AVR is that the CPU is an 8-bit architecture, while the addresses are 16-bit.

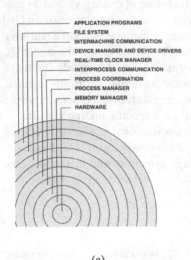

Step	Description
1.	Learn about the new hardware
2.	Build cross-development tools
3.	Learn the compiler's calling conventions
4.	Build a bootstrap mechanism
5.	Devise a basic polled output function
6.	Load and run a sequential program
7.	Port and test the basic memory manager
8.	Port the context switch and process creation functions
9.	Port and test the remaining process manager functions
10.	Build an interrupt dispatcher
11.	Port and test the real-time clock functions
12.	Port and test a tty driver
13.	Port or create drivers for an Ethernet and other devices
14.	Port the network stack, including Internet protocols
15.	Port the remote disk and RAM disk modules
16.	Port the local and remote file system modules
17.	Port the Xinu shell and other applications

(a)   (b)

Fig. 1. (a) Internal structure of Xinu in a multilevel hierarchy. (b) Sequential steps taken when porting Xinu.

Therefore, a C pointer is 16-bit, while the processor's natural data, the word, is 8-bit. Most of the instructions of the AVR ISA take a single clock cycle for execution.

Step 2. The second task consisted in the installation of the development toolchain for the AVR architecture. The selected development computer (host) was a PC with GNU/Linux, which greatly facilitated this task since the Linux distribution used comes with a packaged cross-compiler of C for AVR, binutils (linker, assembler, etc.) for AVR, and the avr-libc C library.

Steps 3 to 6. The calling convention used is the convention already implemented by GCC. The task of compiling, loading and executing a basic program was performed by compiling a C program with gcc and the default linker ld scripts for that microcontroller, then avr-dude command was used for flashing the program on FLASH. Finally, the program was run by the Arduino bootloader already stored in the flash. The complexity lies in assigning, at compile-time, the actual physical ROM (flash) and RAM addresses to the different binary program symbols (e.g., the entry point of the C program or the address for the stack pointer). In our case, this assignment was automatically done via the default ld scripts of the gcc linker for the atmega328p microcontroller.

Step 7. During the fourth task the four Xinu's basic memory management functions were modified and verified. The functions were adapted using the RAM addresses allocations obtained from the previous step, which Xinu uses to set the limits of the available physical memory. The Xinu's compilation system scripts were also modified by adapting the makefiles to use the GCC compiler for AVR.

Steps 8 and 9. This fifth task involved the most of the time and required to port the context switch routine in assembly, which is dependent on the architecture. This routine saves the processor state for a process on its stack and loads a previous state for the process that will continue using the CPU from the stack of the process to be resumed. Several routines for process creation and management were also ported in this task. Once this stage was completed, it was possible to have multiprogramming. Furthermore, the Xinu kernel itself becomes a process, and the details of implementation for converting a single sequential code into several processes are perhaps the most complex to understand. An extra difficulty of utmost importance was encountered in this stage for the whole port: there was no available physical RAM for the components ported in this step. Therefore, alternatives were studied, and by using different techniques simultaneously, the goals of this phase were achieved. These techniques are listed below, which may be of interest for future ports, even if these are used for other operating systems ports to microcontrollers:

1. The compiler has specific options for optimization, and some of them are for reducing the size of the executable.
2. Reduce the size of the data structures being ported. For example, the PID element of the Process Control Block (PCB) data structure of the process management table was reduced from uint32 to a uint8 data type, since it is highly unlikely that there will be more than 255 active processes in this architecture (in fact, there are not enough resources for this to happen). Similarly, other elements of each data structure were analyzed to change the data types to smaller ones, substantially reducing the size of the data structures in RAM without losing their semantics or functionality.
3. Store constants in the read-only program memory (FLASH). For this architecture and compiler, the technique is achieved by prefixing the reserved words "const flash" to the type of a variable or structure being declared. These reserved words indicate to the compiler that the variable or structure will be read-only and should be stored in FLASH memory along with the executable code. An example structure that was stored in FLASH in this way is the devtab[] structure, which is an array of structures where each element of the array represents an I/O device and contains management information and pointers to functions that implement system calls for a particular device (open(), read(), write(), etc.). This entire array of structures does not change at runtime, so it could be declared as a constant and located in the microcontroller's FLASH memory.

By applying these techniques the size of the final executable program was reduced to a few KB. It should be noted that the original version of Xinu requires several MB of RAM when used on general-purpose computers. Finally, when the goal of storing the Xinu executable in FLASH memory was achieved, with available RAM on runtime, a multiprogrammed Xinu system capable of working with concurrent tasks was obtained.

Steps 10 to 12. In this final phase of our port, two I/O device drivers were developed, one to control an AVR hardware timer and the second to control the UART device, which will be used by Xinu as a user interface console. The timer driver will generate an interrupt every millisecond. Depending on the QUANTUM configured in Xinu, after a certain number of interrupts, the Xinu's CPU scheduler will run a context switch to execute another task in a READY state.

4 Results

4.1 Black-Box Testing

Three experimental tests were fulfilled to verify the functionality of all the internal components of the new Xinu port for AVR. As hardware, an Arduino Nano board was used, which presents a USB interface for firmware transfer, and that Xinu uses as a CONSOLE interface at runtime. These three functional testing tests are briefly described below.

First, the programs presented in Chapter 2 of [10] were executed. These programs verify the concurrent execution of processes, the inter-process communication of a producer-consumer example, and the synchronization between processes.

Then, the entire Xinu shell was ported, as well as several UNIX-like tools. This allowed the Arduino Nano board to be used as an old UNIX workstation, with a shell and various utilities. By doing this test we were able to verify almost all the services provided by the ported operating system.

Finally, this Xinu port was under testing to use it as RTOS. On one side Xinu was used as a practical tool in two editions of the Embedded Systems Programming course, from the Bachelor of Computer Science at our university. There, several concepts of real-time systems are studied, and also, how to use an RTOS to develop an embedded system. On the other side, this new port was used to develop an experimental thesis work, where an RTOS was required. The system calculates speed and acceleration of a robot using odometry. This real-time system controls several sensors, a magnetometer and optical encoders among them, whose asynchronous events must report the values obtained using different deadlines for each kind of event, so that the odometry calculation of the robot has an error within the expected margins [18].

4.2 Qualitative Evaluation

This evaluation was carried out with students who are taking the "Embedded Systems Programming" course. Two semantically identical C language programs were shown to the students. The first one developed using FreeRTOS, and the second one using the new Xinu port. Figure 2 contains these examples. The one on the left belongs to FreeRTOS, and the other was developed using Xinu. In the figure, the functions of the API of each RTOS appear in bold, but these examples were presented to the students in plain text, and in an agnostic way, that is, they were not indicated which of the codes belong to FreeRTOS and which one to Xinu (in fact, the name of each RTOS was not mentioned).

These programs are a "hello world" of concurrent programming. Each program contains two producer-consumer tasks that are executed concurrently, and synchronized by two semaphores provided by the RTOS. There is also the 'main' task, which is executed concurrently as well. This is in charge of creating and ending the other two producer-consumer tasks.

Each student answered three questions (short survey):

1. Which of the codes is intuitive (or both). That is, if they intuitively understand, by the name, what each function, belonging to the RTOS API, performs.

```
/* app using RTOS: 3 concurrent tasks */

int n = 0;
SemaphoreHandle_t produced, consumed;

void main(void)
{
    TaskHandle_t xHandle1, xHandle2;
    BaseType_t xReturned1, xReturned2;

    produced = xSemaphoreCreateBinary();
    consumed = xSemaphoreCreateBinary();
    xSemaphoreGive(produced);

    /* Create the tasks */
    xReturned1 = xTaskCreate(cons, "cons",
        256, 1, (void *) 1, 20, &xHandle1);
    xReturned2 = xTaskCreate(prod, "prod",
        256, 1, (void *) 1, 20, &xHandle2);

    /* wait 10 seconds and finish tasks */
    vTaskDelay(10000/portTICK_PERIOD_MS);
    vTaskDelete( xHandle1 );
    vTaskDelete( xHandle2 );
}
/* task prod -- increment n 2000 times */
void prod(void *parameters)
{
    int num = *(int *)parameters;
    int i;

    for( i=1 ; i<=2000 ; i++ ) {
        xSemaphoreTake(consumed);
        n++;
        xSemaphoreGive(produced);
    }
}
/* task cons -- print n 2000 times */
void cons(void *parameters)
{
    int num = *(int *)parameters;
    int i;

    for( i=1 ; i<=2000 ; i++ ) {
        xSemaphoreTake(produced);
        printf("n is %d \n", n);
        xSemaphoreGive(consumed);
    }
}
```

```
/* app using RTOS: 3 concurrent tasks */

int n = 0;
int produced, consumed;

void main(void)
{
    int pid_c, pid_p;

    consumed = semcreate(0);
    produced = semcreate(1);

    /* Create the tasks */
    pid_c = create(cons, 256, 20,"cons",0));
    pid_p = create(prod, 256, 20,"prod",0));

    resume(pid_c);
    resume(pid_p);

    /* wait 10 seconds and finish tasks */
    sleep(10);
    kill(pid_c);
    kill(pid_p);
}
/* task prod -- increment n 2000 times */
void prod(int nargs, char *args[])
{
    int i;

    for( i=1 ; i<=2000 ; i++ ) {
        wait(consumed);
        n++;
        signal(produced);
    }
}
/* task cons -- print n 2000 times */
void cons(int nargs, char *args[])
{
    int i;

    for( i=1 ; i<=2000 ; i++ ) {
        wait(produced);
        printf("n is %d \n", n);
        signal(consumed);
    }
}
```

(a) Version using FreeRTOS API.   (b) Version using Xinu API.

Fig. 2. Examples of a concurrent program: synchronized producer-consumer using a RTOS.

2. Which of the codes presents an easy-to-remember API (or both). That is, if the name of the functions belonging to the RTOS API is easy to memorize or remember.
3. Which of the codes is more readable. In this question, the student must choose only one of the two codes. The code that, according to them, is easier to read and understand.

The qualitative results of this evaluation indicates that the new Xinu port API, as an RTOS, is more attractive to learn and use when compared to other widely used RTOS. For question (a), almost 100% of the students answered that they intuitively recognize what the API of the two RTOS is 'supposed' to do. For question (b), a percentage close to 80% indicated that the Xinu code is easy to remember. Only 10% responded that they would easily remember the presented FreeRTOS API in a simple way. The remaining

10% indicated that they could not remember the name of the functions of either of the two APIs. For question (c) 100% of the students answered that the Xinu code is more readable in this particular example.

4.3 Quantitative Evaluation

The most limited resources on small microcontrollers are memory, and CPU. In particular, when using Xinu on AVR, RAM (composed of 2 KB in atmega328p) becomes the most critical resource, since the RTOS stack and global variables are allocated in RAM. In addition, each task under the RTOS control must have its own stack, which is not shared with the other tasks (processes).

In order to evaluate whether there is enough memory for various tasks[2], when Xinu is running as RTOS, some measurements of different kinds of data allocated in memory were made. In these measurements, the behavior of some internal structures of Xinu was also analyzed, to find out how memory consumption grows for each service or task to be managed.

Setup and Methodology. At a default setup, Xinu manages various processes and semaphores, and contains a reduced set of device drivers. The default system has 4 processes: 2 processes belong to Xinu (null and main), and 2 processes belong to the final embedded system. Main can be repurposed as another task of the final system. In addition, Xinu manages at least 4 semaphores (used for I/O buffers) and 3 I/O device drivers: null, uart, and namespace.

The methodology to evaluate memory consumption was based on the use of the avr-size command, member of avr-toolchain, to know the use of FLASH memory, and freemem(), internal function of Xinu, to measure the use of RAM at runtime. Xinu configuration files were modified, in different tests, to set the number of system components that will be allocated in the main memory, and thus analyze how each one affects memory usage. In order to run these different configurations and obtain consumption measurements basic test programs were developed.

Table 1 shows the memory usage for different setups and components managed by Xinu. The measurements were for RAM and FLASH memory. For each one the memory used by Xinu, and the amount of free available memory, are presented. Results show that for each new process this new version of Xinu uses 97 bytes of RAM, for each semaphore 19 bytes of RAM, and for each device driver 46 bytes of FLASH. As it can be seen in Table 1, for a typical embedded system where there are several processes, semaphores and drivers allocated in memory, there is still available FLASH and RAM memory -at least 50% of RAM and 60% of FLASH- for other purposes.

Stack Memory Usage. The 97 bytes of minimum RAM memory that a process needs is allocated to its stack. An analysis was performed to determine how this stack memory is used. This analysis can be seen in Table 2. The most relevant results show that 32 bytes of stack are necessary to store each context of the process every time Xinu needs to run a context switch. 64 bytes of stack are also required to store variables that belong

---

[2] *Task* and *process* words are synonyms in this work, and are used interchangeably. 'Task' is a term mostly used in RTOS environments, while 'process' is from OS environments.

Table 1. Used and available sizes of RAM and FLASH memories.

Configuration	RAM	FLASH
minimal configuration	932 bytes OS (~45%) 1116 bytes free (~55)	12 KB OS (~39%) 19 KB free (~61%)
5 processes, 4 semaphores, 3 drivers	1029 bytes OS (~51%) 1019 bytes free (~49%)	12 KB OS (~39%) 19 KB free (~61%)
6 processes, 4 semaphores, 3 drivers	1129 bytes OS (~55%) 922 bytes free (~45%)	12 KB OS (~39%) 19 KB free (~61%)
4 processes, 5 semaphores, 3 drivers	951 bytes OS (~47%) 1097 bytes free (~53)	12 KB OS (~39%) 19 KB free (~61%)
4 processes, 6 semaphores, 3 drivers	970 bytes OS (~48%) 1078 bytes free (~52)	12 KB OS (~39%) 19 KB free (~61%)
4 processes, 6 semaphores, 4 drivers	932 bytes OS (~45%) 1116 bytes free (~55)	12 KB OS (~39%) 19 KB free (~61%)

Table 2. Stack memory required for one process

Purpose of stack memory	Size of Stack
process management	64 bytes
calling to printf()	160 bytes
stack memory for saved context	32 bytes (32 registers, SP, PC, and SREG)
local variables, function arguments, return addresses (arch dependent: size of basic types are showed)	char 1 byte, int 2 bytes long 4 bytes, long long 8 bytes
Total	256 bytes

to the process management by Xinu. These two uses of memory per process cannot be minimized. It is also interesting to observe, from Table 2, how much stack RAM memory is required when a process uses some library function. In particular, we analyzed printf(). This library function in Xinu is complex, and makes several nested internal function calls and requires a minimum of 160 bytes of stack for the local variables and arguments of these functions. In summary, a process requires 256 bytes of stack - in RAM memory - to perform some real task and be managed by Xinu.

5   Conclusions and Future Work

In this article we present a description of the work carried out to achieve the port of the academic operating system Xinu, to be used on the AVR (Arduino) architecture, as an academic RTOS. The process required three main tasks. Firstly, the characteristics of real-time operating systems and the internal structure of Xinu were studied. Then, the methodology used to perform other ports was analyzed. Finally, a proposal was selected and executed.

In addition, the resulting work was evaluated through functional testing and quantitative and qualitative evaluation. For functional testing, test programs were executed which used the different services provided by this new RTOS on AVR. In particular, a UNIX-style shell was ported and an experimental thesis project was also developed using this Xinu RTOS. For qualitative evaluation, a survey was conducted with students, where they compared the API of this new port against another widely used RTOS. In that same semester and course, the goal of using Xinu as an academic RTOS was achieved. For quantitative evaluation, the use of RAM memory was analyzed, as it is the most critical resource in the selected microcontroller (its size is 2 KB).

Based on the quantitative results, it was determined that there is 50% of available RAM for processes or tasks with a usable basic configuration. Another interesting result is that one process in the system requires at least 256 bytes of RAM to perform any real task and be managed by Xinu. As for the qualitative evaluation, it was shown that 100% of students in an embedded systems programming course would choose to develop a real-time system using Xinu, when comparing the readability of its API against another particular RTOS.

As future work, it is expected to evaluate its academic impact, for example, by observing the link between courses where the same tool can be used. One possible situation is to use Xinu in introductory subjects to the topic, such as the Operating Systems course. It should be observed there whether the use of the same tool has a better impact on acceptance and streamlines academic paths, achieving more time available to devote to other concepts or topics. We also propose to continue this work performing new ports to other microcontrollers, and promote its use and evaluation in industrial projects.

Software Release. The Xinu kernel source code for AVR, documentation and examples can be downloaded from: http://se.fi.uncoma.edu.ar/xinu-avr/

References

1. Congreso Argentino de Sistemas Embebidos: Libro de artículos y reportes tecnológicos (2020–2022). ISBN 978-987-46297-7-7, 978-987-46297-8-4, 978-987-46297-8-4
2. Laplante, P., Ovaska, S.: Fundamentals of Real-Time Systems. In: Real- Time Systems Design and Analysis: Tools for the Practitioner, pp. 1–25. IEEE (2012). https://doi.org/10.1002/978 1118136607.ch1
3. 2019 Embedded Markets Study Integrating IoT and Advanced Technology Designs, Application Development & Processing Environments. EE Times and Embedded https://www.embedded.com/wp-content/uploads/2019/11/EETimes_Embedded_2019_ Embedded_Markets_Study.pdf, last accessed 07 March 2023
4. Gay, W.: Beginning STM32: Developing with FreeRTOS, libopencm3 and GCC 1st ed. ISBN 978-1484236239. Apress (2018)
5. Di Sirio, G.: ChibiOS/RT - The Ultimate Guide Book (2020). https://www.chibios.org/dok uwiki/doku.php?id=chibios:documentation:books:rt:start, last accessed 07 March 2023

6. Cesium RTOS web page. https://weston-embedded.com/products/cesium, last accessed 07 March 2023

7. VxWorks web page. https://www.windriver.com/products/vxworks, last accessed 07 March 2023

8. Zurita, R., Alvarez, C., Lechner, M., Mora, A.: Versión del Sistema Operativo XINU para la Arquitectura AVR con la Finalidad de ser Utilizado como RTOS Académico. In: Actas del XXVIII Congreso Argentino de Ciencias de la Computación (CACIC 2022), pp. 618–627. ISBN: 978-987-1364-31-2. Editorial de la Universidad Nacional de La Rioja (EUDELAR) (2023)

9. Stankovic, J.: Real-Time Computing Systems: The Next Generation. COINS TECHNICAL REPORT 88–06. Department of Computer and Information Science. University of Massachusetts, Amherst, Ma (1988)

10. Comer, D.: Operating System Design - The Xinu Approach, Second Edition. CRC Press (2015)

11. Khaled, S.: Porting the µC-OS-II Real Time Operating System to the M16C Microcontrollers (2007). https://doi.org/10.13140/2.1.2701.9846

12. Kolhare, N.R., Nitin, I.: Porting & Implementation of features of uC/OS II RTOS on Arm7 controller LPC 2148 with different IPC mechanisms. Int. J. Eng. Res. Technol. 1 (2012)

13. Porting µC/OS-II web page, https://micrium.atlassian.net/wiki/spaces/osiidoc/pages/163 858/Porting+C+OS-II, last accessed 07 March 2023

14. Hsu, H., Hsueh, C.: FreeRTOS Porting on x86 Platform. In: 2016 International Computer Symposium (ICS), pp. 120–123 (2016). https://doi.org/10.1109/ICS.2016.0032

15. Zhang, Y., Lu, F., Kong, X.: VxWorks porting based on MPC8313E hardware platform. In: 2010 International Conference on Computer, Mechatronics, Control and Electronic Engineering, pp. 246–249. (2010). https://doi.org/10.1109/CMCE.2010.5610170

16. IEEE Standard for a Real-Time Operating System (RTOS) for Small-Scale Embedded Systems. (n.d.). https://doi.org/10.1109/ieeestd.2018.84456

17. Gomes, R., Baunach, M.: A model-based concept for RTOS portability. In: 2018 IEEE/ACS 15th International Conference on Computer Systems and Applications (AICCSA) (2018). https://doi.org/10.1109/aiccsa.2018.861286

18. Alvarez, C.: Diseño e implementación de un sistema embebido de navegación por estima para la localización de robots móviles en ambientes de interiores, Tesis de grado de la carrera Lic. en Ciencias de la Computación. Universidad Nacional del Comahue (2022)

Innovation in Computer Science
Education

SETIC: An Educational Software About the Functioning of Computer Parts

Maximiliano Gauthier[1]([✉]) [iD] and Paola D. Budán[2] [iD]

[1] Colegio San Agustín, Mar del Plata, Argentina
maximilianogauthier@gmail.com
[2] Universidad Nacional de Santiago del Estero, Dpto. de Informática, Santiago del Estero,
Argentina
pbudan@unse.edu.ar

Abstract. In this paper, we present the design and development of a prototype called SETIC, a software for teaching information and communication technology (ICT) concepts. SETIC's prototype incorporates several multimedia resources and is intended for secondary school students who need to learn a wide variety of abstract concepts related to ICT. SETIC was designed following the MeiSE methodology that combines a traditional cycle of life system development with agile methods considering a pedagogical point of view as an added value to the software. Although SETIC is not finished, the first evaluations did it by teachers allowed appreciate that SETIC will be a good tool for teaching Informatics concepts.

Keywords: prototype · MeiSE methodology · multimedia resources · educational software · information and communication technology concepts

1 Introduction

In the teaching of technological subjects such as NTICx [1] in secondary education, we observe difficulties in the understanding and assimilation of some concepts related to how computational processes such as executing input, output, processing, and/or storing data are performed by computers. The correct understanding of these concepts is essential for those who want to later pursue an IT degree at higher educational levels. From a pedagogical point of view, It is also recognized that each student has their own preferred way of learning and that some of them may become frustrated and tend to abandon their goals quickly Specifically addressing the particular problem that arises in the 4th year of San Agustin College in the city of Mar del Plata, we propose to implement an Educational Software (ES) prototype whose main objective is to promote the understanding of the computer processes that take place within the computer. The first part of the prototyping and presentation of this ES was carried out and presented at the XXVIII ARGENTINE CONGRESS OF COMPUTER SCIENCE held in the city of La Rioja under the name "SETIC: an Educational Software about the Functioning of Computer Parts" [2].

In this work, we will present the prototyping and development of SETIC (Educational Software for Information and Communication Technologies) showing the progress of its functioning through a mobile device.

The contents SETIC deals with are part of the educational plan of the province of Buenos Aires, specifically of the subject NTICx. It is necessary to clarify that it is only during the 4th year of Secondary School that students come into contact for the first time with this topic. In our opinion, this is far too late, as students have already been through Primary School and half the years that make up Secondary School. As stated in the web:

"We believe that nobody disputes the importance of systematically teaching language and mathematics, along with the basic concepts of other sciences considered indispensable throughout the school years." [3].

As stated before, digital literacy knowledge has no relevance in Primary School and the first years of Secondary School. Furthermore, the teaching of the subjects related to Computer Science depend on each institution's and management team's competencies and interests, and even the teacher's interests as well, thus resulting in extracurricular spaces rather than regulated curricular subjects. In this case, the contents about the functioning of a computer can be tackled in a wide range of approaches, starting with a full theoretical approach (due to a lack of devices for the use of programming) and ending with the use of robotics and 3D printing (in the case of institutions with more economic resources). Under this context, SETIC is being developed as a tool to facilitate students with access to information about Computer Science under different presentations, such as text, images, audio, video, and simulations.

From a technical-informatic point of view, the development of SETIC follows the detailed steps of the MeiSE Methodology [4], which proposes an incremental software development life cycle guided by prototypes, leaving the choice on how to achieve those prototypes to the user's discretion. Thus, the development of SETIC is composed of mini-projects: *(a) Types of computers, (b) Parts of the computer, (c) Peripherals (input, output, I/O, storage), (d) Types of data, (e) Digitization of information,* and *(f) Binary representation of digital data.* Each of these mini-projects focuses on a particular topic related to the NTICx curriculum. In the present extension of our previous work, we present the definition and development for SETIC in general, while the deployment and implementation stage is contextualized in the *Peripherals (input, output, I/O, storage)* and *Parts of the computer mini-projects.*

We structured our work in the following way: firstly, we describe the context of the software application and the general objectives pursued; later, we summarize the chosen methodology for development presenting its general stages. Subsequently, we describe the activities that make up each of these stages and show the developed advances of the ES and its functioning; and finally, we devote the last section to presenting some conclusions of these advances and our future plans.

2   SETIC and Its Application Context

This work is part of the curriculum of the *Educational Software Development* course, which is a mandatory requirement of the *Master's degree in Educational Informatics* offered by the National University of Santiago del Estero[1], Argentina. Within the framework of this curricular obligation, the actual problematic situation could be resolved by developing educational software (ES). Thus, *SETIC* was designed and prototyped, creating the first modules of the ES for subsequent use and testing, considering the population of *4th-year high school students attending the San Agustín School in the city of Mar del Plata*. In this institution, the subject NTICx is taught has 3 sections: A, B, and C. There are 2 teachers for do that. The school has 2 computer rooms. One room equipped with desktop computers, and the other multimedia room with desktop computers, notebooks, and a screen for projecting. In addition, this last room has equipment with 3D printers and educational robotics kits.

When analysing the characteristics of the contents related to information processing that can be accessed through the software, these students require a high degree of abstraction in order to understand them, as all the processes that take place are completely electronic and therefore cannot be tangible or visible in real-time, while being processed at a very high speed. Oftentimes, this leads to a lack of understanding, comprehension, and analysis of the processes. As a result, students end up memorizing most of the content, as the approach to the subject matter is through theoretical conceptual repetition but not empirical. Thus, students remain in a state of uncertainty about what they have learned, without fully understanding and comprehending the process being carried out by the computer. We believe that this approach to digital knowledge (both delayed and very theoretical) is a fundamental factor for students when deciding on their future educational path and which careers to choose later. There is a lack of intermediate digital literacy to bridge the gap between the theoretical and practical, resulting in students failing to understand how a computer really works and dimension how information flows within the computer.

SETIC seeks to find a place between theory and practice and speed the cognitive processes of comprehension by allowing the student to interact with the content in different multimedia formats, removing itself from the abstract part of the concept and demonstrating it visually, creating a situation where meaningful learning can occur and stimulate professional vocations related to informatics. The main objectives of SETIC are the follows: *(i) building a tool that allows the identification of the parts of a computer and the individual functioning of each one of them; (ii) illustrating the differences between input, output, and data storage peripherals; (iii) identifying the main components and the interactions/relationships between them in the process; (iv) showing the functions of each one of the components; (v) simulating the data flow of the computational process from its input to its output, passing through the processing and/or storage.*

In the first article, we informed that this initiative has had the support of the management of the San Agustín School. Nevertheless, between the presentation of the first article and the software design, up to this extension including the development of the first modules and content loading, we contacted other institutions such as Instituto Educativo

---

[1] Accredited according to Ministerial Resolution 2270/2014.

Punta Mogotes, Instituto Club Quilmes, and Instituto Argentino Modelo, all located in the city of Mar del Plata where the subject is taught. These Schools have also opened their doors to SETIC and allowed their teachers and students to test its functionality.

This approach will allow future works to have a broader sample of students' learning preferences (through text, audio, video, images, or simulations), evaluate the results according to the chosen type and create feedback from the educational community of this subject, NTICx.

3   MeiSE: Methodology for the Development of Educational Software

For the initial design and prototyping of SETIC, the MeiSE methodology was selected, considering that *"one of the main problems in the construction of educational software is following a development process that can ensure its quality"* [4]. This methodology presents the necessary stages to balance the technical quality of software with the pedagogical aspects required for it to be considered a didactic tool. The MeiSE methodology achieves this goal by including criteria in its development so that the content can be understood by the student, while attending to didactic characteristics based on psychopedagogical criteria about learning. *"In an educational software, the methodology takes an even more important role, given that besides being able to reach the goals set for the project, the content within the product must really help in the achievement of the necessary competencies for the given level"* [4].

Briefly, the MeiSE methodology consists mainly of two major stages: *definition* and *development*. The first stage is divided into three phases: *the conceptual phase*, during which the system requirements are identified and the development plan is defined; *the initial analysis and design phase*, where the base architecture for the solution is proposed and the pedagogical and communication characteristics that will govern the development are established; finally, *the iterations plan phase*, where the project is divided into functional parts that allow a better control in its development. *The development stage* is divided into three phases: *the computational design phase*, where a detailed computational design of a specific software increment is carried out, which is presented in this; *the development phase*, where the architecture is implemented incrementally; and the *deployment phase*, where the executable product is transitioned to the end-user. As for the platform, we decided on Android given that statistical reports show that in the urban population, there are more adolescent users with 89.5% access to smartphones, while only 61.5% of adolescents have access to computers in their households [6]. These last three stages are repeated iteratively for each software increment. This methodology has been used in works such as [10, 13, 14], inspiring the initial design of *SETIC*.

4   SETIC Development

In the following section we present the activities carried out for the corresponding phases of the *definition and development stages*: conceptual phase, initial analysis and design, and iteration planning; and the *implementation and deployment stage*.

4.1 Conceptual Phase

In this phase, we analyze educational needs and possible solutions (if any), we define software functionality, and establish the initial development plan and quality criteria to obtain learning objects, following the development and quality evaluation methodology [10]. To achieve this, we work with the following artifacts: *an instructional model, a list of requirements, an analysis of solution alternatives, an initial plan,* and *an acceptance model* [4]. The *instructional model* chosen for *SETIC* is the ASSURE model by Heinich et al. [7], based on the constructivist approach and combined with the importance of general student characteristics such as prior knowledge (the "A" in ASSURE, Analyze Learners). This aspect, as we have contextualized, consists of a lack of an ICT-related curriculum in previous years and educational levels before students are faced with NTICx subject, and the context of the student's education (private or public management). In the constructivist approach, the concept of educational influence should be understood as consisting of support aimed at improving the processes related to the constructive activity of the student, its purpose being the generation of the necessary approximation between the meanings constructed by the student and the meanings represented by the curriculum contents [17].

Then, we establish learning objectives (the "S" in ASSURE, State objectives) for the understanding of the subject's contents. Each topic consists of different contents that the student will be able to access in a sequenced manner, and that can be navigated through various multimedia formats, with the possibility of moving back and forth between them. Additionally, the student will have the possibility of returning to topics of interest from any point in the SE, given that each mini-project has a progress chart showing the learning progress from 0% to 100% total and learning progress from each mini-project (illustrated in Figs. 1, 2 and 3).

Fig. 1. The SETIC's initial screen

Fig. 2. The student's progress for devices topic

This progress is achieved once the student takes a self-evaluation, which is found in the assessment module and allows the student to select their preferred self-evaluation method [15].

The evaluation process is done following the CBL model (competency-based learning, known as ABC model in Spanish) and is built upon the concept of "mastery level" of a competency achieved by the student. [16]. These self-evaluations (Fig. 4) will be made using different approaches (multiple choice, true or false, puzzle, drag-and-drop) and will be ludic in their nature, awarding the student "points" for attempts and retries. This score is then kept in the student's profile.

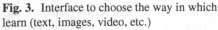

Fig. 3. Interface to choose the way in which learn (text, images, video, etc.)

Fig. 4. Interface to choose the self-evaluation approach.

This progress is achieved once the student takes a self-evaluation, which is found in the assessment module and allows the student to select their preferred self-evaluation method. The evaluation process is done following the CBL model (competency-based learning, known as ABC model in Spanish) and is built upon the concept of "mastery level" of a competency achieved by the student. [19]. These self-evaluations will be made using different approaches (multiple choice, true or false, puzzle, drag-and-drop) and will be ludic in their nature, awarding the student "points" for attempts and retries. This score is then kept in the student's profile, as the Fig. 4 illustrates.

This methodology of evaluating using a device is known as *Computer-Assisted Assessment* (CAA) and refers to the use of technology as a tool to present material to students and automate certain assessment tasks [19]. This technique may involve the use of devices such as computers, tablets, and mobile phones to present information and assess knowledge acquired by students. CAA has become increasingly popular in educational settings due to its efficiency and ability to provide instant feedback to students.

To overcome the previously stated situation in which abstract processes are mainly taught in a theoretical manner, this ES proposes to give them "*visibility*" by representing these processes through interactive simulations where the student will be able to learn through a set of audio-visual stimuli beyond the textual.

Regarding the *initial functional requirements*, we consider that the ES must:

 (i) identify users for the monitoring of their learning process;
 (ii) allow users to select topics they will be working with;
(iii) record the attempts of each user at the activities developed;

(iv) generate an instance of self-evaluation of prior knowledge to compare after going through the ES;

(v) show the progress of each student using the global and per-mini-project progress bar;

(vi) guide the user as to what stage they are in and suggest the next one;

(vii) save all processes and interactions carried out in the human-machine interface, selected learning method (textual, images, video, audio, or simulations), self-evaluation attempts made in quantity or type (multiple choice, true or false, drag-and-drop, or puzzle), paths taken by each user;

(viii) show how data flows in and out of the computer using peripheral devices, their processing, and possible information storage.

From the time of the presentation of the first SETIC prototype [3], several modules were created aggregating it functionalities. Among them is the configuration module, where the ES allows the teacher user to customize certain types of content or to add new ones, as shown in Fig. 5; this new content is then considerer to do the self-assessment. We try to do an intuitive the process to customize. The use of self-assessment as an evaluation technique emerges as an innovative proposal in accordance with democratic values, seeking for the student to take responsibility for their own development and results. [18] Carrying out a correct evaluation generally requires a great effort and dedication on the part of teachers. That is why Information and Communication Technologies (ICT) can play an important role in facilitating the evaluation task itself, for example with the generation of automatic feedback or correction. *SETIC* provides the opportunity to include ICT from the perspective of educational informatics. [23]. Additionally, we incorporated a module that generates learning reports for the teacher, as the Fig. 6 illustrate, showing the results obtained by each student according to the path taken and learning speed based on previous content. Within these new functions, the ES also allows the teacher to manually enter grades for each student (selected in the system) or possible progress for each mini-project if other evaluation instances are carried out by the teacher, such as written or oral exams. These options suggested by teachers give the system versatility to extend its use as a teaching tool.

Regarding the study of *solution alternatives*, we considered two alternatives. *Alternative 1* incorporates the use of video tutorials separated by different topics, in which the student chooses the topic to be addressed, watches the multimedia content in sections, and chooses how to make a self-evaluation for the given topic. *Alternative 2*, on the other hand, uses short educational podcasts that explain the content, followed by a multiple-choice screen where the student must choose the answer based on what was just heard. If a mistake is made, they can choose to listen again or move forward. Each choice will provide a score based on the student's profile in the system. We have decided on Alternative 1, the video tutorial format, because it is closer to the ES's objective of visually demonstrating the computer processes that take place through simulation, presentation, or multimedia explanation.

It is important to note that the SETIC design was planning considering the relation between the future software and ASSURE. The relationship between SETIC and the instructional model procedure of ASSURE is reflected in Fig. 7, where each instance has a close relationship with the design and objectives of SETIC.

Fig. 5. SETIC Interface to customize content

Fig. 6. SETIC results learner report

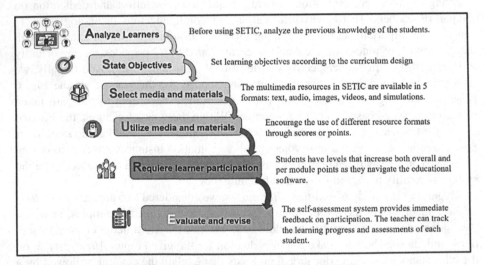

Fig. 7. Relation between SETIC and ASSURE

The ASSURE model considers with the characteristics of the student, their learning styles, and promotes their active and engaged participation. It is a model that teachers can use to design, develop, and plan objectives, to create learning environments suitable for the characteristics of their students. For this reason, it is desirable to design the resources for SETIC under this model.

The *initial development plan* is showed in Fig. 8, while Fig. 9 establishes how was the assign responsible parties for each task made.

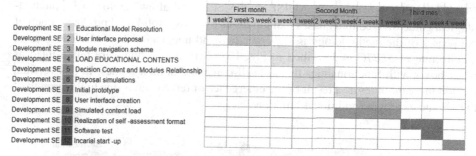

Fig. 8. New development plan for SETIC extension development.

The acceptance model of this STIC extension oversaw a real group of students from the San Agustín Shool, and from other 3 institutions. A sampling of the results will be carried out in the first quarter of work, equivalent to approximately 60 business days.

Project leader	2	3	5	6	9	11	13
Pedagogues	1	3	4	6	10		
Programmers	2	7	8	9	11	12	13
Graphic designer	3	9	10				
Teachers	4	5	10	11	13		
Managers	6	12					
Students	13						

Fig. 9. Tasks and actors responsible for carrying them out.

We have planned to measure the *SETIC's* quality on 3 different levels:

- Level 1 – Evaluation by *Teachers:* ease in incorporating content, possibilities for monitoring the collected data, pedagogical results on didactic proposals, ability to manually add possible evaluations without using the ES. Feedback on the advantages and disadvantages found.
- Level 2 – About the *Management:* involving the management team and their vision on the planning of the subject NTICx and the use of the ES in the institution.
- Level 3 – Evaluation by *Students:* this is the moment where a non-academic sampling will be carried out to measure the influence of the ES and find out if it was helpful for learning, user-friendly, and the students' feedback on the scoring system, opinions on the multimedia and interactive format proposed by SETIC.

4.2 Analysis and Conceptual Design

In this phase, we detail a first architecture of the ES and develop both the educational and communication models. To achieve this goal, we work with artifacts that are related to these models, with a particular emphasis on the interface model, navigation model, and user interface prototype [4]. Just like in the Educational Software "MATH-MOBILE

CONSTRUCTION", using the MeISE methodology [4] allows us to have a methodological guide divided into phases that guides us towards a solid final product. "Each of the phases of the methodology is well specified and understandable" [5]. The general architecture of *SETIC* is described in Fig. 10, where the modules are represented as black boxes with functionalities that are self-contained in their names. In this version, we add more modules as a result of the emergence of recent needs due to the growth of the SE and to provide additional functionality.

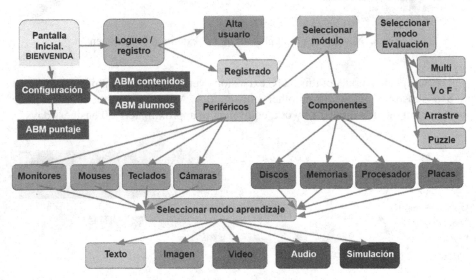

Fig. 10. Modular architecture for *SETIC*

The first *SETIC* prototype was developed in APP INVENTOR 2 [8, 12], as it is a platform that allows for a rapid development of modules for managing users and profiles of the actors involved. In addition, it allows the necessary multimedia resources to be executed locally or at external links to achieve more dynamism in the system and generate a more lightweight platform. The ES was developed following this last premise, given that after an exchange with the users, we discover that a functionality that becomes an advantage for *SETIC* is the possibility of storing material in external repositories that allows the user to access the content publicly in case they encounter any issues (problems with the smartphone, mobile data, storage space, etc.).

Furthermore, we open the opportunity for the extension of *SETIC's* curricular content to the entire educational community, given that the content is available on free servers. Texts and images, for example, can be found in the Blog [9] of the Blogger platform, specifically created for this development, whereas videos and simulations are available on YouTube and audios on Google Podcasts. Another recently-added function regarding the architecture of *SETIC* in the previous article is the configuration module. All the interfaces were thinking to be easy for Professors of any subject. An example of this simple interface is illustrated in Fig. 11, that shows the previous screen to the ones showed in the Fig. 5. This module allows the teacher to manage the software content in a simple way, adding types of content.

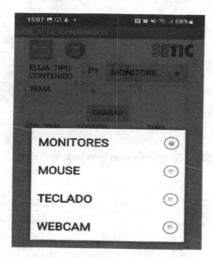

Fig. 11. *SETIC* simple Interface

The curriculum content is created on the various platforms (blogger, YouTube, podcast) and is integrated into *SETIC* by simply adding the link to the different repositories (copy and paste), thus becoming part of the content that will be displayed when the student user accesses the selected options screens. This way, content creation for the teacher becomes easy to access, as it can be done without the need for programming knowledge and can also be created from any type of device (smartphone, tablet, computer, etc.) as these sites are available to be used from a variety of platforms. In addition, the execution of different types of evaluations can be quickly implemented using buttons, checks, drag-and-drop, and puzzle assembling, as it supports object handling with Canvas, screen interactions, and sensors. The Fig. 12 shows the interface architecture.

For the ES to be also used on devices with Windows, in this first stage, the Android emulator BLUESTACK[2] will be installed to run the application without having to create it specifically for Windows. On the other hand, Fig. 13 shows the interface models proposed during the design stage for student users, both for learning activities and self-evaluation activities.

Besides, Fig. 14 shows the interface model for the "Peripherals" screen and self-evaluation activities, as the result of the using of the MeISE for the SETIC development.

Once the student accesses the SE, they choose "start learning" and see the total scores obtained. Afterwards, they select the type of component they want to study from the corresponding screen. The specific component screen also includes an individual indicator of the student's learning for each type of component. Once the student has finished going over the lesson, they can access the evaluation module. It is worth noting

---

[2] https://www.bluestacks.com BlueStacks App Player is designed to allow Android applications to be run on computers with Windows and Macintosh.

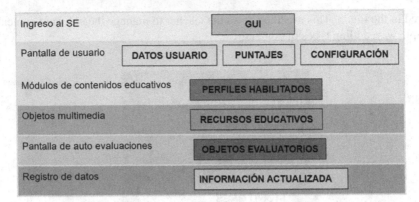

Fig. 12. Interface architecture for SETIC

Fig. 13. Examples of SETIC models interfaces

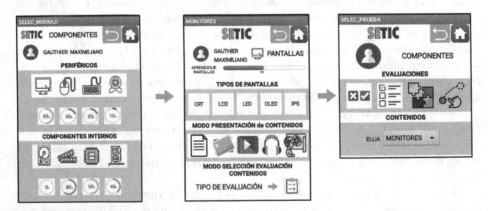

Fig. 14. Model for the "Peripherals" screens and self-evaluation activities

that this module can be accessed later as well. Self-evaluations can be done as many times as the student wishes, but the maximum score obtained for each type of evaluation (true or false, multiple choice, drag and drop or puzzle) will always be the one that is delivered. If the student were to perform another evaluation of a content and evaluation type, even though the system records the attempt, it does not affect the student's final score. The new attempt is saved in the database so that the teacher can see the attempts, retries, content reviews, etc., of each student. In turn, from these records of each attempt, reports with statistics of software-student interaction will be created in future versions of SETIC. Finally, in Fig. 15, we can see the screen models for a user who is already using the application.

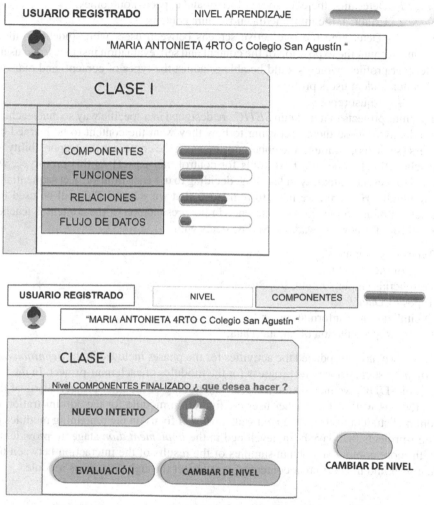

Fig. 15. Interface model for a user who is browsing through *SETIC*

4.3 Iteration Plan

The iterative and incremental development of the project was planned in sequential blocks called *iterations*. These iterations can be planned along with the academic calendar of the NTICx course by the teacher user. Following the proposal of the MeISE methodology [4], the iterations aim to create functional sub-products that can be used after they become available. These sub-products are in the form of mini-projects, each one providing a tangible outcome for users towards the final product, so that the student user can gradually benefit from using the ES. As they use it, their learning outcomes are reflected. For each of these mini-projects, we planned the development of the following routine stages:

Stage 1 - Determine the educational format and expected outcomes;

Stage 2 - Establish the multimedia curriculum content;

Stage 3 - Determine the interactive screens between users with student profiles, taking into account the exposition of the content and self-evaluation instances, and users with teacher profiles, which should be able to adjust the types of content, and manage and monitor student users profiles.

Stage 4 - Adjust reports.

The mini-projects that makeup *SETIC* are designed in a specific way so that teachers can gradually propose them according to how they want the content to be learned by the users (students), although the coherence between the content is the responsibility of the teacher (SETIC does not have tools for control this aspect). In this prototype, we intended to present scalability in learning, deciding to use each mini-project sequentially or individually. However, we need to remember that we want SETIC will be used for the teaching of any topic, so the coherence in the presentation of the content is teacher responsibility for now. Nowadays, SETIC deals with:

(a) Types of Computers,
(b) Parts of the Computer,
(c) Peripherals (Input, Output, I/o, Storage),
(d) Types of Data,
(e) Digitalization of information, and.
(f) Binary Representation of Digital Data.

So far, we have introduced the activities for the phases included in the *definition and development* stage; shown the progress for the modules of each mini-project. In the last version of SETIC, we include the integral functioning of the mini-project "Parts of the computer", as well as the teacher user configuration module for the administration of content and student users. In the next stage, we will focus on the remaining modules of the mini-projects that have been developed in the *implementation* stage, to provide the ES with more content and obtain samples of the results of the interaction between the student user and the curricular content of the subject through the reports module.

4.4   Products Obtained from the First Iterations

For the development of *SETIC*, we expect to develop multimedia resources of various types, depending on the mini-project being addressed. As an illustrative example, if we take the *Peripherals mini-project (input, output, I/O, storage)* as a reference, the multimedia resource that is part of this project is a learning object [11, 13], whose general features can be seen in Fig. 16 and which can be seen in its entirety following the link https://youtu.be/V_z2ZoW6Zv0.

Fig. 16. Multimedia resource created for the *Peripherals* mini-project.

In turn, within this resource, the student has the option of an interactive game. In this game, the learner must click on the indicated components (types of peripherals), and the game will present options to choose from, then giving points for correct or incorrect answers within a certain time limit. When the game is over, a "*score*" is given based on time/accuracy/errors. Although this activity is of a playful nature, it is also an instance of self-evaluation for the student and subsequent evaluation in the ES of the student's evolution and interaction with the activity and content. This is why the type of images incorporated into the game must be truly representative of the content that is being covered and clear in terms of the detailed component. Part of this activity can be seen in the following resource: https://view.genial.ly/629b9bf17dcdb50019b9f470/interactive-content-fichasde-refuerzo-repaso-ampliacion.

To illustrate the navigation model for the user, traversing for "Types of Screens" option it is useful to turn to Fig. 17.

Following technical and pedagogical design principles such as the exemplified activities, the successive iterations in the development of *SETIC* are based on the hypothesis that *the learning process of the included topics is closely related to the inherent difficulty of the level of abstraction that students must handle to understand the process of the "journey" of information from the devices that enter data into the system.* In the case of the "Input Peripherals" mini-project, it is processing in the computer as seen in the "Computer Parts" mini-projects, the processing of information addressed in the "Information Digitalization" mini-project to understand the binary representation of data, the possibilities, and options for saving information shown in the "Storage Devices" mini-project (internal, external, or in the cloud) until its possible output through the devices that display data or information, in the "Output Peripherals" mini-project, in its various formats, which can be textual, auditory, or graphical.

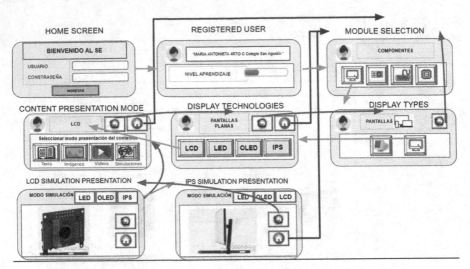

Fig. 17. Navigation model for *Peripherals* mini-project - *Types of screens*

4.5 Development Stage

In this stage of the MeISE methodology [4], we implement the software architecture detailed in Fig. 10, developed in the initial design stage. Over the past 3 months, the functional development of the prototype from the previous article [3] has progressed by means of programming the SE using the App Inventor language [8]. The main screens for each module resulting from the designed iterations were created and represented in the navigation model, as Fig. 18 shows.

For each of these screens, the necessary programming was developed to connect the modules. Some of these modules, or mini-projects, have progressed in their integral functionality. An example of this integration can be seen from the moment the teacher user logs into the system, registers student users with their necessary data such as Last Name, First Name, and ID for identification; username and password so that the student can be uniquely identified in the system; and email for future communication modules. Also, from the main screen, the teacher user can access the complete list of students with their main data for access control, user registration, and if the students forget their password. This module was designed to enable the loading of types of content, contents, and manual learning scores that may be given to students after evaluations outside the ES, as the Fig. 19 illustrates.

4.6 Deployment Stage

The *deployment stage* of the MeISE methodology [4] is the time to test the first versions of the product with users. In our case, *SETIC* has not yet been tested with students, but we have had meaningful exchanges with teachers who have exposed ideas, suggestions, and requirements for practical purposes of the software. From this exchange with teachers, as indicated by the MeISE methodology [4], we returned to the computational design stage to add the improvements that arose and make the corresponding software increment.

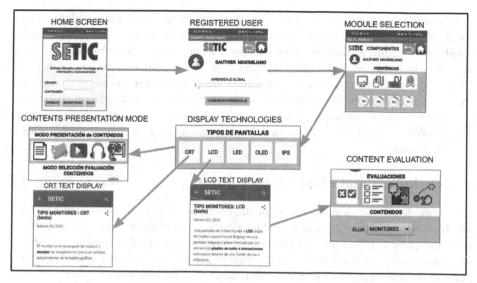

Fig. 18. Navigational model of SETIC

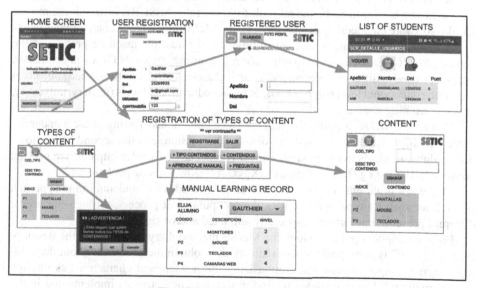

Fig. 19. SETIC module screens

This stage will begin with the use of some mini-projects such as "Types of peripherals" as a complement to the curricular contents of the NTICx subject. In this way, we can evaluate the content, improve functional aspects, or refine the navigation or interface design.

The *evaluation results* regarding the functionality and scope of the software development stage were carried out with colleague teachers. Based on the feedback received from colleague teachers, modifications or additions were made that improved the educational software functions. These improvements were implemented in SETIC, such as the possibility of adding evaluations conducted by teachers outside the software in different formats, which can be oral lessons, written tests, group assignments, etc. With these functions added in the student configuration module, the teacher can see more accurate information reflected in the student's learning evaluation. When loading the student's evaluation that was conducted manually outside the system, the software accumulates the scores of the students and displays it in their learning evaluation progress bar, either in total or in part.

5   Conclusions and Plans for the Future

This work details the design process of the educational software (ES) called *SETIC*, which consists of six mini-projects, and the development of iterations of the *"Peripherals"* mini-project. Using the MeISE methodology, we reached the Development stage, and in this phase, we showed the partial result of the SETIC product, implementing the architecture that emerged from the original idea to its implementation, where a partial test version of the software was obtained with a functional mini-project.

SETIC was created to meet a real need and, although it is intended for a specific subject, it can be used as a pedagogical tool, following the ASSURE instructional model. Unlike software engineering design models, the MeISE model also contemplates activities in which the content is adapted in order to facilitate the teaching process of the subject. *SETIC* is also designed to reinforce self-learning, review NTICx subject matter, or even be used in different leveling and/or articulation experiences for related subjects at the same educational level (high school) or higher educational levels (tertiary, university, courses, training courses).

Nowadays, *SETIC* is going through the Development and Testing phase 2 under the name SETIC 1_1, where the first "1" denotes the version, and the second "1" denotes the available modules in the version. The APK link can be found at https://drive.google.com/file/d/1bZWJYgZtaCeWoh5JssyauXgyU3r2OX8k/view?usp=share_link.

This work highlights the benefits that an ES provides for students in the approach of such an abstract type of content as the computational process, through the use of different presentation formats, especially animated and/or simulated.

From a technical point of view, the MeISE methodology followed for the development of *SETIC* is appropriate since it allows us to obtain the product without demanding programming requirements, emphasizing the pedagogical characteristics through the instructional design included to design the didactic activities implemented in the software. As a future work path, we consider the challenge of prototyping the remaining mini-projects, deepening the evaluation of the tool with different modalities, and generating reports and statistics for monitoring and analysis.

This work highlights the benefits that an ES provides for students in the approach of such an abstract type of content as the computational process, through the use of different presentation formats, especially animated and/or simulated.

From a technical point of view, the MeISE methodology followed for the development of SETIC is appropriate since it allows us to obtain the product without demanding programming requirements, emphasizing the pedagogical characteristics through the instructional design included to design the didactic activities implemented in the software. As a future work path, we consider the challenge of prototyping the remaining mini-projects, deepening the evaluation of the tool with different modalities, and generating reports and statistics for monitoring and analysis.

Some of the ideas that have emerged include the implementation of communication modules between student and teacher users, as well as between students themselves. This led to the creation of the necessary fields to initially record email addresses.

This module can be useful for promoting collaborative and ubiquitous work through SETIC. The feedback and results obtained from this experience will surely motivate us to consider a broader domain related to more abstract interpretation content, covering more curriculum content, and creating the corresponding mini-projects in the ES.

Some of the ideas that have emerged include the implementation of communication modules between student and teacher users, as well as between students themselves. This led to the creation of the necessary fields to initially record email addresses.

This module can be useful for promoting collaborative and ubiquitous work through SETIC. The feedback and results obtained from this experience will surely motivate us to consider a broader domain related to more abstract interpretation content, covering more curriculum content, and creating the corresponding mini-projects in the ES.

in: Libro de Actas del XXVIII Congreso Argentino de Ciencia de la Computación (CACIC 2022), pp.

References

1. Dirección General de Cultura y Educación de la provincia de Buenos Aires / Diseño Curricular para la Educación Secundaria Ciclo Superior. ES4: Nuevas Tecnologías de la Información y la
2. Gauthier, M., Budán, P.: SETIC: un Software Educativo sobre el Funcionamiento de las Partes de un Computador. In: Libro de Actas del XXVIII Congreso Argentino de Ciencia de la Computación (CACIC 2022), pp. 746–755
3. https://cacic2022.unlar.edu.ar/wp-content/uploads/2022/09/FULL-PAPERS-y-SPG-ACE PTADOS-POR-TRACK.pdf
4. Adicra: La informática como materia. https://lainformaticacomomateria.ar/#!/-inicio/
5. Abud, A.: MeiSE: Metodología de Ingeniería de Software Educativo, Vol. 2, N 1 Revista Internacional de Educación en Ingeniería. Instituto Tecnológico de Orizaba, Drizaba, Veracruz, México (2009)
6. Parra Hernández, L.N., Silva Barragán, G.S.: CONSTRUCCIÓN DE MATE-MÓVIL A TRAVÉS DE LA METODOLOGÍA MEISE. México, EduQa (2017)
7. INDEC: Instituto Nacional de Estadísticas y Censos. Acceso y uso de tecnologías de la información y la comunicación. EPH Cuarto trimestre de 2021. Informes técnicos / Vol. 6, n° 89 Argentina (2021). https://www.indec.gob.ar/uploads/informesdeprensa/mautic_05_228 43D61C141.pdf
8. Hernández-Alcántara, M., Genaro, A.-A., Jorge Arturo, B.-T.: Revisión del modelo tecnoeducativo de Heinich y colaboradores (ASSURE) Los Modelos Tecno-Educativos, revolucionando el aprendizaje del siglo XXI, 61–72 (2014)
9. Inventor, MIT App, and M. I. T. Explore: App inventor. línea. Disponible en: http://appinv entor.mit.edu/explore/ (2017). Accedido: 26 may 2015
10. Blog de Setic. Blogger. https://www.blogger.com/blog/posts/5032299877095255895

11. Massa, S.M.: Objetos de aprendizaje: Metodología de desarrollo y Evaluación de la calidad. Diss. Universidad Nacional de La Plata (2013)

12. Ocsa, A., et al.: Propuesta Para El Diseño Y Desarrollo De Aplicaciones M Learning: Caso, Apps De Historia Del Perú Como Objetos De Aprendizaje Móviles. Nuevas Ideas En Informática Educativa TISE, 873–878 (2014)

13. Patton, E.W., Michael, T., Farzeen H.: MIT app inventor: Objectives, design, and development. Computational thinking education, pp. 31–49. Springer, Singapore (2019)

14. Sanz, C., Barranquero, F., Moralejo, L.: Metodología para la creación de Objetos de Aprendizaje CROA. Consultado el 15 de abril del 2017 (2015)

15. Torres-Carrion, P., González González, C., Jaime-Edwin, B.-O.: Diseño de un juego serio para la mejora de la conciencia fonológica de los niños con dislexia. IEEE 11 Congreso Colombiano de Computación (2016)

16. Valdivia, R.C., María Reina, Z.N., Jesús Leonardo, L.H.: Aplicación de TI en el proceso de enseñanza-aprendizaje para la adquisición de conocimientos de matemáticas 1er. grado de educación secundaria "Imat" (2017)

17. Bermúdez, A.-G.-V., Ismael - López, M.T.-M., Francisco - De la Ossa, L.-P., José, M.-R., Tomás - Sánchez, J.L.: Una Definición precisa del concepto "nivel de dominio de una competencia" en el marco del aprendizaje basado en competencias (2011) https://upcommons.upc.edu/handle/2099/11958

18. Serrano, G.-T., José, M., Pons, P., Rosa, M.: El Constructivismo hoy: enfoques constructivistas en educación REDIE. Revista Electrónica de Investigación Educativa, vol. 13, núm. 1, pp. 1–27. Universidad Autónoma de Baja California Ensenada, México (2011). http://www.redalyc.org/articulo.oa?id=15519374001

19. Antonio, F.A.: LA AUTOEVALUACIÓN: UNA ESTRATEGIA DOCENTE PARA EL CAMBIO DE VALORES EDUCATIVOS EN EL AULA. https://dialnet.unirioja.es/descarga/articulo/3441758.pdf

20. Leonardo, C., Lisandro, D., Germán, C., Waldo, H.: Herramienta de Software para Evaluación Semiautomática. Experiencia en un Curso de C#. Instituto de Investigación en Informática LIDI. ttps://core.ac.uk/reader/15775370

A Turing Machine at Secondary School

Jorge Rodríguez[1]([✉])[iD], Gerardo Parra[1][iD], Gabriela Gili[1][iD], Susana Parra[1][iD], Daniel Dolz[1][iD], and Hernán Roumec[2][iD]

[1] Facultad de Informática, Universidad Nacional del Comahue, Buenos Aires 1400, Neuquén, Argentina
{j.rodrig,gparra,susana.parra,ddolz}@fi.uncoma.edu.ar,
gabriela.gili@est.fi.uncoma.edu.ar
[2] Consejo Provincial de Educación Ministerio de Gobierno y Educación de la Provincia de Neuquén, Belgrano 1300, Neuquén, Argentina

Abstract. Currently, Computer Science in the mandatory levels of the education system are acquiring a significantly important role. Therefore, it is a priority to work on the production of educational resources in the area. This article presents an unplugged educational resource, built within the framework of participatory design, aimed at promoting the teaching of concepts related to Turing Machines.

Keywords: Computer Science Education · Secondary School · Turing Machine

1 Introduction

The inclusion of concepts related to Computer Science in the mandatory levels of the educational system is acquiring a significantly important role in recent years. Currently, curricular reforms in this direction are being carried out in numerous countries. Emerging initiatives in recent years aim to provide the student population, at all educational levels, access to the central concepts of the discipline [10,11].

In the Republic of Argentina the situation is disparate, while the initiatives developed by a group of National Universities, the Federal Council of Education, Program.ar and the provincial governments [2–4] drive curricular reforms in some jurisdictions, in most of the country computing is still poorly represented in mandatory education [13].

Current curricular trends for secondary education promote developing a broad journey through the areas of knowledge. In this framework, knowledge related to the area of Computation Theory is considered [17]. Although in the Republic of Argentina initiatives with a certain prevalence of the area of Algorithms and Programming can be observed, it is clear that progressively there is a tendency towards a broader journey through the areas of knowledge [12].

P. Pesado (Ed.): CACIC 2022, CCIS 1778, pp. 295–306, 2023.
https://doi.org/10.1007/978-3-031-34147-2_19

The first contact between students and Computer Science can be challenging. In this sense, unplugged educational resources prove to be an adequate and very interesting option. This is mainly because programming does not need to be learned or a digital device used, and the environment in which they are developed usually has a playful approach that poses challenges for the student [1,16].

Unplugged educational resources were designed as a way to communicate computational concepts in non-formal education spaces, especially as support for scientific dissemination. However, increasingly, schools adopt unplugged educational resources as a way to offer the first contacts with abstract concepts about computing. Nevertheless, there is limited systematic research on their effectiveness in the school environment or about the form they should take to adapt to these institutionalized contexts [1].

On the other hand, although there is a wide range of disciplinary topics covered by this type of resource, there are others that are part of the curriculum proposals and are not yet covered by these collections of resources. This is the case of a set of fundamental concepts in Computation Theory, such as those related to Turing Machines [9].

This work falls within the research and development line aimed at producing didactic resources for teaching Computer Science and evaluating their effectiveness in the secondary education context. In particular, it proposes to work on the development and evaluation of a collection of unplugged educational resources aimed at facilitating the teaching of concepts related to Turing machines and introductory notions of computability [7,9].

In a previous work [14], we suggested the development and use of educational resources aimed at promoting the teaching of concepts related to Turing Machines in the field of secondary education. We described a study carried out in a high school in the province of Neuquén, in the Argentine Patagonia. In the study participated a group of teenagers from different years of secondary education. The aim was to determine whether the activity carried out is appropriate to help understand theoretical concepts about computability and Turing machines. Additionally, whether they considered it a pleasant experience and if they believe that developing a playful experience before formal exposure is appropriate and enjoyable to encourage learning activities.

In this article that extends that work, a more precise description of the purpose of each stage of the process is provided, and the results obtained are presented in greater detail.

The rest of this document is organized as follows. The next section describes the proposed model for facilitating the production of educational resources for teaching Computer Science. Section 3 is dedicated to presenting the results of the study. Finally, it is closed with the conclusions drawn by the research team.

2   Proposed Model

The approach presented in this work is based on four didactic perspectives: CSUnplugged, Experiential Learning, Participatory Design, and Participatory

Action Research. The convergence of these perspectives aims to develop new discipline-based didactic resources validated in the classrooms [1,5,8].

In this context, work is carried out within the framework of methodological approaches based on participatory research and design specifically defined by this research and development line [6]. They are based on the Participatory Design Framing model, an innovative work framework for computer education, where school teachers actively engage in the process of developing educational resources [15].

The cycle in which this model is organized defines a methodological framework structured in four stages.

- **Generation of hypotheses**. The process begins with the definition of some hypotheses about how to support the teaching and learning process. In this stage, some methodological options are adopted for the design of the didactic devices.
  - Promoting collaboration. The use of physical resources acts as a facilitator of group activity.
  - Complexity distribution. Each person assumes responsibility for a piece of the machine. Conceptual complexity is distributed in the group.
  - Learning by playing. The mechanics of the game are transferred to the learning environment in order to achieve better results in disciplinary terms and in the development of soft skills.
  - Learning from experience. Focused on producing abstract and conceptual knowledge by reflecting on concrete experiences.

  On the other hand, a basic mechanics for the game is defined based on successive iterations and a collection of Turing machines that are accessible for students without prior training is selected.
- **Specific design.** The goal is to instantiate the proposal to the concrete situation of teaching and learning in order to make necessary adjustments and advance in the design of the experience.

  At this point, a pair of computer science teachers, who work at the secondary school where the field work is being carried out, are summoned with the intention of recovering their perceptions about the educational resource. In this context, a pilot session is developed with the purpose of evaluating the resource, and informing about the characteristics that are positively valued and about those that require adjustments.

  In these preparatory sessions, the field work is placed over three years of secondary school study, and it is defined that in all cases students without prior knowledge in the field will be working. A two hour class allocation is defined for the development of the activity, that is, 80 min.

  Three adjustments are made to the initial proposal, work is done on the complexity of the Turing Machines to be used by adding a slightly higher complexity machine. Some game mechanics are defined more precisely and the way the machines are represented is modified, adopting a model closer to that used in the discipline area.

- **Mediated Practice.** This moment takes place in the classrooms of selected schools, a practice is carried out mediated by the designed game that expresses the collection of initial conjectures. This instance contributes to validate or suggest adjustments to the initial proposal. In Sect. 2.2 the detailed description of this process can be found.
- **Knowledge retrieval.** After the mediated practice has ended, results of the experience are retrieved. These are used to make necessary adjustments for the improvement of the designed resource and to offer the teaching community new unplugged resources for teaching Computer Science in their classrooms. In another sense, they are used to confirm, adjust, or reject conjectures about the real possibilities of teaching fundamental concepts about Theory of Computation in the field of secondary education. In the Sect.3 results obtained are described.

2.1 A Turing Machine at Secondary School

"A Turing Machine at Secondary School" It is part of a collection of unplugged educational resources designed to facilitate the teaching of concepts related to Turing Machines and introductory notions of computability. This collection aims to use board game mechanics to achieve better learning outcomes. The rules of the games in the collection are defined by the operational mechanisms of Turing Machines.

This proposal is intended for groups of students in secondary education who have no prior disciplinary knowledge in the field of computer science. *"A Turing Machine at Secondary School"* it is outlined to work with multiple teams consisting of 3 to 4 members, and the fundamental idea is to present it as a *game* with specific rules. The estimated duration for the activity is 80 min.

Setup. The materials required to perform the activity include a paper tape divided into cells and a paper triangle to indicate the current position of the tape where the reading and writing head of the machine would point. The head should be able to move on the tape in both directions. Additionally, a card with pre-established rules that determine the operation of the machine is necessary. The rules indicate, given the current state and symbol at the position of the reading head, to which state the machine must go, what symbol should be written in the current position of the tape, and what movement (left or right) should be performed.

Running experience. After organizing the groups, delivering the materials, and presenting the game rules, the game starts by initiating the operation of the machine. The main objective of the activity is to understand the operation of a machine that is not created with technology but executes instructions in the same way as a current computer.

Each group will execute their machine following the rules that were provided to them. If the tape provided to the group contains the input, *"9453"* and the reading and writing head points to *"9"*, a possible rule to apply would be: *(A,9, derecha)*. Informally, this rule could be interpreted as follows: *"the machine moves to state A, writes 9 in the current position, and moves one place to the right."* Then, the values on the tape will be: *"9453"*, But in this case, the current state will be A, and the read-write head will be pointing to the position where the symbol 4 is. At this point, the rule we must apply is in the table corresponding to state A.

Three iterations are projected and, in each opportunity, a different input is used. Each group that correctly predicts the output produced by the machine for the input in play earns 2 points.

These iterations have the purpose of helping to understand the basic operational mechanisms of a Turing Machine, as well as to recognize its constituent parts. In other words, they seek to build meaning by manipulating the educational material prepared for the activity as a group.

The next iteration accumulates 3 points and consists of discovering what the machine being used does, for example *"To determine whether a number is even or odd"* or *"Add one to the number".*

The main objective of this iteration is to recognize and generalize the outputs obtained in the previous steps. Generalization involves reviewing the outputs produced in the previous iterations and generalizing them so that they can be applied to other inputs. This means that students must take the outputs, analyze them, and explain them in a general way so that a variety of outputs can be anticipated. That is, it is about identifying the type of problem that is being solved. This process involves building abstractions, since a collection of outputs produces a more general understanding.

The final iteration is worth 4 points and consists of explaining how the machine manages to solve the problem posed. In this case, the focus is on breaking down the problem into smaller parts in order to understand how they interact and what the complete process is for solving the problem at hand. This process involves developing a deeper understanding of how Turing machines work.

The entire activity is designed to use physical or concrete materials that can be placed on a worktable. Assigning this type of material to a group of students helps to promote debates, focus attention on a topic, and collectively experiment or, in other words, promote collaborative work.

Reflection and formalization. After carrying out the activity, an analysis of the classroom experience is conducted. The goal is to build abstract concepts by understanding the functioning of a formal machine. It is important to demonstrate how the Turing machine, even though it may appear at first glance to be a somewhat rudimentary formal device, had a decisive and fundamental impact on the emergence of the first computer and on the functioning of current computers. Furthermore, it allows the formalization of the intuitive notion of computational procedure, effective procedure, or algorithm.

2.2 Mediated Practice: Fieldwork with Secondary School Students

This educational resource was taken to the classroom with the intention of adjusting it progressively based on comments, suggestions, and revisions made during the fieldwork. This study's main focus is to evaluate the designed educational resource's effectiveness as well as taking note of the secondary school students' feelings towards the learning experience.

The population that participated in the experience consisted of 26 high school students, 12 of whom attend the first and second years of studies and 14 are in their final year. In all cases, these are students without prior knowledge in the area of study. The general age range is 13 to 15 years old for the first group and 16 to 18 years old for the second group.

The experience took place in three different 80-min sessions, with two teachers, carrying out unplugged activities aimed at teaching and learning abstract concepts that would facilitate understanding of the functioning of the Turing Machine. All sessions have a similar structure.

The activity aimed to help students understand specific aspects of formalism. Reflective processes on the experience were considered, as well as the construction of abstract concepts based on linking the machines used during the activity with formal concepts of the Turing Machine.

The experience was organized into four stages: explanation and demonstration of the use of the material, concrete experience, construction of abstract concepts, and application.

Stage 0: Explanation and Demonstration of the use of the Material. In the first instance, a brief explanation of the activity is given and a demonstration of the use of the material (input tapes, reading-writing head, rule cards) for the experience is provided. This stage aims to get the students emotionally and cognitively ready to start the activity. This implies, on the one hand, motivating the students and getting their attention and, on the other hand, presenting the basic rules in order to start playing.

Stage 1: Concrete Experience. In this stage, the experiential phase of the activity is developed. *"Una Máquina de Turing en la Escuela"*. Two machines were used in the activity: the first to determine whether the input value represented an even or odd number, and the second machine to add 1 to an input number. The classroom was divided into groups, and each group was given several tapes, a read-write head, and the written rule cards.

In each group, students distributed the materials to follow the activity and fulfill a role (State A - State S - Head). The student who had the Head performed the reading of the symbol corresponding to the state it was in, and according to the corresponding state, the group partner retrieved the rule, indicated the action to be taken, and established the new state. Upon reaching state H, the end of the sequence, the result was analyzed as a group.

The activity started with the even-odd machine. After testing with two inputs, the 1st and 2nd year classes were able to follow the sequence within the group interaction, obtaining the output correctly. However, a third round was necessary, as well as some guidance from the teachers, for them to fully understand what they were doing. In the experience with the second machine, they were able to easily discover in the first round and with few inputs that the objective was to add 1 to the number represented in the input.

For the group of the last year of high school, they quickly discovered in the first round what each of the machines did, but nonetheless continued with several tests using inputs of different lengths and symbols, since the students expressed that they found the activity entertaining and motivating.

Stage 2: Elaboration of Abstract Concepts. During this stage, a retrospective analysis is carried out on the experience by recovering some particular aspects, such as the fact that a machine has different states and alphabets, and that each state corresponds to a list of actions according to the input symbol. Abstract concepts are constructed by linking the machines used during the activity with the formal concepts of Turing Machines.

Stage 3: Aplication. Finally, in a plenary session, different situations where these concepts come into play were analyzed together. The importance of these concepts in the field of Computer Science was discussed to help recognize the computational power of Turing Machines. The activity was very motivating, entertaining, and easy to follow. High school students were able to appropriate the disciplinary knowledge explored during the activity without difficulty. In the earlier years, they were able to perform the sequences, thus obtaining the expected results, although they encountered some difficulties in understanding the abstract concepts developed.

3   Results

After completing the experience, the participating student population was surveyed about their perception regarding the use of these types of devices and the effectiveness of this didactic resource in terms of constructed learning. The survey was not mandatory, nor was it a component of the subject accreditation process, and it was directed to the entire population that participated in the experience. These surveys' purpose is to acquire information about the educational resource's impact, not for a mark to be assigned by the teachers. The surveys are completed individually and anonimously by each student.

The survey was structured in two sections, the first of which was aimed at recovering perceptions regarding a) usefulness, that is, to what extent students appreciate that the activity developed is useful to help understand concepts about Turing Machines; b) impact, whether they consider it a pleasurable experience or not, and c) organization, whether they consider that developing a ludic experience before the formal exposition is an adequate way to organize learning activities.

This section consists of three questions with the following possible responses: strongly agree, agree, neither agree nor disagree, disagree, and strongly disagree. Below are the results obtained in this section;

Category: Usefulness

Question: The game "A Turing Machine at School" seems to me like a useful tool for learning concepts about Turing Machines.

It is observed that 38% of the surveyed population indicates being very much in agreement with the usefulness of the tool for learning concepts about Turing

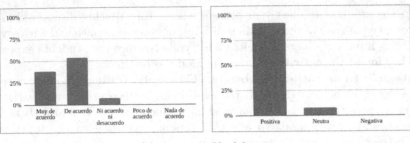

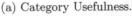

(a) Category Usefulness.

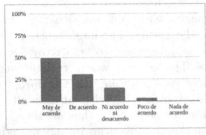

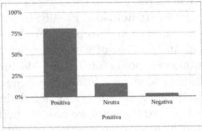

(b) Category Impact.

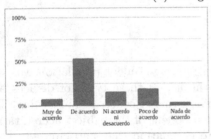

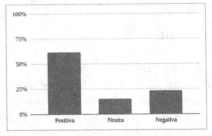

(c) Category Organization.

Fig. 1. Perceptions Section.

Machines, while 54% express their agreement with the same statement, and 8% respond that they are neither in agreement nor disagreement. That is to say, 92% convey a positive appreciation regarding the usefulness of the didactic device Fig. 1a.

Category: Impact

Question: I find the game entertaining and easy to use.

In this category, 50% strongly agree and 31% agree with the statement that the tool is user-friendly and easy to use, 15% prefer a neutral response, and 4% respond that they slightly disagree. In this case, the affirmative responses account for 81% of the total responses Fig. 1b.

Category: Organization

Question: Playing first and then being told about Turing Machines seems like an appropriate way to teach.

Regarding organization, 54% indicate their agreement that the activity's organization is adequate for learning, with 8% of students strongly agreeing with this statement. On the other hand, 19% disagree slightly, and 4% strongly disagree, while the remaining 15% offer a neutral response. Taking into account the accumulated percentages, it is observed that 62% have a positive appreciation of the organization of the learning sequence, while 23% do not consider it appropriate Fig. 1c.

All students express positive views about the usefulness of the tool. However, senior year students express this more strongly, with 17% strongly agreeing and 83% agreeing. Meanwhile, among younger students, 50% strongly agree and 33% agree. Similarly, when it comes to the Impact category, 83% of senior year students strongly agree and 17% agree, while 25% of younger students strongly agree and 33% agree.

With regards to organization, younger students prefer the Concrete experience - Elaboration of abstract concepts sequence more strongly. 17% strongly agree and 67% agree. On the other hand, 50% of senior students prefer a classic structure.

The second section aims to inquire about the knowledge constructed by the student population from their participation in the experience. In this regard, the effectiveness of teaching and learning practices and concepts related to Turing Machines in the context of secondary schools to students without previous knowledge in the area is studied.

This section is organized into three categories: a) Understanding, which involves understanding and interpreting developed concepts, as well as assigning meaning to different elements; b) Applying, which is related to the use of learned practices and concepts to solve particular and concrete cases; and c) Evaluating, which is linked to establishing to what extent it is appropriate to apply learned practices and concepts to particular situations.

This section consists of five questions, each offering the following possible answers: Very sure, I think so, I don't know, I don't think so, That's not the case. The following are the results obtained in this section:

Category: Understanding

Question 01: The Turing machine in the figure has two states: A and S.

Question 02: The Turing machine in the figure can work with letters such as "A", "W", or "T".

It is observed that 76% selected a correct option as an answer, while 13.46% opted for an incorrect option and 9.62% responded that they do not know the answer. The results group the answers to the two questions in the category and accumulate as correct the options "Very sure" and "I think so", as an error to the options "I don't think so" and "That's not the case", and as a neutral response "I don't know" Fig. 2a.

Category: Application

Question 01: In the head position shown in the figure, if the current state is S, the machine moves to state A and moves to the right.

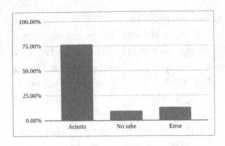

(a) Category: Understanding.

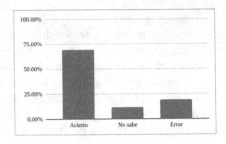

(b) Category: Application.

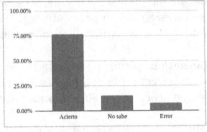

(c) Category: Evaluation.

Fig. 2. Section: Constructed knowledge.

Question 02: In the head position shown in the figure, if the current state is A, the machine moves to state S and moves to the right.

In the Apply category, 69.23% provided a correct answer, 11.54% indicated that they do not know the answer, and 19.23% answered incorrectly. In this case, "Very sure" and "I think so" responses are accumulated as a correct answer for Question 01, and "I don't think so" and "That's not the case" responses are accumulated as incorrect for Question 02 Fig. 2b.

Category: Evaluation

Question 01: One could use a Turing machine, for example, to determine how many digits a number has?

In the Evaluation category, 76.92% provided a correct answer, 15.38% indicated that they do not know the answer, and 7.69% answered incorrectly. In this case, "Very sure" and "I think so" responses are accumulated as a correct answer for Question 01, and "I don't think so" and "That's not the case" responses are accumulated as incorrect for Question 02. Figure 2c.

While the performance of all students is acceptable in all categories, the final year students' performance is notably better than the younger students'. On the one hand, the older students' group presents 93% correct answers in the Understanding category, 71% in the Application category and 76% in the Evaluation category. On the other hand, the younger students' group presents 55% correct answers in the Understanding category, 58% in the Application category and 67% in the Evaluation category.

4   Conclusions and Future Work

This article presents a didactic resource that facilitates the teaching of fundamental concepts in Computer Theory to high school students. The mediated practice carried out in the context of this study provides strong encouraging indications that this type of educational resource has broad possibilities to favor the effective construction of disciplinary knowledge of an abstract nature. On the other hand, the participatory design model defined in the context of this line of research and development offers a valid methodological framework for producing consistent and situated educational resources.

References

1. Bell, T., Vahrenhold, J.: CS unplugged—how is it used, and does it work? In: Böckenhauer, H.-J., Komm, D., Unger, W. (eds.) Adventures Between Lower Bounds and Higher Altitudes. LNCS, vol. 11011, pp. 497–521. Springer, Cham (2018). https://doi.org/10.1007/978-3-319-98355-4_29
2. Consejo Federal de Educación: Res 263/15. Resoluciones CFE (2015)
3. Consejo Federal de Educación: Res 343/18. Resoluciones CFE (2018)
4. Consejo Provincial de Educación: Res 1463/18. Resoluciones CPE (2018)
5. DiSalvo, B., Yip, J., Bonsignore, E., Carl, D.: Participatory design for learning. In: Participatory Design for Learning, pp. 3–6. Routledge (2017)
6. Dolz, D., Martínez, R., Parra, G., Rodríguez, J., Ginez, N.: Recursos educativos desenchufados para la enseñanza de las ciencias de la computación en la escuela secundaria. In: XV TE&ET (2020)
7. Hopcroft, J., Motwani, R., Ullman, J.: Introduction to Automata Theory. Addison Wesley, Languages and Computation (2006)
8. Kolb, A.Y., Kolb, D.A.: Learning styles and learning spaces: enhancing experiential learning in higher education. Acad. Manage. Learn. Educ. 4(2), 193–212 (2005)
9. Lewis, H., Papadimitriou, C.: Elements of the Theory of Computation. Second Edition. Prentice Hall (1998)
10. McGarr, O., Johnston, K.: Curricular responses to computer science provision in schools: current provision and alternative possibilities. Curriculum J. 31(4), 745–756 (2020)
11. Ottestad, G., Gudmundsdottir, G.B.: Information and communication technology policy in primary and secondary education in europe. Second handbook of information technology in primary and secondary education, pp. 1–21 (2018)
12. Rodríguez, J., Cortez, M., Boari, S.: Explorando el lugar de las áreas de conocimiento de las ciencias de la computacion en la escuela secundaria argentina: Una revisión sistemática. Electron. J. SADIO (EJS) 21(2) (jul 2022). https://publicaciones.sadio.org.ar/index.php/EJS/article/view/223
13. Rodríguez, J., Cortez, M.: La posición de las ciencias de la computación en el diseno curricular para la escuela secundaria argentina: Una revisión sistemática. Electron. J. SADIO (EJS) 19(2)
14. Rodríguez, J., Parra, G., Gili, G., Parra, S., Dolz, D., Roumec, H.: Una máquina de turing en la escuela. In: XXVIII Congreso Argentino de Ciencias de la Computación (CACIC) (2022)
15. Sandoval, W.: Conjecture mapping: an approach to systematic educational design research. J. Learn. Sci. 23(1), 18–36 (2014)

16. Taub, R., Armoni, M., Ben-Ari, M.: Cs unplugged and middle-school students' views, attitudes, and intentions regarding cs. ACM Trans. Comput. Educ. (TOCE) **12**(2), 1–29 (2012)
17. Tissenbaum, M., Ottenbreit-Leftwich, A.: A vision of k– 12 computer science education for 2030. Commun. ACM **63**(5), 42–44 (2020)

Digital Governance and Smart Cities

Application Programming Interface Technology to Optimize the Exchange of Information Between Legal Systems

Osvaldo Mario Spositto⬭, Julio César Bossero⬭, Viviana Alejandra Ledesma(✉)⬭, Lorena Romina Matteo⬭, and Sebastian Quevedo⬭

National University of La Matanza, Department of Engineering and Technological Research, Florencio Varela 1903, La Matanza, San Justo, Buenos Aires, Argentina
`{Spositto,jbossero,vledesma,lmatteo,jquevedo}@unlam.edu.ar`

Abstract. Building Expert Systems is an attempt to capture the experience of people who are experts in a subject and incorporate it into computer programs. This task is based on finding out what they know and how they use their knowledge to resolve problems. Law and legal reasoning is one of the new targets for Artificial Intelligence systems. This work is a continuation of previous work, where a prototype of Expert Systems called Experticia was designed and implemented by a public University of the Argentine Republic, aims to improve the resolution of judicial files, optimizing time and minimizing data loading errors. Experticia, in its first version, interacts with the Integral System of the Judicial Branch of the Province of Buenos Aires, in an asynchronous way.

This article presents part of the work carried out within the framework of a research that aims to optimize the exchange of information between both systems. For this purpose, the use of Application Programming Interfaces is proposed to synchronously access the information of the judicial files.

First, the technologies used are described, then their specification and design, and finally, the implementation details and the tests performed are explained.

The results indicate the feasibility of incorporating this technology in the new version of the Experticia.

Keywords: Artificial Intelligence · Expert Systems · Application Programming Interfaces · Web Services

1 Introduction

This paper is a continuation of the work presented at the XXVIII Argentine Congress of Computer Science (CACIC), held at the Capital Headquarters of the Department of Exact, Physical and Natural Sciences of the National University of La Rioja (UNLaR), from October 3 to 6, 2022, organized by the Network of Universities with Degrees in Computer Science (RedUNCI) and the UNLaR, under the title *"Development of Application Programming Interfaces applied to a Legal Expert System"* [1]. In this work, a modification made to a prototype of a Legal Expert System was presented.

© The Author(s), under exclusive license to Springer Nature Switzerland AG 2023
P. Pesado (Ed.): CACIC 2022, CCIS 1778, pp. 309–323, 2023.
https://doi.org/10.1007/978-3-031-34147-2_20

In 2020, the National University of La Matanza (UNLaM), through researchers from two departments, the Engineering and Technological Research Department and the Law and Political Science Department, with a close collaboration of the Execution Court N°2 of the Morón Judicial Department, presented the PROINCE[1] project entitled "Design and Implementation of an Expert System to Support the Process of Dispatch of Procedures of a Judicial Body", whose objective was the design and construction of a prototype of an Expert System (ES).

This project would be used for the systematization and optimization of several of the judicial processes that are currently carried out manually or semi-automatically in the Judicial Branch of the Province of Buenos Aires. Given the importance of the project, in the same year, the Supreme Court of Justice of the Province of Buenos Aires (SCBA) signed a reciprocal collaboration agreement with the UNLaM for the development of Experticia.

During these years, the aforementioned research teams have been working continuously together with specialists from the provincial legal area and technicians from the SCBA.

Experticia is an example of a knowledge-based system. Salvaneschi in [2] states that ES were the first commercial systems to use a knowledge-based architecture.

The project was born as a need that arises from the Execution Court No. 2 of the Judicial Department Morón, province of Buenos Aires. When faced with repetitive and time-consuming tasks. The original idea of the ES is to take the experience of the "experts in justice" to build a knowledge base, with standardized models, which can then be applied by the operators in the different judicial bodies from the user interface provided by the system (see Fig. 1).

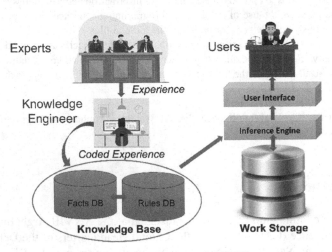

Fig. 1. Basic structure of a ES [1].

---

[1] Incentive Program for Research Teachers of the Secretariat of University Policies, implemented by the Secretariat of University Policies of the National Ministry of Education.

In the initial stage of the project, a prototype was built, a desktop version, whose functionality provided support to justice operators in making decisions for the resolution of a judicial file, particularly those related to the criminal jurisdiction, the jurisdiction where the application is currently operating. Among the potential benefits of Experticia that can be mentioned: Allows the standardization of different processes for the dispatch of proceedings, streamlining and reducing loading times, as well as minimizing errors, both during decision making and data entry. Also, the efficiency in training new agents was proven. Descriptions of the development progress and tests performed have been described and published in several papers [3–7].

As explained in [1], algorithmically Experticia is based on decision theory [8], using binary decision trees. These are constituted by a series of decisions or conditions organized in a hierarchical way. Figure 2 shows the graphical representation of a binary tree.

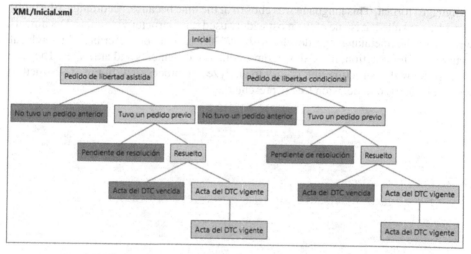

Fig. 2. Graphical representation of a binary decision tree.

The first judicial processes, which were developed to be incorporated to the prototype, were the probation request, in the work published in 49 JAIIO [4]. It can be observed how the process is decomposed in several steps, until its resolution is reached. In [5] and [6] it is also explained how these data can be used with different Data Mining algorithms to predict its resolution. As mentioned above, it was initially implemented in a desktop version. At this stage of testing, it has provided highly satisfactory results in the Criminal Execution Court No. 2 of Morón [7].

At the beginning of the project, it was stipulated that Experticia should be integrated, asynchronously, with the Multi-fence and Multi-Instance Assisted Management Computer System, better known in the judicial environment as Augusta[2]. The system was developed by the Department of IT Development of the Sub-secretariat of IT Technology of the SCBA. It is worth mentioning that this system is used in all the courts of

---

[2] https://www.scba.gov.ar/paginas.asp?id=39889.

312   O. M. Spositto et al.

the Province of Buenos Aires. Augusta registers all the data of the cases starting with the lawsuit and then records all the procedural steps, the parties or persons involved, annexed documentation and all the information that contributes to the management of the case. It assists the agency's office with a library of models specific to the agency and/or generic models. The system has the possibility of scheduling due dates and/or milestones, as well as the option of calculating judicial deadlines.

In this processing, the data that makes up the information of the case (in the context of Experticia, this data has been called *"essential data"*), is taken from Augusta asynchronously and manually dumped in Experticia to perform the corresponding process. After completing all the steps indicated in the corresponding tree, the new information produced by the ES is updated again in Augusta, in the same way, that is to say, asynchronously.

It is important to clarify, at this point, that Experticia stores locally the code of the composition of the decision trees. These are constructed in XML (Extensible Markup Language) format. This language was chosen at the time because, according to the bibliography consulted, it is one of the most widely used semi-structured formats. Documents written in this metalanguage developed by W3C[3] have a self-describing hierarchical structure of information, formed by atoms, compound elements and attributes. They are extensible, with a structure that is easy to analyze and process [9]. In Fig. 3, a structure written in XML of a decision tree is presented.

Fig. 3. Structure written in XML of a decision tree.

Based on the acceptable results obtained in the experimentation carried out in the Criminal Execution Court No. 2 of Morón, a new PROINCE project was presented this year under the title *"Legal Artificial Intelligence: The Evolution of Experticia towards a*

---

[3] https://www.w3.org/.

Predictive Justice Model". In this project, it is proposed to upgrade the current desktop system to a new version.

In this opportunity, a web development, the new system will have the same modules, corresponding to the management of the resolution of the dispatches associated with the cases, but the exchange of information between the systems will be carried out synchronously.

For Experticia to connect and interact with Augusta, an application programming interface (API) was built. An API is a set of subroutines, functions, and procedures (or methods, in object-oriented programming) that offers a certain library to be used by other software as an abstraction layer. In this way it can directly take the essential data from a cause, and even return and store information in Augusta when necessary.

Following this objective, the web architecture presented in Fig. 4 was proposed. As can be seen, it is a software architecture for applications that require real-time and bidirectional communication between server and clients.

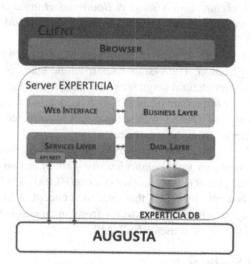

Fig. 4. Structure ES Web.

At the end of 2022, the research group implemented new processes for the exchange of information between both systems. By means of different API's, in this opportunity, the decision tree models, already built and residing locally in Experticia, are sent to Augusta in XML format. Through a process, these structures are converted into a new format to be stored in Augusta. The format chosen is JavaScript Object Notation (JSON).

This process is only used to transfer models built in XML. From now on, the new trees will be built and stored only in Augusta.

Finally, the work is completed by presenting a new API for the transfer of these JSON structures to Experticia.

2 Research Background

Several works related to Artificial Intelligence (AI) applied to justice or some processes involving judges or court rulings were found. The papers presented by this research team name and described them [3–7]. Regarding the use of web services applied to justice, we present a brief summary of the following works:

- *Bob Slaski & Gerry Coleman. (2012). Accelerated Information Sharing for Law Enforcement (AISLE) Using Web Services. Available at:* https://bja.ojp.gov/sites/g/files/xyckuh186/files/media/document/aisle_web_services.pdf

  Abstract: The National Law Enforcement Telecommunications System (NLETS) provides a network for criminal justice information sharing across North America. NLETS is defining new XML-based standards and web services under the Accelerated Information Sharing for Law Enforcement (AISLE) project. AISLE implemented an XML message router (XMR) that provides operational web services capabilities.

- *Seeam, Preetila & Teckchandani, Nishant & Booneyad, Hansha & Torul, V. & Seeam, Amar. (2018). Employment Law Expert System. 1–6.* https://doi.org/10.1109/ICONIC.2018.8601271.

  Abstract: Presents an ES to assist the people of Mauritania with queries they may have about labor legislation. The system uses machine learning techniques, speech recognition/synthesis and natural language processing to converse with users through a web interface. It was implemented in HTML5, CSS3 and JavaScript to create the front-end application, and a REST web service API was created so that user queries and responses generated from the inference engine.

- *Behzadidoost, R., Hasheminezhad, M., Farshi, M. et al. A framework for text mining on Twitter: a case study on joint comprehensive plan of action (JCPOA)- between 2015 and 2019. Qual Quant (2021).* https://doi.org/10.1007/s11135-021-01239-y

  Abstract: This is a rule-based ES that uses the concept of fingerprinting in judicial sciences. The system fingerprints tweets from an emerging topic. To detect the untagged tweets of the topic, it uses REST API.

3 About Expert Systems

According to [10], ES are computer systems that emulate the decision-making capacity of a human expert. They belong to the field of artificial intelligence and can be identified as programs that reproduce the performance of one or more experts in a given field of activity (domain).

Let us recall that the term artificial intelligence was used by John McCarthy[4] in 1955, and he defined it as *"the science and engineering of making intelligent machines"*. AI is the intelligence displayed by machines or computer programs [11].

It is also the name of the academic field that studies how to create computers and computer programs capable of behaving intelligently. In the book Artificial Intelligence. A Modern Approach the authors [8] define this field as *"the study and design of intelligent agents"*, in which an intelligent agent is a system that perceives its environment and performs actions that maximize its chances of success.

---

[4] http://www-formal.stanford.edu/jmc//.

In the early 1960s, the first work on what are now called "*expert*" systems began. Initially, the aim was to build intelligent machines with great reasoning and problem-solving power. It was imagined that, from a small set of norms or rules of reasoning introduced into a powerful computer, systems of greater than human capacity would be created.

We find in [12] that the name ES derives from the term "*knowledge-based expert system*".

An ES employs human knowledge captured on a computer to re-solve problems that normally require human experts. Well-designed systems mimic the reasoning process that experts use to re-solve specific problems. Such systems can be used by non-experts to improve their problem-solving skills. ESs can also be used as assistants by experts. Furthermore, these systems can perform better than any individual human expert making decisions in a specific, narrow area of Experticia, referred to as a domain.

Taking as a starting point some authors [11, 12], an ES is mainly composed of three parts. Figure 5:

- A user interface: this is the system that allows a non-expert user to query (question) the ES system and receive advice. The user interface is designed to be as simple as possible to use.
- A knowledge base - This is a collection of facts and rules. The knowledge base is created from information provided by human experts.
- An inference engine - This acts as a search engine, examining the knowledge base for information that matches the user's query.

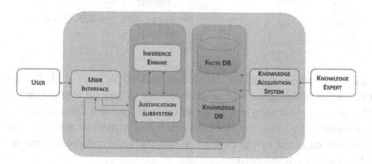

Fig. 5. Structure of an ES [11].

4 Application Programming Interfaces Considerations

An API is code that allows two software programs to communicate with each other [13]. The API dictates the correct way for a programmer to write code that requests services from an operating system (OS) or other application. These are implemented through function calls composed of verbs and nouns.

An API is composed of two related elements. The first is a specification that describes how information is exchanged between programs, in the form of a request for processing and return of the necessary data. The second is a software interface written to that specification and published in some form for use [13].

To realize it, for this project, we resorted to layered programming [14], where the service layer (also called business layer) consists of the logic that performs the main functions of the application: data processing, implementation of business functions, coordination of various users and management of external resources such as, for example, access to databases. On top of this layer, Web Services (WS) and API operate [15]. It is not the purpose of this paper to highlight the differences between the two concepts, but some of them are briefly described in Table 1 [16 and 17].

Table 1. Some differences between WS and API.

WS	API
• It is a collection of open source protocols and standards used to exchange data between systems or applications	• It is a software interface that allows two applications to interact with each other without the user's participation
• They are mainly based on standards such as SOAP (Simple Object Access Protocol), XML-RPC (short for Extensible Markup Language Remote Procedure Call) and REST (Representational Estate Transfer) for communication	• It is used for any communication style
• Only supports the protocol HTTP (*Hypertext Transfer Protocol*)	• Protocol support HTTP/HTTPS (*Hypertext Transfer Protocol Secure*)
• Support XML	• Admit XML y JSON (*JavaScript Object Notation*)

From the comparison, it can be concluded that all WS are API, but not all API are WS [18]. When building an API, it is necessary to rely on a set of definitions and protocols that are used to design and integrate the application software. These interfaces are usually considered as the contract between the information provider and the user, where the content required by the consumer (the call) and the content required by the producer (the response) is established.

4.1 Why use the REST API?

As detailed in [1], the API implemented in Experticia, conforms to the limits of the REST (Representational State Transfer) architecture, this term is an acronym, whose translation into English means Representational State Transfer. This web development architecture can be used in any HTTP client [19]. According to the bibliography consulted, it is simpler than other existing architectures, such as XML-RPC or SOAP. This simplicity is achieved because it employs a web interface that uses hypermedia for the representation and transition of information. The main advantage of this architecture is that it has provided the web with greater scalability, i.e., it supports a greater number of components and the interactions between them [13].

REST implementations also rely on the notion of a limited set of operations that both client and server fully understand from the outset. In the HTTP protocol, the operations are described in the *"initial line"*, and the main operations used in HTTP are as follows [19]:

- GET: returns the information identified by the request URI[5].
- PUT: requests that the enclosing entity be stored in the supplied request URI.
- POST: requests that the origin server accept the attached entity in the request as a new subordinate of the resource identified by the request URI.
- DELETE: requests that the origin server delete the resource identified by the request URI.

The first three operations are read-only, while the last three are write operations [19].

An API that uses the REST architecture is called RESTful API which uses the JSON text format to exchange data.

4.2   About JSON Data Modeling

JSON is a format based on the data types of the JavaScript programming language [20]. As a semi-structured[6] data format language, it has become one of the main data exchange formats on the World Wide Web in recent years and gained popularity in database community research [21]. As each JSON object is a set of key-value pairs, such a document can be naturally represented as a data tree structure called a "JSON tree". A value can be an atomic value such as a string, an integer, a number, an array, or a null value. To capture the composition structure of JSON data, each value can be returned as a set of JSON objects. This language agnostic format, i.e., with programming aspects that are independent of any specific language, can be used for example in: Node.js, Python, Ruby, PHP, .NET, Java, etc. [22].

4.3   Design Pattern REACT

A design pattern that works with API aims to hide the complexity of the internal implementation and presents a simple interface to clients. One of several existing design patterns [23, 24] is the Model View Controller (MVC), which is commonly used to implement user interfaces, data and control logic. It emphasizes a separation between business logic and its visualization.

This *"separation of concerns"*[7] provides a better division of labor and improved maintainability. The three parts of the MVC software design pattern can be described as follows:

- Model: Handles data and business logic.

---

[5] Universal Resource Identifier.

[6] Semi-structured data does not have a defined schema. They do not fit into a ta-table/row/column format but are organized by means of labels or "tags" that allow them to be grouped and hierarchies to be created. They are also known as non-relational or NoSQL.

[7] Is a design principle for separating a computer program into distinct sections, such that each section focuses on a delimited interest.

- View: Handles design and presentation.
- Controller: Routes commands to the models and views.

For this project, REACT[8] (also called React.js or ReactJS) was used, which is an open source JavaScript library designed to create user interfaces with the goal of facilitating single-page application development [25]. This library is intended to help developers build applications that use data that changes all the time. REACT only handles the user interface in an application; it is the View in a context where the MVC pattern is used [24].

5 Experimental Evaluation

Microsoft's Visual Studio 2019[9] was selected as the integrated development environment (IDE) for this experimental programming. It has numerous features that support various aspects of software development: editing, debugging and compiling code, and then publishing an application.

Apart from the standard editor and debugger provided by most IDEs, Visual Studio includes compilers, code completion tools, graphical designers and many more features to facilitate the software development process.

The coding was done in C#[10], which is an object-oriented programming language developed by Microsoft that has been designed to compile various applications running on.*NET Framework 4.5*.

Finally, for API testing, Postman[11] was used, which is an application that allows requests to be made and test data to be obtained. Postman is an HTTP client that provides the possibility of testing HTTP requests through a graphical user interface, by means of which different types of responses are obtained that must later be validated. Figure 6 shows the architecture proposed in this work.

Regarding the way Experticia communicates with Augusta, calls are used by requests as if it were a URL with parameters, for example:

```
.../api/Expediente/ListarBasico?IdOrganismo
={idOrganismo}&NroExpediente={nroExpediente}
```

The creation of JSON objects involves writing data:

- Data is separated by commas.
- The data is written in pairs, with the data name or attribute first and then the data value.
- JSON objects are surrounded by braces "{}".
- Square braces "[]" store arrays, including other objects.

---

[8] https://reactjs.org/.

[9] https://docs.microsoft.com/es-es/visualstudio/get-started/visual-studio-ide?view=vs-2022.

[10] https://docs.microsoft.com/es-es/dotnet/csharp/tour-of-csharp/.

[11] https://www.postman.com/.

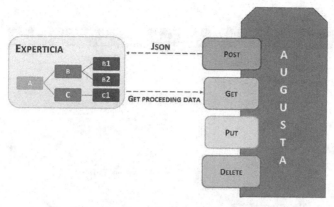

Fig. 6. Proposed architecture for data exchange.

Figure 7 below shows a fragment of the data in JSON format used in Experticia:

```
 1    [
 2      {
 3          "idExpediente": 112298,
 4          "idOrganismo": 1862,
 5          "prefijo": "LC",
 6          "numero": 9609,
 7          "sufijo": "1",
 8          "letraReceptoria": null,
 9          "numeroReceptoria": null,
10          "anioReceptoria": null,
11          "caratula": "DE ARMAS BAQUERO, EDISON ALEJANDRO S/ INCIDENTE DIGITAL DE LIBERTAD CONDICIONAL ",
12          "fechaInicio": "2021-03-18T18:32:14.93",
13          "fechaRadicacion": "2021-07-01T00:00:00"
14      },
```

Fig. 7. Fragment of the data in JSON format used in Experticia.

One advantage that JSON has over XML is that the resulting code is more lightweight. To store the same information using JSON reduces the size since it does not produce data redundancy, and this results in a higher speed when transmitting the information [20].

Figure 8 shows the screen with a list of several feasible causes to be solved. After selecting the cause, Experticia contacts Augusta to request an update of the cause. He completes the essential data that may be missing and resolves the case by applying the corresponding process model. Experticia returns a result, such as an electronic document like a parole request. The data, which was completed in Experticia, is stored, and sent back to Augusta via another API.

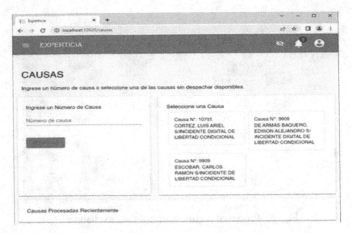

Fig. 8. Experticia screen for the selection of a case.

At the end of the year 2022, a new API was developed, whose function is to decentralize the decision trees, which until now have been stored locally in Experticia. The import of the trees stored in Augusta is done in JSON format. Figure 9 shows the structure of a binary tree written in JSON.

```
Esquema: <No se seleccionó ningún esquema>
1  [{"name":"1","desc":"Nuevo pedido de libertad condicional","type":"Tree","path":"","fecha":"","comp":"","ffin":"","auto":"","children": [
2
3    {"name":"2","desc":"Fecha del hecho","type":"FechaHecho","path":"","fecha":"06/08/2017","comp":"0","ffin":"","auto":"","children": [
4      {"name":"3","desc":"Hecho desde el 6/8/2017","type":"Art14","path":"","fecha":"","comp":"","ffin":"","auto":"1","children": [
5        {"name":"4","desc":"Con veda del art. 14 CP (ley 27375)","type":"Documento","path":"Rechazo 16","fecha":"","comp":"","ffin":"","auto":"1","children": []},
6        {"name":"5","desc":"Sin veda del art. 14 CP (ley 27375)","type":"Item","path":"","fecha":"","comp":"","ffin":"","auto":"0","children": [
7          {"name":"6","desc":"Con radicación en sala 1","type":"Item","path":"","fecha":"","comp":"","ffin":"","auto":"","children": [
8            {"name":"7","desc":"Socioambiental vigente","type":"Documento","path":"Modelo se piden informes 40","fecha":"","comp":"","ffin":"","auto":"","children": []},
9            {"name":"8","desc":"Sin socioambiental vigente","type":"Documento","path":"Modelo se piden informes 41","fecha":"","comp":"","ffin":"","auto":"","children": []}
10         ]},
11         {"name":"9","desc":"Sin radicación en sala 1","type":"Documento","path":"Modelo se piden informes 42","fecha":"","comp":"","ffin":"","auto":"","children": []}
12       ]}
13     ]},
14     {"name":"10","desc":"Hecho anterior al 6/8/2017","type":"FechaHecho","path":"","fecha":"03/06/2004","comp":"0","ffin":"","auto":"0","children": [
15       {"name":"11","desc":"Hecho desde el 3/6/2004","type":"Art14","path":"","fecha":"","comp":"","ffin":"","auto":"1","children": [
16         {"name":"12","desc":"Con veda del art. 14 CP (ley 25892)","type":"Documento","path":"Rechazo 17","fecha":"","comp":"","ffin":"","auto":"1","children": []},
17         {"name":"13","desc":"Sin veda del art. 14 CP (ley 25892)","type":"Item","path":"","fecha":"","comp":"","ffin":"","auto":"0","children": [
18           {"name":"14","desc":"Con radicación en sala 1","type":"Item","path":"","fecha":"","comp":"","ffin":"","auto":"","children": [
19             {"name":"15","desc":"Socioambiental vigente","type":"Documento","path":"Modelo se piden informes 43","fecha":"","comp":"","ffin":"","auto":"","children": []},
20             {"name":"16","desc":"Sin socioambiental vigente","type":"Documento","path":"Modelo se piden informes 44","fecha":"","comp":"","ffin":"","auto":"","children": []}
21           ]},
22           {"name":"17","desc":"Sin radicación en sala 1","type":"Documento","path":"Modelo se piden informes 45","fecha":"","comp":"","ffin":"","auto":"","children": []}
23         ]}
24       ]},
25       {"name":"18","desc":"Hecho anterior al 3/6/2004","type":"Item","path":"","fecha":"","comp":"","ffin":"","auto":"0","children": [
26         {"name":"19","desc":"Con radicación en sala 1","type":"Item","path":"","fecha":"","comp":"","ffin":"","auto":"","children": [
27           {"name":"20","desc":"Socioambiental vigente","type":"Documento","path":"Modelo se piden informes 46","fecha":"","comp":"","ffin":"","auto":"","children": []},
28           {"name":"21","desc":"Sin socioambiental vigente","type":"Documento","path":"Modelo se piden informes 47","fecha":"","comp":"","ffin":"","auto":"","children": []}
29         ]},
30         {"name":"22","desc":"Sin radicación en sala 1","type":"Documento","path":"Modelo se piden informes 48","fecha":"","comp":"","ffin":"","auto":"","children": []}
31       ]}
32     ]}
33   ]}
34 ]}
```

Fig. 9. JSON code extract from a binary tree.

The following Fig. 10 shows the graphical representation in Experticia of the code shown above.

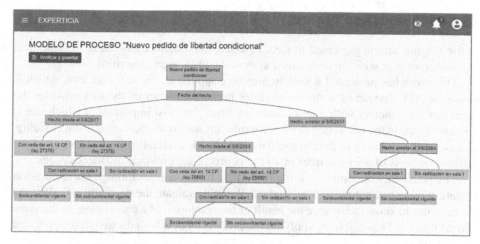

Fig. 10. Experticia graphical representation of a binary tree.

6   Results Obtained

This new version of Experticia is currently in the testing stage. Table 2 shows the time taken by the system for the initial query of a case, the details of which are given in the same table. These results were those mentioned in [1].

Table 2. Detail of the actions together with their respective times.

Process	Times
Request from Augusta information about a case	**1202 ms**
Receive from Augusta data containing parties involved in the case	**143 ms**
Update the data of the case in Experticia to be processed and send such information to the operator	**15 ms**
Total time taken to add the new case to Experticia with the pertinent verifications	**1360 ms**

These are very preliminary tests, the times arise from the average of 20 cases consulted. As can be seen, the most time consumed corresponds to the request of the case, which has demanded approximately 88% of the total time, this at first glance might seem excessive.

However, when it is considered that it is not a request for an isolated piece of data, but is bringing the history of a case, it could be considered a totally acceptable time.

As for new processes related to decision trees, it was shown that the API development technique aims to provide a framework within which these systems can exchange information without the need for user intervention.

7 Conclusions and Future Work

In the original article presented in CACIC 2022, the modifications made to Experticia and its interaction with the centralized system Augusta, were described.

This work has presented a new architecture applied to this software tool, which is based on API. The set of software modules proposed as part of the tool provides the agents of the judiciary with a set of functionalities, the most important of which are: i) improved time in the resolution of files, minimizing the errors that occur in data loading, ii) ease in the updating of data in the Augusta and iii) availability and execution of the different models of decision trees in all the courts of the province of Buenos Aires.

The possibility of complementing Experticia functionalities through the application of data mining techniques will be studied. We will evaluate the possibility of allowing the operator to know in advance the result of the resolution of a proceeding, in the same way as it would be possible by applying the process models with the assistance provided by Experticia.

Acknowledgments. Thanks are due to the Department of Engineering and Technological Research of the National University of La Matanza, this work is financed within the framework of the PROINCE C249 project.

References

1. Spositto, O., et al.: Desarrollo de Interfaces de Programación de Aplicaciones aplicadas en un Sistema Experto Jurídico. (CACIC 2022). UNLaR. Argentina (2020)
2. Salvaneschi, P., Cadei, M., Lazzari, M.: Applying AI to structural safety monitoring and evaluation. IEEE Expert - Intelligent Systems, pp. 24–34. London (2009)
3. Spositto, O., et al.: Inteligencia Artificial aplicada al Poder Judicial. XXII Workshop de Investigadores en Ciencias de la Computación (WICC 2020), U. N. de la Patagonia Austral (UNPA), pp. 7-11. ISBN: 978-987-3714-82-5 (2020)
4. Spositto, O., et al.: Sistema Experto para Apoyo del Proceso de Despacho de Trámites de un Organismo Judicial. XIV Simposio de Informática en el Estado (SIE 2020) - JAIIO 49. Facultad de Ingeniería de la UBA. ISSN: 2451-7534, pp. 17–29 (2020)
5. Spositto, O., et al.: Metodología para evaluar un modelo de Justicia Predictiva. 8vo. Congreso Nacional de Ingeniería Informática y Sistemas de Información (CoNaIISI 2020). UTN. - Facultad Regional San Francisco. ISBN 978-950-42-0202-8, pp. 527–535 (2020)
6. Spositto, O., et al.: Experticia. Un Modelo de Sistema Experto aplicada al Poder Judicial. XXIII. Workshop de Inv. Cs. de la Computación (WICC 2021). Univ. Nacional de Chilecito, La Rioja. ISBN: 978-987-24611-3-3; 978-987-24611-4-0, pp. 113–118 (2021)
7. Spositto, O., et al.: Experticia, un sistema experto para dar apoyo al despacho de trámites asociados al expediente judicial. Suplemento de derecho de la alta tecnología. el-dial.com biblioteca jurídica online. ISSN: 2362–3527. Available at: https://www.eldial.com/nuevo/lite-tcd-detalle.asp?id=14162&base=50&id_publicar=&fechapublicar=08/11/2021&indice=doctrina&suple=DAT (2021)
8. Russell, S., Norvig, P.: Inteligencia artificial, un enfoque moderno. Pearson (2004)
9. Magdaleno, D., et al.: Recuperación de información para artículos científicos soportada en el agrupamiento de documentos XML. Revista Cubana de Ciencias Informáticas 10(2), 57-72. Recuperado en 11 de febrero de 2023, de http://scielo.sld.cu/scielo.php?script=sci_arttext&pid=S2227-18992016000200005&lng=es&tlng=es (2016)

10. Isizoh, A.N., Alagbu, E.E., Nwosu, F.C., Nwoye, C.G., Ogbogu, E.N.: Applications and analyses of expert systems in decision management. J. Inventive Eng. TECHNOL. (JIET) **1**(5), 78–85 (2021)

11. Badaro, S., Ibañez, L., Agüero, M.: Sistemas Expertos: Fundamentos, Metodologías y Aplicaciones. Ciencia y Tecnología 13, 349–363 (2013) https://doi.org/10.18682/cyt.v1i 13.122

12. Turban, E.: Decision Support and Expert Systems: Management Support Systems. Prentice-Hall (2003)

13. Amodeo, E.: Principios de diseño de APIs REST (desmitificando REST). Available at: https://qdoc.tips/introduccionapisrestpdf-pdf-free.html (2013)

14. De la Torre Llorente, C. y otros.: Guía de arquitectura en N capas orientadas al dominio con Net 4.0. ISBN: 978-84-936696-3-8 (2010) Available at: https://sistemamid.com/panel/uploads/biblioteca/2018-06-12_04-26-49144688.pdf (2010)

15. Mestras, J.: Protocolos y arquitecturas de aplicaciones en internet Aplicaciones Web/Sistemas Web. Dep. Ingeniería del Software e Inteligencia Artificial Facultad de Informática. Universidad Complutense Madrid. Available at: https://www.fdi.ucm.es/profesor/jpavon/web/10-Int roduccion-ProtocolosInternet.pdf (2012)

16. Tidwell, D., Snell J., Kulchenko, P.: Programming Web Services with SOAP. O'Reilly First Edition. ISBN: 0-596-00095-2b. Available at: https://docer.com.ar/doc/5sn10 (2001)

17. Verma, S.: APIs versus web services. Available at: https://blogs.mulesoft.com/dev-guides/apis-versus-web-services/ (2018)

18. Beltran, C.: Diferencia entre API y Servicio Web. Available at: https://medium.com/beltranc/diferencia-entre-api-y-servicio-web-5f204af3aedb (2019)

19. Diseño de API RESTful. Available at: https://www.ibm.com/docs/es/zos-connect/zosconnect/3.0?topic=apis-designing-restful (2021)

20. Paiva, R.: Cómo transferir archivos a través de REST para almacenar en una propiedad. Parte I. Available at: https://es.community.intersystems.com/post/c%C3%B3mo-transferir-archivos-trav%C3%A9s-de-rest-para-almacenar-en-una-propiedad-parte-1 (2021)

21. Introducción a JSON Available at: http://www.json.org/json-es.html (2015)

22. IBM Business Automation Workflow. Formato JSON (JavaScript Object Notation) Available at: https://www.ibm.com/docs/es/baw/20.x?topic=formats-javascript-object-notation-json-format (2022)

23. Gamma, E.: Patrones de Diseño. Addison Weskey ISBN: 9788478290598 Available at: http://docer.com.ar/doc/sx5s500 (2017)

24. Stephen, W.: Descripción de los modelos, vistas y controladores (C#). Available at. https://docs.microsoft.com/es-es/aspnet/mvc/overview/older-versions-1/overview/unders tanding-models-views-and-controllers-cs (2022)

25. ASP.NET MVC 4 Release Notes. Available at: https://docs.microsoft.com/en-us/aspnet/whi tepapers/mvc4-release-notes

Author Index

Printed in the United States
by Baker & Taylor Publisher Services